The Collector's Encyclopedia of
HEISEY GLASS
1925-1938

Neila Bredehoft

COLLECTOR BOOKS
A Division of Schroeder Publishing Co., Inc.

COVER

#352 FLAT PANEL humidor, marked Benson & Hedges - zircon, #1430 ARISTOCRAT low footed candy jar - cobalt (Stiegel Blue), #361 IRWIN ash tray and cigarette container - marigold, #1189 YEOMAN individual cream and covered sugar - moongleam.

Additional copies of this book may be ordered from:

Collector Books
P.O. Box 3009
Paducah, KY 42001

or

Heisey Collectors of America, Inc.
P. O. Box 27
Newark, OH 43055

@ $24.95 Add $2.00 for postage and handling.

Acknowledgments

Original Heisey catalogs, price lists and other factory information were researched from the Heisey Collectors of America, Inc., archives. Information on color ingredients and their chemical reactions was provided by the Corning Museum of Glass Library, Corning, New York. For this I wish to thank Norma P.H. Jenkins and her staff.

I also wish to thank members of the Research and Archives Committee of HCA for their assistance in planning the scope and format of this book:

Tom Bredehoft	Sharon Metcalf
Tom Felt	W. Alwyn Miller
Joseph D. Lokay	Bob O'Grady
Jack Metcalf	Louise Ream

Other persons contributing to the book include:
Jim Earnshaw
Eileen and George Schamel
Janice and Norman Thran
Betty and Burl Whaley
Bill Barnard

A special thank you is given to those collectors and members of HCA who allowed their glass to be photographed for this book and also to the people who helped carry glass during the two photography sessions.

All of the above people, and many others, have my heartfelt thanks for the time, effort and knowledge they contributed.

Neila Bredehoft

Preface

"The age of color is here . . . We are living in an age in which color has reached an ascendancy in the scheme of things not hitherto dreamed of.

"Now that cannisters for the kitchen are to be had in bright colors, now that can-openers have colored handles and brooms have colored handles, and now that the housewife has a kitchen as colorful and as pleasant to be in as her living room, does one believe that color in the home is merely a fad that will die out, and that the housewife soon will go back to a drab kitchen with its unpromising and cheerless and colorless equipment of the olden days?

"So everyone is becoming color conscious. And womens clubs and schools everywhere are taking up the subject of color harmony--the proper blending of tones. Of course the women started with proper color harmony in their attire first, but they have passed that stage now and are matching lamp shades with drapes, and they are matching glassware with china, all according to definite color schemes. The effects they are attaining are beautiful and are undoubtedly a decided improvement over the old order of things. That shows the trend of the times and it provides a background which one must consider if he contemplates the subject of colored glass.

"But that is not all. The colored glass era has not yet reached its heights. Despite the fact that some beautiful shades have been presented by the importers and manufacturers, even finer shades are to come. Just this year some new shades which were superior to anything heretofore shown were brought out. For example, one need only look at the blue attained by the Fostoria Glass Co. and the Economy Glass Co., or the lovely pink that is presented by the New Martinsville Glass Mfg. Co., or some of the exquisite shades to be seen from the productions of A. H. Heisey & Co., or the color tones achieved by half a dozen other companies.

"In these columns recently appeared an article on colored glasswares from the viewpoint of the manufacturer. As an amplification of the idea developed in this article, to the effect that the manufacturers are bending all their efforts toward the making of colored glass, to the detriment of crystal in many respects, the following letter sent out to the trade by A.H. Heisey & Company a short time ago is well worth reading.

"The letter:

As a keen merchandiser you have watched with interest the current craving for color in everything. Not only in automobiles and wallpaper but refrigerators, stoves, kettles, sinks, and bathtubs, are being regaled in tints that rival the flowers in grandmother's garden.

"When people want color, sell it to them, feature glassware in colors. Play up strong this spring and summer the wonderful color of Heisey's glassware--the enchanting tints of Flamingo, Hawthorne and Moon Gleam. Make displays of them. Show them in your windows. Bring home to your customers their rich beauty and quality and how they harmonize with individual decorative ideas.

"Here is one of the outstanding glassware manufacturers in America urging colored glass as strongly as possible, upon those who perhaps may have been thus far unaware of the present tendencies. It is not likely that A.H. Heisey & Company would urge colored glassware in this fashion if it had not gone into the subject deeply first and noted the signs of the times.

"*Table Talk,* the little illustrated publication of A.H. Heisey & Company, also stresses colored glass, in much detail.

"And A.H. Heisey & Company are by no means the only factory doing this. It seems everyone is doing it, and with good reason.

"There are a few things to be said from the standpoint of the few who still cling to the idea of crystal, of course. One cannot doubt the surpassing beauty of a fine engraving or cutting on the highest grade of rock crystal. It has stood in a class by itself for many years and will continue to stand in a class by itself. Its beauty is recognized everywhere. But the highest grade of rock crystal with its beautiful engraving or cutting is beyond the reach of the masses. In plain English, it costs too much to reach the bulk of trade.

"Crystal in a good lead glass of moderate price also is of transcendent beauty, but it certainly is a moot question as to whether it is more attractive than colored glass of the same quality, and as a matter of fact, the colored glass gets all the better of the comparison in some shades and tints.

"In lower priced glass, the colored glass seems to be far ahead of crystal from the standpoint of beauty, in the opinion of unbiased observers, for here the outstanding features of crystal--its metallic glow, its sparkling clearness, are to a great extent missing and the color makes up for it bountifully.

"Another argument advanced by those who prefer to think of the returning reign of crystal as something imminent is the criticism that manufacturers are foisting colored glass on the market because colors cover a multitude of sins that show up in the crystal. While it may be true that the number of pieces discarded in colored glass is smaller than in the case of crystal, due to the failure of imperfections to show so readily in colored glass at the same time this would seem to be more than offset by the difficulty in obtaining a good color batch on the part of the manufacturer. In the opinion of most people with whom the writer has talked, there is little advantage gained one way or another.

"So apparently colored glass is here to stay and will remain very much in evidence, to the detriment of crystal, except in the very highest grades of rock crystal."

by W.H. Nicholas
CHINA, GLASS & LAMPS
June 18, 1928

Table of Contents

Introduction

When the Heisey Company started making glass in 1896, it produced patterns with table sets, oils (cruets), toothpick holders, syrups, nappies (bowls), and various other standard items typical of glassware of the turn of the century. Most of these early patterns were imitation cut patterns—meaning that they had the same motifs of the expensive cut glass, but were made by the more inexpensive process of pressing glass into a mold. Heisey also made a full line of tumblers, shot glasses and several novelties—all mainstays of any glass house of the time.

In a few years, candlesticks and vases were added to production. Early in its history Heisey introduced its first colonial pressed pattern—#300 Peerless. An instant success, the pattern heralded a new era of design—actually a return to the early colonial blown pieces with their simple scallops, panels and flutes. These colonial patterns (of which there were many) became the primary production of the company for well over a decade and they are still what many people think of when they think of Heisey glass.

By 1915, glassware styles were changing. People were using fewer table sets, toothpicks and syrups—seeming to regard these as old fashioned. These items disappeared from patterns not really to be replaced. Heisey patterns became assortments of nappies, plates, oils, creams and sugars and miscellaneous matching pieces. Soda fountain glass was selling well. The Heisey Company was in a transitional phase.

The gap left by the disappearance of staple items convinced the company to open a decorating shop at this time. Etched glass was popular and Heisey began decorating their wares. At first they etched their pressed items—baskets, lavender jars and candlesticks.

As the etching department grew and demand for etched ware also grew, Heisey began producing excellent blown stemware—often decorated with needle, pantograph or plate etched designs. The blow shops became extremely important to the company and blown stemware and sodas remained good sellers for the Heisey Company. During this period, some cutting was done at Heisey's although this seems to have been minimal compared with etching.

This brings us to the early to mid-1920's—the focus of this book.

Stemware was selling well. New patterns were introduced yearly. However, times were changing again. More and more customers preferred the bright new colors (often pastels) beginning to permeate the housewares market.

While the Heisey Company produced colored glass during all periods of its life, early, middle and late, the middle years saw the introduction of the most unusual colors and those which are most sought today. These were developed through the efforts of Heisey's chemist, Emmett Olsen. Because more colors were produced during this span of about 14 years, from 1925 to 1938, this period is called the "Color Era" by most Heisey glass collectors.

Even though this was Heisey's most prolific period in regards to color, the company still made far less colored glass than did several other glass companies such as Cambridge and Fostoria. These companies in particular produced huge quantities of colored glass. At the Heisey Company quality was always of prime importance and often this resulted in smaller output than many other competing firms. It is this quality that has attracted so many collectors to Heisey glass, so that today it is the most popular glass collectible in the United States.

Heisey began its second color production period about 1923 or 1924 when it made a few items in vaseline. Even now, no actual documentation has been found in price lists or ads naming this color or even indicating that it was made. In 1925, the Heisey Company produced its first two pastel colors in massive amounts—Moongleam (green) and Flamingo (rose pink). While these colors were made by most American companies producing colored glass, the Heisey colors are distinctive. Moongleam is a dark yellow-green in early pieces and shades to a softer glowing green in later production. Flamingo contains an orange-red tone in combination with the rose pink—a shade suggested by its name. Marigold is a strong brassy color with much more verve than the yellows being produced by other companies. Even Heisey's Sahara (yellow) which replaced the strong Marigold had a brightness and warmth often lacking in the products of other companies.

Heisey was very proud of its Hawthorne, the company's first attempt at a lavender color. Again, the color was not exactly what the company had in mind, so continuing experimentation (and the fortunate acquisition of a glass formula from Europe) resulted in the introduction of Alexandrite—the most expensive color produced by Heisey. Dozens of mentions of this fantastic new color are found in contemporary accounts in trade journals. The dual colorations produced by Alexandrite, ranging from an orchid-red to an orchid-blue made it unlike any other color made in the United States at that time.

By 1933, Heisey began a trend away from the popular pastel colors to deeper shades and introduced its vivid orange-red Tangerine and the deep, pure Cobalt, which was called Stiegel Blue by the company.

Heisey Amber of this period is a tawny color and glows with an inner life. It too is a deep vibrant color. The last color made during this period was Zircon—a lovely turquoise blue-green which the company spoke of as reminding one of the sea.

By this time, color was becoming passe and crystal was returning to the fore. Even though Heisey produced large amounts of color during this period, their largest production by far was in crystal. Regular customers in the industrial trade, hotel trade, companies using items for mounting plus the large production for cuttings—both by Heisey and by others—insured the continued production of crystal glass in large amounts. And, of course, there were also many people who always preferred their glassware to be crystal.

Color Trends of the 1920's and 1930's

Contemporary trade journal accounts give an interesting history of the styles and trends of glassware during the twenties and early thirties. There was quite a lot of discussion about the colors being produced by almost every glass company then in business. There must have been some reluctance to accept this as a true desire of homemakers however, since there is some undercurrent of trying to dispel the idea that colored glass was only a fad and that it was, in truth, a staple commodity. It is unclear from reading these reports as to whether the reluctance stemmed from the jobbers and trade buyers or from interior designers or someone else. Certainly the housewife was buying colored glass and showed no sign of being ready to stop.

In 1928, a general article called "Modern Table Glassware" appeared in *China, Glass & Lamps*. In part it said:

> "Of late years, along with the inevitable reaction from the heavy stodgieness and stolidity of the century's closing years, has come an awakening appreciation of the charm of glass. Perhaps the appeal of glorious color, so striking in glass, accounts for it: like the rousing consciousness for colors in interiors. Perhaps it is the airy grace, the impalpable transparency of glass. At any rate, the pendulum of favor has completely swung from the massive atrocities in the cut glass of the period, to the free, graceful beautiful glass we enjoy today.
>
> "Clean of line, glass is seemingly as ephemeral as a soap bubble; and like that bubble, of many and varied colors, colors which are daily growing in number and charm. Blue in varying tones was some years ago in wide favor; then amethyst displaced it. Rapidly came amber and green, which colors maintain a deserved respect, because of their adaptability. Rose, canary, sapphire, in quick succession—no color today is unrepresented. Certainly the profusion of hues blown is evidence of the astounding popularity of colored glass.
>
> "For even a little colored glass on a table makes imperative the use of more. Green glass goblets seem to demand green glass bowls, and candlesticks, and compotes. So it has happened that not only dominant decorative elements are fashioned, but incidental pieces; even small nut dishes, salt cups, pepper pots have been made with the ensemble idea in mind.
>
> "And glass is selected to 'go with' certain tones of china. The hostess with a sense of fitness (her name is legion, today) has a glass service for each of her dinner services. She does not dream of using gold-banded glass with brightly informal pottery; neither would she use gayly colored glass with stately china. For her severely formal tables she uses glittering crystal, etched or cut, engraved or gold decorated . . ."

With small changes, the above article could have been written about Heisey glass exclusively. Certainly the descriptions of small accessory pieces made in colors and patterns to match large table services coincided with Heisey's production. Harry M. Bortz, a Heisey representative, said in 1928:

> "Previous to the war, colored glass would have been looked upon as 'off color'. All glassware was crystal, and the lines were not nearly so extensive as they are now."

In a review of the market for 1928 and a forecast for 1929, *China, Glass & Lamps* again commented:

> ". . . Transparent colored wares continued to find a healthy and steady market in 1928. Several factories went more into colored wares than they had previously. However, in the better grades of wares there was a moderate, but clearly outlined, trend toward crystal and color combinations and crystal alone. In 1927, the pink or rose shade of glass made its debut in strong fashion. There was no outstanding new shade in 1928. The pink continued to hold the lead with the green coming behind. Other shades, while interesting in various shapes, did not have the popular appeal of the pinks and greens . . ."

In October, 1929, the reports were much the same:

> "Most manufacturers of blown and pressed glassware for table, home and decorative uses find themselves busier than at any previous time this year and the outlook is for full production from now until it is too late for Christmas-sale shipments . . .
>
> "Blown stemware and table ware is in good demand with colored glass and combinations of color and crystal having the call. Pink or rose glass still predominates in the production list . . . However, several factories report increasing demand for crystal. This is especially true of those making blown stemware and those decorating a certain quantity of their production in their own decorating departments."

In 1930, a buyer for a large eastcoast department store gave these thoughts on his experiences in buying glass:

"Nothing can shake the popularity of rose pink. At least ⅔ of the glassware sold in (the) store is in that shade . . . although with the approach of warm weather, green is creating a greater demand for itself. This, of course, is only to be expected, since the coolness of green lends itself naturally to the attractive serving of summer fruits and vegetables.

"Amber rates third in the list of favorites, while blue, even in warm weather, proves itself a poor seller . . .And, surprisingly enough, black, even combined with crystal is considered too somber. . ."

Even though the trade journals remained remarkably silent about the deepening Depression which was certainly making itself felt in the glass industry, the Heisey Company was apparently trying any way possible to sell glass. A rather humorous (from today's vantage point) account taken from Table Talk shows just how the company suggested that its customers merchandise Heisey glass.

"Color in glassware is more in demand than ever before. In line with this tremendous trend, Heisey makes rich offerings of wonderful tints that the trade might satisfy their customers.

"In selling glassware, capitalize the tendency toward brightness and you will be well repaid. Feature the fascinating colors of Heisey's Glassware. Make sure you have an ample stock.

"Tell your customers they can have complete glassware services in color. Give them the idea of having different colors for different times, and thus you can sell them two or three sets instead of one."

By 1931, the stronghold pink glassware had on the market seemed to be waning:

"In colored glassware, the colors of topaze (sic), green and amber appear to be in most popular request, and some distributors are of the opinion that the green glassware lines have a slight edge on some of the other colors. Syndicate stores have sold enormous quantities of green glassware, such as tumblers, salts and peppers, plates and other items, while department stores have also had an active request for the greens. Many users of glassware for scheme purposes have demanded green glassware to the exclusion of most all other colors." (*Crockery & Glass Journal*, June, 1931.)

In 1933, *Crockery & Glass Journal* published an interesting survey of some of the leading glass producers of the day concerning the sale of colored glass as opposed to crystal:

"The Trend is Not Away From Color
"Say most glass men, denying rumor that the movement of popular taste is away from color to crystal.
"Buyers and the public at large still believe in colored glassware, according to information an inquiring reporter obtained from the New York representatives of some of the leading glass manufacturers. To summarize the matter briefly it is as good as ever, and holds its proportion of total sales, as in the past. Literally, too, color is 'still going strong,' for the strong shades are particularly good, Ruby red, Ritz blue, and dark green are on the upswing; topaze (sic) is generally good, as are amethyst and amber, and there is now as ever, a certain activity in pale green, particularly in the two tone stemware.

"Cambridge Glass Co.
"The Cambridge Glass Co. is strong for color, as anyone entering their New York showroom can see in the glance of an eye. They have 'thirteen colors, of which crystal is one', to quote their own words. They do not consider color in glass on the wane, as a stylist here and there may be heard to remark, but hold that it is still the life of the trade. They say the sales scope of potential market of any piece of glass is multiplied directly by the number of colors in which it is made. The bright colors are best with them, especially in novelties, while crystal combined with the high shades sells well in stemware. They find too an interesting sectionalism displaying itself in the sales figures of the various colors. For that reason it is necessary to have all shades to meet the sectional demands.

"Morgantown Glass Works
"D. King Irwin, New York representative for the Morgantown Glass Works and the Paden City Glass Co., finds color still better than crystal in both his lines. He says the strong colors are best, perhaps because the market for the pale shades in the higher priced lines has been greatly curtailed by the inundation of cheap goods flooding the counters of the ten cent stores. He thinks perhaps the people who buy solely on a price basis would not appreciate the strong colors anyhow, since it takes taste to set a table in these colors. He finds crystal moves very well in the cheaper cut stemware.

"Heisey Glass Co.

"The Heisey Glass Co. reports that topaze (sahara) is still their leading color though their high shades are also very popular. Pale green holds up well in two-tone stemware with the colored stem and crystal bowl, and there is always a certain demand for the all over pale green, particularly in the spring and summer, since it is suggestive of coolness. Amethyst, too, is popular with them, and as for their new high shade, tangerine, they are oversold on it. In crystal they find the etched and Early American patterns very good."

By March of 1935, the trends of colored glass had changed. Several representatives were interviewed in the Merchandise Mart in Chicago and stated:

". . . The trend to crystal announced more than a year ago is actually stronger today, with colored glass lines being confined to luncheon and informal service.

". . . U.S. Glass Co., declares that for some time now crystal has been the big thing.

". . . A. H. Heisey & Co. finds that colors are continuing to lose ground to crystal.

". . . Tinker Brothers are selling a great deal of crystal, deep reds and deep blues. Pastel and light tints are falling off rapidly.

". . . Fostoria Glass Co. reports plain, simple designs as the best sellers. A modified modern design in crystal is being used almost entirely for formal tables. For luncheons, colors are still used, but the colors are very deep rather than the pastels. . ."

So it can be seen from contemporary accounts, that the Heisey Company responded quickly to trends of the times; in fact, they helped set them. When pink and green were popular, they produced their Flamingo and Moongleam. Topaz, as it was called in the trade, was filled by their Sahara yellow. When styles changed to deeper shades, Heisey brought out Tangerine and Cobalt. A last attempt in color, namely Zircon, seems to have been out of step with the times, and it was dropped after a short time. Again, crystal glass was king and the Heisey Company returned to complete crystal production.

Prohibition and Changing Glassware Styles

The end of prohibition in 1933 began a new phase in American glass making. A new gamut of styles and beverage glasses were now deemed necessary for the home bartender and hostess. This created many fascinating new shapes and pieces in the Heisey line. Beer mugs, decanters, pilsners and other specialty containers became popular for the home bar.

As early as 1931, reports of the products of the Heisey Company included the following:

"The wine decanter, be it in crystal or in color, is fitted with a ground in cut crystal glass stopper, which adds very much to its appearance."

Anticipating the repeal of prohibition, Heisey was beginning to expand its line of liquor wares. It had continued to produce lines of stemware which included all types of wines, cocktails and cordials during prohibition, but now the company added several decanters and accessory pieces to its line.

In August of 1931, the #4222 Steeplechase cocktail set was described in literature as available with a "Lalique" style foot—indicative of the frosted base found on both the cocktails and the mixer.

In 1932 one of the most innovative of the Heisey designs brought out was the all-glass cocktail shaker (#4225). This was completely new with its glass stopper and strainer and patented by the company. Its design and the design for the mold were the inspired work of Ray Cobel, head of Heisey's mold shop and their master mold maker. The cocktail shaker proved to be such a popular design that it remained in the Heisey line until the factory closed in 1957. Imperial Glass continued to make the cocktail shaker for some time after that.

Two other very popular items with today's collectors were brought out in this time period. First, the #1231 rum pot was introduced as a "water jug". Price lists indicate it was available with or without a stopper. As with earlier rum pots the lid on the Heisey jug is fixed and cannot be removed. Filling the vessel must be done through the spout.

The second item was the #4163 pretzel jar. In 1931 the company offered a $100.00 prize to any employee of a store selling Heisey for the best original glassware design. The result was the pretzel jar which used the twisted pretzel as a finial. The design was submitted by Florence Green, secretary to E.G. Nock, head of Heisey's New York sales room. Her design was accepted without change.

In order to see the development of new drinking wares throughout the glass industry, several quotes from either trade journals or the Heisey *Table Talks* are quite informative. This first quotation is purportedly written by "Kay", assistant editor to a trade publication in April, 1933:

"I don't mind telling you that after making the rounds this month I feel very much like Barroom Bess—with mugs, jugs, steins, Weiss beers, Hoffman House goblets, Pilsner ales and complete shell lines all dancing madly together before my eyes . . .Anyone and everyone who could possibly get together a line has done so—and all of those who have been working along beer lines for the past six months or so . . . are sitting proudly back and just putting a few finishing touches to their collections.

"Of course the big beer problem so far as you are concerned is what on earth your dear public is going to use at home by way of steins and glasses . . ."

In *Pottery, Glass & Brass Salesman* in April, 1933, the following was said about Heisey:

"Several New Styles of Beer Mugs Just Put on the Market"

"To their already large array of beer mugs A.H. Heisey & Co., of Newark, Ohio, have recently made several interesting additions. These include both plain and fancy styles in a number of different sizes. One new line of 16 ounce mugs shown in rather thin glass comes in two forms—one a typical barrel shape, and the other barreled in the lower portion and slightly concave near the top. It is interesting to note that a considerable choice of handle is offered, some much heavier than others and some inclined to be fanciful, while others are plain. The mugs themselves are in crystal glass, and can be had with handles in crystal or else cobalt blue, green or ruby.

"Another new number is a 12-ounce Colonial idea—that is, absolutely plain in the upper portion and paneled in the lower part. A little somewhat out-of-the-ordinary twist is given by having every third panel puntied. The handle of this mug shows the upper part extending out straight and then turning sharply to return to the body in a graceful curve. Both of these types have already met with considerable favor." (References are probably to #4163 or #3406 and #3407. The Colonial mug with punties is the #1404 Old Sandwich.)

The Heisey *Table Talk* of 1933 also inspired their salesmen to take full advantage of selling the new lines:

"Good Glassware Makes the Beverage More Inviting

"The American woman, noted for her discriminating taste, has learned, during the past decade, to enjoy beer and wine. This means quite a little to those of us who are concerned with the task of producing and supplying her with appropriate glassware in which to serve these beverages . . .

"Beer really is more enjoyable when served in glasses or mugs of crystal clearness. The clear glass reflects the tints of the amber beverage—emphasizing the quality of the drink. Muddy, distorted glass makes the beer seem muddy too . . .

"No matter how heavy the mug, nor how thin and dainty the glass, each of these patterns is regular Heisey quality. The clear, transparent glass is free of distortion and possesses that inimitable 'ring' that only fine glassware can give you."

The extent to which Heisey produced drinking glassware is further clarified by the following: (from 1933)

". . . Other new offerings include two new shapes in Pilsner glasses. One is quite conventional, with optic bowl set on a figured button, and this again on a plain foot. The other shows the bowl, also slightly optic, almost cylindrical in form, being a bit narrower at the foot than at the top. It is set directly on the base, which is plain." (#3386 Diamond Rose and an unknown, previously unidentified pilsner— unfortunately, the photocopy of the ad is too poor to reproduce. The piece illustrated is exactly as described.)

Again, Heisey spoke to its salesmen and store representatives:

"More Glasses Necessary

"The American buffet will soon be competing on even terms with the fabulously furnished sideboards of Merry England. The up-to-the-minute host or hostess will soon be serving not only beer, but wines and quite probably liquers as well. Different wines demand different glasses. The delicate goblet, the tiny wine glass, flagons and liquer glasses will be necessary in the home of those who desire to be socially correct.

"And since cocktails will always be served, regardless of whether their ingredients are strictly legal, the Heisey cocktail shaker in several beautiful designs, is also an important buffet accessory."

Standard pattern lines of the time also reflected the new market with various bar items and accessory items being integral parts of several lines. Old Sandwich (#1404) incorporates three sizes of beer mugs, a popcorn bowl, an oval decanter and bar glasses—all liquor related—along with its more traditional items. Ipswich (#1405) and Ridgeleigh (#1469) had cocktail shakers matching the line—two of the few patterns to include this item.

It is important to remember that this period was in the depths of the Depression, and certainly glass houses were having their fair share of hard times. Heisey suffered equally or possibly more than many since its wares were more expensive and thus were considered to be more luxuries than necessities. Certainly the company eagerly looked forward to the repeal of prohibition and saw an opportunity for creating a whole new market with all styles of drinking glassware and accessories. Ice buckets, martini pitchers, cocktail shakers, decanters, sherry bottles and bitters bottles were only some of the variety of wares produced by the company in the '30's. The demand was there and some of these items remained standard in the Heisey line until the demise of the company.

Sandwich-Inspired Patterns

About 1925, Heisey began making several new items which were either faithful reproductions or newly designed forms of old Sandwich Glass Company patterns.

According to information from early articles in *Antiques* and Heisey's own *Table Talk*, the Heisey Company had become the repository of many original Sandwich Company models. According to the article in *Antiques*, March, 1927, the models had originally been given to A.H. Heisey. Since he died in 1922, the models had apparently been kept for several years by the company. Renewed interest in early American glass, especially lacy Sandwich, prompted the company to unearth the models and adapt their patterns to new wares.

To quote the article in *Antiques:*

"At some time in its history, the Sandwich glass factory had its models carved in mahogany. When the concern ceased operation, although the greater part of its records of all kinds were destroyed, several barrels of wooden models were preserved by one of the company's staff. In due course, these models came into possession of the late James E. Johnston, of Sandwich, who turned them over to Colonel A.H. Heisey, founder of the firm of A.H. Heisey & Company, glass manufacturers, of Newark, Ohio. The extensive interest in old Sandwich patterns led recently to investigation of the entire cache. As a result, the contents of three of the original barrels were found intact. . ."

It should be carefully noted here that these were wooden models from the Sandwich Company, not actual molds. Confusion has existed about this in the past, leading many to think that the Heisey Company produced its designs from the actual molds used by Sandwich. This was not true since Heisey never did have the original molds. The models were used as full-size pieces to guide the mold makers in producing molds and were not used in making glass. The models were estimated to be from the 1850 to 1870 era.

In *Table Talk*, Heisey said about the models:

"Highly treasured is the collection of original models of Sandwich glass owned by A.H. Heisey & Company. They came into our possession through a former Heisey salesman, Mr. Johnson, who was related to the owners of the Sandwich Glass Company.

"These models are estimated to be between sixty and one hundred years old (in 1928). They were carefully and accurately made of mahogany and from them, templates or patterns were formed, from which in turn the actual molds were produced for giving shape and design to the glass."

Several of the patterns and items made by Heisey are known to be almost exact reproductions of Sandwich glass. These include the #110 Sandwich Dolphin candlestick, the #1238 Beehive plate, and the #1236 Eagle plate. Several other items were included in a small brochure which was being designed to specifically advertise the Sandwich-inspired pieces. Other items Heisey included in this booklet include the #10 Oak Leaf coaster, the #1237 Sandwich Star plate, the #1234 Stippled Diamond plate and the #109 Petticoat Dolphin candlestick. Experts at the Sandwich Museum state that the Petticoat Dolphin was not a Sandwich design and was probably midwestern in origin—possibly Northwood. The Heisey dolphin candlestick (#110) differs from the original Sandwich design in several ways. The most apparent of which is the larger scales on the Heisey product. Heisey's Beehive plate has larger stippling than the original Sandwich version.

It is likely that Heisey used some creative marketing descriptions in attributing all these designs to Sandwich. Probably the "Early American" influence was enough for them to include many of these items such as the Stippled Diamond plate in their "Sandwich inspired" designs. The appearance of the stippled effects on some of these pieces plus their obvious inspiration from older glass seems to be the reason Heisey included them in the same category.

The #10 Oak Leaf coaster seems to be copied from the leaf in the edge of the #1238 Beehive plate (Sandwich's Beehive design.) The Heisey copy of the Beehive plate is a good reproduction of the Sandwich original. Duncan Miller made a very similar plate, but it lacks the leaf in the outer border and it has a ground and polished bottom rim—something which the original Sandwich pieces and the Heisey plates do not have. The #1236 Eagle plate also seems to be a faithful copy of the Sandwich original. Another plate was made by Heisey which is not shown in catalogs but is an exact copy of the original Sandwich design. This is the #8071 Sandwich Hairpin, the number and name both of which have been given to the piece. Several of these plates have been found in the Newark area, some with original Heisey labels, but it is unknown whether they were marketed.

The Sandwich-inspired plates are not marked with the Diamond H, possibly because they were considered reproductions even in their own time. The Stippled Diamond plate is marked however, also seeming to indicate that while Heisey said it was a Sandwich copy, they did not really consider it one. Some collectors have thought the Eagle plates to be marked in the central design, but this "mark" does not seem to actually be a Diamond H, but a small mold flaw.

Other patterns which were inspired by original Sandwich designs were #1404 Old Sandwich and #1405 Ipswich. These were openly advertised by Heisey as modern forms inspired by the original Sandwich designs for which they owned the original models. The Old Sandwich pattern (first called Early American Thumbprint in Heisey ads) was the Sandwich Pillar pattern. The inspiration for the #1405 Ipswich pattern was the Comet pattern. Both are faithfully reproduced. #1433 Thumbprint and Panel is also a copy of an early Sandwich pattern, but Heisey did not seem to advertise it as such. It is a very short line of about five items. It is also possible that #1425 Victorian was inspired by some of the Sandwich models since it is very similar to many early "block" patterns, including some of the block-style goblets shown with the Sandwich models owned by Heisey.

Another item which probably had its inspiration in early American glass is the #367 decanter. In the book, *American Glass*, a similar glass decanter engraved with the words "New England Glass Co. Boston Mass." is shown. Although it has a cut neck and faceted knop, the decanter bears a remarkable resemblance to Heisey's #367 Prism Band decanter.

It is unfortunate to report that the wooden Sandwich models in which Heisey took such pride no longer seem to exist. According to reports, they were being shipped west for a special exhibition and were lost en route. Nothing has been heard about them since. It would indeed be a magnificent find if by some miracle they would eventually be unearthed. Their loss was certainly a sad day for the history of American glass.

Optics

Optics are decorative effects used in glass to enhance its reflective qualities. The transparent medium of glass lends itself to the use of varying thicknesses of glass which is essentially how optics are achieved. While optics are effective in crystal glass, they greatly add to the beauty of colored transparent glass—especially in stemware where the bowls of items catch the light and if filled, the liquid also adds to the sparkle created.

Optics are possible in both pressed ware and blown ware. In pressed ware, optics tend to be heavy and easily felt. Optic effects in blown ware are often delicate and subtle, especially if the item is also etched or cut. It is not so much noticed, but if not there, the lack of brilliance is apparent.

Heisey used several different optics during the period of 1925 to 1938.

CHECKER: This optic was developed about 1927 and used in conjunction with a few stem lines, primarily in hawthorne. It is occasionally found in flamingo. The effect is that of squares about one inch in size further divided into tiny vertical lines which gives a vague checkerboard effect. The optic is often very delicate and can be overlooked. (abbreviated c/o)

DIAMOND: Probably the most popular optic used by Heisey. Used on some pressed patterns, but mainly on blown ware. Stem lines, sodas, jugs, tumblers, vases and many other items were available with this optic. It consists of diamond-shaped motifs repeated over and over throughout the item. (abbreviated d/o)

MEDIUM: A vertical panel optic of medium width. Not regularly used by the company, but it was offered on several stemware lines on a special order basis. (abbreviated m/o)

NARROW: A vertical panel optic of narrow width. Most often used prior to this period, often in pressed stemware and sodas. (abbreviated n/o)

RAMSHORN: A Heisey innovation for the #3365 Ramshorn stemware patented in 1927 by Ray Cobel. It is likely that the patent was for the unusual optic. It is a swirl optic which is narrow at the bottom and widens greatly to the top of the bowl.

SATURN: A fairly wide horizontal optic developed by Heisey for its use about 1936. The effect achieved is of rings in the glass, thus the name, Saturn. It is a copy of imported glass, especially Swedish. Used both on pressed ware and blown ware. Used extensively with the zircon color. (abbreviated s/o)

SWIRL: A medium wide optic which partially encircled an item in a spiral or swirl design. Beginning at the bottom of an item, it angled up the side of the bowl and ended at the top before completing a circle. In contrast to Ramshorn optic, it remained the same width for its entire length. Actually this optic was used on only a few items and for a short period of time and thus is somewhat difficult to find today.

WAVY LINE: A variation of Saturn optic used very rarely in some #1485 Saturn items. The rings of the saturn optic also undulate in a wavy fashion around the piece of glass. Illustrated only on a few large pieces of Saturn such as floral bowls.

WIDE: A vertical panel optic of fairly wide width. In popularity, it probably rivaled diamond optic. Heisey used it on many stem lines and items such as ball vases. (abbreviated w/o)

In general, Heisey's optics are found on the interior of items. This is especially true of blown items since the glass was first blown into an optic mold to create the optic and then blown into a smooth-sided mold, causing the optic to remain on the interior and resulting in a smooth exterior.

All names used in describing the optics are the original Heisey terms.

The Unknowns

Most items and patterns made during the 1925-1938 period are shown in this book. There are some omissions. The most notable is the #1489 Puritan pattern which is a transitional pattern made almost exclusively in crystal and which will appear in a subsequent book.

Other omissions are not arbitrary but are due to a lack of information. From various sources many pattern numbers are known, often with descriptions of pieces. Some of these are very detailed, while others are vague. All share one important feature—no illustrations are known to exist of these wares. Certainly some of these items must match items collectors have found marked with the Diamond H but for which original numbers are not known—resulting in numbers being assigned by researchers.

Many of the "unknowns" are intriguing—prime examples being three blown items listed with cobalt/crystal combinations: #4075, #4076 and #4077.

The following unknowns will remain a puzzle for years to come. Descriptions used are quoted exactly from original records except in cases where "full line" or "stem line" are used to shorten the listing.

115 3″ candlestick, moongleam & flamingo	
500 vase	1925
1001 bowl cover, optic (rose in 1926)	1924

1024 marmalade	1924
1122 8″ plate "new"	1923
1126 plate, 7″ green	1925
1190 ash tray "new"	1924
1235 plate, green	1925
1240 plate, green	1925
1316 10 oz. goblet, optic	1923
1407 8″ vase, moongleam, flamingo, sahara	ca. 1931
1407 variety tray, moongleam, flamingo, sahara	
1409 plate, moongleam, flamingo, sahara	ca. 1931
1410 cream soup & plate (cereal set) moongleam, flamingo, sahara	1931
1422 puff box and cologne	
1461 10½″ plate	ca. 1935
2000 8″ nappy	1925
2001 3 oz. whiskey	1924
2003 traveler's glass*	1924
2935 tumbler, clear and rose	1926
3002 traveler's glass*	1924
3003 traveler's glass*	1924
3003 tumbler and water bottle for B & O Railroad	1924, 1925
3009 finger bowl, optic	1924
3055 sodas, full line	ca. 1933-1940
3056 9 oz. soda, w/o, moongleam, flamingo, sahara	1933
3313 footed soda, d/o sahara	1933
3356 soda, handled & footed	1924
3358 8 oz. goblet, optic	1925
3374 12 oz. ftd. tumbler	ca. 1929
3382 ice tea, d/o	1925
3385 goblet	mid 1930
3402 10″ bowl, alexandrite	1930
3439 10 oz. goblet, special	1925
3439 11 oz. goblet	1925
3441 goblet, d/o	1925
3441 goblet, d/o green foot	1926
3500 bell	1925
3618 4 oz., 4½ oz. parfait, optic	1926
3875 ash tray, crystal & green	1924, 1925
3877 9″ candlestick	1924
3931 8″ nappy "new"	1924
3939 goblet	1923
4003 3½ oz. cocktail	ca. 1937-1943
4009 8″ plate "new"	1925
4033 cologne	1923
4047 KNICKERBOCKER stem line	1934-1937
4075 2½ oz. cocktail, blue foot	
4076 3 oz. cocktail, optic, blue foot	
4077 9 oz. footed tumbler, blue bowl	
4093 goblet, plain, w/o, s/o	1937
4094 3½ oz. cocktail	ca. 1938
4137 sherbet liner	1925
4138 sherbet liner	1925
4168 oval jug, "all bad"	1924
4170 jug, d/o moongleam	1930
4184 78 oz. jug, d/o sahara	1930

*Several numbers were found for traveler's glasses. One of these has been found with a Heisey label but there is no way of knowing which number is correct for this particular glass.

Rose refers to flamingo, green to moongleam and blue to cobalt.

As can be seen by the above list (which is not complete) many, many items are known to have been made, but because many are blown ware numbers (those over 2000), most will probably never be able to be properly identified.

As is apparent from the entries, often quite a lot is known about an item. In one instance (#4047 Knickerbocker) the original number, name, period of production and items made are all known. It is listed in price lists but not illustrated. Because of this, it may always remain a mystery. In other cases, even colors, sizes, and optics are known, but the piece is still unknown. Much of this information is found in factory turn books which contain daily records of production of the company, but also some of the items were listed in catalogs but no pictures accompanied the descriptions.

It would be tempting to try to match the descriptions found with pieces known to be Heisey, but this is inviting disaster and also would provide erroneous information to collectors. Better to let a little mystery remain in the world of Heisey collecting.

Very recently the Heisey Collectors of America obtained the existing Heisey molds and all paper information from the Heisey Company which had been the property of Imperial Glass Corporation. Much new information regarding original numbers and new pieces will be available from this treasure trove in the future. A few late corrections were able to be added to this book before it went to press. Possibly several of the "unknowns" listed above will no longer be unknown in the next few years.

Heisey Personalities

While the workers of the A.H. Heisey & Company numbered in the hundreds throughout its life, a few of these stand out and deserve special mention for their contributions during the color period. Many other people also made major contributions, but since space is limited, only a few are listed here.

E. Wilson Heisey

Wilson Heisey, son of A.H. Heisey, became the second president of the A.H. Heisey & Company in 1922 following the death of his father.

Wilson Heisey is credited with the introduction of color into the Heisey line. He worked closely with Emmett Olson in the development of Heisey's colors during the middle years.

Mr. Heisey's other interests included baseball, hunting and politics.

By the time of his death in 1942, the color era of Heisey glass was over and crystal glass again was in the forefront.

Emmett E. Olson

Emmett Olson began working for the Heisey Company in 1919 as a stopper fitter.

Wilson Heisey soon introduced him to the color room where the ingredients for making and controlling colors were prepared. This became Mr. Olson's main interest in the glass industry and he eventually became Heisey's chemist.

About 1921, Olson visited the B.F. Drakenfeld Co. of Washington, PA, several times to learn about color chemistry and technology. He returned to this company several times each year for many years.

While Olson learned much from this association, he also did much of his own experimentation at the Heisey Company and is credited with developing most of Heisey's pastel colors.

Emmett Olson continued to work for Heisey until the plant closed.

Louise Adkins

Louise Adkins began work at A.H. Heisey & Company when the factory began production in 1896. At first she worked in the gold decorating department. Soon she was promoted to take charge of the stock room.

Subsequently she became supervisor of the sample department, the cutting and grinding department and the blowing and finishing department.

It is said that she loved decorated glassware and was an enthusiastic supporter of the development of cuttings and engravings by Heisey.

Miss Adkins held positions of great responsibility in the Heisey Company at a time when few women were in executive positions in industry. She continued to work until her retirement in 1951, completing over 55 years of employment with the Heisey Company.

Others of the talented people who worked for the Heisey Company were the designers. Because of these people, the Heisey Company was always one of the leaders in new designs for the industry. They employed designers of the highest caliber and thus the quality of their product was superior to most other glass companies.

Walter Von Nessen

During the color period, several designers worked for the Heisey Company. Most renowned of these was Walter Von Nessen, a Dutch architect and designer in his own right. He was contacted to do some design work for the Heisey Company by Rodney C. Irwin, then the sales manager. The first items designed by Mr. Von Nessen were to be items for a special display in the Metropolitan Museum of Art's exhibition of Modern Art and Housefurnishings. Every item on display in this exhibit had to be a new item never before on the market. Mr. Von Nessen was able to take several items from the current Heisey line and with small alterations, create new items for the display. Many of these were cut or etched in modernistic designs. This display was held in November, 1934. Some of the items which were the result of Mr. Von Nessen's designs were a vase made from the #4206 Optic Tooth vase with the "claws" left off and the #4056 salad bowl, which was adapted from the #4045 ball vase. At this time, he also designed the teardrop-shaped stopper for the #4036 decanter.

Heisey was apparently quite pleased with the efforts of Walter Von Nessen since he went on to create several new patterns for the company. The most well known of these are: #1495 Fern, #1488 Kohinoor, #1483 Stanhope and at least the 2 light candlestick in #1485 Saturn. He may, in fact, have had the inspiration for the entire Saturn line, but this is not known to be certain.

Carl Cobel

Another designer for Heisey was closely associated with Walter Von Nessen. Carl Cobel had begun to work for Heisey when he was still in high school and eventually became part of Mr. Von Nessen's studio in New York. Mr. Cobel designed many of the silhouette etchings of the mid-1930's which proved to be so popular, especially on barware. He also designed the #490 Maytime etching placed on Stanhope and possibly designed #491 Frosty Dawn and #494 Swingtime. He was most likely associated with Von Nessen at this time since the etchings were developed expressly for Stanhope.

Josef O. Balda

Josef Balda designed several etchings and some early stemware for Heisey. He was a free-lance designer who lived in the Newark area and assigned many of his designs to the Heisey Company. He also did designs for some of the other glass companies. He is known to have designed #3315 Polonaise stemware, #3350 Wabash stemware and the #4166 jug. He also designed #387 Augusta etching, #413 Renaissance etching, #440 Frontenac etching, #439 Pied Piper etching and #671 Entente cutting, #674 Adams cutting and #680 Crusader cutting. In addition, he may have designed the stems on which these decorations appear in the patent drawings. This is unclear.

Andrew J. Sanford

Andrew J. Sanford was Heisey's primary designer during the colonial years and is responsible for many of the colonial patterns. He also designed many of the sanitary syrups, light shades and baskets. Some of the items he designed were in the following patterns: #352 Flat Panel, #393 Narrow Flute, #468 Octagon with Rim, #451 Cross Lined Flute and #473 and #475 Narrow Flute with Rim. He also designed several early colognes—including #489, #490, #491 and #492. He was a prolific designer for the Heisey Company.

Rodney C. Irwin

Rodney Irwin held several patents which he assigned to the Heisey Company. He is best known as Heisey's sales manager rather than a designer. He is credited with the design for the #361 "Irwin" ash tray/cigarette holder and the #4044 New Era goblet and plate.

Ray C. Cobel

Ray C. Cobel, the father of Carl Cobel, held only a few designs in his own name, but from information from other former employees, it is likely that he designed many of the patterns and items produced by the company. Ray Cobel was head of the mold-making shop for many years and he was a master craftsman in this department. He is credited with the designs of #3365 Ramshorn stemware, the #15 Duck floral block, the #1486 Coleport soda line, and the #4225 "Cobel" cocktail shaker which proved so popular.

Clyde S. Whipple

Clyde S. Whipple, a Heisey salesman, held a few design patents for Heisey, mainly some early colonial tumblers and several liners -- #1222, #1226 and #1228.

While the majority of the patents in this time period list either E. Wilson Heisey or T. Clarence Heisey as designers, it is highly unlikely that they were responsible for the designs. It is much more likely that their positions in the Heisey Company required that they sign the legal documents necessary for obtaining patents on various Heisey products.

A.H. Heisey & Company History

Much has been written about Augustus H. Heisey and his remarkable achievements in the handmade glass industry. Much more has been said about the A.H. Heisey & Company of Newark, Ohio, producers of "The Finest in Glassware--Made in America by Hand". However one cannot publish a book about this fine company without giving a brief history of the man and his factory.

Augustus H. Heisey was born in Hanover, Germany, on August 25, 1842 and emigrated to America with his family in 1843. They settled in Merrittown, Pennsylvania, where he attended school. His father died while he was still young and his mother returned to Germany leaving him with a sister. After his graduation from the Merrittown Academy, he worked for a short time in the printing business. In 1861 he began his lifelong career in the glass industry by taking a job as a clerk with the King Glass Company of Pittsburgh. On August 21, 1862, he enlisted in the 155th Pennsylvania Infantry and fought with the Union Army during the Civil War. At the war's end, he had been promoted to Captain of Company C.

After his discharge in June, 1865 he returned to his position with the King Company but a short time later joined the Ripley Glass Company as a salesman. It was here that he earned his reputation of "the best glass salesman on the road".

George Duncan had already become a part owner of the Ripley Company and by 1873, was the sole owner. In the meantime Heisey had met Duncan's daughter, Susan, whom he married in 1870. On April 14, 1874, Duncan deeded a one-fourth interest in the company to each of his children, his son James and Susan Heisey. Terms of the sale were "one dollar and natural love and affection". The name of the company was changed to George Duncan & Sons at that time.

George Duncan died in 1877 and on May 6, 1879, Heisey and James Duncan completed the purchase of his one-half interest and thus became sole owners of the company. The Duncan firm made fine handmade glass which is quite collectible today. Augustus Heisey applied for and obtained several design patents during this time.

In 1891 most glass companies were having great financial difficulties and the United States Glass combine was formed to save them. George Duncan & Sons became a part of U.S. Glass and Heisey became the commercial manager.

In 1893, after a short time out west in the mining industry, Heisey began to formulate plans for his own glass company. He chose Newark, Ohio, because the Newark Board of Trade was actively seeking industry, there was an abundance of natural gas nearby and plenty of low cost labor was available. Construction of the factory at 301 Oakwood Ave. began in 1895 and it opened in April of 1896 with one sixteen-pot furnace. The factory subsequently had three furnaces and employed nearly seven hundred people. There was a great demand for the fine glass and Heisey sold it all over the world.

The production in the early years was confined to pressed ware, much of it of such fine quality and sharpness of design that it appeared to be cut. Much bar and hotel ware was also made. In the late 1890's, Heisey revived the colonial patterns with flutes, scallops and panels which had been so popular earlier in the century. These were so well accepted that from that time on, at least one colonial line was made continuously until the factory closed.

In late 1900, the trademark was designed by a son, George Duncan Heisey, and the famous "H within a diamond" was registered in late 1901. The registration papers noted that the mark had been in use since November, 1900. Heisey was proud of it and insisted that all of the glass be marked. In the late years, less of the glass was marked than formerly, but today's collectors are fortunate that so much of it bears the Diamond H.

The Heisey Company was the pioneer in advertising glassware in magazines nationally and did so as early as 1910. In 1914 they began to make blown ware which they called "Heisey's American Crystal". Not content with traditional pulled stemware, they became the first glass company to make fancy pressed stems. This idea met with approval and most hand-wrought stemware today is made in this manner.

A. H. Heisey died in 1922 and after his death, his son, E. Wilson, became president. He was responsible for most of the colored Heisey glass which is so popular among today's collectors. Some colored glass had been made earlier but first pastel colors, and later deeper ones such as tangerine and cobalt, were in their heyday during the twenties and early thirties. When Wilson Heisey died in 1942, colored glass had all but disappeared from the market.

After his death another son of A.H. Heisey, T. Clarence Heisey, became the president. The war years curtailed the glass industry considerably. During the forties and fifties, the famous Heisey figurines were made. There was some resurrection of colored glass in the last few years. By this time foreign competition was taking its toll and many glass companies were once more in trouble. Increasing costs and other problems led to the company's demise and when Heisey closed the doors for Christmas vacation in 1957, they never opened again except to sell out the existing stock.

The old factory still stands today but the proud smokestacks with their Diamond H's are gone and little is left to remind one of those glorious years when the "Finest in Glassware" was being made in Newark.

The Imperial Glass Corporation of Bellaire, Ohio, bought the existing molds in 1958. They have used only a small portion of them, mostly patterns being made when Heisey closed. Prior to January 1, 1968, part of this glass was still being made with the Heisey mark, but at that time Imperial announced that they would no longer use it. Today's glass is either marked with Imperial's I.G. or not all all. Imperial Glass went out of business in 1984 and all of its assets were sold by a liquidator in 1985. The HCA was fortunate in being able to purchase most of the existing Heisey molds formerly in the possession of Imperial.

Heisey owed its beauty to an excellent glass formula, high quality raw materials, and to the way it was finished—fire polishing, and grinding and polishing the bottoms of most pieces. Glass made today is heavier, duller and not ordinarily as well finished on the bottom and is inclined to have sags in it. A careful study should enable any collector to tell the difference.

Heisey Collectors of America, Inc.

In 1969, a group of nine Heisey Collectors from in and around Newark, Ohio, met and formed the Newark Heisey Collectors Club in order to share their finds and their knowledge. On the occasion of the 75th anniversary of the founding of A.H. Heisey & Company in 1970, the group was asked to put on a display at the Buckingham House in the Sixth Street Museum Park to benefit the Licking County Historical Society. Thousands of visitors came from all over the United States to see the exhibit.

The Newark Club was asked again in 1971 to put on a display in conjunction with the Land of Legend Festival, an annual event. This display was held in one of the local schools and an antique show was added. Proceeds were shared with the Land of Legend Festival Committee and the Historical Society. The Heisey Club issued a souvenir plate made by Imperial in a Heisey mold and the receipts from these plates and the club's share of the admission to the other events were set aside for a future museum.

A short-lived national club for Heisey Collectors operating out of California announced its intention to dissolve in July, 1971. There was so much interest in a new national club to be based in Newark that the Newark group, by then having 20 members, voted to organize such a club. On October 15, 1971, the Heisey Collectors of America, Inc., a non-profit corporation dedicated to the collection and preservation of the products of the A.H. Heisey & Company was founded. Membership was opened to collectors nationwide on January 1, 1972. From that small beginning, there are now thousands of members representing all fifty states, the District of Columbia and Canada. There are also many study groups from coast to coast chartered by HCA.

One of the goals of the organization, stated in the Constitution, was to found a museum in Newark, Ohio, for preserving Heisey glass. In July of 1973, the club was offered as a gift one of Newark's oldest and finest homes to use as a museum. The house, built in 1831 for Samuel Dennis King, a prominent attorney, had been lived in by members of the King family for all the intervening years. It was now to be torn down, along with the entire block where it stood, to make way for a motel.

The house was accepted by the Club and was moved to its new site in the Sixth Street Museum Park in September 1973. After extensive renovation and repair, and the addition of lighted cabinets throughout, the museum was opened in September, 1974, and was dedicated in June, 1975, during the HCA's annual convention.

The beautiful old Greek Revival house with its eight rooms of Heisey glass, and other memorabilia, tools, etc. in its lower level, has become a mecca for Heisey collectors. Everyone who loves fine glass, and Heisey in particular, should pay a visit to this fine museum which has already delighted thousands of visitors from all over the U.S.A. and the world.

How Heisey Glassware Was Made

The origin of glass is almost completely lost in the past. Probably glass has been made for 3500 or 4000 years. The story told by Pliny, ancient historian, of the discovery of glass relates how some Phoenician merchants, having landed or been shipwrecked on the coast of Palestine, were preparing their repast. Finding no stones on the sandy beach upon which to place their pots, they brought cakes of nitre from their cargo for that purpose. The nitre thus being submitted to the heat of the fire, combined with the sand on the shore, produced transparent streams of an unknown liquid which hardened when cool. Such was the origin of glass.

It's a pretty story and somewhat plausible, but the glass thus made must have been greatly different from that we know today. Yet the base of all glass is now, and always has been silica. The fact is, glass cannot be made commercially without the use of sand.

Since about one-half of the earth's crust is silica, it would seem to be a very simple thing to make glass. But the fact is, only a very small amount of silica is pure enough to be used in the manufacture of glass. Even the purest silica obtainable must be washed and treated to remove minute impurities.

The silica used in Heisey glass is carefully selected sandstone, crushed, washed and treated several times until it contains less than four-tenths of one percent foreign matter. This is necessary in order to produce a fine quality of glass.

While silica is the base of glass, many other materials are used in conjunction with the sand. Some of these are sodium carbonate, sodium nitrate, lime, potash, lead, zinc and borax. The most used alkali in glass making is sodium carbonate or soda ash. This is a flux for the sand.

Lime is necessary in glass to make it insoluble. The limestone deposits in Northern and Western Ohio are the purest of the many deposits in America, and it is from here that Heisey secures its lime. The limestone is selected with great care, burned and ground to the proper fineness.

Sodium nitrate, or nitre, is imported from Chile. It is purified, or separated from its deposits, by boiling in large receptacles of water, then run into pans, cooled and allowed to crystalize. Nitre is used to speed up the melting process.

Potash is brought from the Strassfurth deposits in Germany. In its natural state, it is contaminated with several other substances which must be eliminated. Potash when used in the proper proportions with lead, gives to glass its bell-like ring. The lead ores mined in Missouri furnish most of the lead used in glassmaking. It is used in the form of litharge, or red lead, and has the property of increasing the brilliance of glass and also imparting resonance, or ring, to it.

Zinc is necessary for glass to withstand sudden changes of temperature. It comes from New Jersey and Missouri.

But Borax is a product of the deserts of California, where it is found as Colmanite or Razorite. From these ores the borax is extracted and refined, reaching the manufacturer with a purity of over 99%.

The materials above are known as heavy chemicals in the glass industry. The constitute probably 98% of the total ingredients in glass. The remainder is largely made up of the coloring or decolorizing chemicals.

How are the beautiful colors in glassware produced? Certain materials which may be called "coloring chemicals" are added to the other materials described above. These chemicals are usually metallic oxides (the "rust" of various metals) and in most instances only a very little is needed to give the desired tint.

Even in the purest sand there is a trace of iron, which would give the glass a slight green tinge. The iron is neutralized by adding manganese, which comes principally from Java or the Caucasus. Selenium gives glass a reddish color, depending on the amount used. A certain quantity is added to produce a rose tint. This material is derived from copper.

Chrome oxide gives a green color and is obtained from New Caledonia. Yellow results from the use of cerium, which comes from monazite sand found in the interior of South America. It takes four months to get the sand to the United States, then a long, expensive process to separate the cerium from the sand.

The Heisey colors—Flamingo rose, Moongleam green, Sahara golden yellow and Alexandrite amethyst—are known for their delicacy, purity and distinctiveness. Only the finest materials, scientifically blended and proportioned, can produce such outstanding, "different" tints. The chemicals that give the Alexandrite color, for instance, comes from a very rare lead ore, of which only a comparatively small amount is in existence. Heisey spares no pain in making their colored glass of the highest possible quality.

The various materials from which glass is made are mixed together. This is called the "batch". As mentioned above, these materials are silica or sand, lime, potash, lead, coloring materials, etc.

The mixing has to be done with great scientific care so as to get the right proportions. Too much sand or too little potash, for example, will keep the batch from melting properly. Incorrect quantities of other materials will affect the quality or the color.

To secure and maintain the highest quality and the delicate colors, the formulas for mixing the batch for Heisey glass have been prepared very painstakingly and are strictly followed.

The fact that Heisey glass contains potash and lead means that it is of the best. Only the finest glass has these elements, which give it a pure texture, ringing tone and brilliancy.

And Heisey's Sahara glass—that wonderful golden color—is the only colored glass that rings like a bell. Try it by snapping it with your finger.

Fire is the transforming element in glass-making, just as it is in making iron or steel. The "batch" of materials mixed together is put into furnaces to be melted by intense heat.

Pot furnaces are used for making high quality glass such as Heisey ware. They are so called because they contain on the average six or eight good-size vessels or "pots". The furnaces are round with an immense chimney through the center, about the base of which the fire burns. The pots are arranged in a circle around the fire, with small openings to the outside. Through these openings the batch is placed, then the pots are sealed so that air and flames cannot reach the materials while being melted. The melting of the materials is known as "fusing", and the heat necessary to bring this about is around 2500 degrees F.

After a while the batch becomes a hot, boiling, thick liquid. Then "fluxes", or materials containing oxygen are added and the temperature of the furnace increased, to remove air bubbles from the molten glass. This is known as the "fining process". The fusing and the fining take about 24 hours.

The best fuel for glass furnaces is natural gas, since it does not give off smoke or impurities and furnishes an even temperature. The gas used in making Heisey glass is obtained from nearby wells. It is pumped in by special compressing machinery in the quantities needed. This machinery, as well as the entire Heisey factory, is operated by electricity, which is generated in Heisey's own power plant.

After the melting process is finished, the "metal" (as glass-workers call the molten glass) is ready to be shaped into the many various forms which we know as table ware. There are two methods for doing this, blowing and pressing.

Hand-blowing is the more ancient method. The Egyptians long ago used it, and the best glass of all ages has been produced by this process. It is the only way in which to obtain the beautiful, dainty and graceful pieces such as Heisey's fine stemware. In other words, these pieces are the result of true handcraft, because the glassblower must necessarily be a skillful artist, a master in making glass.

The glassblower's most important tool is an iron blow-pipe, about five feet long. One end of this is dipped into the molten glass in the furnace pot. Some of the metal clings to the pipe, and the worker transforms it into the shape he wants by blowing his breath through the pipe. He also rolls, twirls and pulls the material, working swiftly and in a fascinating way with his trained mind and fingers.

Molds are used to aid in shaping some pieces while blowing. The molds are made of metal in the shape the glass is to take and lined with cork. The blower takes up molten glass on his pipe as before, thrusts it into the mold, expands it with his breath, while the mold helps to give it the desired form. This is also a handcraft operation.

Watching the production of blown stemware can be a most fascinating experience.

The gathering boy dips the blow pipe into the pot of molten glass and gathers a glob which is trimmed to the right amount. He passes the rod to the glass blower who stands upon a throne above the mold. He blows a bubble and inserts it into the open mold which is then shut by the mold boy. The blower expands the bubble inside the mold to form the bowl. The stem maker applies the molded stem to the base of the bowl, and the foot maker casts the foot, freehand, to the base of the stem. This process leaves a "blowing bubble" between the bowl and the blowing rod. When the glass has cooled enough, the rod is broken from this bubble and the stemware is now ready to leave the blowing shop and go to the finishing room.

When a piece such as a goblet has been blown, it looks elongated, somewhat like a bottle. The top or neck is later cracked off evenly by turning it before a small, hot flame. Then the edges are smoothed off by emery wheels and the heat from a flame.

Many glassware items, like flower bowls, candlesticks, plates, nappies, Early American ware, etc., are made by pressing. This is an interesting process.

A solid iron rod from 4 to 6 feet long, called a "punty" is heated at one end, which is in the shape of a knob. The heated end is then dipped into a pot of molten glass. The workman now rotates the "punty" slowly at first, then faster and faster until he has gathered up sufficient glass or metal to form the article to be made. It is suspended in droplike fashion from the end of the "punty" from which it is placed in the mold.

Molds for pressed ware are usually made of cast iron, in the correct shape and size. The inside of the mold is cut in the pattern desired for the outside of the finished article. A plunger is forced into the mold, pressing the soft glass against the sides of the molds. The plunger shapes the inside of the article while it is pressing the outside into the design of the mold. The temperature of mold and plunger is carefully regulated, by streams of air blown against them, to prevent cracking or roughening the surface of the glass.

Heisey glass made by this process is of high quality, because of the fine ingredients in the glass and the skill used in making it. Heisey craftsmen have also contributed what they know as "pressed, blown lead-potash glass." A variety of Heisey items are of this kind. Handwork and blowing are used in producing them, as well as molds.

As a result this Heisey glass is different from ordinary pressed ware, because the lead and potash in it give it the wonderful ring and brilliancy that only high-quality ware has. Hand-blowing it in the molds adds a finer finish, too.

Here also should be pointed out the difference between the blown ware and ordinary pressed ware. Blown ware is thinner, daintier, more sparkling and more graceful.

After the various glassware items have been given their shape by hand blowing or pressing methods, they are placed in long, tunnel-like kilns, called lehrs, to be tempered or annealed.

This is an important process in the making of glass, because it is through tempering or annealing that the glassware receives its strength, durability and consistent texture. The items are placed in one end of a lehr and as they keep moving on the continous platform, slowly, almost imperceptibly, they are gradually cooled from a temperature of 1100 or 1200F. This permits an even, uniform contraction of the molecular composition of the glass, which was expanded by the heat.

The lehrs in the Heisey glassworks are of the most modern, advanced type, being entirely automatic and thermostatically controlled. This does away with any necessity for manipulation and makes absolutely certain that all articles placed in the lehrs will receive the correct amount of heat at all stages of the tempering process. It is another example of the great care that is taken to maintain the uniform, high quality of Heisey glass.

In order to increase the luster, the piece is held for a few moments in the intense heat of the "Glory Hole". This is known as fire polishing. The "Glory Hole" is the name given to one of the openings in the furnace, with its hot flame. One of the real features of Heisey glass is the fire polish given to it. Extra fuel is used to make the flame more intense. The workmen have acquired through the years a high skill in the art of handling this operation.

The "Glory Hole" is also used to aid in giving the desired shape to some pieces or to restore pliability in case a piece has cooled off too much to be easily worked, particularly in producing blown ware.

Additional polishing is also done on wheels of different kinds. Some of these are emery wheels, or buffing wheels, which are padded with wool. Then there are cork wheels and circular brushes with stiff fibers. Certain polishing materials are used in connection with the wheels, such as powdered pumice-stone, "rough" and putty powder.

Grinding is also done on similar wheels, to remove any rough edges that may be present in the glass. Thus, the glass, when it has gone through the different finishing operations, is smooth and sparkling.

To a large extent, glass is beautiful because its smooth surface has great brilliance and sparkles in the light. When it has been blown or molded into shape, it has considerable natural polish but this needs to be heightened by additional processes to bring out its full charm.

Especially is this true of pressed glass, the surface of which is dulled when it comes into contact with the sides of the metal molds which chill the glass rather quickly.

> . . .Excerpts from an article written by the Heisey Company in the early 1930's to be sent to Heisey's retail dealers.

Book Format

The pattern pages of this book have been taken from several original Heisey catalogs from the years 1925-1938. Using several sources caused unavoidable duplication of some illustrations, although every attempt was made to keep this to a minimum. Catalog pages were chosen since photography would have been an impossibility—many more items could be illustrated than could have been assembled for photographs. The catalog pages vary in format. Earlier pages were horizontal and later ones were vertical. Occasionally these catalog pages contain errors—usually of spelling or of captioning. These errors are corrected in the text pages accompanying the catalog illustrations.

The "Miscellaneous" Section created problems since many of the items shown there would have been more appropriately placed in other categories. Since cutting the catalogs was an unacceptable solution, the alternative chosen was to print the pages intact and cross-reference the entries as much as possible.

Another decision involved organization of the book itself. Format begins with the major pressed tableware patterns of the period, followed by the major stemware patterns. These sections are each arranged in numerical order using Heisey pattern numbers. Following these, several specialized categories are shown: ash trays, baskets, candlesticks, and others. These are arranged alphabetically by subject.

The color section shows representative samples of all the Heisey colors produced during this time period. Some items are shown more than once, but often this was for better detail. An entire page is devoted to each Heisey color. Also individual photographs are shown of the experimental colors such as light blue, unusual shades, and bi-colored items. Table settings are also shown in some colors. Large cabinet photographs are shown of stemware and beer mugs. This permits comparison of various sizes and styles. Full captions are included for these items.

Text pages accompany each major pattern. An outline format is used for each pattern.

1. HEADING: Contains the Heisey pattern number, the name of the pattern and whether the name is an original company name or one which has been given by researchers. The original Heisey Company name is always given preference over any applied name. Pattern numbers in the 7000's or 8000's have been given by researchers for ease of reference and are not original with Heisey.

2. DATES: Lists the beginning and ending dates of the patterns. Occasionally a few pattern items survived past the date when most pieces ceased being available. Dates used as discontinued dates are usually when the majority of the pattern was no longer available. Exceptions are noted. Dates can possibly be misleading by a span of a few months to a few years, depending on the time span between Heisey catalogs. Dates given are best estimates from information available for study.

3. COLORS: Lists the colors found in the pattern. Mention of rare or unusual colors is made here. If only a few items are known in specific colors, every attempt to list these items is made. Crystal is assumed on all lines unless specifically noted as "not listed in crystal."

4. DECORATIONS: Notation is made if the pattern was decorated by the Heisey Company. Mention of decorations by other companies is included if known. Specific Heisey decorations are not listed since these are covered in other books.

5. MARKED: Information is given to indicate if MOST pieces of a pattern are marked with the Diamond H or are unmarked. Location of the mark is mentioned if it is in an unusual location (other than the bottom of the item). Location of marks on stemware is fully decribed. IMPORTANT: The designation "yes" after marked means that it is usual to find pieces marked. Exceptions always exist and often items are found both marked and unmarked. Occasionally an item has not been available for study and the word "unknown" is used.

6. COMMENTS: Pertinent information about the pattern is contained in this section. Special features or unusual items in the pattern are also mentioned. Sometimes more explanation of color and color availability in the pattern is listed here.

7. IMPERIAL REISSUES: This section states whether Imperial Glass has reissued any pieces in the pattern along with dates and colors made. More detailed information on this subject is contained in the book, *Heisey By Imperial*.

8. AVAILABILITY: This is a judgmental decision based on the opinions of several people as to whether most pieces in the pattern are easy or difficult to find. It is not meant to indicate the availability of individual items. The terms used are COMMON, MODERATELY AVAILABLE and SCARCE.

Two other categories are included on pages where they apply. OPTIC indicates if items of the pattern were available other than plain. This usually applies to stemware but occasionally to pressed ware too. Various optics were used by Heisey and most were made during this time period. A full discussion of Heisey optics is contained in the section, OPTICS. PATENTS indicates pieces of the pattern which were patented by Heisey, the patent number, when applied for, when granted and the designer. Often either E. Wilson Heisey or T. Clarence Heisey were listed as designers. In reality, it is unlikely that they were the designers of these patterns. It is far more likely that they simply signed the legal papers necessary for the patent applications.

One final, important note needs to be made about color. In the individual discussions of the colors beginning and ending dates are listed. In all actuality, the beginning date is listed as when the color was first marketed. Development and experimentation were certainly carried on for a fairly long period before this date. Also, the ending date indicates when the color was no longer listed in company price lists. In actuality, the company did produce matching and special orders for many years after the color was technically out of production. Archives in the Heisey Museum contain references to an order for Tangerine in the 1950's.

Heisey Colors

Vaseline
Circa 1923-1924

At some time in the early twenties, Heisey began its return to color production with experimentation in vaseline glass. A bright vaseline-colored glass had been made by Heisey early (ca. 1899 or 1900) and was called Canary. It is possible that the later production was a variation of the old canary formula. Both are uranium-based, yellow-green glass and fluoresce under black light.

No documentation in original factory catalogs or old ads has been found indicating whether this color was ever produced beyond the experimental stage. The fact that pieces being made in the early twenties exist in the vaseline color indicates the approximate time of development of the color. Pieces are found in vaseline with the patent date of 8/30/21 impressed in the mold. Also since several colonial pieces are found, the production period would seem to be before the development of such dinnerware patterns as Twist and Empress. The last item to be designed which is found in vaseline is the #1201 Laverne floral bowl, thought to have been new in 1923 or 1924. Thus best estimates for the time of production for vaseline seem to be circa 1923-1924.

According to former employees' reminiscences, the color was not pleasing to company executives. This may indeed be true since there seems to be no one pattern with many pieces found in vaseline. Rather, individual pieces found are from many patterns and this may indicate that the company was searching for a pleasing combination of pattern and color.

Since the pieces also vary so greatly in depth of color, it is possible that some experimentation in differing shades was done. Another possibility may be that the color was judged to be unattractive to Heisey's customers and thus never marketed.

The name "vaseline" is a term used by today's collectors to describe the color. Vaseline items produced by Heisey in the 1920 era are usually much paler when compared to vaseline items made by other companies. While some pieces do glow with the yellow-green cast usually associated with the color, many more are very pale, some hardly distinguishable from crystal at first glance.

Vaseline items are not easy to find and are usually quite expensive. Probably the most often seen pieces are the #1020 Phyllis cream and sugar. Several #3345 Mary 'n' Virg stems have been found—some entirely vaseline, others with a crystal bowl and vaseline stem and foot. Pieces of #473 Narrow Flute with Rim, #465 Recessed Panel and #350 Pinwheel and Fan are sometimes found in vaseline.

Vaseline should not be confused with Heisey's ovenware or bakeware. Heisey called this product its "Visible Cooking Ware" and produced it for a short time in the teens. These pieces often have a slightly yellow shade, but they are not true vaseline glass.

Moongleam
Late 1925-1935

Production records of the Heisey Company indicate that on March 14, 1925, the #3357 King Arthur goblets were made in green. This was the first mention of color in the records of this period, making Moongleam the first Heisey production color of the twenties. The glass shop, headed by L. Kime, made these historic items.

Moon Gleam (it was spelled as two words much of the time by Heisey) was described as "the green of moonlight on the sea" in old ads.

Early pieces of moongleam bear a striking resemblance to Heisey's old emerald green, made during the late 1890's. In fact, moongleam may be an adaptation of the old emerald formula. So closely are the two related, it is difficult to tell the difference with the naked eye. The best method of separating the colors is by comparing the known production periods of the pieces in question. The 1890's pieces are emerald while 1920's pieces are moongleam—no matter how similar they might be in appearance. Emerald and moongleam do react differently under ultraviolet light. Zircon and limelight are other greenish colors made by Heisey, but since they are a turquoise-blue-green, usually they pose no problem to the collector.

Later pieces of moongleam are not so deep in color as are the early pieces. The later shade seems to be less of a yellow green and somewhat more subdued. Certainly the company revised the formula for moongleam to come up with this new shade. By 1929, the formula seems to have stabilized to a pleasant, soft green. This shade is the color most often seen in #1252 Twist and #1401 Empress. Some of the earlier patterns are found in both shades of green. These include #1170 Pleat and Panel, several stemware patterns such as #3357 King Arthur and #3355 Fairacre and quite a number of the individual accessory pieces. The #1020 Phyllis cream and sugar, the #5 Patrician candelabrum and other early pieces are found in the early moongleam shade.

Heisey's moongleam formulae included copper scale (a mixture of cupric oxide and cuprous oxide) and green oxide chrome as coloring agents. Both of these are the sources of the green color. Glass using copper and chromium oxide yields different shades of blue-green depending on the quantities in the mix. Chromium oxide is also sometimes added to glass to modify the green color in copper glass. The melting point of the mix also may affect the color since a lower melting point tends to result in a bluish color rather than green.

Moongleam was a very popular color during its time. It is probably the third most available color to today's collectors. Since its life spanned several years, many patterns and pieces are available. Almost any type piece was made in moongleam—ash trays, candlesticks, colognes, floral bowls, and water sets to name only a few. Later patterns available in moongleam include #1404 Old Sandwich, #1405 Ipswich, #1428 Warwick and a limited number of items in #1425 Victorian.

Moongleam was featured in a great many luncheon sets and water sets. Desirability of the color was spurred by numerous articles in women's magazines of the time promoting the use of green glass as the perfect color for summer entertaining. Green glass had a cooling effect in the summer heat according to the authors who helped set the style trends of the 1920's and 1930's.

In 1929, Heisey spoke of moongleam in this way:

> "Moon Gleam by Heisey has always proved to be a green of charming distinction. One of the many points in its favor is that it harmonizes so satisfactorily with any other green, or color schemes that go well with green. Moon Gleam has a deep brilliancy, too, a demonstration of the quality with which it is created."

Flamingo
Late 1925-1935

Very soon after introducing moongleam, Heisey began making flamingo. With it, the company had its most successful color as far as sales were concerned. Today it is the most commonly found color made by Heisey. While flamingo was the official name always used in ads and trade reports, a simple "rose" was used to refer to the color in company records.

The first pieces of flamingo listed in turn books were made during the week of December 19, 1925. These items included the #107 candlesticks, the #112 candlesticks and #406 5" nappies for plates.

A distinctive orange-red tone in pink glass is responsible for the name "flamingo" which is very apt, since it truly has the shade of the flamingo bird. Heisey produced a special label for some of its flamingo ware and it featured the bird prominently in a diamond-shaped label. Many collectors today like to add a piece of flamingo to their collections which still bears this distinctive label.

Heisey described flamingo as "the rose tint of tropical plumage" in old ads. In 1926 they advised their salesmen in a letter, saying: "We note in most cases that you are sending orders in flamingo with the word rose. We know this is much easier, but there are and will be quite a few roses on the market, so that if we call ours Flamingo the public will think of our product as something distinctive from ordinary rose. And it is, as far as anything we have seen so far is concerned."

As the company indicated, much flamingo is distinguishable from pink glass made by other companies. Today's Heisey collectors are often able to tell a piece of Heisey flamingo from other companies' products. Early pieces, however, tend to be of a paler rose and lack some of the orange tone typical in most items and these early pieces are more difficult to identify by shade alone. Of course, it is always safest to identify Heisey by patterns rather than colors. Flamingo is also found in a great many shades of color and sometimes matching patterns can be difficult if exact matches in color are needed.

Heisey's flamingo color is characterized by wide variations in shade and hue. It ranges from a mild pink, sometimes tinged with orange, to a nearly brown, muddy color. This is caused by the use of selenium as a coloring agent. Although selenium is what made flamingo pink, it also had some unpleasant side effects—glass containing selenium has a tendency to burn out, changing the hue of the glass as it sits in the furnace. It is also possible that color changes can occur during the annealing process. Also, in order to maintain consistent coloration when using selenium, it is critical to provide identical furnace conditions for each batch of glass, as well as identical ingredients. The difficulty of controlling these conditions is probably what led to the differences in the flamingo Heisey we see today.

Flamingo continued to be a color in great favor with the homemaker for a number of years. This is typical of the experience of other companies who also indicated that their primary color sales came from pink or rose colored glass. This is mentioned in several references in contemporary accounts.

Several of the major patterns found in flamingo include #1170 Pleat and Panel, #1252 Twist, #1401 Empress, with more limited production in #1428 Warwick, #1404 Old Sandwich and #1405 Ipswich. Stemware in flamingo was quite popular—either in solid color or in combination with crystal. Many patterns were made including #3357 King Arthur, #3355 Fairacre, #3370 African, #3365 Ramshorn, #3324 Delaware and others. In rare instances, flamingo was used in combination with moongleam—usually in #3481 Glenford, a barware and soda line. Apparently some experimentation in using old molds occurred since a few pieces of the old #325 Pillows pattern have also been found in flamingo.

In 1929 Heisey described flamingo as "One of the most popular colors brought out in recent years is Flamingo by Heisey. In its many patterns and multitude of pieces, this distinctive rose tint has remained from the beginning unexcelled in brilliancy, fire and uniformity. Customers see and realize these unusual characteristics of Flamingo and hence it has an appeal that not only endures but grows stronger."

Amber
Circa 1926+

Amber as a Heisey color in this period is not listed in company price lists, although a few items are listed in old turn ledgers for the latter part of 1926. Many of these items seem to have been made for Fred Harvey. (See HARVEY AMBER ITEMS Section.) An entry was also found for the #1170 Pleat and Panel oil bottle in amber. Other hand-written notations in the 1938 catalog refer to the #1417 Arch tumbler in amber.

Other items during this period were made in amber although production seems to have been limited. Possibly these pieces were special orders or sample items only. The easiest items found in amber which were apparently not for Fred Harvey are the #1404 Old Sandwich beer mugs. The #110 Sandwich Dolphin candlesticks are also sometimes found in amber, but these are quite scarce.

The Heisey Company used a carbon ingredient as the coloring agent in their amber glass. Even though the coloring agents are cheap in a carbon-based glass, there are some production problems, especially during the melting process, in keeping the glass clear and free from inclusions and bubbles. There is some indication that early amber production may have contained selenium in the formula. Amber or topaz colored glass (rather than pink glass) can be made from selenium if furnace conditions are controlled differently.

Finding Heisey amber items from this period is difficult. Production, except for the Fred Harvey restaurants, was limited and collectors should consider themselves fortunate to own amber items from this period. Later in 1952 Heisey again marketed a limited line of amber items. While not plentiful, they are more available than the 1930's pieces.

Hawthorne
1927-1928

Heisey introduced hawthorne to the trade in 1927 with a huge fanfare, including devoting a complete issue of their *Table Talk* to the new color. *Table Talk* was their monthly newsletter mailed to salesmen and customers. The quotes from this May, 1927, issue describe the color and the wares completely.

"Heisey's Hawthorne Glassware appeals to people. This was ascertained before putting it into extensive production and before releasing it to the trade.

"People are delighted with Hawthorne because it looks so exquisite on the table—the rare, elusive tint adds a new charm that is wonderfully delightful. And it is such beautiful glassware! The finest quality of blown and pressed items made by Heisey craftsmen. . .

"A wide variety of Heisey's fine glassware comes in the new Hawthorne color—the beautiful amethyst tint that is proving its popularity. Selections can be made for a complete table service in a number of patterns. . .

"Pieces for every occasion and purpose can be had in the Hawthorne tint. A few of them are bouillon cups and plates, service plates, salad plates, coffee cups and saucers, sandwich plates and dessert plates . . .

"A complete selection of glasses is offered, such as goblets, sherbets, saucer champagnes, fruit and oyster cocktails, parfaits, tumblers, and soda and ice tea glasses. Jugs or pitchers of different designs are included. Then there are a variety of accessories, as, for instance, comports, flower bowls, candlesticks, salts and peppers, mayonnaise dishes, nut and bon bons, condiment dishes, and many more. The smoker may have cigarette jars and ash trays and for the dressing table, there are perfume bottles and powder containers."

In spite of this extravagant introduction, hawthorne apparently was not the sales success that Heisey anticipated. Its life span was only one year. The color is an attractive shade of lavender, especially when set on a white tablecloth. As with many of Heisey's other colors, it also is found in several shades. Unfortunately for hawthorne, some of the shades tend to be a muddy color and lack the delicate tint of lavender the company was striving for. Most stemware tends to be of a pleasing shade and some is a vibrant amethyst.

During this period, Heisey began producing a new optic which they called "checker optic." This is primarily found in hawthorne stemware and blown sodas. This optic is composed of alternating squares of about 1 inch which are divided into fine lines. This effectively gives the impression of a checkerboard, although the effect is very delicate and not at all strong.

Hawthorne was also used in combination with moongleam in a few instances, mainly in the #4206 Optic Tooth pattern, which has moongleam bases with hawthorne bowls. A few pieces in #3361 Charlotte stemware are known with moongleam stem and foot and hawthorne bowls. Any piece in these two color combinations should be considered rare.

Patterns found in hawthorne include some items in #411 Tudor, #417 Double Rib & Panel, #1184 Yeoman, #1229 Octagon and #1231 Ribbed Octagon. Stemware patterns include #3324 Delaware, #3360 Penn Charter (both with checker optic), #3333 Old Glory, #3366 Trojan and several soda lines.

As with flamingo, Heisey used a special label on some of their hawthorne glass and this is an added attraction to many collectors.

Marigold
1929-1930

Early in 1929, Heisey brought out a new color in new patterns for the trade shows. This color was their first attempt in yellow—a color which was proving popular for other companies. As usual, Heisey was not content to make the standard soft yellow widely used by machine glass houses and other cheaper glass manufacturers. Heisey's yellow was a strong, vibrant shade which they aptly named marigold.

Contemporary trade journal reports described the color fully:

"One of the distinctive new colors put on the market this season is unquestionably the 'marigold' which A.H. Heisey & Co., Newark, Ohio, has just produced. The Heisey concern has been working on this marigold for many months, and has certainly produced a tone that is well worth while. It is a distinct though lightish yellow, with a touch of green about it. As a matter of fact, it is somewhat suggestive of the plumage of the canary that shows a bit of the green in its feathers. This green suggestion, however, is so slight that it can only be seen when the items are studied carefully and held in just the proper light. Under ordinary illumination the color is true yellow. The green touch, incidentally, was no mistake, but was put in with deliberation and adds much to the tone. Here is a color, by the way, that is absolutely up to date and novel, and is a real addition to the Heisey color range. In it is produced a full line of wares, both pressed and blown; and whether the item is a delicate bit of stemware or an imposing bowl, the color shows equally well on both." (Pottery, Glass & Brass Salesman, January 31, 1929.)

The description here is quite accurate, especially indicating the green tint most easily seen on the edges of marigold pieces. It is usually a fairly strong yellow-green almost of the same shade as the green seen in depression glass. Occasionally, in certain lights, a piece will show an amber-red tinge on the edges rather than the green tinge.

Marigold proved to be immediately popular with both the Heisey salesmen and the buying public. The following statement was made by George A. Granville, the New England representative for the Heisey Company and was printed in the Heisey Company publication, Table Talk:

". . . In one of the large stores I opened up this Marigold line and placed it on a table awaiting the attention of the buyer. He looked it over, admitted it was good-looking, but was not sufficiently interested to buy it.

". . . A customer was interested in the glassware on display. . . she liked the color and the etching appealed particularly to her, and to quote her, she said: 'Regardless of the low price it is certainly the most beautiful etching and glassware I have seen in a long time.' The buyer then gave me a nice order for stock. When he saw what a big appeal the Marigold color in etching 447 has, he wanted to be in a position to offer it to other customers." (Etching 447 is Heisey's Empress.)

The #1252 Twist pattern in marigold was a very popular line for Heisey. Also in *Table Talk*, they reported that entire tea rooms in large hotels were furnished entirely with marigold Twist.

In spite of all this popularity, marigold was doomed to a short life. This was not due to a diminished popularity, but because the glass tended to be unstable. Even while working or mixing the glass, it had a tendency to "spit" at the workers, making it dangerous to be around. Even today, marigold is often found in an unstable state. Sometimes pieces are found with a crazing or "crizzling" that can be from just a slight amount to a level in which the entire piece is semi-opaque.Some items become so badly deteriorated that flakes of glass fall from the pieces. It is doubtful that all marigold glass will eventually deteriorate, but collectors should be aware that once a piece has evidence of crazing, it will never become clear, and in all probability, may deteriorate further.

Because of the problems of manufacture, the Heisey Company continued experimentation to find a stable yellow color and this eventually led to their very popular sahara color which was introduced in 1930.

Heisey's marigold color resulted from using sodium uranate and cadmium sulphide as coloring agents. Uranium in glass, under oxidizing conditions, produces a yellow glass which is strongly fluorescent. Cadmium sulphide gives glass a yellow color and an orange fluorescence—so this is probably responsible for the variety of marigold now referred to as "gold". It is possible that the instability of some marigold items is the result of unusually large crystals being formed during the production of the glass, causing it to become excessively brittle.

Gold

A variation of marigold exists which is readily separated from most marigold with the use of a black light. Under the black light, the gold variation will fluoresce a bright orange—entirely different from the usual color which is a strong yellow green.

It is doubtful that gold (which is what modern collectors call the variation) was an intentional variant of marigold. It is more likely that it was an early formula and was used for a very short time—possibly only as an experimental batch. Few items have been found in gold, but they are all items which are listed in price lists as marigold—another indication that the company did not view it as an independent color. Collectors today are fortunate to find a piece of gold, but again, it should be considered an oddity—not a rarity. Its value and interest are in the striking color variation—most easily seen under the black light as mentioned before. It is not considered a Heisey production color but a shade, although more striking in variation than shades found in other Heisey colors.

Sahara
1930-1937

After the difficulties with marigold, Heisey continued experimentation to make a stable yellow color. In 1930 they succeeded with their popular sahara. It was probably the most successful of Heisey's colors in terms of sales with the exception of flamingo.

Sahara yellow used both red lead and cerium hydrate as the principal coloring agents. Cerium and titanium oxide (also an ingredient in sahara) produce a yellow color in glass.

The glass trade was impressed with the Heisey sahara as evidenced by a report in March, 1932: "In the 1932 Heisey line a step forward has been made that cannot be stressed too strongly. This is the feat of producing the sparkling gold Sahara color in ringing, resonant lead glass. Until achieved by Heisey the production of golden yellow glass commonly called topaz in lead glass was considered an impossibility. Heisey had likewise succeeded in making pressed lead glass giving to the pressed table pieces the clear ringing glass of lead glass stemware."

Sahara is a brilliant, glowing yellow glass still popular today with many collectors. Contemporary trade journal accounts highly praise sahara:

> "Sahara—this is a golden yellow, and, as the name would indicate, it suggests the golden sands of
> the dessert. It is a rich and attractive tone. . . (It) is one of the most charming colors of its type on
> the market. It looks well in the plain, but carries ornamentation to splendid advantage."

As suggested by the previous report, much sahara was decorated with various Heisey etchings. In fact, sahara with Old Colony etching is a specialty of many of today's collectors.

In *Table Talk*, the Heisey Company described sahara thus:

> "The subtle, warm glow of the new Sahara golden tint provides a high point in your glassware displays
> from the very start. It surpasses we believe in depth and strength of tone anything of a yellow hue
> now being offered. It is lighter, more sparkling and more delicate than the widely favored Marigold
> color."

In various Heisey ads of the time, sahara was described as "bright with the golden tone of sunshine . . .," and "a bright hue of yellow desert sand," and "the yellow of sunny sands." The company continued to tie the feeling of warmth of sun and sand to the name "sahara" in most of its advertising. Obviously, this was effective since Sahara is fairly easy to locate today and still remains very popular with collectors.

Patterns found in sahara include #1401 Empress, #1404 Old Sandwich, #1405 Ipswich, #1425 Victorian and #1428 Warwick among many others. Stemware in #3389 Duquesne, #3380 Old Dominion, #3390 Carcassonne and #3397 Gascony among others are found in sahara.

Alexandrite
1930-1935

In 1930, Heisey was successful in introducing their new lavender color replacing the unsuccessful hawthorne. Alexandrite was an instant success and is one of the most lovely of the Heisey colors. It shades from a warm orchid-red to a cooler orchid-blue. When introduced, fluorescent lights were not in use and the company did not realize that the glass had a rather unattractive greenish-blue tint when viewed under this lighting. This does not detract from it in the eyes of most collectors, however. It is an easy way to distinguish hawthorne from alexandrite for the person who is unsure of the two colors.

Heisey described alexandrite in this way in *Table Talk*:

"The intriguing color of the glass, Alexandrite, greatly heightens the effect. Alexandrite is an outstanding Heisey achievement in glassware tinting. Flashing with the delicate glow of treasured amethyst, it is a dainty, tantalizing purple. It is the only amethyst color in glass which remains brilliant under artificial light. Also as one looks at it from different angles, one sees a powder blue tint, then a ruby glow, and again the amethyst is prominent. These qualities coupled with the fashionableness of the glass, place it in a favored position with discriminating customers."

Heisey also used this description in ads of the time:

"When you see this new Alexandrite glassware by Heisey, you are struck with the wonder of its soft, elusive radiance. Tinted like some rare orchid petal, the fleeting glow of the sapphire, it is an American triumph for exclusive American tables."

The remark about "exclusiveness" may have been in reference to the fact that alexandrite was the most expensive of Heisey's colors. Even tangerine, which commands high prices today, was not as expensive to produce. Because of this, Heisey promoted the color as acceptable and proper for their prestige trade.

Pottery, Glass & Brass Salesman gives the following report of alexandrite—interesting because of the excellent description of the color but more importantly, indicating that Heisey did indeed obtain the formula from Europe—certainly from Moser who was producing a similar color:

"It is not going too far to say that 'Alexandrite' is as striking a color as has ever made its appearance in glassware and the more it is studied, the more its richness becomes apparent and the difficulties that surround its manufacture are appreciated. It is a foreign invention brought to this country with rare progressiveness by the Heisey Co. . .

"The complexity of its nature is best seen under artificial light. When viewed from one angle the powder blue is most in evidence. A little twist and the ruby becomes prominent. Again, a turn and it is the amethyst that is outstanding. By its very nature the color will appeal most to the high-class, exclusive trade, and has already found a considerable market in this field."

This variation in color is properly termed "dichroic" or "dichromatic" glass. This means that the glass shows different colors depending on the angle of the light falling on it or transmitted through it. This is due to the presence of neodymium in alexandrite as a coloring agent. To quote W.A. Weyl from *Colored Glasses:*

"It is extremely difficult to describe the colours of glasses containing oxides of neodymium or praesodymium or both. The characteristic delicate purple of a neodymium glass might look to the untrained observer like a combination of selenium pink with traces of cobalt oxide, but so soon as the two types of glass are compared in artificial light, the observer is impressed by the tremendous difference; for the neodymium glass appears as a brilliant red, whereas the specimens containing other colourants possess a noticeable grey content which makes them look dull in artificial light. Perhaps the most attractive feature of neodymium glasses is their 'dichroism.' The colour sensation not only varies with the type of illumination, but also with the thickness of the glass layer. In thin layers or with low concentration of neodymium these glasses are blue, in thick layers or with high concentrations, red. This play of colour is purposely accentuated in the Moser glasses by their form and deep cutting. They are shaped into forms which allow some of the light to pass through thin layers, whereas the rest follows a much longer path."

Koloman L. Moser was a glass-worker and designer from Karlsbad, Bohemia, in the early 1900's who developed "Alexandrit" glass, among other types.

Heisey made many patterns in alexandrite. The main pattern for pressed ware was #1401 Empress. Stemware was made in #3390 Carcassonne and #3381 Creole plus a few other patterns which are more difficult to find. Several accessory pieces were also made in alexandrite, including vases, ball vases, jugs, some colonial items (including a few stems) and candlesticks. A few rare pieces are known in an alexandrite/sahara combination—notably in Carcassonne and the #134 Trident candlesticks.

Tangerine
1932-1935

Heisey's most elusive production color of this period viewed from today's standpoint is tangerine. Many collectors count themselves lucky to own even one piece in this color and those who are able to assemble table settings are indeed fortunate.

In 1932 the Heisey line introduced bolder, deeper colors. Pastels were beginning to wane and Heisey decided to promote tangerine and cobalt blue. Tangerine is an apt name for the color since it is most often found in a deep orange red typical of the tangerine fruit. Sometimes the color deepens to almost a true red. This shade is referred to as "red side" by Heisey collectors, and usually commands a price premium since it is in much less supply.

Tangerine is a flashed or struck color—meaning that the true color does not appear until the article of glass is reheated in the glory hole. Then the true orange-red appears. This is also why there are so many shadings in this particular color—a little overheating or underheating resulted in a different shade. Occasionally a piece of tangerine is found with an almost amberina shading. A few plates have been seen in which the centers were a deep yellow with the edges being tangerine. This again is due to the reheating process in the glory hole.

Again, old ads and trade journal reports describe the color and the items made in the new tangerine:

"A.H. Heisey & Co. have just introduced a new color which they call 'Tangerine'. This is made in a full stemware line which offers a fancy crystal foot and stem. It also is made in flatware. The Heisey firm is the first to produce this color which is most unusual and very beautiful." (August, 1932).

Gascony sodas and stemware are described in the following account:

"A great point is made of a new color at Heisey's that's as startling a departure as you could want—Tangerine—a clear, yet deep shade that's very gay and appetizing—just the tone to offer a good color harmony with much of the new dinnerware and the new linens. You may have this at present in two ranges—a tall stem line, No. 3389, the one with the hexagonal slightly tapered stem and the slightly cupped-in flared optic-type bowl and the low-footed No. 3397 line that has the hexagonal base—just the bowls are colored in both style ranges. You may retail goblets around $7.00 a dozen. In a little while you'll be able to have this new color in bridge sets, candlesticks, vases, bowls and other decorative pieces. . . 19 piece bridge sets will retail for $9.00."

By December, 1932, Heisey was bringing out their new Spanish stemware in tangerine. A report noted the following:

"Spanish Stemware in Heisey's Tangerine
"New Spanish shapes in stemware with crystal stems and bowls of Heisey's new tangerine will make a table as exotic as the blaze of colors in a Senorita's embroidered shawl. The hostess who wants something different in table settings will find it in these new designs. . ."

While the new color was heralded by the trade and apparently enjoyed at least a short period of popularity, it seems to have lost favor quickly. By 1935, it was no longer listed as available in price lists. Of course, as with other colors and lines, the company continued to offer matching pieces for some time after this date.

As indicated from the trade reports, several styles of stemware were available in tangerine—the first available was #3389 Duquesne, followed shortly by #3397 Gascony and #3404 Spanish. Pressed ware is usually found in the #1401 Empress pattern. Candlesticks (#134) were also made in tangerine. The actual availability of tangerine items is small, possibly due to the difficulty of maintaining the quality of the glass and the consistency of the color. The many variations of shading found in examples today indicate that the company had difficulty producing the color in quantities in the same shade. A few unusual blown bottles or vases are known in tangerine—mostly in the deeper "red side". The #4224 ivy vase is sometimes found in tangerine, although it is not listed in price lists and some experts are uncertain that it is a Heisey product. A very unusual #351 14 oz. pilsner has also been found in tangerine. A few items in #1404 Old Sandwich are also known in the color.

Blown tangerine items sometimes have a semi-opaque quality to them which is difficult to describe—possibly this condition also results from either difficulty with the formula or maintaining the proper mix. Tangerine items also often seem to have several bubbles or other small defects in blown bowls of stemware especially. None of these factors seem to decrease the value of items in this popular color and collectibility remains very high.

Stiegel Blue
(Cobalt)
1933-1941

Heisey continued in the vein of producing strong colors when it began production of Stiegel blue in 1933. This color is called simply cobalt by modern collectors.

Cobalt or Stiegel blue obtained its color from black oxide copper (cupric oxide) and cobalt black oxide. Powdered blue is probably a mixture of cobalt oxide and alumina and was also used. Restrictions in the use of cobalt for non-military or non-necessary use during the period of World War II probably hastened the end of Heisey's cobalt production.

Cobalt is extremely popular with today's collectors and it seems somewhat surprising that more mentions of the new color were not found in accounts of the time. Perhaps it was popular enough without much advertising.

In January, 1933, the two major trade publications both offered small reports about the new color.

"One of the outstanding lines in Heisey's offerings for 1933 is a Cobalt blue line of stemware with exceptionally heavy ball stems in crystal, a reproduction of an old Spanish design. In this blue, also, come many odd pieces, vases, candelabra, cocktail shakers and bowls.

"Among the novelties are four styles in beer mugs which may be had in crystal or colors including the new Cobalt blue and a ball jug which. . . is made all in one piece." (*Crockery & Glass Journal*)

". . . a new complete range of table and stemware in a blue color which is a new Heisey product. Strangely enough, while Heisey has always pioneered in colors, the concern has never before brought out a deep blue. This is a real royal blue. It might even be referred to as a cobalt. Certain it is that it would tie up well with a dinnerware service carrying a rich cobalt band. Possibly the concern had that in mind when the color was produced.

"Stemware is made with crystal stem and foot, jugs with crystal handles, and the candlesticks are hung with crystal bobeches." *(Pottery, Glass & Brass Salesman)*

The stem line referred to is #3404 Spanish. It is interesting to note that Spanish is also referred to as "French Provincial" in some early reports. The "ball jug" referred to is the #1231 Ribbed Octagon rum pot—a very desirable item in colors.

Heisey cobalt is a very rich, deep blue. It appears almost opaque in heavier pieces. Combined with crystal it is truly striking.

Stemware is most often found in the #3404 Spanish pattern although there was some production in #3390 Carcassonne and #4044 New Era also. Several vases, jugs, barware, candlesticks and other occasional items were made in cobalt also. Pressed tableware patterns such as #1404 Old Sandwich, #1405 Ipswich, #1401 Empress, #1425 Victorian and #1428 Warwick also contain items made in cobalt, but often the entire pattern line was not available in the color.

Zircon
1936-1939

Zircon is a lovely turquoise blue-green. It is quite attractive, especially when combined with saturn optic, as it often is. The Heisey Company apparently did not advertise the new color heavily as very few references are found in old ads or trade journal accounts.

Zircon used the ingredients of powdered blue, copper scale (a mixture of cuprous oxide and cupric oxide) and green oxide of chrome to produce its bluish-green shade. By use of different amounts of colorants and different melting conditions, zircon rather than cobalt or green was produced.

Zircon was introduced in 1936 and listed in catalogs until 1939. Experimentation apparently was carried out sporadically through the years by the company resulting in its return in 1955 under the name of limelight. As with most other Heisey colors, there is variation in shade of zircon items. Some collectors refer to "zircon-blue side" or "zircon-green side" depending on how they see the color of individual pieces. Although Heisey probably used several formulae over the life of the color, no attempt was made (by the company) to differentiate among the shades.

A few pieces are known in unusual tints—a #1445 Grape Cluster floral bowl and #1469 Ridgeleigh candlesticks to mention only two.

Heisey introduced zircon concurrently with saturn optic, so many of the lines using this optic were made in zircon. Patterns found in zircon include #1485 Saturn, #1495 Fern, a few pieces in #1469 Ridgeleigh and blownware in #4083 Stanhope, #4085 Kohinoor, #4090 Coventry and #4091 Kimberly. Accessory pieces such as candlesticks, ball vases and jugs were also made. A special production of saturn optic ball vases in both crystal and zircon which were specially engraved by Emil Krall were also brought out during this time. These are especially noteworthy since they are some of the few items in color Heisey advertised as available with engravings.

Zircon was soon phased out of the Heisey line. Color in glassware had lost some of its popularity even before zircon had been introduced. Possibly the color was not popular. The coming of World War II and the government restrictions on critical materials also curtailed many glass colors and products.

Experimental Colors

Along with all the production colors of this period, the Heisey Company, under the direction of chemist, Emmett Olsen, did rather extensive experimentation in colors other than those finally reaching the market.

Light Blue

This lovely shade of pale blue was never more than an experimental color at Heisey's. According to Paul Fairall, a long-time Heisey employee, the color was not marketed because of its similarity to Cambridge's moonlight blue.

Only a few items are known to exist. Some of the pieces made include the #393 Narrow Flute individual cream, the #355 Quator individual ash tray, the #134 Trident two-light candlestick (with crystal foot), the #1469 Ridgeleigh star relish, goblets in #3324 Delaware and several pieces in #3404 Spanish stemware and #4085 Kohinoor stemware. Kohinoor stems seen have crystal bowls with light blue stems and feet. Spanish stemware has been seen both with the bowl crystal and light blue stem and foot and with the bowl light blue and crystal stem and foot.

Small nappies have been found in #406 Coarse Rib and #398 Hopewell. In the case of the Hopewell nappies, the color does not appear solid, but is mottled and streaked. An unusual pair of #1483 Stanhope two-light candlesticks is also known in light blue.

A few other pieces have been seen, but all items are very difficult to find.

Opalescent Gold

A few pieces of this unusual color have been found. It appears to be a variation of marigold/gold with an opalescent edge, indicating a reheating after molding. Pieces found to date have been candlesticks, namely #112 Mercury and #118 Miss Muffet.

Gold Ruby

Gold ruby glass was produced in very limited quantities by Heisey on an experimental basis during this time period. Very few items are known. Gold was the coloring agent in this glass. Contrary to whimsical belief, gold pieces were not tossed in the mix to produce the color. The gold had to be dissolved in aqua regia or be in another form such as a chloride before it could be introduced into the glass batch. At Heisey's the gold was added by using ingots of gold ruby glass and heating them with the colorless glass. As with some gold ruby produced by other companies (including Steuben), two of the Heisey pieces known are not a solid pink color, but are mottled with colorless glass.

Only three pieces of Heisey gold ruby are known at this time: a #3390 Carcassonne water pitcher in which the pink color is solid, a #338 14" carnation vase and a #4220 Janice vase.

Red

True red was made in only very small quantities by the Heisey Company. It was certainly experimental, with possibly only a few or even one small pot being mixed. Some of the beer mugs (#4163) have been found with true red handles. Sometimes collectors confuse the darker tangerine items with red, but they are only a variation of tangerine. True red items are very rare.

Bi-Colored Heisey Items

The Heisey Company produced very few items in glass of two colors. It often combined its colors with crystal, but the use of two colors in one item is considered rare.

Most often seen are the flamingo/moongleam and moongleam/hawthorne combinations. The #3481 Glenford sodas and tumblers are occasionally found with flamingo bowls and moongleam feet. The #4206 Optic Tooth pattern is sometimes found with hawthorne bowls and moongleam feet.

One stem line, #3361 Charlotte, has only been found in a combination of moongleam stem and foot with hawthorne bowl.

Other items seen include the #134 Trident candlestick in a combination of sahara and alexandrite. A few pieces of #3390 Carcassonne stemware have also been seen in this combination.

Another rare combination is zircon/sahara. A few items in #3390 Carcassonne stemware and #3380 Old Dominion stemware have been seen. These items have been found with zircon bowls, sahara stems and vice versa.

Collectors are fortunate to own even one example of these rare Heisey color combinations.

Odd Shades of Colors

Almost all of Heisey's colors during this period have been found in unusual tints and shades. Most of this was probably due to the experimentation in colors done by Heisey's chemist, Emmett Olson. Even though extensive work was done on Heisey's colors through this process, some of the color variations were almost certainly also due to difficulties in maintaining ideal production conditions: i.e. ingredients in the batch, furnace conditions, melting conditions and other factors.

Included in the color section of the book is a photograph of several zircon pieces in unusual shades. None of these pieces comform to the usual color, zircon. Some of the items such as the #1445 Grape Cluster floral bowl are a very deep shade of zircon, while others such as the #1401 Empress pieces are very light. There is some indication that even the chemist referred to zircon as "zircon, green side" or "zircon, blue side" during his experiments with the color.

Tangerine is another color which shows wide variations of color. Collectors now call the very deep red shade, "tangerine, red side" to differentiate it from the more normal orange-red hue. Some items have almost an amberina-like coloration—meaning that they shade from a yellow-amber to red. This is due to the reheating process. Not all areas of these pieces were heated the same amount, causing a wide variation of color. Some of the pieces which show this most strikingly are the #337 Touraine sherbet and the #1252 Twist plate. Another variation of tangerine is the opaque tangerine slag rose bowl (#4157) pictured in the color section. This is the only type of slag glass ever produced by Heisey.

Flamingo and moongleam are also found with wide variations in shade. These are readily apparent in the color section, as are the variations in hawthorne.

For more detailed information on color variations, see the discussions under each individual color.

Vaseline

ROW 1: #3345 MARY N VIRG goblet, #473 NARROW FLUTE WITH RIM 5″ footed almond, #353 MEDIUM FLAT PANEL vase, #341½ PURITAN jug; **ROW 2:** #350 PINWHEEL & FAN nappy, #1020 PHYLLIS cream and sugar, #465 RECESSED PANEL candy jar and cover, #1184 YEOMAN oval preserve; **ROW 3:** #1193 INSIDE SCALLOP nappy, #351 PRISCILLA extra high footed shallow bowl, #1201 LAVERNE floral bowl

Moongleam

ROW 1: #3480 KOORS two handled vase, crystal with moongleam handles - not a production item, #3368 DIAMOND ROSE goblet, crystal stem and foot, #1252 TWIST oil & stopper, #465 RECESSED PANEL candy jar and cover, #1408 (7043) PANEL & DIAMOND POINT goblet, #367 PRISM BAND decanter; **ROW 2:** #1020 PHYLLIS sugar & cream (early moongleam), #125 LEAF DESIGN candleblock, #1020 PHYLLIS sugar & cream; **ROW 3:** #8040 EVA MAE candlestick, #352 FLAT PANEL lavender jar or humidor with silver overlay, #4224 STEEPLECHASE cocktail and cocktail mixer (frosted bases, crystal bowls), #4045 BALL vase, wide optic; **ROW 4:** #50 ADENA flared floral bowl with block, #1413 CATHEDRAL flared vase with #9009 Artic etching, #1184 YEOMAN handled bon bon, #1200 YEOMAN individual ash tray, #1406 FLEUR DE LIS plate, #411 TUDOR luncheon goblet.

Moongleam

ROW 1: #1404 OLD SANDWICH ice lip pitcher, solid moongleam block, #1183 REVERE candlevase, #1405 IPSWICH candy jar and cover, #1428 WARWICK horn of plenty vase; **ROW 2:** #4215 DOROTHY vase, diamond optic, #473 NARROW FLUTE WITH RIM two-compartment relish, #500 OCTAGON sugar and cream, crystal with moongleam handles, #141 EDNA candlestick; **ROW 3:** #353 MEDIUM FLAT PANEL toothbrush holder, #300½ PEERLESS tumbler, #1401½ EMPRESS plate, #1401 EMPRESS oil, crystal with moongleam stopper and foot, #1401 EMPRESS pitcher - variant without dolphin feet; **ROW 4:** #1170 PLEAT & PANEL high footed compotier and cover, #1170 PLEAT & PANEL goblet, #416/109 HERRINGBONE/PETTICOAT DOLPHIN compote, #4224 IVY vase with #9009 Arctic etching, #1445 GRAPE CLUSTER floral bowl

Flamingo

ROW 1: #353 MEDIUM FLAT PANEL vase, #300½ PEERLESS bar glass, #300 PEERLESS low footed goblet or tumbler, #300 PEERLESS sherbet, #341 PURITAN tankard pitcher, #300½ PEERLESS tumbler, #351 PRISCILLA footed ale; #341 PURITAN sherbet; **ROW 2:** #1184 YEOMAN cigarette ash tray, #14 KINGFISHER flower block, #1001 CASWELL sugar sifter and cream, #1252 TWIST oil and stopper, #1184 YEOMAN bridge smoking set; **ROW 3:** #7007 ANGULAR CRISS CROSS tumbler, #1201 PHILIP MORRIS match stand ash tray, #130 ACORN candlestick, #1403 HALF CIRCLE individual cream and sugar, #433 GRECIAN BORDER handled custard (punch cup); **ROW 4:** #463 BONNET basket, #412 TUDOR footed tankard pitcher, #412 TUDOR footed handled ice tea, #3355 FAIRACRE vase, #2517 TEARDROP pitcher

Note the wide variation in shades of flamingo.

Flamingo

ROW 1: #7089 CLOVERLEAF snack plate, #1433 THUMBPRINT & PANEL vase, #1428 WARWICK one-light candlestick, #1420 TULIP vase, #1404 OLD SANDWICH popcorn bowl; ROW 2: #500 OCTAGON variety tray; #1405 IPSWICH candy jar and cover; #1184 YEOMAN crescent salad plate, #1010 DECAGON relish; ROW 3: #136 TRIPLEX candlestick, #516/3 vase, #111 CHERUB candlestick, #1225/109 RIDGE & STAR/PETTICOAT DOLPHIN comport, #325 PILLOWS water bottle - an experimental piece

Hawthorne

ROW 1: #1191 LOBE handled spice dish, #406 COARSE RIB low foot jelly, #15 DUCK figurine in floral block, #1170 PLEAT & PANEL spice tray; **ROW 2:** #121 PINWHEEL candlesticks, #4203 EMOGENE vase, #3480 KOORS pitcher, #1186 YEOMAN individual ash tray, #479 PETAL sugar and cream, **ROW 3:** #417 DOUBLE RIB & PANEL basket, #354 WIDE FLAT PANEL footed hotel cream and sugar, #461 BANDED PICKET basket, #1186 YEOMAN puff box and cover

38

Marigold

ROW 1: #500 OCTAGON nappy, #1229 OCTAGON footed mayonnaise diamond optic, #393 NARROW FLUTE individual sugar, #355 QUATOR cream and sugar; **ROW 2:** #1252 TWIST cream soup, #500 OCTAGON basket, #357 DUCK ash tray, #1401 EMPRESS salt, #501 FOGG floral box; **ROW 3:** #361 IRWIN ash tray and cigarette container, #350 PINWHEEL & FAN nappy, #411 TUDOR footed grapefruit, #1210 FROG handled cheese plate; **ROW 4:** #1252 TWIST high footed compote, #1252 TWIST saucer champagne, #1252 TWIST cocktail, #1252 TWIST goblet, #3368 ALBEMARLE goblet, crystal stem, #128 LIBERTY candlestick

Sahara

ROW 1: #140 CROCUS candlestick; #1447 ROCOCO candlestick, #3397 GASCONY sugar and cream, #3485 IRENE jug;
ROW 2: #1483 STANHOPE celery tray, #1447 ROCOCO sugar and cream, #1401 EMPRESS tumbler, dolphin footed;
ROW 3: #1189 YEOMAN individual cream and covered sugar, #1184 YEOMAN mustard and cover, #1184 YEOMAN individual cream, #1415 TWENTIETH CENTURY cereal bowl, #1469 RIDGELEIGH cigarette box and cover, #1469 RIDGELEIGH round cigarette holder; ROW 4: #1445 GRAPE CLUSTER two-light candlestick, #1405 IPSWICH oil and stopper, #1252 TWIST French dressing bottle and stopper; #1430 ARISTOCRAT tall candy jar and cover; #4223 SWIRL vase, #4225 COBEL cocktail shaker, #450 Chintz etching

Alexandrite

ROW 1: #3381 CREOLE goblet, #3381 CREOLE saucer champagne, #3381 CREOLE footed soda, #1150 COLONIAL STAR plate, #3416 BARBARA FRITCHIE cordial, crystal stem and foot, #3405 COYLE beer mug; **ROW 2:** #3381 CREOLE finger bowl, #3381 CREOLE cordial, #3381 CREOLE wine, #1184 YEOMAN candy box, bottom only - etched and cut, #1000 marmalade and cover, #1401 EMPRESS ash tray; **ROW 3:** #1401 EMPRESS cup and saucer, #6 mayonnaise ladle, #1401 EMPRESS mayonnaise, dolphin footed - Miniature candlesticks, full cut - whimsies, #1401 EMPRESS cream soup and underplate; **ROW 4:** #300 PEERLESS low footed goblet or tumbler, #4027 CHRISTOS decanter, #373 OLD WILLIAMSBURG goblet, #1306 COMET LEAF goblet, #301 OLD WILLIAMSBURG two-light candelabrum, crystal prisms, #135 EMPRESS candlestick

Alexandrite

ROW 1: #3390 CARCASSONNE jug, #3390 CARCASSONNE saucer champagne, #3390 CARCASSONNE whimsey pitcher made from decanter, #3390 CARCASSONNE cocktail, #3390 CARCASSONNE short goblet, #3390 CARCASSONNE tall goblet, #3390 CARCASSONNE bar, #3390 CARCASSONNE flagon; ROW 2: #3368 ALBEMARLE goblet, #4045 BALL vase, 12″, wide optic, #4044 NEW ERA candlestick; ROW 3: #1413 CATHEDRAL flared vase, #1252 TWIST ice bucket, #1428 WARWICK horn of plenty vase

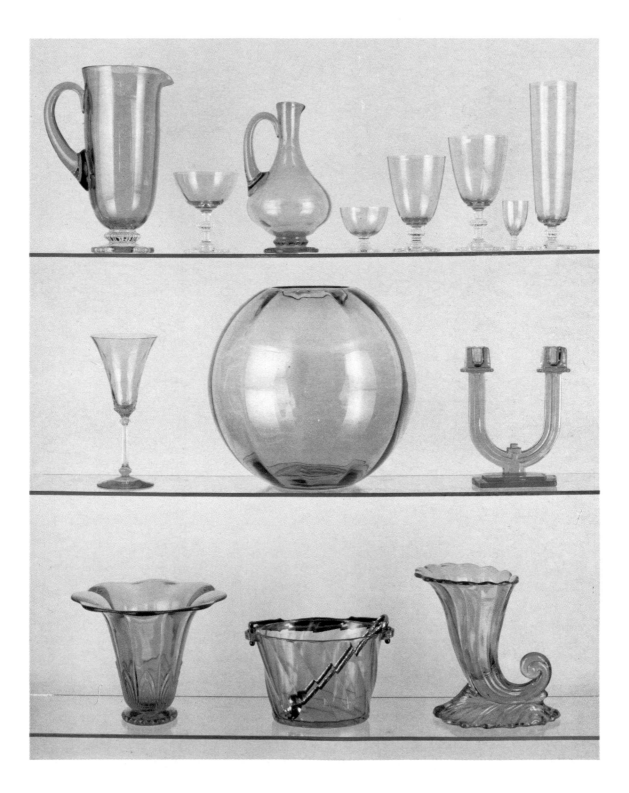

Amber

ROW 1: #3404 SPANISH saucer champagne, #3397 GASCONY goblet, #1186 YEOMAN individual ash tray, #3390 CAR-CASSONNE saucer champagne, #201 HARVEY COLONIAL tumbler, #353 MEDIUM FLAT PANEL footed soda; ROW 2: #1170 PLEAT & PANEL oil and stopper, #337½ TOURAINE sherbet, narrow optic, #586 soda, narrow optic, #586 juice, narrow optic, #588 soda, #1404 OLD SANDWICH beer mug; ROW 3: #337 TOURAINE parfait, narrow optic, #4049 OLD FITZ hot whiskey, #1125 STARBURST plate, #337 TOURAINE goblet, narrow optic, #1417 ARCH tumbler; ROW 4: #353 MEDIUM FLAT PANEL hall boy tray, #4165 SHAW jug, cut, #353 MEDIUM FLAT PANEL hall boy jug

43

Cobalt

ROW 1: #1405 IPSWICH candlevase, crystal insert and prisms, #1433 THUMBPRINT & PANEL two-light candlestick, #1433 THUMBPRINT & PANEL vase, #4224 IVY vase; **ROW 2:** #4044 NEW ERA goblet, #3390 CARCASSONNE footed soda, #3397 GASCONY decanter, crystal foot and stopper, #3397 GASCONY floral bowl, crystal foot; **ROW 3:** #1428 WARWICK horn of plenty floral bowl, #1413 CATHEDRAL two-handled vase, #1440 ARCH floral bowl

Cobalt

ROW 1: #1404 OLD SANDWICH decanter, #393 NARROW FLUTE bitters bottle, #3359 PLATEAU sherbet, crystal foot, #142 CASCADE candlestick, crystal foot; **ROW 2:** #1421 HI LO vase, #1533 WAMPUM floral bowl, #1425 VICTORIAN cream and sugar, #1445 GRAPE CLUSTER one-light candlestick, crystal base, #10 muddler; **ROW 3:** #4225 COBEL cocktail shaker, #110 SANDWICH DOLPHIN candlestick, #4165 SHAW jug, Bottle-vase - not a production item

Tangerine

ROW 1: #3404 SPANISH goblet (2) - one on red side, #3404 SPANISH saucer champagne, #3404 SPANISH cocktail, #8066 LARSON bottle-vase - experimental, #3389 DUQUESNE oyster cocktail, #3389 DUQUESNE wine, #3389 DUQUESNE parfait; **ROW 2:** #3397 GASCONY oval floral bowl, #1401 EMPRESS cream & sugar, #1401 EMPRESS salt, #4230 favor vase, #3389 DUQUESNE finger bowl; **ROW 3:** #134 TRIDENT candlestick, crystal base, #1417 ARCH tumbler with 4 toes, #1401 EMPRESS cup and saucer, #3397 GASCONY sodas (2), #3397 GASCONY wine, #3397 GASCONY saucer champagne, #3397 GASCONY goblet; **ROW 4:** #1404 OLD SANDWICH plate, #1404 OLD SANDWICH oyster cocktail, #1404 OLD SANDWICH soda, #1401 EMPRESS two-handled sandwich plate, #1401 EMPRESS square plate, Diamond shaped advertising sign, crystal

46

Zircon

ROW 1: #4085 KOHINOOR soda, #4085 KOHINOOR goblet, #1495 FERN three-compartment relish, #1404 OLD SAND-WICH soda, #3390 CARCASSONNE vase, saturn optic; **ROW 2:** #4090 COVENTRY goblet, #4083 STANHOPE saucer champagne, #4083 STANHOPE goblet, #4083 STANHOPE wine, #1469 RIDGELEIGH oval floral bowl; **ROW 3:** #1496 MAHABAR cigarette box, #1496 MAHABAR square ash tray, #1485 SATURN cocktail, #1485 SATURN saucer champagne, #1485 SATURN mustard and paddle cover, #1485 SATURN violet vase; **ROW 4:** #1495 FERN two-light candlestick, #1485 SATURN two light candleblock, #352 FLAT PANEL cigar jar and cover, marked Benson & Hedges, #4085 BALL vase, saturn optic

Zircon - Odd Shades

These pieces are pictured together to show the wide variation in the Zircon color.

BACK: #1445 GRAPE CLUSTER floral bowl, #110 SANDWICH DOLPHIN candlestick; **MIDDLE:** #1401 EMPRESS triplex relish, #1425 VICTORIAN three compartment relish, #1469 RIDGELEIGH one-light candlestick; **FRONT:** #1401 EMPRESS bon bon, #1485 SATURN two-compartment relish (normal color)

Bi-Colored Items

BACK: #4206 OPTIC TOOTH vase - hawthorne bowl, moongleam foot; **MIDDLE:** #134 TRIDENT candlestick - sahara arms, alexandrite foot, #3361 CHARLOTTE saucer champagne - hawthorne bowl, moongleam foot, #3361 CHARLOTTE goblet - hawthorne bowl, moongleam foot; **FRONT:** #3481 GLENFORD tumbler - flamingo bowl, moongleam foot

Experimental Light Blue

Back: #1483 STANHOPE two-light candelabrum; **MIDDLE:** #134 TRIDENT candlestick, #3404 SPANISH sherbet, #3324 DELAWARE goblet, #4085 KOHINOOR low goblet; **FRONT:** #393 NARROW FLUTE individual cream, #355 Quator individual ash tray

Cobalt

BACK: #4059 ALLEN water bottle - crystal with cobalt stripes (experimental item), #4223 SWIRL vase; **MIDDLE:** #2323 NAVY bar glass (2) - 1 with sham, #2323 NAVY tall soda, #2323 NAVY saucer, #419 SUSSEX goblet; **FRONT:** #2323 NAVY plate, #2323 NAVY cup

Tangerine Variations

BACK: #4157 STEELE rose bowl in opaque tangerine slag, #8066 LARSON experimental bottle/vase - almost red; **FRONT:** #337 TOURAINE sherbet, #1229 OCTAGON Mayonnaise, diamond optic - almost amberina, #1252 TWIST plate - almost amberina

See discussion under the TANGERINE color for reasons for the wide color variations.

Goblets

ROW 1: #3362 CHARTER OAK goblet - marigold bowl, crystal stem, #3362 CHARTER OAK goblet - moongleam, #3362 CHARTER OAK goblet - flamingo, #3362 CHARTER OAK goblet - hawthorne, #3324 DELAWARE goblet - hawthorne, #3324 DELAWARE goblet - flamingo, #3386 DIAMOND ROSE goblet - moongleam bowl, crystal stem and foot, #4044 NEW ERA goblet - cobalt bowl, crystal stem and foot; ROW 2: #3350 WABASH goblet - sahara bowl, #3350 WABASH cocktail - zircon bowl, #3350 WABASH goblet - flamingo, #3350 WABASH goblet - experimental gold stem, #3350 WABASH goblet - moongleam stem, #3350 WABASH goblet (2) - hawthorne - Note color variation; ROW 3: #3397 GASCONY goblet - tangerine bowl, #3397 GASCONY goblet - sahara, etched, #3357 KING ARTHUR goblet - flamingo stem, cut, #3357 KING ARTHUR goblet - moongleam stem, #3357 KING ARTHUR cocktail - moongleam stem, #3357 KING ARTHUR goblet - flamingo, etched, #3373 MORNING GLORY goblet - flamingo, #3379 PYRAMID saucer champagne - flamingo; ROW 4: #3333 OLD GLORY goblet - hawthorne, #3389 DUQUESNE goblet - sahara, #3320 RITZ goblet - moongleam foot, etched, #3390 CARCASSONNE low-footed goblet - moongleam foot, #4083 STANHOPE goblet - zircon bowl and foot, crystal stem, #4085 KOHINOOR footed soda - all zircon, #4090 COVENTRY goblet - zircon, #4085 KOHINOOR goblet - zircon bowl

Goblets

ROW 1: #3381 CREOLE goblet - alexandrite bowl, #3381 CREOLE goblet - sahara bowl, #3381 CREOLE goblet - all alexandrite, #3370 AFRICAN goblet - flamingo, #3370 AFRICAN goblet - moongleam stem, #3366 TROJAN goblet - flamingo, #3366 TROJAN goblet - hawthorne, #3365 RAMSHORN goblet - flamingo; ROW 2: #3361 CHARLOTTE goblet - hawthorne bowl, moongleam stem and foot, #3325 RAMPUL goblet - hawthorne, #3390 CARCASSONNE goblet - sahara, etched, #3390 CARCASSONNE goblet - alexandrite bowl, #3390 CARCASSONNE goblet - cobalt bowl, #3360 PENN CHARTER goblet - flamingo, #3360 PENN CHARTER goblet - hawthorne, checker optic; ROW 3; #3312 GAYOSO goblet - flamingo, #2516 CIRCLE PAIR goblet - moongleam, #3359 PLATEAU goblet - flamingo, #3376 ADAM goblet - flamingo, #3404 SPANISH goblet - sahara bowl, #3404 SPANISH goblet (2) - tangerine bowl - note color variation, #3404 SPANISH goblet - cobalt bowl; ROW 4: #3368 ALBEMARLE goblet - marigold bowl, #3368 ALBEMARLE goblet - alexandrite, #3368 ALBEMARLE goblet - moongleam stem, #3380 OLD DOMINION short stem goblet - sahara, etched, #3380 OLD DOMINION short stem goblet - flamingo, #3380 OLD DOMINION tall stem goblet - moongleam bowl, #3380 OLD DOMINION tall stem goblet - moongleam stem

52

Beer Mugs

ROW 1: #1404 OLD SANDWICH 18 oz.: cobalt, sahara, moongleam, crystal, amber, flamingo; ROW 2: #1404 OLD SAND-WICH: crystal (14 oz.), sahara (12 oz.), flamingo (12 oz.), crystal (12 oz.), moongleam (12 oz.); ROW 3: #3405 COYLE - alexandrite, #3408 JAMESTOWN: sahara handle, tangerine handle, moongleam handle, cobalt handle; ROW 4: #4163 WHALEY: sahara handle, etched, flamingo handle, moongleam handle, red handle, etched, cobalt handle, etched; ROW 5: #3407 OVERDORF cobalt with crystal handle - variant handle, #3407 OVERDORF crystal with cobalt handle, #412 TUDOR sahara, #1434 TOM & JERRY crystal, #1426 CLOVER ROPE sahara, #1426 CLOVER ROPE cobalt

Colonial Pieces in Color

BACK: #393 NARROW FLUTE banana split - flamingo; #353 MEDIUM FLAT PANEL ice cream or candy tray - flamingo; **MIDDLE:** #300 PEERLESS low-footed goblet - flamingo, #300 PEERLESS sherbet - flamingo, #372 MCGRADY sanitary syrup - sahara, #300½ PEERLESS bar - flamingo, #300 PEERLESS schoppen - flamingo, #351 PRISCILLA ale - flamingo; **FRONT:** #341 PURITAN sherbet - flamingo, #394 NARROW FLUTE domino sugar - sahara, #300½ PEERLESS tumbler - moongleam

Ash Trays

BACK: #364 RHOMBIC - moongleam, #361 IRWIN ash tray and cigarette container - flamingo, #411 TUDOR cigarette jar and ash tray cover - moongleam, #357 DUCK - flamingo; **MIDDLE:** #363 WINGS - moongleam, #1488 KOHINOOR bridge ash tray - zircon, #442 MALTESE CROSS - flamingo, #1187 YEOMAN - amber stain with silver overlay, #1180 TREFOIL - moongleam; **FRONT:** #1488 KOHINOOR - zircon, #1425 VICTORIAN - sahara, #439 FATIMA - moongleam, #1186 YEOMAN - hawthorne, #358 SOLITAIRE - marigold (gold variant)

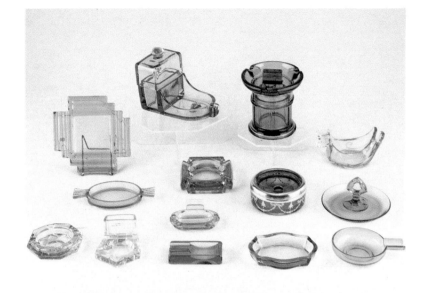

Colognes

BACK: #487 HEXAGON STEM - amber stain, gold decoration, #516 FAIRACRE variant with applied crystal foot - moongleam, #515 TAPER - flamingo, #515 TAPER - hawthorne, #517 CIRCLE PAIR - flamingo; **FRONT:** #485 HEXAGON STEM - moongleam, #516 FAIRACRE - flamingo, #516 FAIRACRE - moongleam, #1186 YEOMAN puff box and cover - hawthorne, #4035 SEVEN OCTAGON - flamingo, #4034 SEVEN CIRCLE - flamingo, #1405 IPSWICH - crystal, #4035 SEVEN OCTAGON - moongleam

Decorations on Heisey by Other Companies

All of these decorations were done by outside decorating companies and were not done by the Heisey Company. During the twenties and thirties, Heisey sold many blanks to such companies and it is possible to find Heisey glass with very unusual stains, enamels, silver and gold and other types of decorations.

BACK: #353 MEDIUM FLAT PANEL vase - enamel, #352 FLAT PANEL lavender jar - moongleam with silver overlay, #4209 OVAL vase - marigold stain, #1229 OCTAGON cheese plate - enamel and cut; MIDDLE: #485 Dunham nappy - enamel decoration by Charleton, called "Ebony Swirl", #1184 Yeoman covered candy - enamel and gold, #1223 FLUTED BORDER nappy - marigold stain, #411 TUDOR cigarette jar - amber stain and silver overlay; FRONT: #341½ OLD WILLIAMSBURG compote - yellow and blue iridized, #468 OCTAGON WITH RIM celery - enamel and gold, #353 MEDIUM FLAT PANEL ash tray - amber stain with engraving, #4035 SEVEN OCTAGON cologne - lavender iridized.

Salts and Peppers

BACK: #1404 OLD SANDWICH - sahara, #1404 OLD SANDWICH - flamingo, #1404 OLD SANDWICH - moongleam, #12 SMALL EIGHT FLUTE - flamingo, #12 SMALL EIGHT FLUTE - moongleam, #42 ELEGANCE - flamingo, #46 CHESHIRE - flamingo; MIDDLE: #1401 EMPRESS - moongleam foot, #1401 EMPRESS - marigold, #1401 EMPRESS - sahara, #1401 EMPRESS - tangerine, #1252 (#54) TWIST - sahara, #1252 (#54) TWIST - moongleam, #1252 TWIST - sahara; MIDDLE: #53 TALL INDIVIDUAL - moongleam, #53 TALL INDIVIDUAL - flamingo, #12 SMALL EIGHT FLUTE - amber, #51 DRUM - moongleam foot, #48 KOORS - flamingo; FRONT: #23 SHORT PANEL - sahara, #23 SHORT PANEL - moongleam, #1469½ RIDGELEIGH - amber, #49 YORKSHIRE - moongleam foot, #49 YORKSHIRE - flamingo, #47 SPOOL - moongleam

Cigarette Sets

In mid-1937 Heisey introduced its new "Mahabar" line. This consisted of the #1496 cigarette box and cover and round or square ash trays. These were available in crystal, zircon and sahara. Collectors today know these items as part of #1503 Crystolite pattern. Actually these items were the forerunners of the Crystolite table ware pattern and were the basis for the entire line which was introduced in late 1937 or early 1938. Mahabar was shown in a September, 1937 issue of TABLE TALK, Heisey's small publication.

BACK: #1496 RIDGELEIGH square ash tray - sahara, #1469 RIDGELEIGH round cigarette holder - sahara, #1496 MAHABAR cigarette box - sahara; MIDDLE: #1469 RIDGELEIGH round cigarette holder - zircon, #1496 MAHABAR cigarette box - zircon, #1496 MAHABAR square ash tray - sahara; FRONT: #1469 RIDGELEIGH cigarette box - sahara, #1496 MAHABAR square ash tray - zircon, #1496 MAHABAR round ash tray - zircon

Dolphin Comports

These comports use the #109 Petticoat Dolphin candlestick as a base combined with three different plates as tops. They were made circa 1925.

LEFT TO RIGHT: #109 PETTICOAT DOLPHIN lamp - flamingo, #416/109 HERRINGBONE/PETTICOAT DOLPHIN comport - moongleam and crystal, #1225/109 RIDGE & STAR/PETTICOAT DOLPHIN comport - flamingo and crystal, #1185/109 YEOMAN/PETTICOAT DOLPHIN comport - flamingo with gold decoration

Vases

TOP BACK: #21 ARISTOCRAT one-light candelabrum - moongleam, #4026 SPENCER decanter - moongleam, #2517 TEARDROP vase - hawthorne; **TOP FRONT:** #4205 VALLI vase - flamingo, #4162/4 GENIE vase - moongleam, #4215 DOROTHY vase - moongleam; **BOTTOM BACK:** #516/1 vase - hawthorne, #4207 MODERNE vase - moongleam, #3485 IRENE vase - flamingo; **BOTTOM FRONT:** #4196 RHODA vase - flamingo, cut, #133 SWAN HANDLED floral bowl and block - sahara, cut, #4204 JOYCE vase - flamingo

Favor Vases

All six shapes were made in all six colors.

BACK: #4227 flamingo, #4229 moongleam, #4232 cobalt; **FRONT;** #4231 sahara, #4230 tangerine, #4228 crystal

Baskets

BACK: #463 BONNET - flamingo, #461 BANDED PICKET - hawthorne; **FRONT:** #500 OCTAGON - marigold, #417 DOUBLE RIB & PANEL - moongleam

Miscellaneous Goblets

BACK: #1423 SWEET AD O LINE - crystal, #8005 GALAXY - flamingo, #3386 DIAMOND ROSE - flamingo; **MIDDLE:** #3373 MORNING GLORY - flamingo, #3394 SAXONY - crystal; **FRONT:** #419 SUSSEX - moongleam, #3379 PYRAMID saucer champagne - flamingo

Tumblers & Sodas

BACK: #1417 ARCH tumbler - cobalt, #3484 DONNA - moongleam, diamond optic; **MIDDLE:** #2516 CIRCLE PAIR soda - marigold; **FRONT:** #1485 SATURN tumbler - zircon, #299 toddy - sahara, #3362 CHARTER OAK tumbler - flamingo

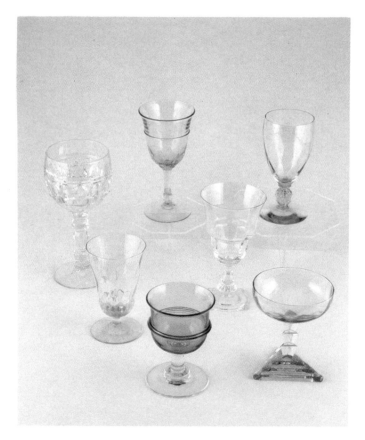

Table Settings

Moongleam. All items are from #1404 OLD SANDWICH pattern. **BACK:** Sherbet and plate, comport, salt & pepper, soda or ice tea, ice lip pitcher; **FRONT:** individual ash tray, sundae and plate, saucer champagne

Flamingo. BACK: #516/3 vase, #3355 FAIRACRE vase, #3312 GAYOSO Russian coffee, #3312 GAYOSO goblet, #3350 WABASH compote and cover; **FRONT:** #1184 YEOMAN cup and saucer, #1184 YEOMAN dinner plate, #52 SHORT INDIVIDUAL salt and pepper

Table Settings

Marigold. All items are from the #1252 TWIST pattern; **BACK:** Oyster cocktail, saucer champagne, goblet; **MIDDLE:** individual bon bon, cup and saucer; **FRONT:** dinner plate, salad plate, cream soup

Cobalt (Stiegel Blue). BACK: #1430 ARISTOCRAT low-footed candy, #301 OLD WILLIAMSBURG three light candelabrum; **MIDDLE:** #1183 (#1184) REVERE individual salt, #3404 SPANISH oyster cocktail, #3404 SPANISH cocktail, #3404 SPANISH goblet; **FRONT:** #1401 EMPRESS dinner plate - crystal, #1401 EMPRESS salad plate

Sahara.   All items are from the #1447 ROCOCO pattern; **BACK:** cigarette box, five-part relish, footed cheese; **FRONT:** sugar and cream

Sahara. BACK: #1405 IPSWICH footed juice, #1405 IPSWICH footed ice tea, #1231 RIBBED OCTAGON rum pot; **FRONT:** #1405 IPSWICH oil, #1405 IPSWICH salad plate

Table Settings

Hawthorne. BACK: #15 DUCK and floral block, #417 DOUBLE RIB & PANEL basket, #3366 TROJAN saucer champagne, #3366 TROJAN wine, #3366 TROJAN goblet; **FRONT:** #52 SHORT INDIVIDUAL salt & pepper, #1184 YEOMAN dinner plate, #1184 YEOMAN salad plate, #1184 YEOMAN cup and saucer, #1229 OCTAGON individual nut dish

Alexandrite. BACK: #4220 JANICE vase, #4045 BALL vase, Mermaids etch, #1445 GRAPE CLUSTER two light candlestick; **MIDDLE:** #1401 EMPRESS salt & pepper, #3381 CREOLE finger bowl, #1401 EMPRESS individual nut, dolphin footed, #3381 CREOLE cordial, #3381 CREOLE goblet, #1401 EMPRESS cup and saucer; **FRONT;** #1401 EMPRESS dinner plate, #1401 EMPRESS salad plate, #1401 EMPRESS cream soup

Table Settings

Tangerine. BACK: #4045 BALL vase, #3404 SPANISH goblet, #3404 SPANISH cocktail, #3404 SPANISH saucer champagne, #1401 EMPRESS cup and saucer; **FRONT:** #1401 EMPRESS dinner plate - crystal, #1401 EMPRESS salad plate

Zircon. BACK: #1485 SATURN wine, #1485 SATURN goblet, #4085 (#4161) KOHINOOR jug; **MIDDLE:** #1485 SATURN covered mustard, #1485 SATURN parfait, #1485 SATURN oyster cocktail, #1485 SATURN oil; **FRONT:** #1485 SATURN salad plate, #1485 SATURN sherbet, #1485 SATURN cup and saucer

Lamps. #4206 OPTIC TOOTH, flamingo - engraved by Emil Krall, #21 ARISTOCRAT electro portable lamp, early moongleam

Decanters. #4027 CHRISTOS - alexandrite, cobalt, moongleam, sahara, #3380 OLD DOMINION wines, sahara (2), flamingo (2), alexandrite (2)

Pressed Patterns

The major pressed ware patterns of the 1925-1938 era consisted mostly of tableware patterns which were available in either dinner or luncheon sets. These patterns comprised the great bulk of Heisey's production and sales.

Most major patterns contained a variety of sizes of plates, accessory pieces, and matching stemware. At first this stemware was pressed and thus sturdy and durable just as the matching service pieces were. Patterns such as #406 Coarse Rib, #411 Tudor, #1170 Pleat & Panel, #1252 Twist and #1401 Empress fall into this category. This practice continued through the early 1930's and patterns such as #1404 Old Sandwich, #1405 Ipswich and #1425 Victorian had many pieces of stemware, most of which were produced in vast quantities.

By 1936, Heisey began producing pattern lines with both pressed stemware and blown stemware beginning with #1469 Ridgeleigh. Most major patterns after this time offered the hostess the choice of the heavier, more durable pressed stemware or the more delicate and fragile blown-ware.

A few patterns strayed from this standard and included no stemware at all, such as #1428 Warwick—mainly vases and candlesticks—and #1495 Fern—a pattern consisting entirely of accessory pieces.

Major lines which proved to be of tremendous interest to the buying public were enlarged almost beyond imagination. The #1469 Ridgeleigh, for instance, had at least 6 styles of candleholders and 10 or more ash trays. Combined with all other conceivable useful or decorative objects able to be made of glass, the Ridgeleigh pattern becomes one of the largest lines ever made by Heisey.

By contrast, there are many minor patterns which consist of only a few pieces. For instance, #1415 Twentieth Century was made only in several sizes of sodas, a milk pitcher and a cereal bowl and plate. Many other minor patterns consisted of from one to a dozen different pieces. These are often found in the MISCELLANEOUS Section of the book or scattered through other sections since their limited production was not important enough for the company to devote entire pages in catalogs to them.

By studying the catalog pages closely, it is evident that Heisey often used basic shapes in several patterns. Again, the Ridgeleigh line shows this quite well. Many items were either redesigned to be compatible with Ridgeleigh or old molds were given new life by adaptation into the line. Examples include the #133 Swan Handled floral bowl, #501 floral box, and the #1170 Pleat and Panel oil and low-footed comport. All these reappear in Ridgeleigh with the repetitive ridges characteristic of the pattern. Careful attention to basic Heisey shapes will reveal other patterns in which shapes or details are changed slightly to conform to a new pattern. With new molds costing hundreds of dollars each, it is quite apparent why old molds were not scrapped if new uses could be found for them.

With the introduction and development of almost 20 patterns in pressed ware alone over the 13 year period from 1925-1938, it can be seen how prolific the Heisey Company was. Considering many factors such as the number of pieces in patterns, all the miscellaneous areas of production such as candlesticks, floral bowls, vases and various other items, it becomes very apparent that the Heisey Company was a thriving, active business during this period. When remembering that this was in a time of national economic depression, it becomes even more impressive that the company was able to continue and even succeed in an area of selling devoted to relatively luxurious items.

In an analysis of a week's production from October 31 to November 5, 1925, the total production was 124,117 pieces. These were produced by 24 shops, only 4 of which produced blown ware exclusively. Primary production of the company was pressed ware. Pressed stemware, tumblers and plates seemed to be items made in greatest quantities. This particular week was taken at random from the factory turn books, but it seems typical of most entries of the time.

#355 QUATOR - name given by researchers

Dates: 1913-1935
Colors: Footed cream and sugar in moongleam, flamingo, marigold and sahara. Individual ashtray in experimental light blue
Decorations: The hotel cream and sugar are often found cut or etched. Often the decoration was done by decorating companies, not by Heisey.
Marked: Most items
Comments: An unusual, short pattern in which most pieces are square, including the nappies. Most of the production was before the color era, so few items are found in colors. The footed sugar doubles as a bon bon dish. The individual ashtray in experimental light blue is an unusual item. (See ASHTRAYS Section for illustration.)
Imperial Reissues: None
Availability: Common to moderately available

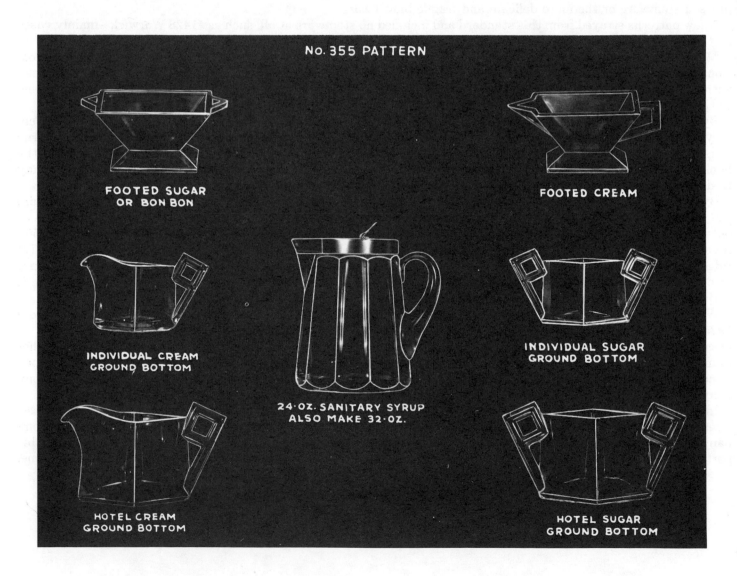

#406, 407 COARSE RIB - name given by researchers

Dates: 1923-1937. Nappies remained until at least 1944
Colors: Many items made in moongleam and flamingo. A few pieces were made in hawthorne. A plate is known in true marigold. A few small nappies are known in experimental light blue.
Decorations: Usually seen undecorated. Some items were decorated by outside firms—gold trim on flamingo, silver on moongleam. The marigold-appearing pieces were stained by a firm calling the treatment "Cathedral Glass". These pieces are not the bright, deep color of true marigold but a duller, less colorful shade which was achieved by staining crystal glass. The relish and celery found with this stain are usually seen in metal holders. The marigold stain is often found on the 9″ and 12″ celeries, the mustard and cover, two-handled jelly, ice jug and may be found on other items as well.
Marked: Most Pieces
Comments: A good, utilitarian pattern which is available in many shapes. The moongleam items are often of the early moongleam, which is very close to emerald in depth of color. The ½ gallon jug was made with an ice lip and had an original factory number of 408.
Patents: #72064 for high footed jelly—applied for 3/19/23 and granted 2/22/27. #66630 for plate—applied for 3/21/23 and granted 2/17/25. #66853 for nappy—applied for 3/22/23 and granted 3/24/25. E. Wilson Heisey was listed as designer on all three patents.
Imperial Reissues: The large chip and dip tray in crystal and cobalt marked with the Diamond H. This one-piece item was not originally made by Heisey.
Availability: Moderately available

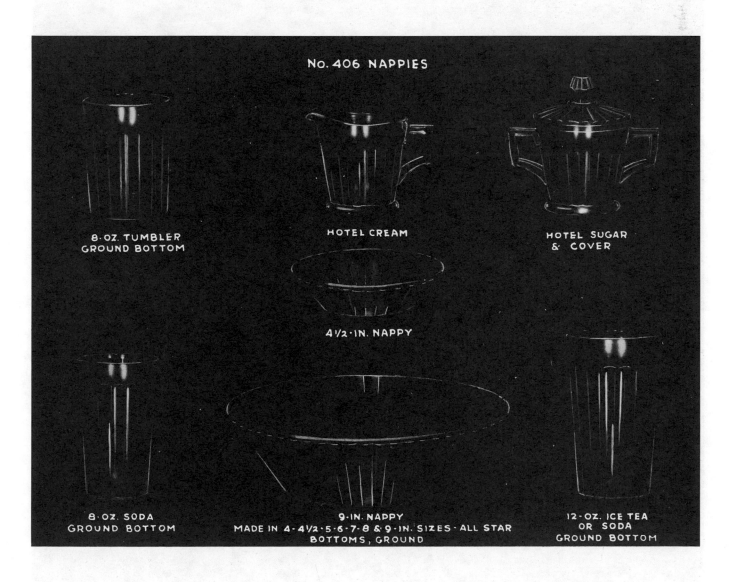

NO. 406 NAPPIES

8·OZ. TUMBLER
GROUND BOTTOM

HOTEL CREAM

HOTEL SUGAR
& COVER

4½·IN. NAPPY

8·OZ. SODA
GROUND BOTTOM

9·IN. NAPPY
MADE IN 4·4½·5·6·7·8 & 9·IN. SIZES · ALL STAR
BOTTOMS, GROUND

12·OZ. ICE TEA
OR SODA
GROUND BOTTOM

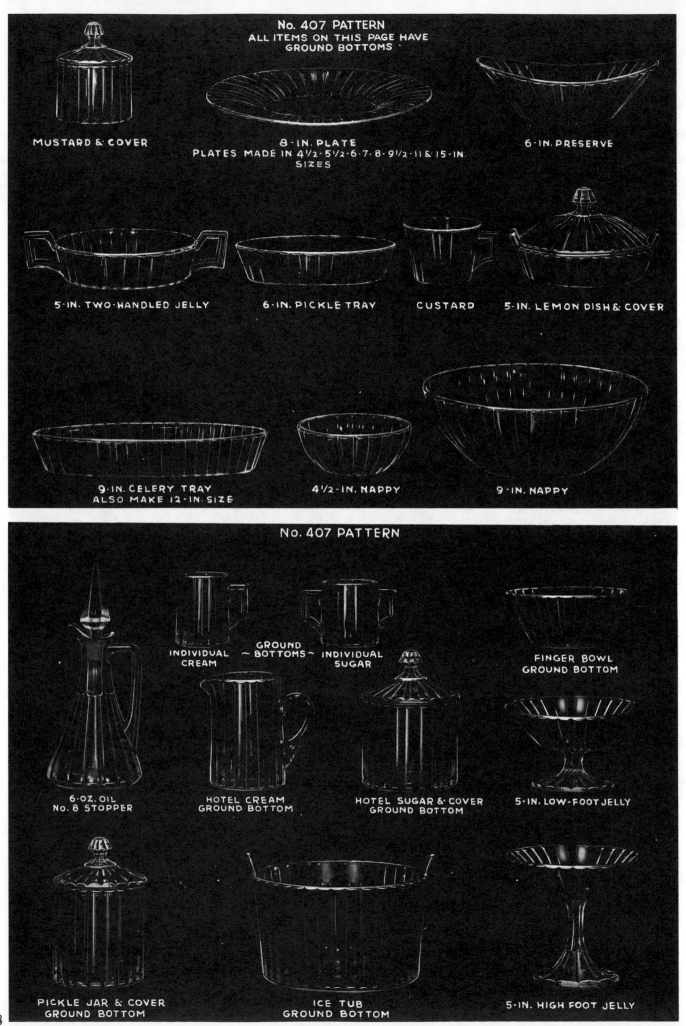

No. 407 PATTERN
ALL ITEMS ON THIS PAGE HAVE GROUND BOTTOMS

MUSTARD & COVER

8-IN. PLATE
PLATES MADE IN 4½-5½-6-7-8-9½-11 & 15-IN. SIZES

6-IN. PRESERVE

5-IN. TWO-HANDLED JELLY

6-IN. PICKLE TRAY

CUSTARD

5-IN. LEMON DISH & COVER

9-IN. CELERY TRAY
ALSO MAKE 12-IN. SIZE

4½-IN. NAPPY

9-IN. NAPPY

No. 407 PATTERN

INDIVIDUAL CREAM

GROUND ~ BOTTOMS ~

INDIVIDUAL SUGAR

FINGER BOWL
GROUND BOTTOM

6-OZ. OIL
No. 8 STOPPER

HOTEL CREAM
GROUND BOTTOM

HOTEL SUGAR & COVER
GROUND BOTTOM

5-IN. LOW-FOOT JELLY

PICKLE JAR & COVER
GROUND BOTTOM

ICE TUB
GROUND BOTTOM

5-IN. HIGH FOOT JELLY

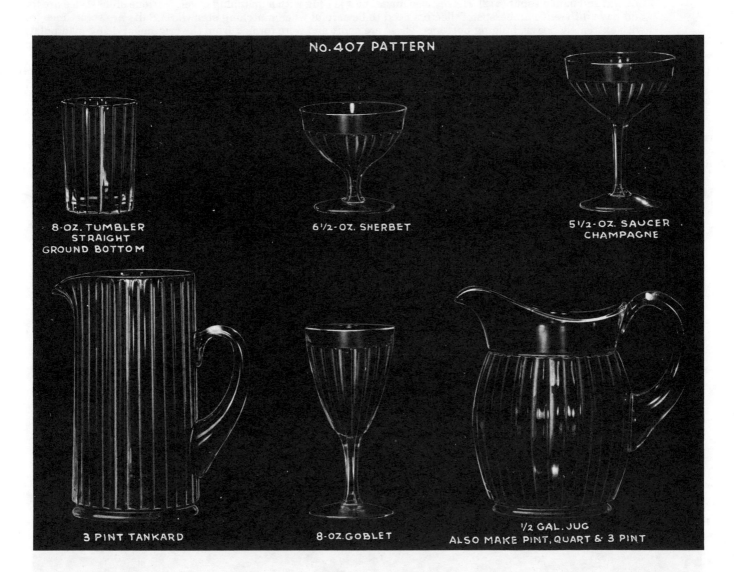

No. 407 PATTERN

8-OZ. TUMBLER
STRAIGHT
GROUND BOTTOM

6½-OZ. SHERBET

5½-OZ. SAUCER
CHAMPAGNE

3 PINT TANKARD

8-OZ. GOBLET

½ GAL. JUG
ALSO MAKE PINT, QUART & 3 PINT

#411, 412, 413, 414 TUDOR - original Heisey Co. name

Dates: 1923-1939

Colors: Many items made in moongleam and flamingo. A limited number made in hawthorne. The grapefruit is known in marigold.

Decorations: Heisey used some simple cuttings on some pieces. Sometimes pieces are found with colored stains done by other companies.

Marked: Most pieces

Comments: Early researchers called this pattern "Rib & Panel" and "Wagon Wheel" before the original company name was found. Tudor is a large pattern which includes many interesting pieces such as the cigarette jar and ashtray cover, individual almond and banana split (412). Heisey also made the #411 jug with a matching cover. Various stem styles are found and have different numbers, so collectors need to be careful when matching stemware. Salts are sometimes found with extremely heavy, bulging bottoms. These are short and were formed from the original style by manipulation. They are considered somewhat of an oddity. Several items were made in the mid-1950's for Dohrmann Commercial. These included standard items and also an oil with a screw top (illustration not available.)

Patents: #71064 for #411 goblet - applied for 3/12/23 and granted 9/14/26. #63947 for #411 plate - applied for 3/14/23 and granted 2/12/24. #68857 for #411 floral compotier - applied for 3/15/23 and granted 11/24/25. #66288 for #411 two-handled mint - applied for 3/20/23 and granted 12/23/24. #64183 for #411 soda - applied for 5/24/23 and granted 3/11/24. #70224 for #411 nappy - applied for 5/31/23 and granted 5/25/26. #66233 for #411 flared tumbler - applied for 6/2/23 and granted 12/16/23. T. Clarence Heisey listed as designer on all patents.

Imperial Reissues: The #411 jug and cover in crystal from 1959 to 1961 for Fisher-Bruce & Co., Philadelphia.

Availability: Common to moderately available.

Note: This pattern could be easily confused with McKee's Lenox pattern.

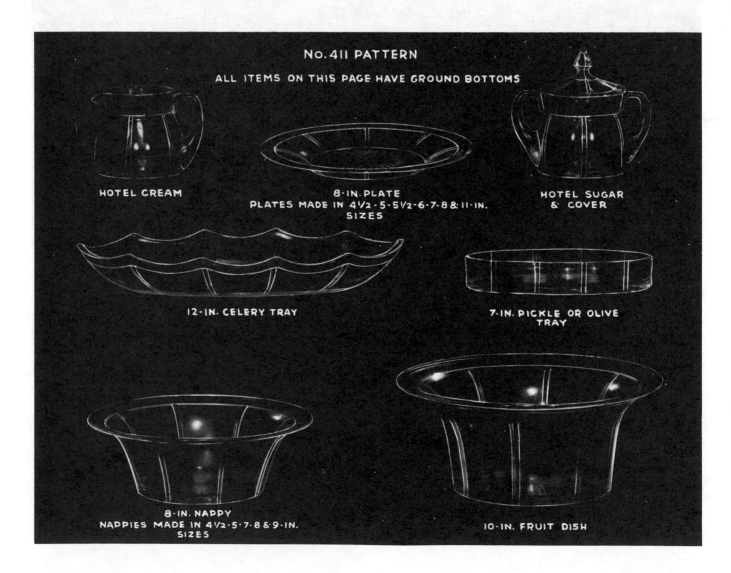

No. 411 PATTERN

ALL ITEMS ON THIS PAGE HAVE GROUND BOTTOMS

HOTEL CREAM

8-IN. PLATE
PLATES MADE IN 4½-5-5½-6-7-8 & 11-IN. SIZES

HOTEL SUGAR & COVER

12-IN. CELERY TRAY

7-IN. PICKLE OR OLIVE TRAY

8-IN. NAPPY
NAPPIES MADE IN 4½-5-7-8 & 9-IN. SIZES

10-IN. FRUIT DISH

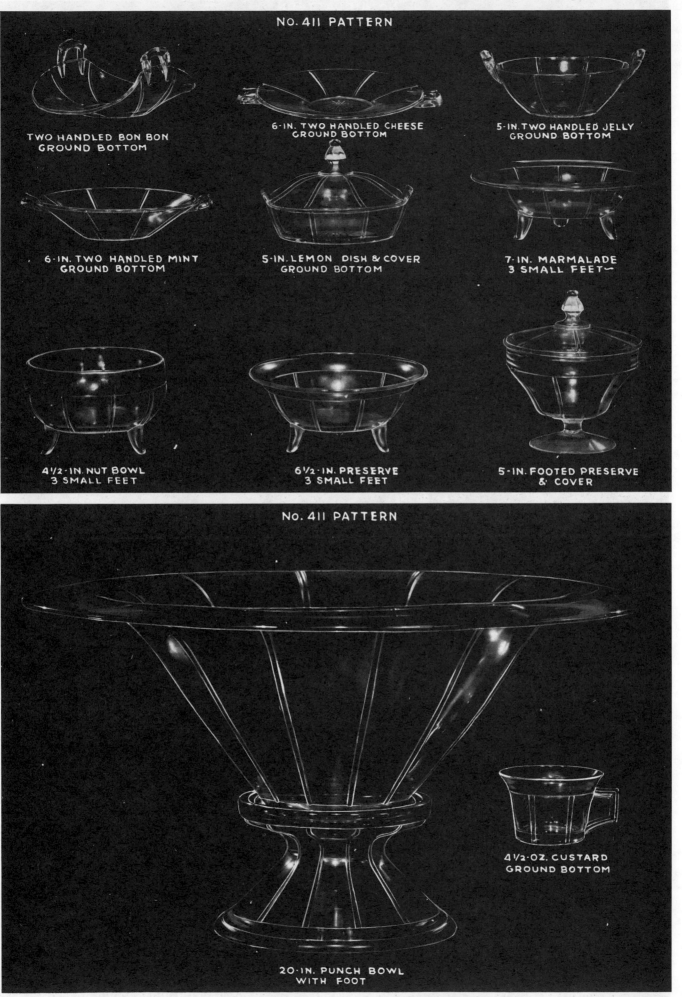

TWO HANDLED BON BON
GROUND BOTTOM

6-IN. TWO HANDLED CHEESE
GROUND BOTTOM

5-IN. TWO HANDLED JELLY
GROUND BOTTOM

6-IN. TWO HANDLED MINT
GROUND BOTTOM

5-IN. LEMON DISH & COVER
GROUND BOTTOM

7-IN. MARMALADE
3 SMALL FEET

4½-IN. NUT BOWL
3 SMALL FEET

6½-IN. PRESERVE
3 SMALL FEET

5-IN. FOOTED PRESERVE
& COVER

NO. 411 PATTERN

20-IN. PUNCH BOWL
WITH FOOT

4½-OZ. CUSTARD
GROUND BOTTOM

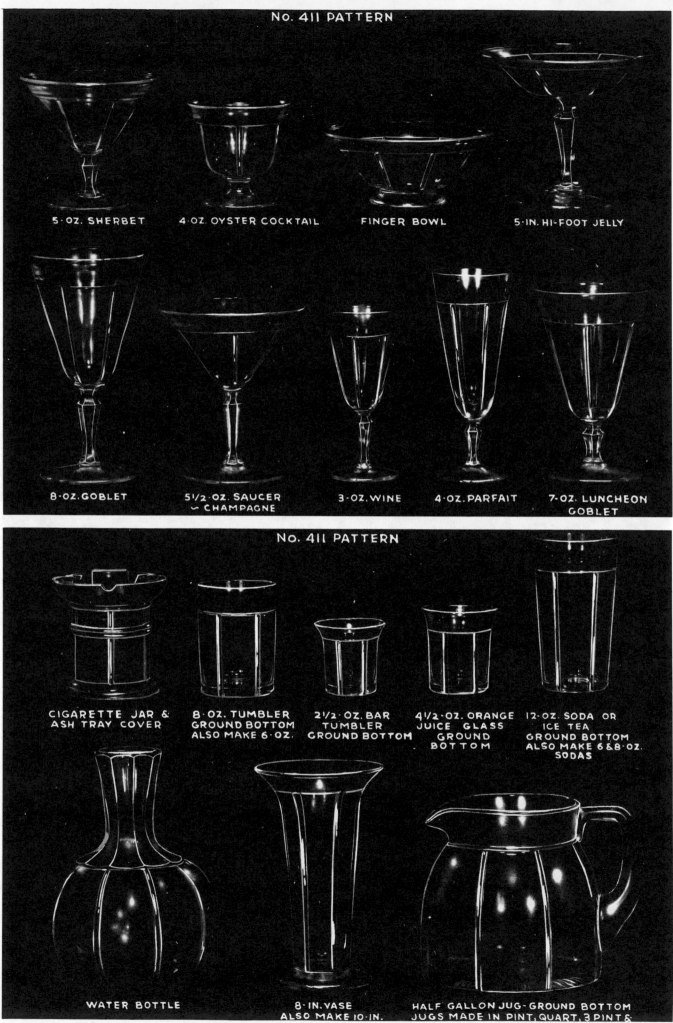

5·OZ. SHERBET

4·OZ. OYSTER COCKTAIL

FINGER BOWL

5·IN. HI·FOOT JELLY

8·OZ. GOBLET

5½·OZ. SAUCER
~ CHAMPAGNE

3·OZ. WINE

4·OZ. PARFAIT

7·OZ. LUNCHEON
GOBLET

No. 411 PATTERN

CIGARETTE JAR &
ASH TRAY COVER

8·OZ. TUMBLER
GROUND BOTTOM
ALSO MAKE 6·OZ.

2½·OZ. BAR
TUMBLER
GROUND BOTTOM

4½·OZ. ORANGE
JUICE GLASS
GROUND
BOTTOM

12·OZ. SODA OR
ICE TEA
GROUND BOTTOM
ALSO MAKE 6 & 8·OZ.
SODAS

WATER BOTTLE

8·IN. VASE
ALSO MAKE 10·IN.

HALF GALLON JUG·GROUND BOTTOM
JUGS MADE IN PINT, QUART, 3 PINT &

NO. 411 PATTERN

SALT OR PEPPER WITH No.1 SANITARY TOP

SALT OR PEPPER WITH No.3 SANITARY TOP

SALT OR PEPPER WITH No.43 TOP

SALT OR PEPPER WITH NICKLE TOP

GRAPE FRUIT CENTRE

MUSTARD & COVER GROUND BOTTOM

INDIVIDUAL ALMOND

6½-IN. GRAPE FRUIT GROUND BOTTOM

MAYONNAISE & 5½-IN. PLATE

SUGAR DISPENSER WITH SILVER TOP

6-OZ. OIL No.7 STOPPER, PRESSED OR CUT ALSO MAKE 4-OZ.

5-IN. FOOTED GRAPE FRUIT

NO. 412 PATTERN

8-OZ. TUMBLER GROUND BOTTOM

8-IN. FOOTED BANANA SPLIT

12-OZ. HANDLED FOOTED ICE TEA ALSO MAKE 10-OZ. FOOTED SODA, HEAVY, LIKE ABOVE, BUT WITHOUT HANDLE

7½-OZ. GOBLET

6-OZ. SAUCER CHAMPAGNE

5-OZ. SHERBET

4½-OZ. PARFAIT

73

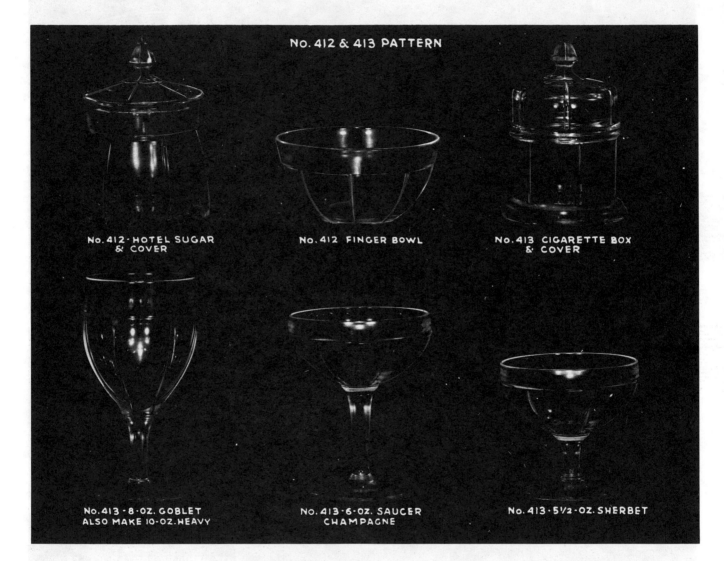

No. 412 & 413 PATTERN

No. 412·HOTEL SUGAR
& COVER

No. 412 FINGER BOWL

No. 413 CIGARETTE BOX
& COVER

No. 413·8·OZ. GOBLET
ALSO MAKE 10·OZ. HEAVY

No. 413·6·OZ. SAUCER
CHAMPAGNE

No. 413·5½·OZ. SHERBET

74

6 oz. Saucer Champagne

8 oz. Goblet

5½ oz. Low Footed Sherbet
Also made 3½ oz.

10 oz. Heavy Goblet

10½ oz. Footed Soda
Heavy

#413 stemware

#473 NARROW FLUTE WITH RIM - name given by researchers

Dates: 1915-1933. #475 nut dish remained until 1935.

Colors: A few items were made in flamingo and moongleam. The #475 nut dish was also made in hawthorne. A few items are known in vaseline, but these are scarce.

Decorations: Occasionally some pieces are found with a simple cutting on the plain band around the top. Some items are also found with various colored stains applied by other firms.

Marked: Usually. The #475 nut dish sometimes contains a patent date as does the dice sugar.

Comments: An interesting pattern containing many unusual items, but by this period, most of these were out of production. Colored items are desirable, especially since this pattern is basically colonial in nature and thus most production was only in crystal. See COLONIAL PIECES IN COLOR for a few other items. Other companies made similar items, especially the dice sugar and cream, so it is best to buy these items only with the Diamond H. A dice sugar has been seen with the mark on one of the small panels, rather than in the bottom as is usual.

Patents: #47738 for basket applied for 3/1/15 and granted 8/17/15. #49224 for 2-handled tray applied for 6/11/15 and granted 6/20/16. #48614 for #475 fruit dish applied for 11/3/15 and granted 2/22/15. Andrew J. Sanford listed as designer for all patents

Imperial Reissues: None

Availability: Moderately available

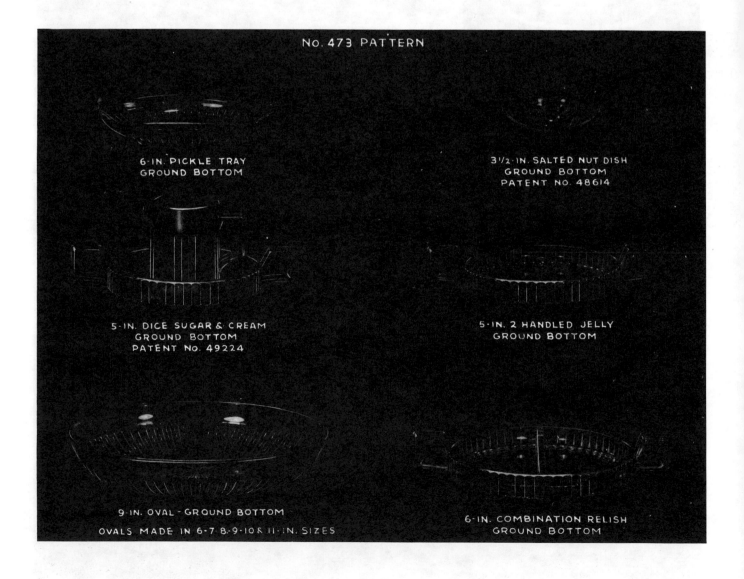

NO. 473 PATTERN

6-IN. PICKLE TRAY
GROUND BOTTOM

3½-IN. SALTED NUT DISH
GROUND BOTTOM
PATENT NO. 48614

5-IN. DICE SUGAR & CREAM
GROUND BOTTOM
PATENT NO. 49224

5-IN. 2 HANDLED JELLY
GROUND BOTTOM

9-IN. OVAL - GROUND BOTTOM
OVALS MADE IN 6-7-8-9-10 & 11-IN. SIZES

6-IN. COMBINATION RELISH
GROUND BOTTOM

#500 OCTAGON - name given by researchers

Dates: 1928-1935. The ice bucket and variety tray were made for several years longer.
Colors: All items made in moongleam and flamingo. Several were made in sahara and marigold. The variety tray was made again in 1955 to 1957 in dawn as part of the #1183 Revere pattern.
Decorations: The ice bucket and variety tray were used for many etchings by Heisey. The variety tray was also used for many Heisey cuttings. The frozen dessert is sometimes found with a simple floral cutting.
Marked: Usually. The frozen dessert is not marked.
Comments: A utilitarian pattern with a few desirable items. The ice bucket, variety tray and basket (see BASKET Section) are desirable. The cream and sugar are sometimes found with moongleam handles. The frozen dessert is similar to ones made by other companies. Heisey's has a small rectangular thumbprint in the bottom.
Patents: #78024 for ice bucket applied for 5/31/28 and granted 3/19/29. E. Wilson Heisey listed as designer.
Imperial Reissues: None
Availability: Common

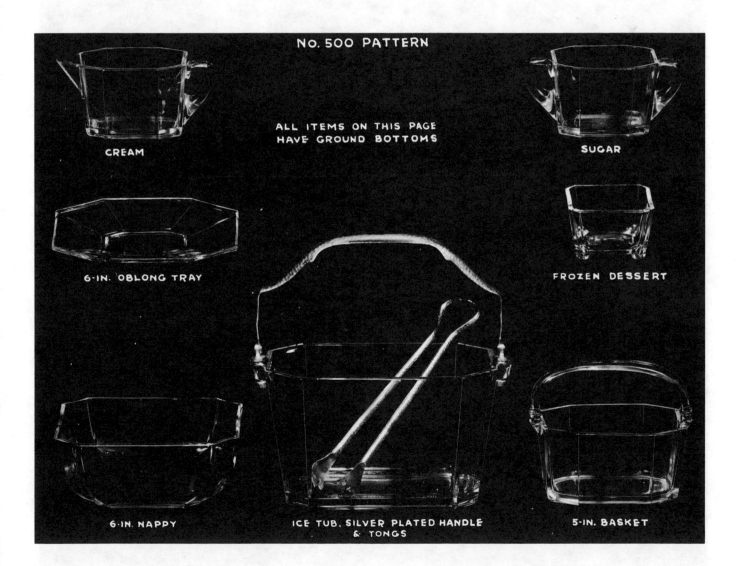

NO. 500 PATTERN

ALL ITEMS ON THIS PAGE HAVE GROUND BOTTOMS

CREAM

SUGAR

6-IN. OBLONG TRAY

FROZEN DESSERT

6-IN. NAPPY

ICE TUB, SILVER PLATED HANDLE & TONGS

5-IN. BASKET

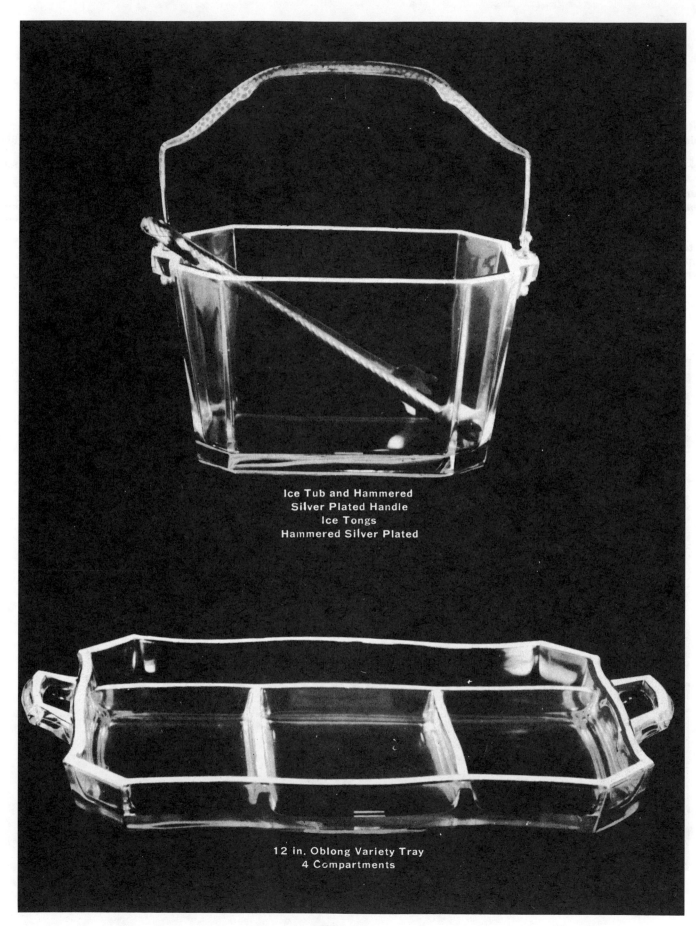

Ice Tub and Hammered
Silver Plated Handle
Ice Tongs
Hammered Silver Plated

12 in. Oblong Variety Tray
4 Compartments

#500 pattern

#1170 PLEAT & PANEL - name given by researchers

Dates: 1925-1937
Colors: All items listed in moongleam and flamingo. Spice tray is known in hawthorne. Ice jug made in sahara. Oil bottle was made in amber. Price lists indicate the oil was offered for sale in crystal with moongleam stopper and in moongleam with crystal stopper.
Decorations: Several simple Heisey cuttings (usually florals) for which original numbers have not been found
Marked: Most items
Comments: Originally, this pattern began as a plate. The number is derived from a series of plate numbers. Apparently the pattern was attractive enough that other items were quickly added. This is the first pattern in which Heisey made a luncheon service. Items made in moongleam are found in both the early, deep moongleam and the later paler shade. See MISCELLANEOUS Section for ice jug and spice tray.
Imperial Reissues: None
Availability: Moderately available

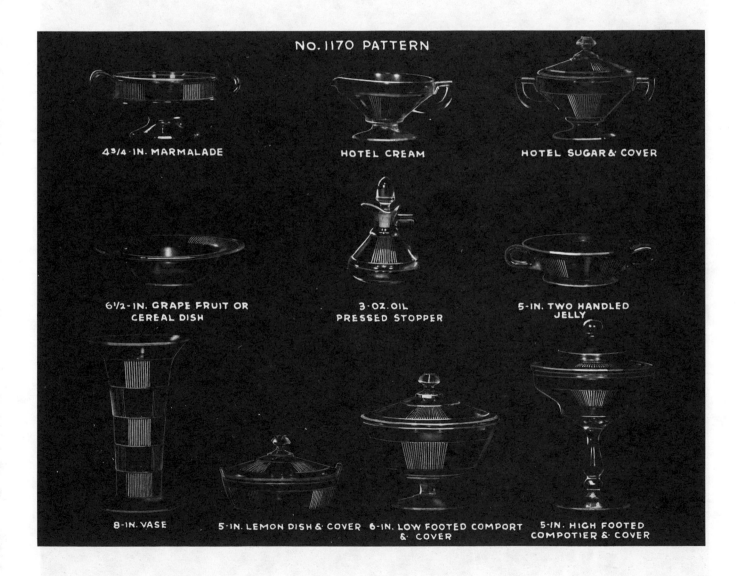

NO. 1170 PATTERN

4¾-IN. MARMALADE   HOTEL CREAM   HOTEL SUGAR & COVER

6½-IN. GRAPE FRUIT OR CEREAL DISH   3-OZ. OIL PRESSED STOPPER   5-IN. TWO HANDLED JELLY

8-IN. VASE   5-IN. LEMON DISH & COVER   6-IN. LOW FOOTED COMPORT & COVER   5-IN. HIGH FOOTED COMPOTIER & COVER

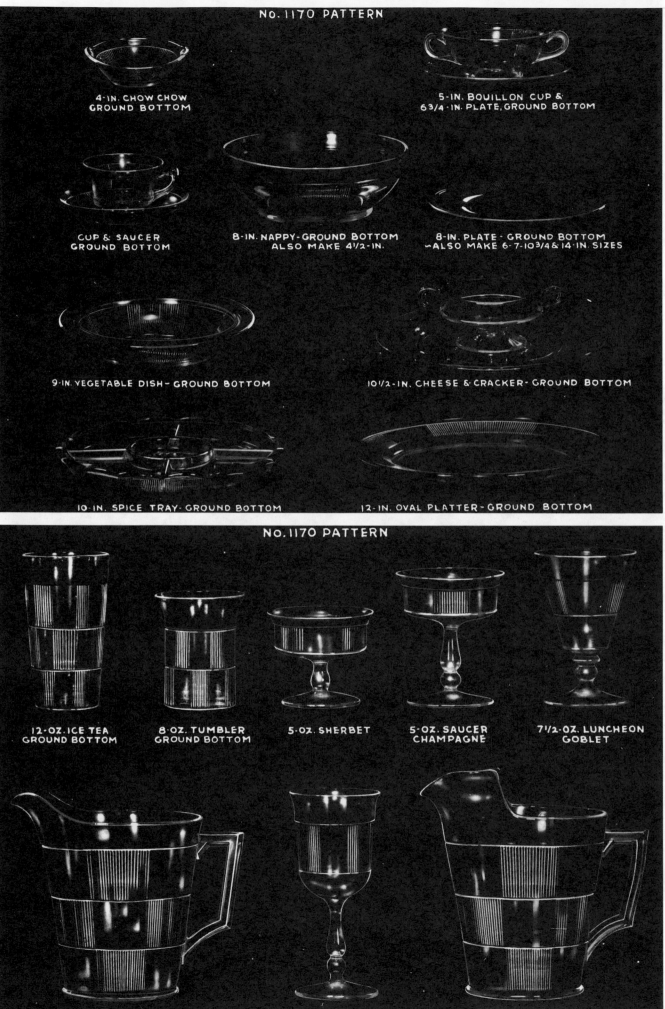

4-IN. CHOW CHOW
GROUND BOTTOM

5-IN. BOUILLON CUP &
6¾-IN. PLATE, GROUND BOTTOM

CUP & SAUCER
GROUND BOTTOM

8-IN. NAPPY-GROUND BOTTOM
ALSO MAKE 4½-IN.

8-IN. PLATE - GROUND BOTTOM
-ALSO MAKE 6-7-10¾ & 14-IN. SIZES

9-IN. VEGETABLE DISH - GROUND BOTTOM

10½-IN. CHEESE & CRACKER - GROUND BOTTOM

10-IN. SPICE TRAY - GROUND BOTTOM

12-IN. OVAL PLATTER - GROUND BOTTOM

No. 1170 PATTERN

12-OZ. ICE TEA
GROUND BOTTOM

8-OZ. TUMBLER
GROUND BOTTOM

5-OZ. SHERBET

5-OZ. SAUCER
CHAMPAGNE

7½-OZ. LUNCHEON
GOBLET

3 PINT JUG

8-OZ. GOBLET

3 PINT ICE JUG

#1184, 1185, 1186, 1187, 1189 YEOMAN - original Heisey Co. name in later years

Dates: 1913-1957

Colors: Many items made in moongleam and flamingo. Several items made in marigold and sahara. Limited number available in hawthorne. The footed bouillon and 5″ oval lemon are found in vaseline. The candy box and cover was made in alexandrite. 6¼″ & 8″ plates in amber; 8″ plate and individual salt in cobalt.

Decorations: Heisey used many pieces for various etchings and cuttings. Several pieces are also found with decorations done by outside firms in various manners.

Marked: Most items.

Optic: Plain or diamond optic in many pieces.

Comments: Several items in the line were originally listed as Pattern #1182 (mainly those available in hawthorne.) Yeoman seems to be a catch-all pattern of simple designs for tableware. Usually numbers up to #1189 are considered to be part of Yeoman. In the pages used here the individual salt is listed as #1184 Yeoman even though it is called #1183 Revere in most other catalogs. Due to the simplicity of the pieces, it is quite likely that many of them were designed especially for etchings and cuttings. Note that the #1023 cream and sugar became part of the Yeoman pattern. See the MISCELLANEOUS Section for other Yeoman items. Some ashtrays are also found in the ASHTRAY Section. Unusual items include trays with ring handles, saucer footed syrup, and hors d' oeuvre. Small basket-shaped trays are popularly called "Bowtie" and eagerly sought. The egg cup is unusual. The tumbler cover is often overlooked by collectors. A 9″ grill plate was listed but not illustrated.

Patents: #1184: #47573 stack sugar, cream and butter applied for 10/10/14 and granted 7/13/15. #50666 for oval nappy applied for 2/16/17 and granted 4/24/17. #1189: #65870 for celery applied for 2/8/21 and granted 10/28/24. #66461 for footed bowl applied for 2/8/21 and granted 1/20/25. Andrew J. Sanford listed as designer on all patents

Availability: Common

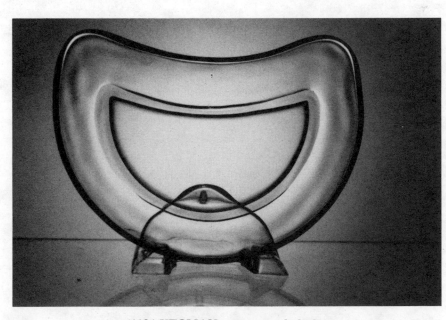

#1184 YEOMAN crescent salad plate

#1186 YEOMAN covered puff box with insert

No. 1184 PATTERN

4½-IN. NAPPY - DIAMOND OPTIC
GROUND BOTTOM
ALSO MADE PLAIN

6-IN. VEGETABLE DISH
DIAMOND OPTIC - GRD. BOTTOM
ALSO MADE PLAIN

13-IN. CELERY TRAY - DIAMOND OPTIC
GROUND BOTTOM
ALSO MAKE 9-IN. SIZE

9-IN. OVAL BAKER - DIAMOND OPTIC
GROUND BOTTOM - ALSO MADE PLAIN

8-IN. OYSTER COCKTAIL PLATE
GROUND BOTTOM - ALSO MAKE 9-IN. SIZE
PLAIN OR DIAMOND OPTIC

9-IN. VEGETABLE DISH AND COVER
DIAMOND OPTIC - GROUND BOTTOM
ALSO MADE PLAIN

12-IN. OBLONG TRAY - FIRE POLISHED BOTTOM

12-IN. OVAL PLATTER - DIAMOND OPTIC - ALSO
MAKE 15-IN. SIZE. GROUND BOTTOM - PLAIN OR DIAMOND OPTIC

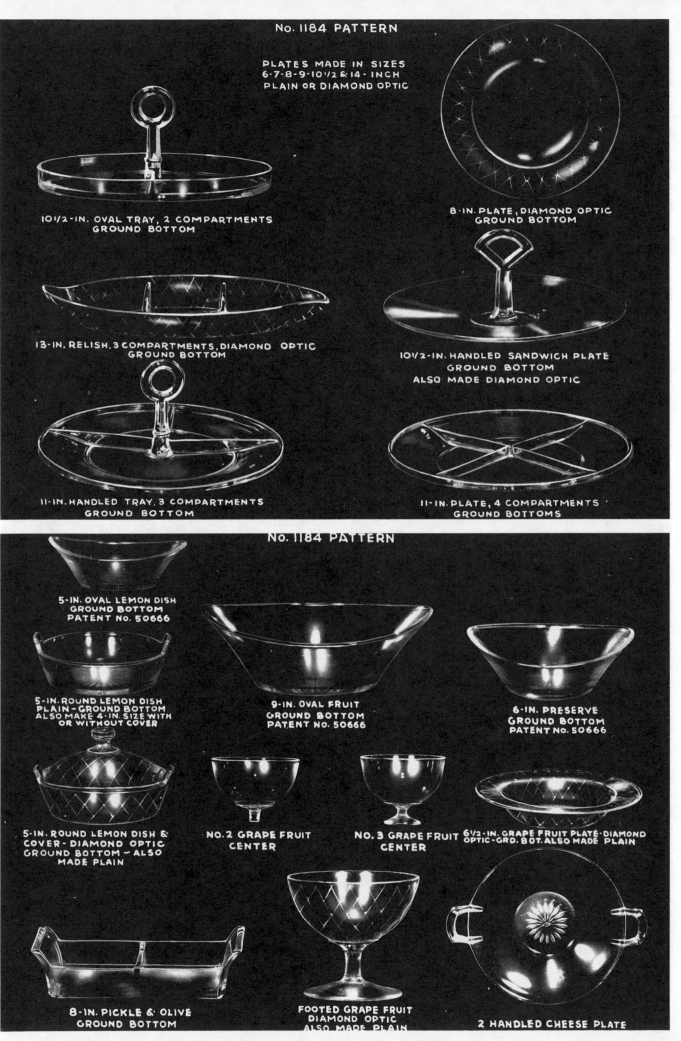

No. 1184 PATTERN

PLATES MADE IN SIZES
6·7·8·9·10½ & 14 · INCH
PLAIN OR DIAMOND OPTIC

10½-IN. OVAL TRAY, 2 COMPARTMENTS
GROUND BOTTOM

8-IN. PLATE, DIAMOND OPTIC
GROUND BOTTOM

13-IN. RELISH, 3 COMPARTMENTS, DIAMOND OPTIC
GROUND BOTTOM

10½-IN. HANDLED SANDWICH PLATE
GROUND BOTTOM
ALSO MADE DIAMOND OPTIC

11-IN. HANDLED TRAY, 3 COMPARTMENTS
GROUND BOTTOM

11-IN. PLATE, 4 COMPARTMENTS
GROUND BOTTOMS

No. 1184 PATTERN

5-IN. OVAL LEMON DISH
GROUND BOTTOM
PATENT No. 50666

5-IN. ROUND LEMON DISH
PLAIN · GROUND BOTTOM
ALSO MAKE 4-IN. SIZE WITH
OR WITHOUT COVER

9-IN. OVAL FRUIT
GROUND BOTTOM
PATENT No. 50666

6-IN. PRESERVE
GROUND BOTTOM
PATENT No. 50666

5-IN. ROUND LEMON DISH &
COVER · DIAMOND OPTIC
GROUND BOTTOM — ALSO
MADE PLAIN

NO. 2 GRAPE FRUIT
CENTER

NO. 3 GRAPE FRUIT
CENTER

6½-IN. GRAPE FRUIT PLATE · DIAMOND
OPTIC · GRD. BOT. ALSO MADE PLAIN

8-IN. PICKLE & OLIVE
GROUND BOTTOM

FOOTED GRAPE FRUIT
DIAMOND OPTIC
ALSO MADE PLAIN

2 HANDLED CHEESE PLATE

83

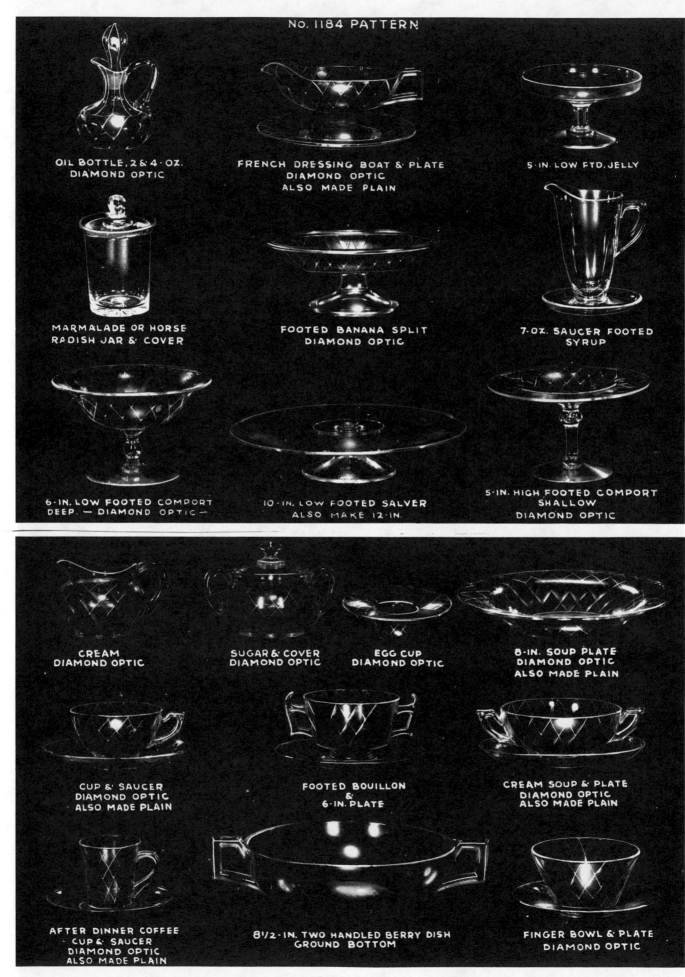

OIL BOTTLE, 2 & 4-OZ.
DIAMOND OPTIC

FRENCH DRESSING BOAT & PLATE
DIAMOND OPTIC
ALSO MADE PLAIN

5-IN. LOW FTD. JELLY

MARMALADE OR HORSE
RADISH JAR & COVER

FOOTED BANANA SPLIT
DIAMOND OPTIC

7-OZ. SAUCER FOOTED
SYRUP

6-IN. LOW FOOTED COMPORT
DEEP. — DIAMOND OPTIC —

10-IN. LOW FOOTED SALVER
ALSO MAKE 12-IN.

5-IN. HIGH FOOTED COMPORT
SHALLOW
DIAMOND OPTIC

CREAM
DIAMOND OPTIC

SUGAR & COVER
DIAMOND OPTIC

EGG CUP
DIAMOND OPTIC

8-IN. SOUP PLATE
DIAMOND OPTIC
ALSO MADE PLAIN

CUP & SAUCER
DIAMOND OPTIC
ALSO MADE PLAIN

FOOTED BOUILLON
&
6-IN. PLATE

CREAM SOUP & PLATE
DIAMOND OPTIC
ALSO MADE PLAIN

AFTER DINNER COFFEE
CUP & SAUCER
DIAMOND OPTIC
ALSO MADE PLAIN

8½-IN. TWO HANDLED BERRY DISH
GROUND BOTTOM

FINGER BOWL & PLATE
DIAMOND OPTIC

#1184 pattern

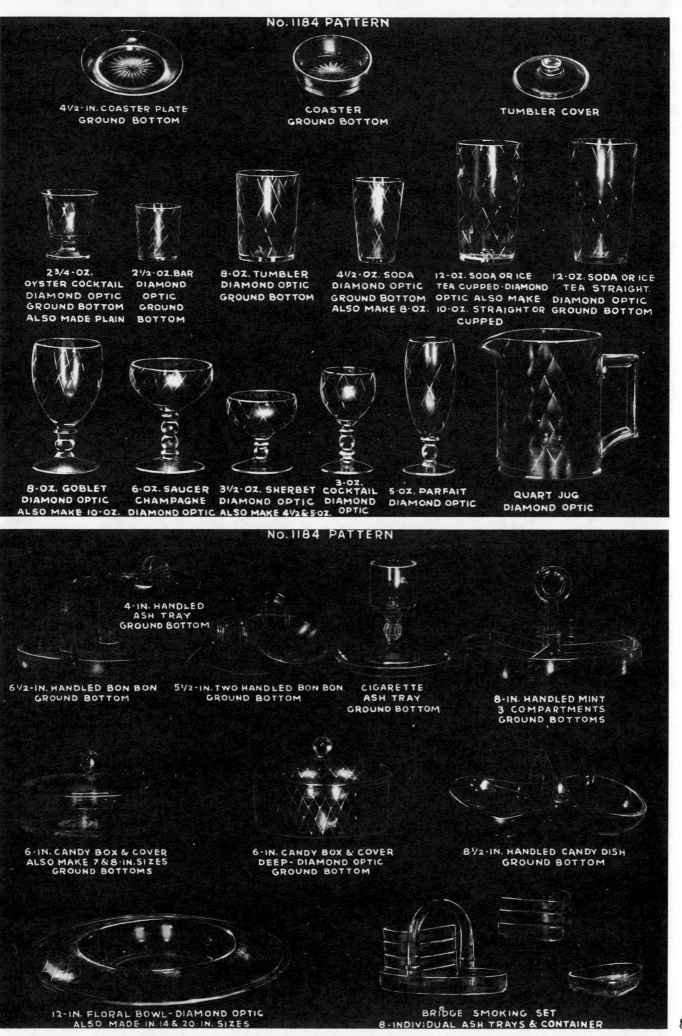

No. 1184 PATTERN

4½-IN. COASTER PLATE
GROUND BOTTOM

COASTER
GROUND BOTTOM

TUMBLER COVER

2¾-OZ.
OYSTER COCKTAIL
DIAMOND OPTIC
GROUND BOTTOM
ALSO MADE PLAIN

2½-OZ. BAR
DIAMOND
OPTIC
GROUND
BOTTOM

8-OZ. TUMBLER
DIAMOND OPTIC
GROUND BOTTOM

4½-OZ. SODA
DIAMOND OPTIC
GROUND BOTTOM
ALSO MAKE 8-OZ.

12-OZ. SODA OR ICE
TEA CUPPED-DIAMOND
OPTIC ALSO MAKE
10-OZ. STRAIGHT OR
CUPPED

12-OZ. SODA OR ICE
TEA STRAIGHT.
DIAMOND OPTIC
GROUND BOTTOM

8-OZ. GOBLET
DIAMOND OPTIC
ALSO MAKE 10-OZ.

6-OZ. SAUCER
CHAMPAGNE
DIAMOND OPTIC

3½-OZ. SHERBET
DIAMOND OPTIC
ALSO MAKE 4½ & 5-OZ.

3-OZ.
COCKTAIL
DIAMOND
OPTIC

5-OZ. PARFAIT
DIAMOND OPTIC

QUART JUG
DIAMOND OPTIC

No. 1184 PATTERN

4-IN. HANDLED
ASH TRAY
GROUND BOTTOM

6½-IN. HANDLED BON BON
GROUND BOTTOM

5½-IN. TWO HANDLED BON BON
GROUND BOTTOM

CIGARETTE
ASH TRAY
GROUND BOTTOM

8-IN. HANDLED MINT
3 COMPARTMENTS
GROUND BOTTOMS

6-IN. CANDY BOX & COVER
ALSO MAKE 7 & 8-IN. SIZES
GROUND BOTTOMS

6-IN. CANDY BOX & COVER
DEEP-DIAMOND OPTIC
GROUND BOTTOM

8½-IN. HANDLED CANDY DISH
GROUND BOTTOM

12-IN. FLORAL BOWL-DIAMOND OPTIC
ALSO MADE IN 14 & 20-IN. SIZES

BRIDGE SMOKING SET
8-INDIVIDUAL ASH TRAYS & CONTAINER

Cigarette Box & Ash Tray Cover

No 1023 Hotel Cream
Plain or Diamond

Hotel Sugar & Cover
Plain or Diamond Optic

Individual Salt
Ground Bottom

Tumbler Cover

7 x 10 in. Relish Tray

Finger Bowl

3½ x 4½ in. Relish Tray Inserts

4 oz. Fruit Cocktail
Diamond Optic

2 oz. Oil &
No. 1 P/S Ground In
Diamond Optic
Also made 4 oz.

13 in. Hors' D' Oeuvre Base
Center & Cover

12 oz. Footed Soda
Diamond Optic
Also made 5 oz.

#1184 pattern

#1229 OCTAGON - name given by researchers

Dates: 1925-1937
Colors: Moongleam, flamingo, hawthorne, marigold and sahara. Very scarce in tangerine
Decorations: Cut and etched by Heisey; also decorated extensively by other companies in various manners
Marked: Most pieces are unmarked. Individual nut dishes are marked. Large sandwich and muffin plates are sometimes marked on the handle.
Comments: An all-purpose pattern of accessory pieces. As such it was often used for early plate etchings such as Empress. The footed bowl is unusual. Similar pieces are made by many companies, but the handles on most Heisey pieces are distinctive.
Optic: Available plain or diamond optic
Patents: #1,774,871 applied for on 4/17/28 and granted 9/2/30 by Ray C. Cobel for the open handles pressed with the item in one mold
Imperial Reissues: None
Availability: Common

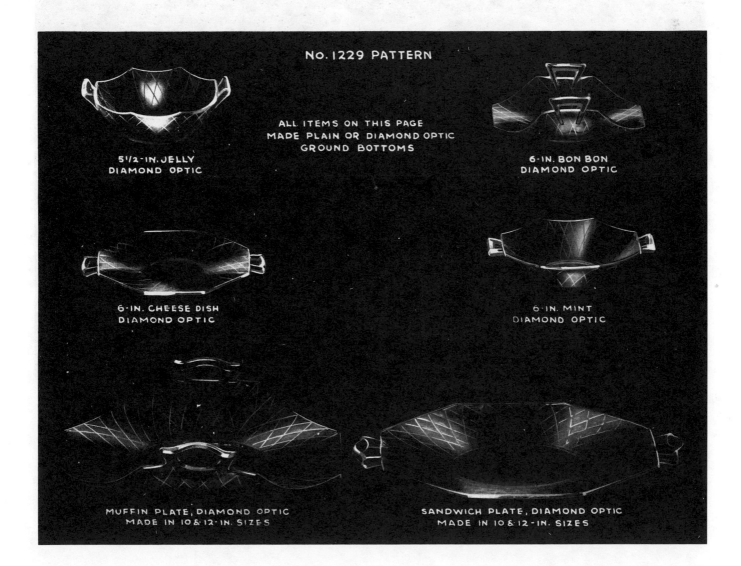

NO. 1229 PATTERN

ALL ITEMS ON THIS PAGE
MADE PLAIN OR DIAMOND OPTIC
GROUND BOTTOMS

5 1/2 - IN. JELLY
DIAMOND OPTIC

6 - IN. BON BON
DIAMOND OPTIC

6 - IN. CHEESE DISH
DIAMOND OPTIC

6 - IN. MINT
DIAMOND OPTIC

MUFFIN PLATE, DIAMOND OPTIC
MADE IN 10 & 12 - IN. SIZES

SANDWICH PLATE, DIAMOND OPTIC
MADE IN 10 & 12 - IN. SIZES

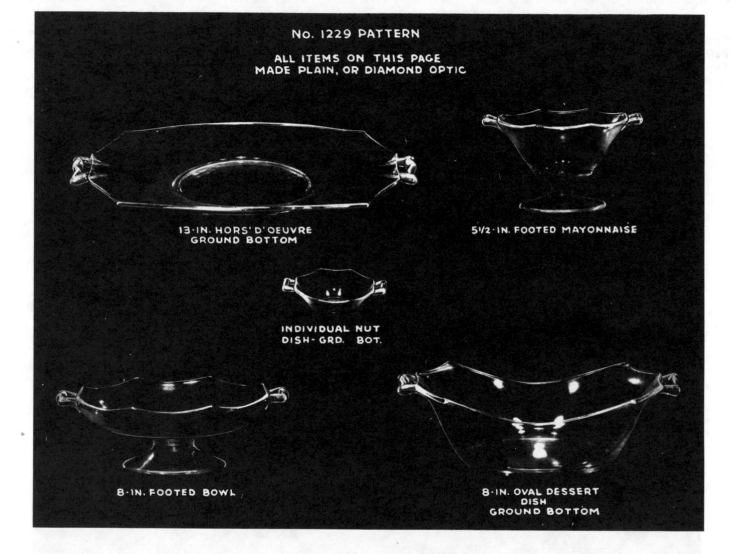

No. 1229 PATTERN

ALL ITEMS ON THIS PAGE
MADE PLAIN, OR DIAMOND OPTIC

13-IN. HORS' D' OEUVRE
GROUND BOTTOM

5½-IN. FOOTED MAYONNAISE

INDIVIDUAL NUT
DISH- GRD. BOT.

8-IN. FOOTED BOWL

8-IN. OVAL DESSERT
DISH
GROUND BOTTOM

#1231 RIBBED OCTAGON - name given by researchers

Dates: 1925-1936
Colors: Moongleam, flamingo and hawthorne. Cream and sugar and 10½″ sandwich plate also in sahara. The water jug (rum pot) was made in crystal, moongleam, flamingo, sahara and cobalt.
Decorations: Not usually found decorated
Marked: Some items
Comments: A transitional pattern with cups, plates, after-dinner cups (demitasse) and accessory pieces suitable for luncheon sets. The trefoil handled sandwich plate is interesting and usually marked. It is similar to the #1180 ashtray shown in the ASHTRAY Section. The cup shown in catalogs appears to be the #1186 cup. Cups with panels similar to the panels on the other pieces have been seen. These are thought to be the original #1231 cups. The water jug - usually called a rum pot by collectors - is the most desirable piece in the pattern and was made circa 1933 to 1937 and is unmarked. It was available both with and without a plain stopper for the spout. Examples have been seen with the "lid" portion both plain and with colonial style panels.
Imperial Reissues: None
Availability: Moderately available
Note: Similar to McKee's Octagon Edge pattern

#1231 RIBBED OCTAGON water jug (rum pot). Also made with a stopper

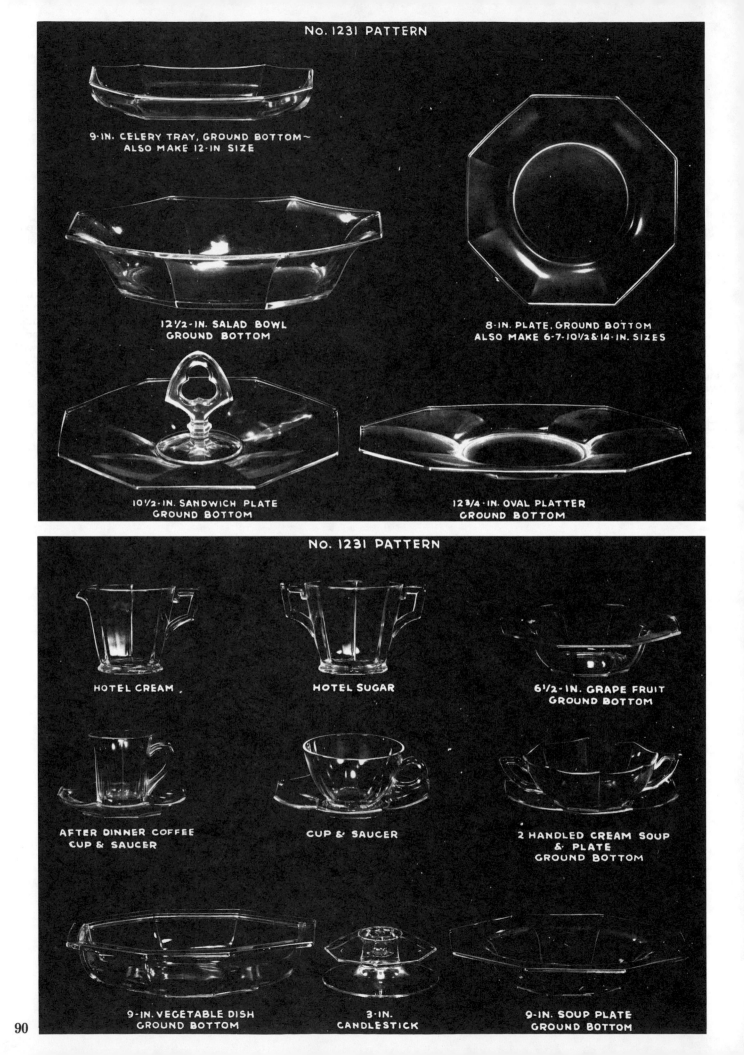

No. 1231 PATTERN

9-IN. CELERY TRAY, GROUND BOTTOM~
ALSO MAKE 12-IN SIZE

12½-IN. SALAD BOWL
GROUND BOTTOM

8-IN. PLATE, GROUND BOTTOM
ALSO MAKE 6-7-10½ & 14-IN. SIZES

10½-IN. SANDWICH PLATE
GROUND BOTTOM

12¾-IN. OVAL PLATTER
GROUND BOTTOM

No. 1231 PATTERN

HOTEL CREAM

HOTEL SUGAR

6½-IN. GRAPE FRUIT
GROUND BOTTOM

AFTER DINNER COFFEE
CUP & SAUCER

CUP & SAUCER

2 HANDLED CREAM SOUP
& PLATE
GROUND BOTTOM

9-IN. VEGETABLE DISH
GROUND BOTTOM

3-IN.
CANDLESTICK

9-IN. SOUP PLATE
GROUND BOTTOM

#1252 TWIST - name given by researchers

Dates: 1928-1937; 4″ nappy until 1957

Colors: Flamingo, moongleam, marigold, sahara. A few items were made in alexandrite. A few plates are known in tangerine (almost an amberina.) The small nappy is known in dawn

Decorations: Some early cuttings by Heisey - usually florals. Original numbers for these have not been found

Marked: Most pieces

Comments: A large pattern line originally developed from a design for a plate. Consists of almost any serving piece or ornamental item plus a full line of stemware. Only a nappy survived until 1957. The majority of the items were discontinued by 1937. Contemporary reports described the pattern as "attractively moderne but not bizarre" in 1929. The "lighting" handles are found on several pieces and are distinctive. Unusual pieces include the Kraft cheese plate, the small individual bon bon, the utility plate and the nasturtium bowl. A #1252½ cup was also made - this with a plain top rim for ease of drinking. Originally the flat salt was #54. A footed salt was also made, the foot being similar to the feet found on stemware. In early ads, the #129 candlestick was shown with the pattern. Note that there are three styles of creams and sugars. There is a cover known for the oval hotel sugar, but this is rare. A tall (about 12″) footed piece with molded threads on the top has been seen. This is a cocktail shaker to be fitted with a metal lid.

Patents: #79885 for plate applied for 9/10/28 and granted 11/12/29. #79716 for bowl applied for 5/1/29 and granted 10/29/29. T. Clarence Heisey listed as designer for both

Imperial Reissues: The 4″ nappy was made from 1957 to 1966 and probably marked with the Diamond H. It was made in crystal

Availability: Common

#1252½ TWIST cup

#1252 TWIST individual cream and sugar. The sugar is the same as the footed almond.

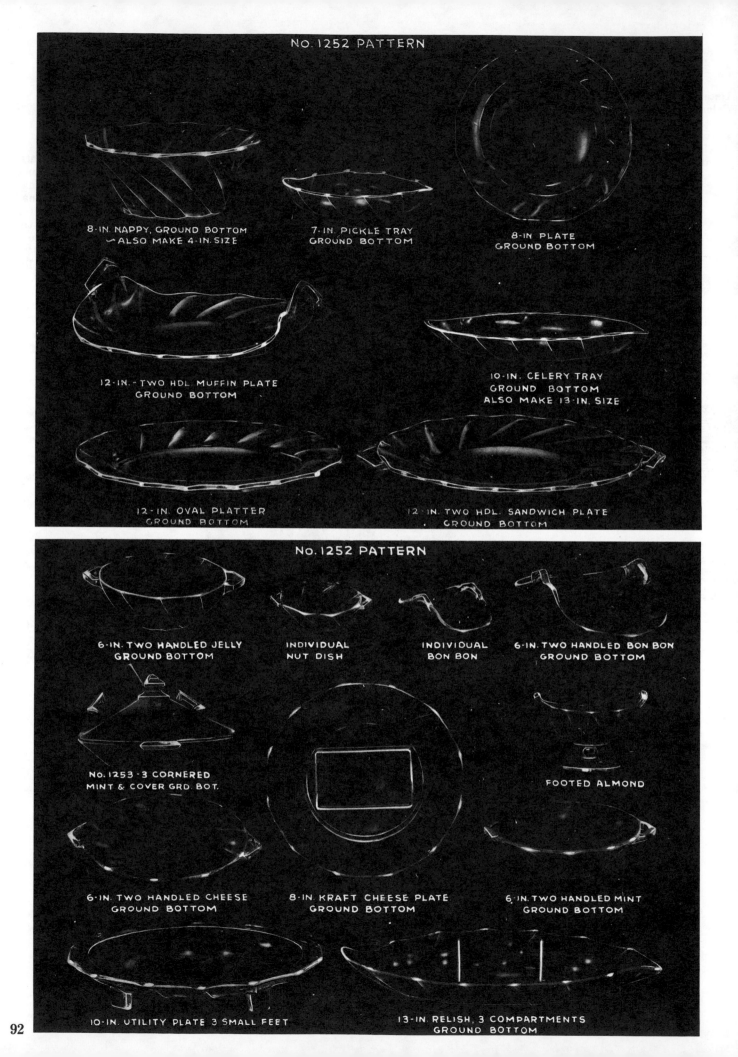

8-IN. NAPPY, GROUND BOTTOM
—ALSO MAKE 4-IN. SIZE

7-IN. PICKLE TRAY
GROUND BOTTOM

8-IN PLATE
GROUND BOTTOM

12-IN.—TWO HDL MUFFIN PLATE
GROUND BOTTOM

10-IN. CELERY TRAY
GROUND BOTTOM
ALSO MAKE 13-IN. SIZE

12-IN. OVAL PLATTER
GROUND BOTTOM

12-IN. TWO HDL. SANDWICH PLATE
GROUND BOTTOM

No. 1252 PATTERN

6-IN. TWO HANDLED JELLY
GROUND BOTTOM

INDIVIDUAL
NUT DISH

INDIVIDUAL
BON BON

6-IN. TWO HANDLED BON BON
GROUND BOTTOM

No. 1253 - 3 CORNERED
MINT & COVER GRD. BOT.

FOOTED ALMOND

6-IN. TWO HANDLED CHEESE
GROUND BOTTOM

8-IN. KRAFT CHEESE PLATE
GROUND BOTTOM

6-IN. TWO HANDLED MINT
GROUND BOTTOM

10-IN. UTILITY PLATE 3 SMALL FEET

13-IN. RELISH, 3 COMPARTMENTS
GROUND BOTTOM

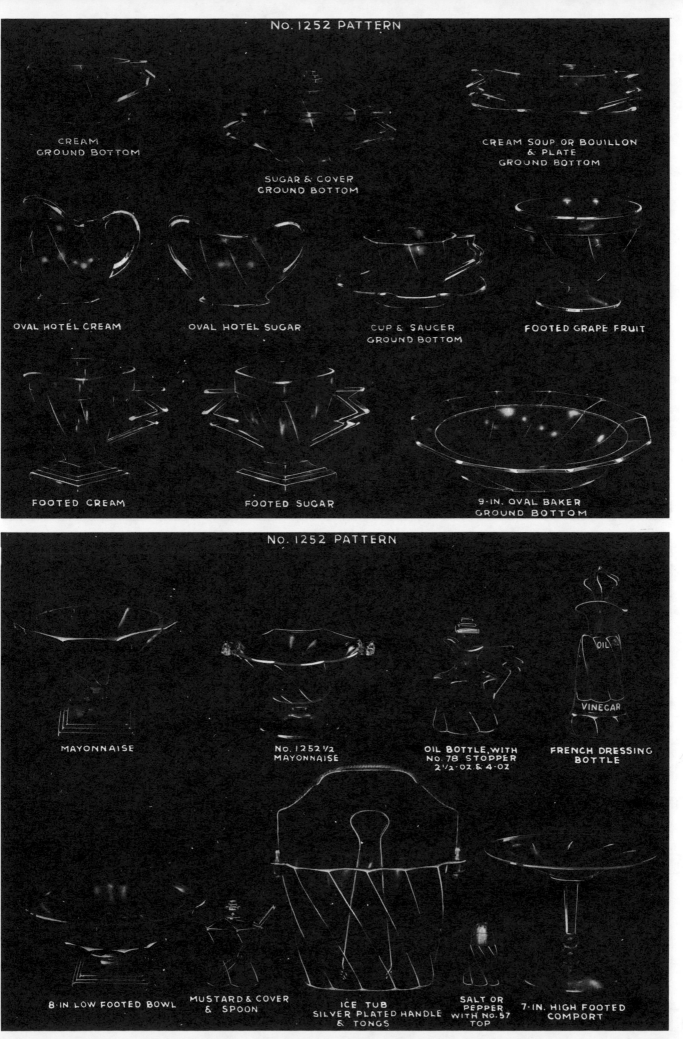

No. 1252 PATTERN

CREAM
GROUND BOTTOM

SUGAR & COVER
GROUND BOTTOM

CREAM SOUP OR BOUILLON
& PLATE
GROUND BOTTOM

OVAL HOTEL CREAM

OVAL HOTEL SUGAR

CUP & SAUCER
GROUND BOTTOM

FOOTED GRAPE FRUIT

FOOTED CREAM

FOOTED SUGAR

9-IN. OVAL BAKER
GROUND BOTTOM

No. 1252 PATTERN

MAYONNAISE

No. 1252½
MAYONNAISE

OIL BOTTLE, WITH
No. 78 STOPPER
2½-OZ. & 4-OZ.

FRENCH DRESSING
BOTTLE

8-IN. LOW FOOTED BOWL

MUSTARD & COVER
& SPOON

ICE TUB
SILVER PLATED HANDLE
& TONGS

SALT OR
PEPPER
WITH No. 57
TOP

7-IN. HIGH FOOTED
COMPORT

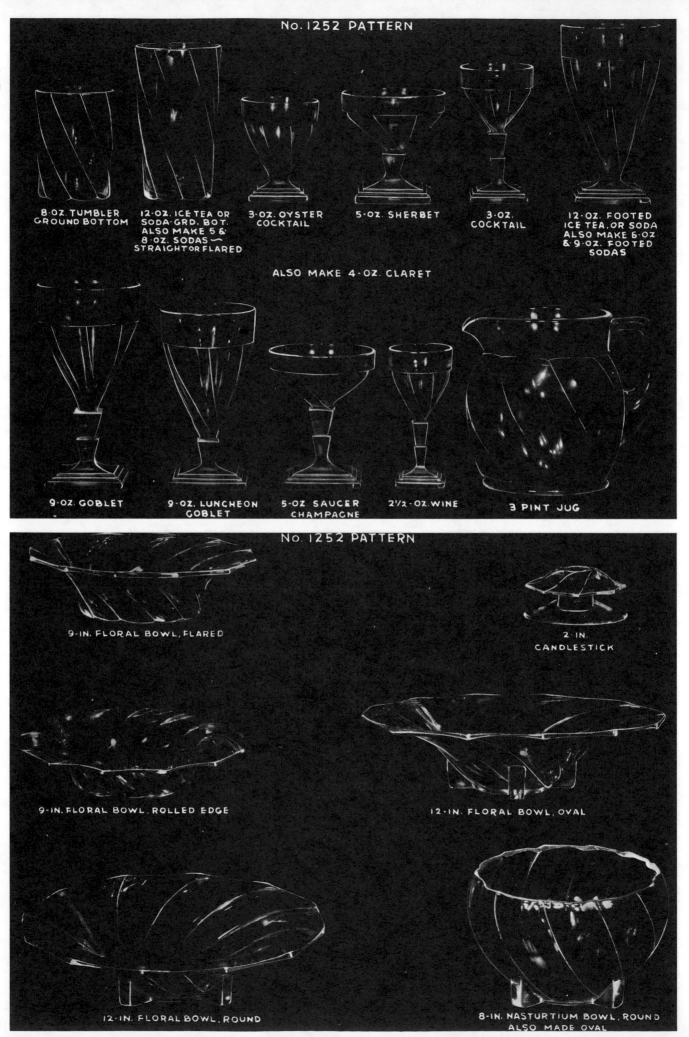

No. 1252 PATTERN

8-OZ. TUMBLER GROUND BOTTOM

12-OZ. ICE TEA OR SODA-GRD. BOT. ALSO MAKE 5 & 8-OZ. SODAS — STRAIGHT or FLARED

3-OZ. OYSTER COCKTAIL

5-OZ. SHERBET

3-OZ. COCKTAIL

12-OZ. FOOTED ICE TEA, OR SODA ALSO MAKE 6-OZ & 9-OZ. FOOTED SODAS

ALSO MAKE 4-OZ. CLARET

9-OZ. GOBLET

9-OZ. LUNCHEON GOBLET

5-OZ. SAUCER CHAMPAGNE

2½-OZ. WINE

3 PINT JUG

No. 1252 PATTERN

9-IN. FLORAL BOWL, FLARED

2-IN. CANDLESTICK

9-IN. FLORAL BOWL, ROLLED EDGE

12-IN. FLORAL BOWL, OVAL

12-IN. FLORAL BOWL, ROUND

8-IN. NASTURTIUM BOWL, ROUND ALSO MADE OVAL

94

#1401 EMPRESS - original Heisey Co. name

Dates: 1930-1938
Colors: Moongleam, flamingo, sahara. Many items in alexandrite. Several items in tangerine and cobalt. Salt and pepper known in marigold
Decorations: Widely used for Heisey etchings and cuttings. Some pressed pieces cut by Pairpoint in "Boswell" gray design.
Marked: Many pieces are marked although some have never been seen with a mark. The dolphin footed items, if marked at all, will be marked on the back of one of the dolphin feet.
Comments: One of the most popular Heisey patterns when it was first brought out and continues to be collected avidly today. Extensive line of many, many different items. Early Heisey ads also referred to it as "Lilies of France" pattern. Do not confuse the name Empress (for the pattern) with the same name for a Heisey etching. Unusual items include the Lion Head bowl, the punch bowl, the #1401½ plate and the dolphin footed items which form a specialty in themselves. Note the lemon dish with the dolphin finial. A #1401½ cup was also made - this has a plain rim. Also a variation of the jug and cream and sugar is known without the dolphin feet - these have usually been found in moongleam and may be an early design for the pattern. After 1938, many of the pieces were made with an internal optic only in crystal. At this time, this was declared a new pattern - #1509 Queen Ann. Some items like the triplex relish were continued without the optic so in reality are identical to Empress. When these pieces are found in crystal, only the presence of a etching or cutting could positively identify these pieces as either Empress or Queen Ann. #1402 refers to a matching Empress round sandwich tray.
Patents: #81388 for floral bowl applied for 3/29/30 and granted 6/17/30. #82887 for plate applied for 10/27/30 and granted 12/23/30. #82888 for bowl, ring handled applied for 10/27/30 and granted 12/23/30. T. Clarence Heisey listed as designer on all patents.
Imperial Reissues: The dolphin footed (3 toed) candlesticks in Sunshine Yellow in 1981 for Collectors Guild. Marked with CG in a circle between 2 of the dolphin feet. The dolphin footed floral bowl and jug were also made, but technically these were from Queen Ann molds since they have optic. However, since they were made in colors, we are mentioning them here. The bowl was also made in Sunshine Yellow and the jug was made in green. Both are marked CG in a circle. The jug is not tooled in at the top as are Heisey ones, and the bowl has an uneven, pulled rim quite unlike Heisey bowls.
Availability: Common

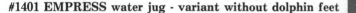

#1401 EMPRESS water jug - variant without dolphin feet

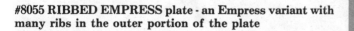

#8055 RIBBED EMPRESS plate - an Empress variant with many ribs in the outer portion of the plate

NO. 1401 PATTERN

MADE CRYSTAL, MOONGLEAM, FLAMINGO, SAHARA
AND ALEXANDRITE

8-IN. NAPPY, GROUND BOTTOM
ALSO MAKE 4½-IN.
SIZE

10-IN. SALAD BOWL, GROUND BOTTOM

8-IN. PLATE, GROUND BOTTOM
ALSO MAKE 4½-6-7-9-10½
& 12-IN.

6-IN. FOOTED COMPORT

8-IN. SQUARE PLATE, GROUND BOTTOM
NO. 1401½

NO. 1401 PATTERN

7½-IN. FOOTED NAPPY

6-IN. GRAPE FRUIT
SQUARE TOP- GROUND BOTTOM

7-IN. TRIPLEX RELISH
GROUND BOTTOM

13-IN. HORS'D'OEUVRE, GROUND
BOTTOM

8-IN. SQUARE PLATE, GROUND BOTTOM
ALSO MAKE 6-7-8 & 10½-IN.

10-IN. OVAL DESSERT-GROUND BOTTOM

NO. 1401 PATTERN

NO. 1401½ CUP & SAUCER

AFTER DINNER COFFEE
CUP & SAUCER

CUP & SAUCER

BOUILLON & PLATE

13-IN. CELERY TRAY, GROUND BOTTOM
ALSO MAKE 10-IN.

14-IN. OVAL PLATTER, GROUND BOTTOM

CREAM SOUP & PLATE

NO. 1401 PATTERN

INDIVIDUAL
NUT DISH

6-IN. FOOTED JELLY
2 HANDLES

5½-IN. FOOTED
MAYONNAISE

6-IN. FOOTED MINT

6-IN. BON BON
GROUND BOTTOM

6-IN. CANDLESTICK

SALT OR
PEPPER
NO. 57 TOP

5-IN. PRESERVE · 2 HDLS.

MUSTARD
& COVER

13-IN. PICKLE & OLIVE · 2 COMPARTMENTS
GROUND BOTTOM

4-OZ. OIL
NO. 83 STOPPER

97

No. 1401 PATTERN

FOOTED CREAM

INDIVIDUAL CREAM

INDIVIDUAL SUGAR

**FOOTED SUGAR
3 HANDLES**

**12-IN. 2 HANDLED SANDWICH PLATE
GROUND BOTTOM**

**12-IN. SQUARE SANDWICH TRAY
GROUND BOTTOM**

**12-IN. 2 HANDLED MUFFIN PLATE
GROUND BOTTOM**

No. 1401 PATTERN

15-IN. FOOTED PUNCH BOWL

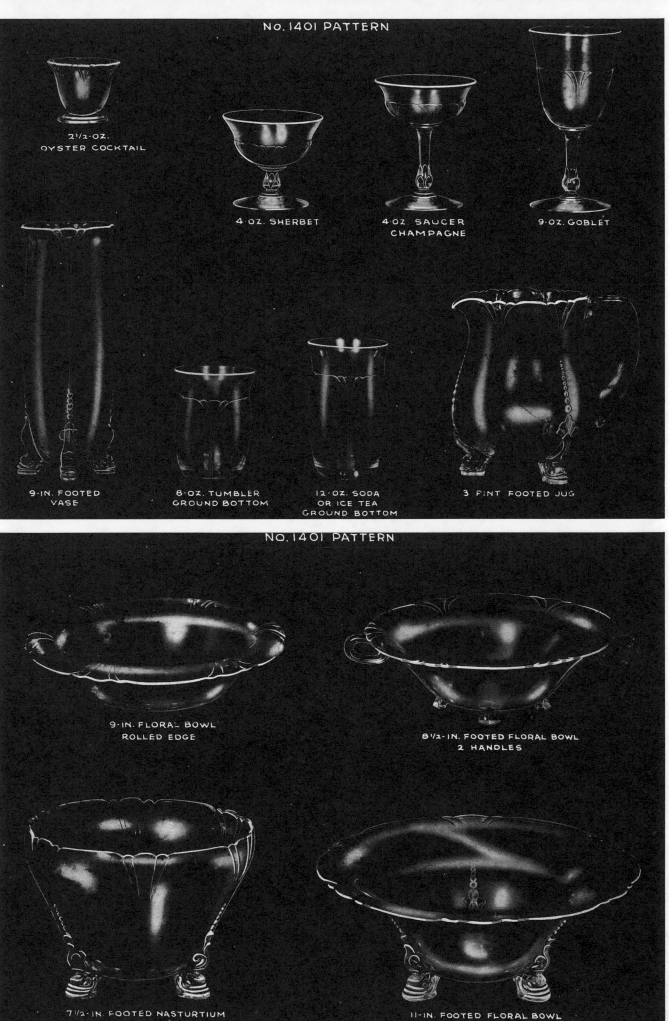

NO. 1401 PATTERN

2½-OZ.
OYSTER COCKTAIL

4-OZ. SHERBET

4-OZ. SAUCER
CHAMPAGNE

9-OZ. GOBLET

9-IN. FOOTED
VASE

8-OZ. TUMBLER
GROUND BOTTOM

12-OZ. SODA
OR ICE TEA
GROUND BOTTOM

3 PINT FOOTED JUG

NO. 1401 PATTERN

9-IN. FLORAL BOWL
ROLLED EDGE

8½-IN. FOOTED FLORAL BOWL
2 HANDLES

7½-IN. FOOTED NASTURTIUM
BOWL

11-IN. FOOTED FLORAL BOWL

99

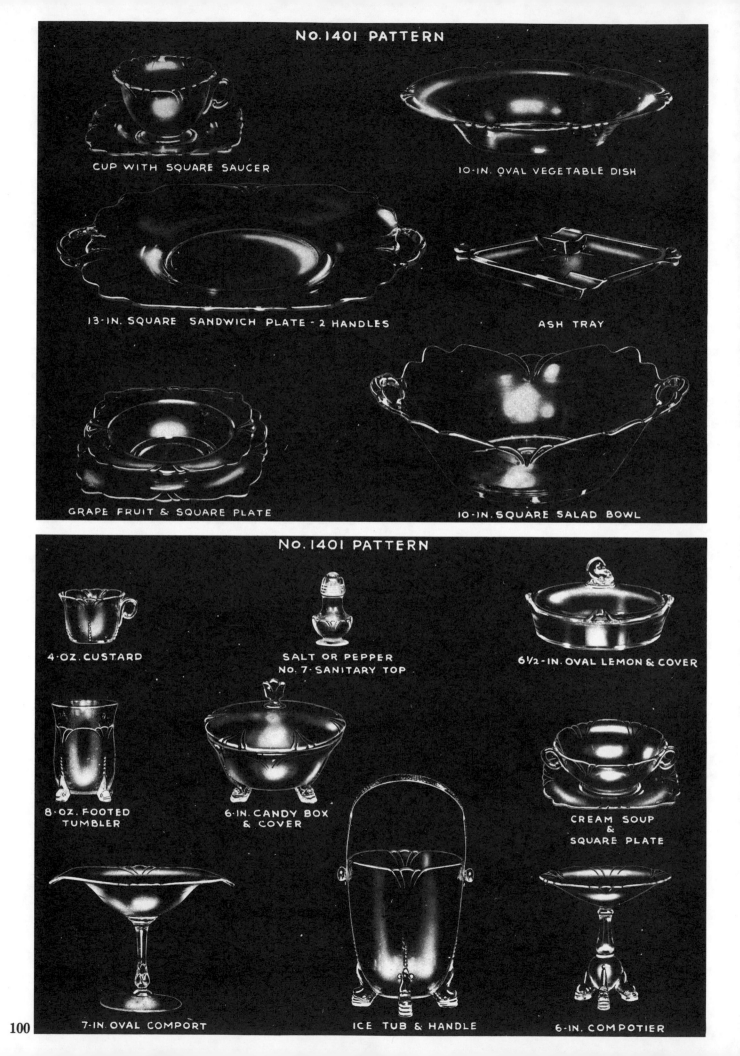

No.1401 PATTERN

CUP WITH SQUARE SAUCER

10-IN. OVAL VEGETABLE DISH

13-IN. SQUARE SANDWICH PLATE - 2 HANDLES

ASH TRAY

GRAPE FRUIT & SQUARE PLATE

10-IN. SQUARE SALAD BOWL

No.1401 PATTERN

4-OZ. CUSTARD

SALT OR PEPPER
NO. 7 SANITARY TOP

6½-IN. OVAL LEMON & COVER

8-OZ. FOOTED
TUMBLER

6-IN. CANDY BOX
& COVER

CREAM SOUP
&
SQUARE PLATE

7-IN. OVAL COMPORT

ICE TUB & HANDLE

6-IN. COMPOTIER

100

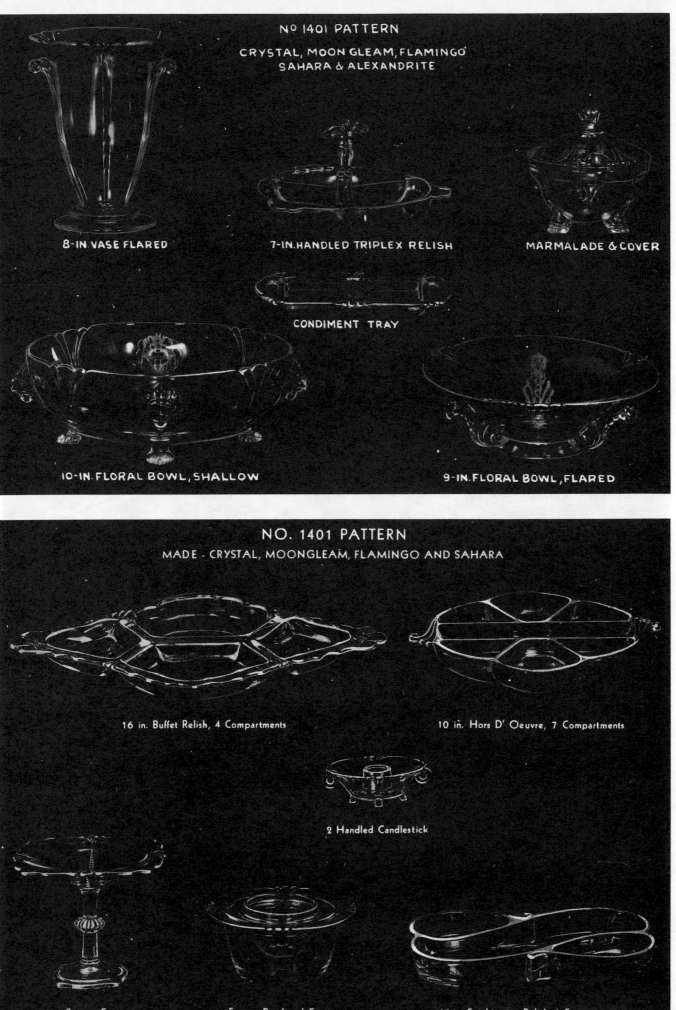

Nº 1401 PATTERN

CRYSTAL, MOON GLEAM, FLAMINGO
SAHARA & ALEXANDRITE

8-IN. VASE FLARED

7-IN. HANDLED TRIPLEX RELISH

MARMALADE & COVER

CONDIMENT TRAY

10-IN. FLORAL BOWL, SHALLOW

9-IN. FLORAL BOWL, FLARED

NO. 1401 PATTERN
MADE - CRYSTAL, MOONGLEAM, FLAMINGO AND SAHARA

16 in. Buffet Relish, 4 Compartments

10 in. Hors D' Oeuvre, 7 Compartments

2 Handled Candlestick

6 in Square Comport

Frappe Bowl and Center

10 in. Combination Relish, 3 Compartments

7 in. Triplex Relish
Center Handle

10 in. Combination Relish
3 Compartments

10 in. Triplex Relish

7 in. Triplex Relish
Ground Bottom

13 in. Hors D'Oeuvre

#1401 EMPRESS pattern

102

#1404 OLD SANDWICH - original Heisey Co. name

Dates: 1931-1956
Colors: Moongleam, flamingo and sahara. A few items were made in cobalt. Scarce in tangerine and zircon. In this pattern, flamingo and moongleam are difficult colors to find. Beer mugs are found in amber.
Decorations: Unusual to find any decoration
Marked: Most items are marked
Comments: Heisey copied this pattern from the original Sandwich glass pattern called Pillar. Old Sandwich is an adaptation in modern shapes. In a few early ads Heisey called this Early American Thumbprint, but this name was quickly dropped and Old Sandwich took its place. Unusual items include the three sizes of beer mugs, plus the cream pitchers made from them; the popcorn bowl; candlestick; cigarette holder and the oval sherry bottle. One mention was found in an old price list of a basket made from a footed soda. This is an unusual item. A round cream and sugar were also made. The floral bowl was made in two manners - one has a well to accept the floral block and the other does not. See the MISCELLANEOUS Section for the pilsner and other sections for various other items. Old Sandwich seems to go against normal color availablity in several pieces. For instance, even though most of the pattern is difficult to find in flamingo, the salt and peppers are relatively easy to find in this color. The individual ashtray is most commonly found in cobalt with moongleam and flamingo being difficult to find. Incidentally, this item was always called an individual ashtray by Heisey, not a butter pat or a salt dip as many people today call it. Sometimes the oils are found with Maltese Cross stoppers. These were probably made for use in churches. Heisey did supply the oils with these stoppers.
Imperial Reissues: 15 items in crystal - mostly stems and sodas
Availability: Common to moderately available

#1404 OLD SANDWICH round cream and sugar

4 oz. Claret

2½ oz. Wine

3 oz. Cocktail

4 oz. Oyster Cocktail

6 oz. Sundae

10 oz. Low Footed Goblet

5 oz. Saucer Champagne

4½ oz. Parfait

4 oz. Sherbet

6 in. Square Plate
Ground Bottom
Also made 7 & 8 in.

10 oz. Low Footed Tumbler

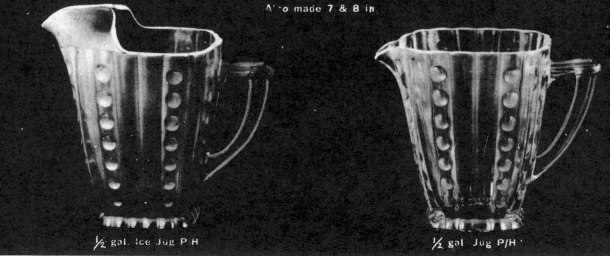
½ gal. Ice Jug P/H

½ gal. Jug P/H

#1404 OLD SANDWICH pattern

Oval Cream

Oval Sugar

Cup & Saucer

1½ oz. Bar
Ground Bottom

8 oz. Soda or Ice Tea
Ground Bottom
Straight or Cupped
Also made 5, 10 & 12 oz.

6½ oz. Toddy

12 oz.
Footed Soda or Ice Tea

8 oz. Tumbler
Ground Bottom
Straight or Cupped

6 in. Candlestick

6 in. Comport

#1404 OLD SANDWICH pattern

Salt or Pepper
No. 20 Top

Individual Ash Tray

2½ oz. Oil & No. 85 P/S

Catsup Bottle & No. 3 P/S

11 in. Round Floral Bowl
Footed

No. 22 Floral Block

12 in. Oval Floral Bowl
Footed

Finger Bowl

#1404 OLD SANDWICH pattern

18 oz. Cream

12 oz. Cream

14 oz. Cream

14 oz. Beer Mug

18 oz. Beer Mug

12 oz. Beer Mug

Cigarette Holder

1 pt. Decanter & No. 98 P/S

Footed Pop Corn Bowl
Cupped

#1404 OLD SANDWICH pattern

#1405 IPSWICH - original Heisey Co. name

Dates: 1931-1946; reissued in crystal from 1951-1953

Colors: Moongleam, flamingo, sahara. Center vase and floral bowl in cobalt and the goblet is known in alexandrite

Decorations: No, although the centerpiece and vase was placed on a metal filagree base by a decorating company

Marked: Most items

Comments: A copy of the Sandwich glass pattern, Comet. Heisey used the motif on modern shapes. Originally the name was Early American Scroll but this was quickly changed to Ipswich. Moongleam and flamingo are difficult to find today even though listed in company price lists. Unusual items include the cocktail shaker, candlestick, cologne with #91 stopper (made 1939-1944+) and the centerpiece and insert and the oil. Old trade journal accounts state that in August of 1932 new centerpieces, a footed fruit bowl, footed oil and sauce dish were added to the line. Apparently these items were not made early in the pattern's life. Maltese Cross stoppers are also sometimes found in Ipswich oils. (See discussion under #1404 Old Sandwich.)

Imperial Reissues: Two sizes of candy jars and a footed bowl were made in amber, heather, verde, antique blue, mandarin gold and moonlight blue. The candy jar and cover was also made in milk glass. The pecan bowl (with a ruffled edge) was not originally made by Heisey. All these items may be marked with the Diamond H.

Availability: Common to moderately available

#1405 IPSWICH cologne with #91 stopper

Finger Bowl & 6 in. Plate

4 oz. Sherbet

Sugar

Cream

2 oz. Oil
Footed & No. 86 P/S

10 oz. Tumbler
Ground Bottom
Straight or Cupped

4 oz. Saucer Champagne

7 in. Square Plate
Ground Bottom
Also made 8 in.

4 oz. Oyster Cocktail

8 oz. Footed Soda.
Also made 5, 10 & 12 oz.

12 oz. Schoppen

10 oz. Goblet

#1405 IPSWICH pattern

11 in. Floral Bowl

Footed Center Piece
with Vase and "A" Prisms

6 in. Candlestick

½ lb. Candy Jar & Cover
Also made ¼ lb.

1 qt. Cocktail Shaker
with No. 1 Strainer & No. 86 P/S

½ gal. Jug
Stuck Handle

#1405 IPSWICH pattern

#1415 TWENTIETH CENTURY - original Heisey Co. name

Dates: 1931-1937; reissued from 1955-1957 in dawn
Colors: Moongleam, flamingo, sahara, dawn. Sodas found in cobalt
Decorations: Cutting #878 Sea Glade
Marked: Yes, most items
Comments: A short pattern line. Items in moongleam and flamingo are more difficult to find than other colors. The cereal bowl is the most difficult item to locate and was not made in dawn. The plate appears to be a plain plate and does not carry the basic quatrefoil pattern. The pattern may have been difficult to release from the mold since often the four small feet do not sit flat. The pitcher has been seen without the four vertical ribs.
Imperial Reissues: None
Availability: Moderate—dawn is the easiest color to find

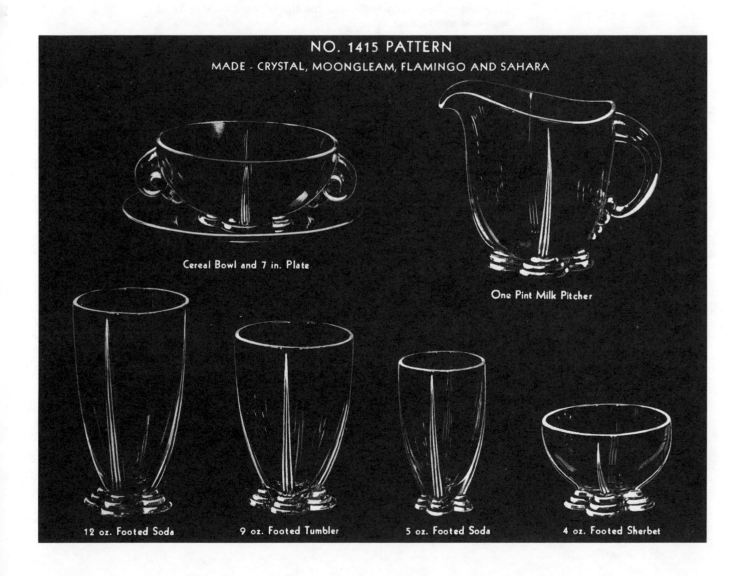

NO. 1415 PATTERN
MADE - CRYSTAL, MOONGLEAM, FLAMINGO AND SAHARA

Cereal Bowl and 7 in. Plate

One Pint Milk Pitcher

12 oz. Footed Soda   9 oz. Footed Tumbler   5 oz. Footed Soda   4 oz. Footed Sherbet

#1425 VICTORIAN - original Heisey Co. name

Dates: 1933-1953

Colors: Sahara and cobalt. A few pieces are known in a light zircon. Also scarce in an unusual green shade. Goblets and sherbets are listed in flamingo and moongleam.

Decorations: None

Marked: Most items

Comments: This pattern is a modern adaptation of several old "waffle" type patterns made by George Duncan's Sons, among others. Items to beware of are cruets with smooth handles, which were made by Duncan and the water bottle, which is also probably Duncan and was never made by Heisey. Even though listed in price lists, sahara items are difficult to find and cobalt items are very hard to locate. Early items were the goblet and sherbet listed in moongleam, flamingo, sahara and cobalt. In fact these items were the only items of the pattern listed in 1933. The pattern includes stemware, some barware and accessory pieces plus table service. A ½ gallon jug was also made which is not illustrated. Unusual items include the rose bowl, the triplex bowl and the #1425½ condiment tray set. Old ads sometimes called the pattern "Old Colony" and "Wayside Inn". Occasionally, dealers today refer to the pattern as "Block" or "Waffle Keg". In an early Heisey ad, the pattern was called "Squares".

Imperial Reissues: Eight items in stemware, sodas, nappy and plate. These items were made in crystal, amber, azalea, and verde and marked with the Diamond H.

Availability: Moderately available

8 in. Nappy

10½ in. Floral Bowl

2 lt Candlestick

13 in. Sandwich Plate

Cheese Holder

7 in. Plate
Also made 8 in.

12 in. Cracker Plate

#1425 VICTORIAN pattern

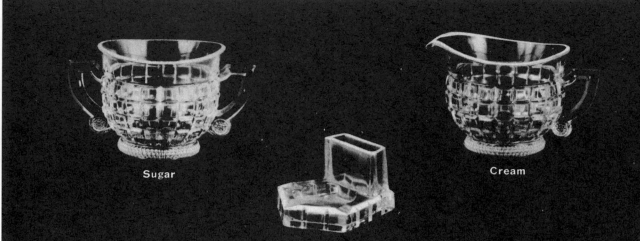

Sugar

Individual Cigarette Holder & Ash Tray

Cream

Salt or Pepper & No. 339 Metal Top

Salt or Pepper & No. 43 Metal Top

Salt or Pepper & No. 643 Metal Top

Salt or Pepper & Nickel Top

Salt or Pepper & No. 1 Sanitary Top

12 in. Celery Tray

#1425 VICTORIAN pattern

114

4 oz. Claret

3 oz. Cocktail

2½ oz. Wine

Finger Bowl & 6 in. Plate

8 oz. Old Fashion Cocktail

2 oz. Bar

10 oz. Footed Tumbler

5 oz. Saucer Champagne

5 oz. Oyster Cocktail

5 oz. Sherbet

12 oz. Soda
Straight or Cupped
Also made 5 oz

12 oz. Footed Soda

9 oz. High Footed Goblet

9 oz. Goblet

#1425 VICTORIAN pattern

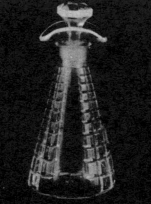

French Dressing Bottle
& No. 7 P/S

6 in. Footed Vase

4 in. Vase

5½ in. Vase

6 in. Cigarette Box & Cover

3 oz. Oil Bottle & No. 7 P/S

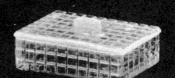

4 in. Cigarette Box & Cover

27 oz. Rye Bottle & No. 99 P/S

9 in. Footed Vase

#1425 VICTORIAN pattern

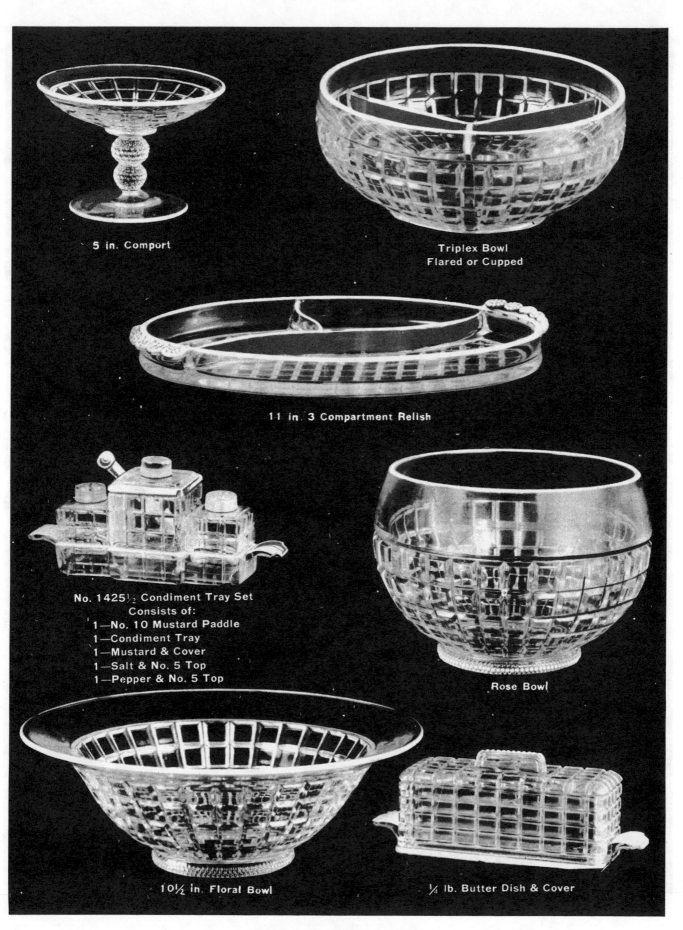

5 in. Comport

Triplex Bowl
Flared or Cupped

11 in. 3 Compartment Relish

No. 1425½ Condiment Tray Set
Consists of:
1—No. 10 Mustard Paddle
1—Condiment Tray
1—Mustard & Cover
1—Salt & No. 5 Top
1—Pepper & No. 5 Top

Rose Bowl

10½ in. Floral Bowl

¼ lb. Butter Dish & Cover

#1425 VICTORIAN pattern

Punch Bowl

5 oz. Custard

21 in. Buffet Plate

#1425 VICTORIAN pattern

2 light Horn of Plenty Candlestick

Horn of Plenty Individual Vase

Horn of Plenty Individual Candlestick

9 in. Horn of Plenty Vase
Also made 5 & 7 in.

11 in. Horn of Plenty Floral Bowl

Horn of Plenty Cigarette Holder

#1428 WARWICK - original Heisey Co. name

Dates: 1933-1957   **Colors:** Moongleam, flamingo, sahara and cobalt. Rare in alexandrite
Decorations: Some pieces have satin finish on bases. Occasionally decorated with cuttings by Heisey.
Marked: Yes
Comments: Also referred to as Horn of Plenty. In early years there was a difference in the small candlestick and the individual vase. Later the candlestick looked like the vase but was called a candlestick. In the early candlestick, the glass comes into the center leaving an opening just large enough to hold a candle. Again, normal color availability is different in this pattern. In this case, sahara and cobalt items are much easier to find than the other colors. Moongleam is next most available and flamingo the scarcest. Beware of a fake 7″ vase in crystal in very poor, yellowish glass.
Imperial Reissues: Although not listed or advertised in their regular line, Imperial made the 1-light candlestick, the 2-light candlestick and the 7″ vase in heather and verde. Items seen have been marked with the Diamond H.
Availability: Common

#1447 ROCOCO - original Heisey Co. name

Dates: 1934-1938

Colors: Sahara. Scarce in cobalt. The combination mayonnaise and relish was made in limelight in 1956.

Decorations: Occasionally found with a Heisey cutting

Marked: Most items

Comments: The pattern has an unusual design for its time period, being very "busy". The oval "jewels" are unusual and distinctive. They are raised on all pieces except the candlestick which has an oval opening. The entire pattern is not plentiful. Sahara items are difficult to find and other colored items are more difficult. Unusual items include the comport, the candlestick, the footed soda and combination mayonnaise and relish and cover. Note the four tiny feet on the salt, footed soda and cream and sugar. The footed cheese remained in the Heisey line as the center portion of a #1509 Queen Ann cheese and cracker until 1957. This is found with Orchid and Rose etchings among others. It is sometimes incorrectly identified as a "Knee & Step" comport rather than as a true piece of Rococo. A variant plate was made circa 1939 with a stippled background. It is #1512 and has been named Stippled Rococo.

Imperial Reissues: The souvenir plates made for HCA from 1971 to 1976 were made from the Rococo plate mold. These plates bear the IG trademark and a Diamond H plus the date of issue. Colors used were amberglo, blue haze, verde, nut brown, ultra blue and crystal.

Availability: Moderately available to scarce

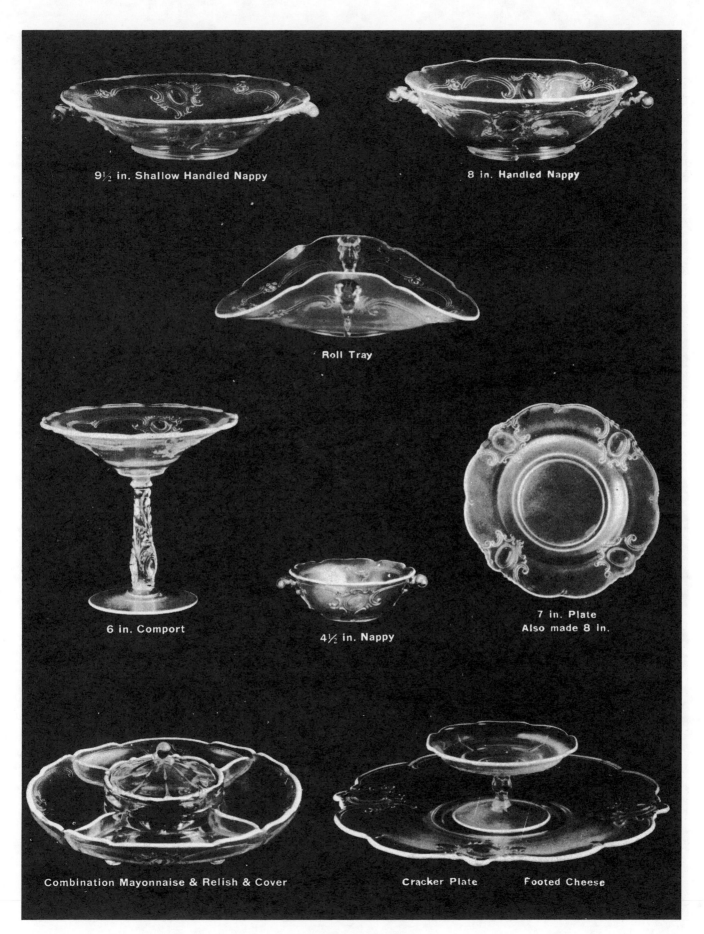

9½ in. Shallow Handled Nappy

8 in. Handled Nappy

Roll Tray

6 in. Comport

4½ in. Nappy

7 in. Plate
Also made 8 in.

Combination Mayonnaise & Relish & Cover

Cracker Plate

Footed Cheese

#1447 ROCOCO pattern

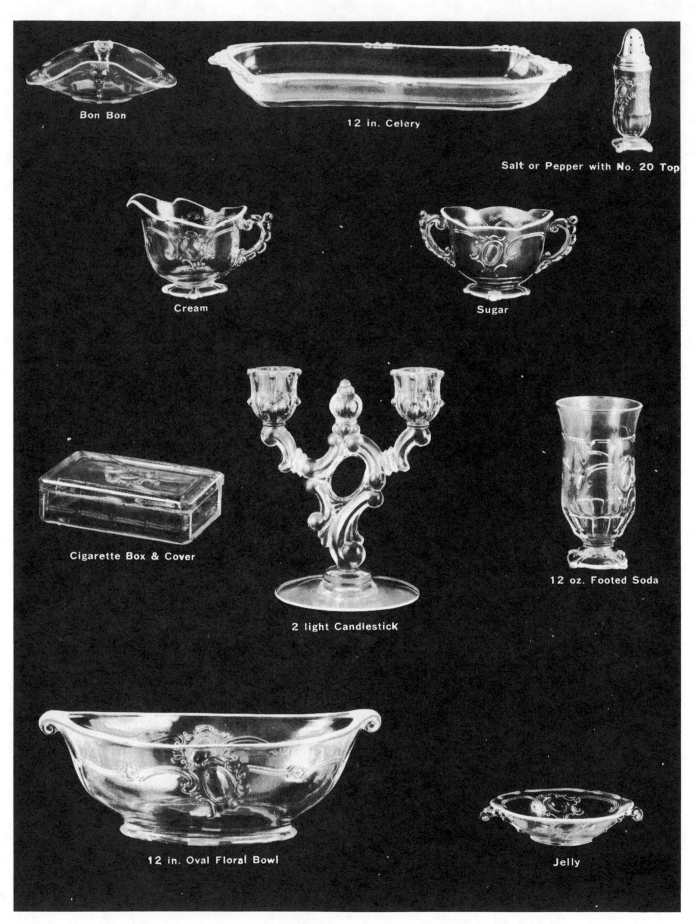

Bon Bon

12 in. Celery

Salt or Pepper with No. 20 Top

Cream

Sugar

Cigarette Box & Cover

2 light Candlestick

12 oz. Footed Soda

12 in. Oval Floral Bowl

Jelly

#1447 ROCOCO pattern

#1463 QUAKER - original Heisey Co. name

Dates: 1935-1938
Colors: Crystal only
Decorations: No
Marked: Yes, with a small Diamond H.
Comments: This particular pattern seems to be a reissue of nappies and plates made from them from the old #355 Quator pattern. Old Quator pieces will have the large Diamond H and a full ground bottom. Also, plates were not listed in the Quator pattern, only in Quaker.
Imperial Reissues: None
Availability: Scarce

8 in. Nappy
Star Bottom
Also made 4½, 7 & 9 in.

9 in. Plate
Star Bottom
Also made 5, 10 & 11 in.

#1469, 1469½, 1469¾ RIDGELEIGH - original Heisey Co. name

Dates: 1935-1944. Some pieces survived until 1957

Colors: A few items in zircon and sahara in 1937. Very scarce in cobalt, experimental light blue and amber.

Decorations: Sometimes found with silver overlay and other types of decoration done by decorating companies. The 8″ plate was etched with #602 Simplex. The 6″ square ashtray was used for several special etchings for promotional items by various companies and organizations. This ashtray was also offered with Fish, Hunting Scene, Dog and Horse etchings by Heisey. Heisey Cuttings: Usually the 7″ and 8″ square plates and sometimes a few other pieces were cut with some cuttings. The 2-light candlestick was sold with a cutting, although there is no known illustration of this cutting.

Marked: Most pieces

Comments: A very, very large pattern line. Many styles of candlesticks and candelabra were made. Several of these were designs by Carl Cobel. The pattern seems to have originated with the icicle-shaped decanter which was originally numbered #1457 but became part of the #1469 pattern later. Several of the pieces are adaptations from molds from other patterns including the Swan Handled bowl (#133), the 8″ floral bowl (#501 box), the oblong trays (#473), the marmalade and cover (#393), the mustard (#417), the oil and low footed comport (#1170) and others. Interesting items include the 1-pint decanter (icicle), the 10″ 5-compartment relish (star), the 7″ ball vase with flared top, the cocktail shaker, the card suit ashtrays, the perfume, the roly poly, the covered cigarette holder and the oval cigarette box. Many collectors admire the brilliance reflected from the ridged glass and the great variety of pieces available in the pattern. Stemware is not easy to find especially in all the different sizes. Two types of salts are known. The double cone shape is #1469½ and not shown in catalogs but is listed in original material. Sometimes these are found with a Diamond B mark—made by Bryce who obtained the equipment and molds from Heisey. The sahara and zircon pieces were made at the same time as the #1497 Mahabar (which became Crystolite) items were made. The star relish is known in experimental light blue and the #1469½ salt in amber. The cigarette holder is sometimes seen in cobalt and thought to be Heisey rather than Imperial.

Look-Alikes: The Fenton Co. made their Sheffield line (bowls most often found) in a light blue similar to Heisey's light blue. Be aware of these. Fenton also made the card suit ashtrays; the bottoms of these do not have the ridges of the true Heisey Ridgeleigh ones. Heisey's are usually marked with the Diamond H. Libbey and Fostoria and possibly other companies also made items similar to Ridgeleigh. Often seen is a cream and sugar in yellowish, poor quality glass. This set is a mid-size, larger than Heisey's individual set and smaller than the regular size. The sides of Heisey's have a low curve while the look-alike has a straight side from handle to lip.

Patents: #99085 for oval cigarette box applied for 1/24/36 and granted 3/24/36. #99798 for vase applied for 2/26/36 and granted 5/26/36. #101630 for diamond shaped ashtray applied for 3/6/36 and granted 10/20/36. #99799 for swan bowl without handles applied for 3/7/36 and granted 6/26/36. T. Clarence Heisey listed as designer for all patents.

Imperial Reissues: The cigarette holder, the 2½″ inch square ashtray, and a cigarette lighter were made in heather and charcoal. These are marked with the Diamond H. A 3½″ coaster and the ring tree made from the coaster (not originally made by Heisey) were made in crystal, plum, sunshine yellow and ultra blue. These are marked with ALIG. The 6½″ ball vase (which Imperial called an Iris Vase) was made in crystal, plum, sunshine yellow, ultra blue satin and ultra blue in 1981-1982. These are also marked ALIG.

Availability: Common to moderately available.

#1469 RIDGELEIGH roly poly glass on cocktail rest

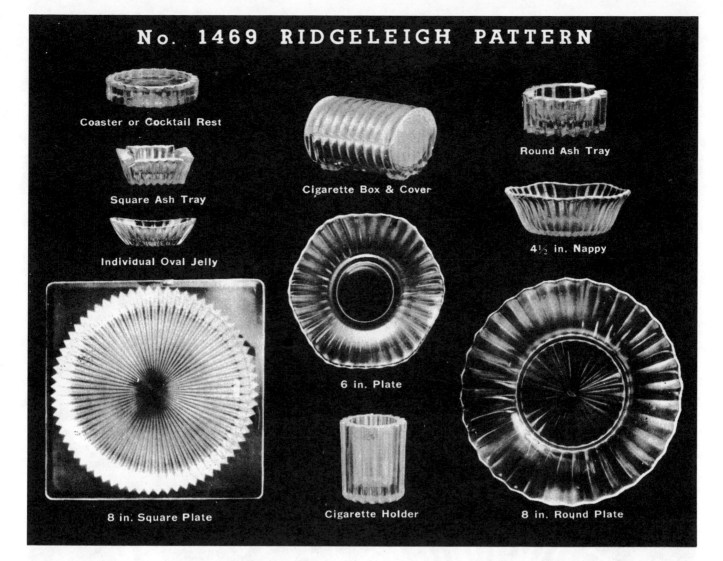

No. 1469 RIDGELEIGH PATTERN

Coaster or Cocktail Rest

Square Ash Tray

Individual Oval Jelly

8 in. Square Plate

Cigarette Box & Cover

6 in. Plate

Cigarette Holder

Round Ash Tray

4½ in. Nappy

8 in. Round Plate

#1469½ RIDGELEIGH salt shaker, double cone shape

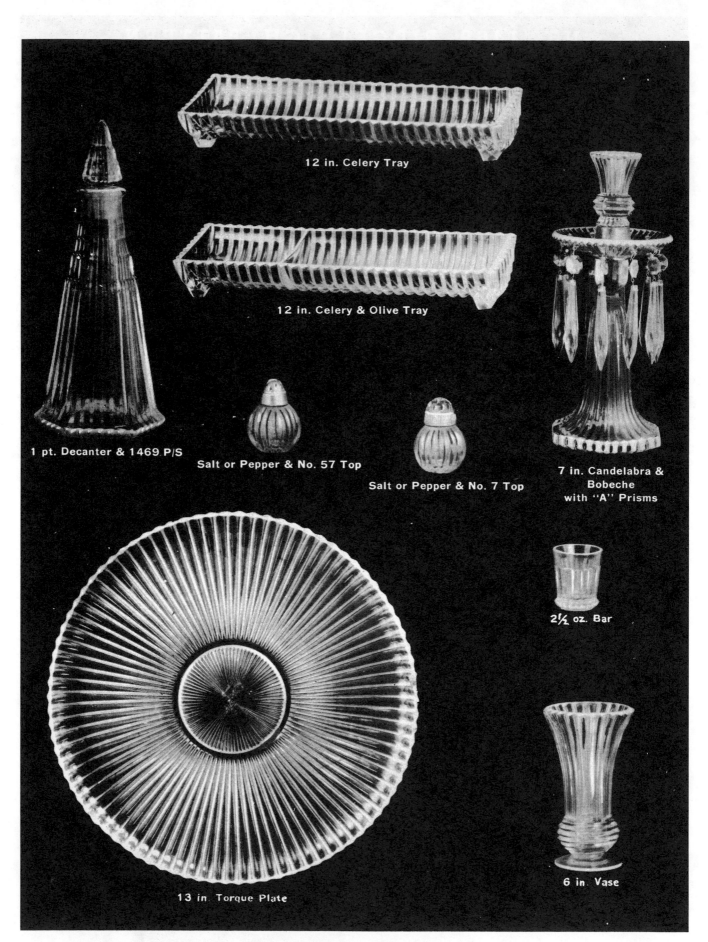

12 in. Celery Tray

12 in. Celery & Olive Tray

1 pt. Decanter & 1469 P/S

Salt or Pepper & No. 57 Top

Salt or Pepper & No. 7 Top

7 in. Candelabra & Bobeche with "A" Prisms

2½ oz. Bar

13 in. Torque Plate

6 in. Vase

#1469 RIDGELEIGH pattern

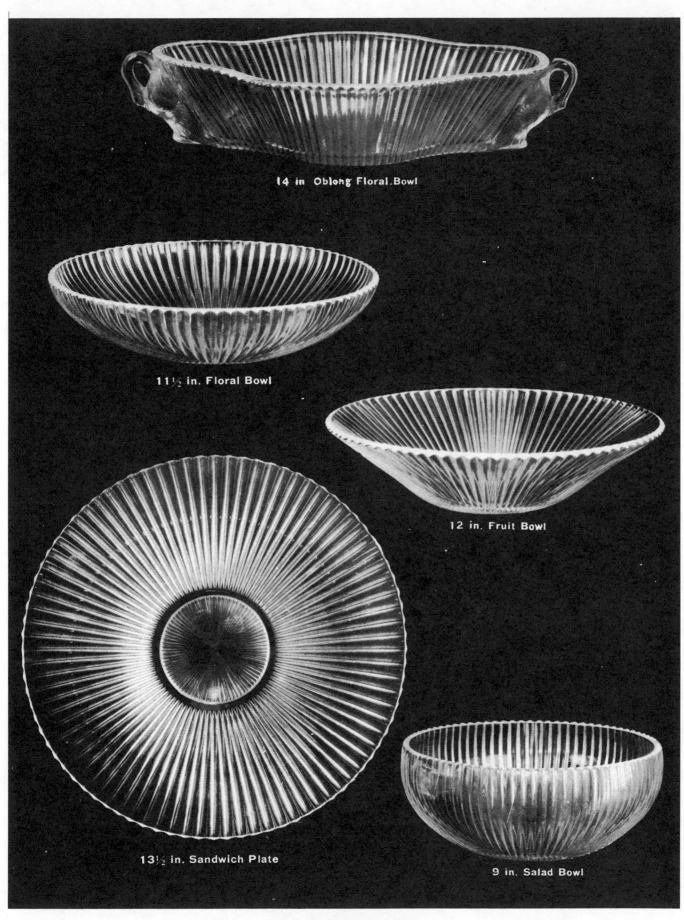

14 in. Oblong Floral Bowl

11½ in. Floral Bowl

12 in. Fruit Bowl

13½ in. Sandwich Plate

9 in. Salad Bowl

#1469 RIDGELEIGH pattern

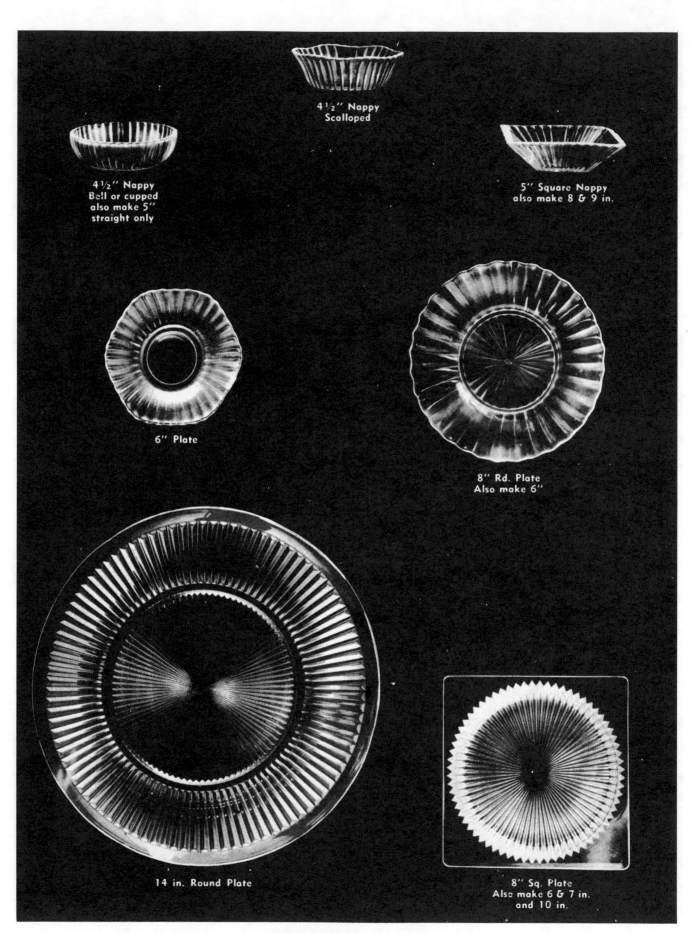

4 1/2" Nappy
Scalloped

4 1/2" Nappy
Bell or cupped
also make 5"
straight only

5" Square Nappy
also make 8 & 9 in.

6" Plate

8" Rd. Plate
Also make 6"

14 in. Round Plate

8" Sq. Plate
Also make 6 & 7 in.
and 10 in.

#1469 RIDGELEIGH pattern

13 in. Torte Plate
Also make 11 & 18 in.

13½ in. Sandwich Plate
Also make 11½ in.

14 in. Torte Plate
Also make 20 in.

#1469 RIDGELEIGH pattern

10 in. Desert 2 Hdld.

8 ½ in. Berry Bowl Cupped

9 in. Salad Bowl

11 in. Salad Bowl

11 in. Cone Beverage
Bowl

12 in. Fruit Bowl
Also make 10 in.

#1469 RIDGELEIGH pattern

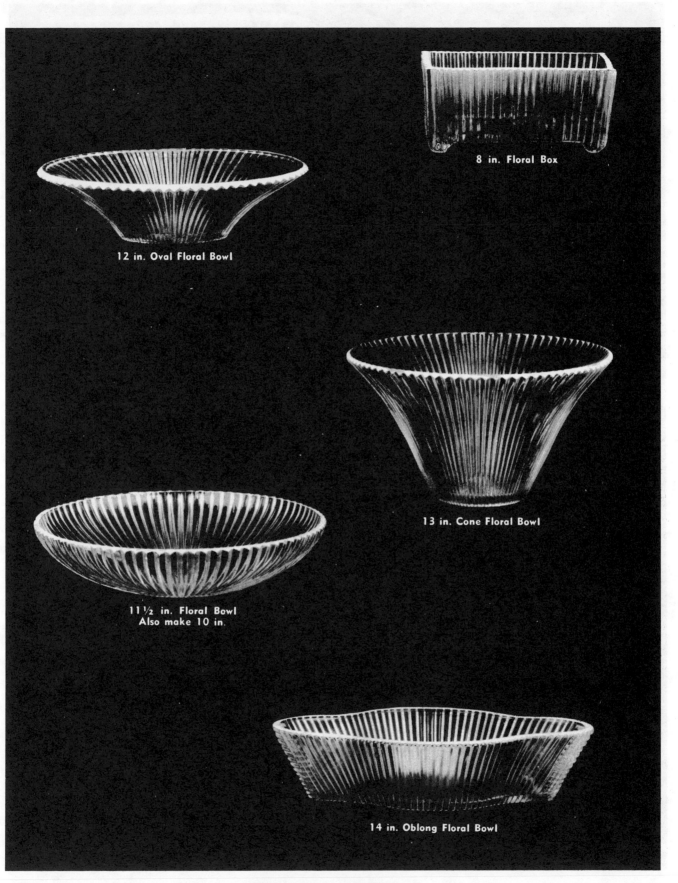

8 in. Floral Box

12 in. Oval Floral Bowl

13 in. Cone Floral Bowl

11½ in. Floral Bowl
Also make 10 in.

14 in. Oblong Floral Bowl

#1469 RIDGELEIGH pattern

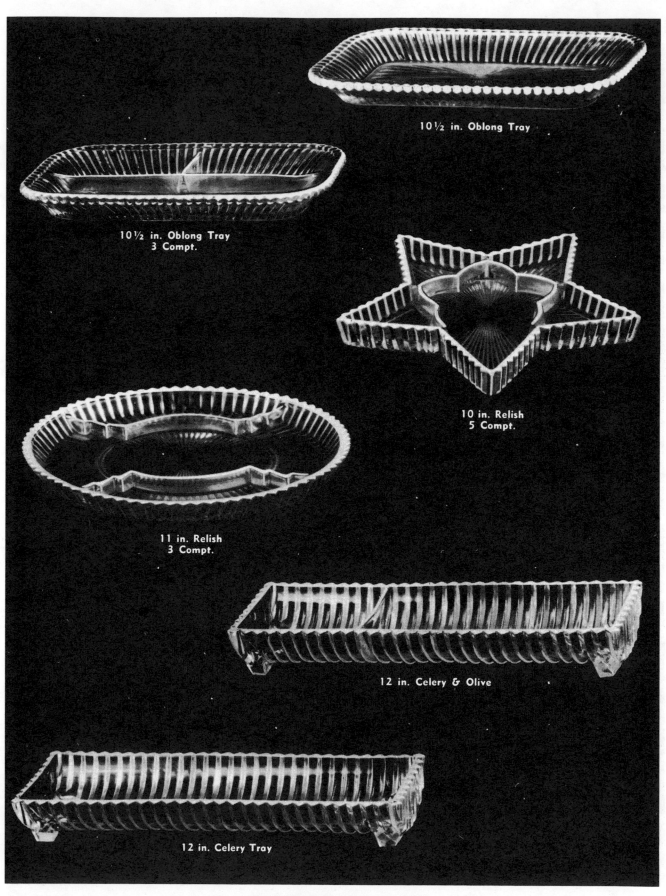

10½ in. Oblong Tray

10½ in. Oblong Tray
3 Compt.

10 in. Relish
5 Compt.

11 in. Relish
3 Compt.

12 in. Celery & Olive

12 in. Celery Tray

#1469 RIDGELEIGH pattern

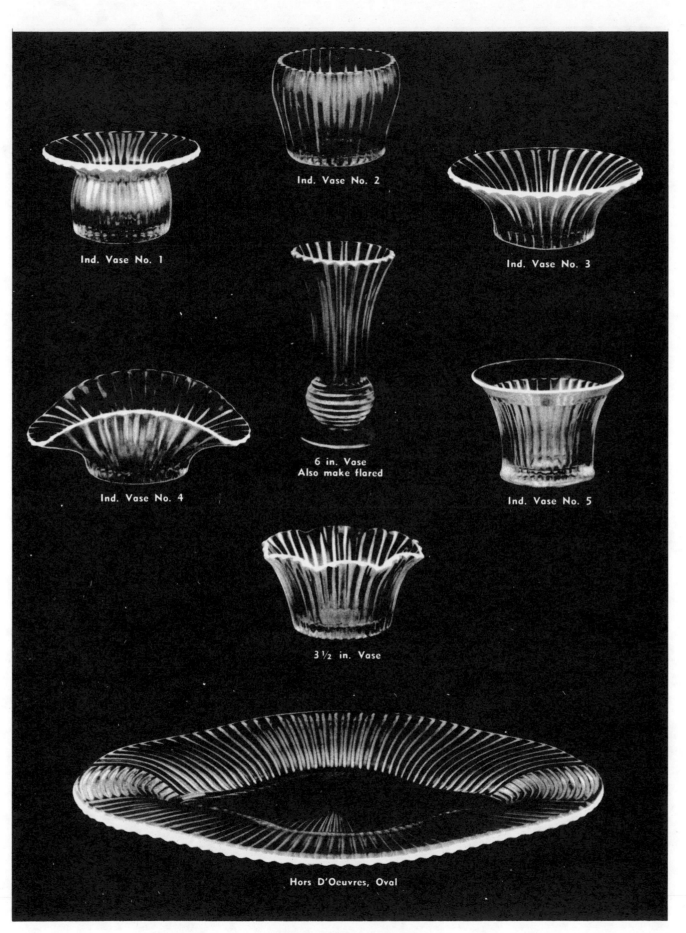

Ind. Vase No. 2

Ind. Vase No. 1

Ind. Vase No. 3

6 in. Vase
Also make flared

Ind. Vase No. 4

Ind. Vase No. 5

3½ in. Vase

Hors D'Oeuvres, Oval

#1469 RIDGELEIGH pattern

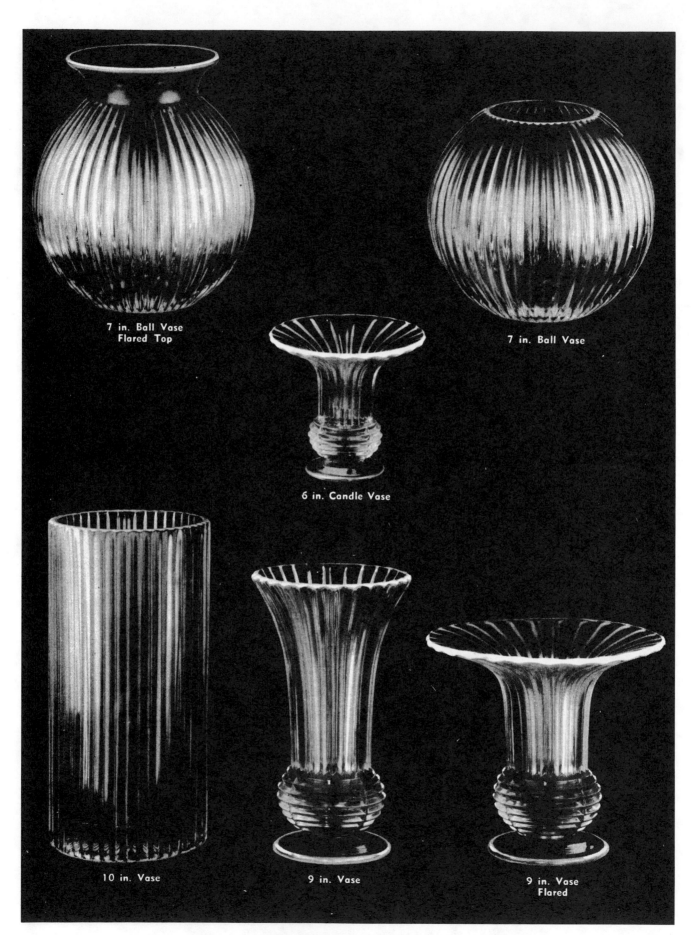

7 in. Ball Vase
Flared Top

6 in. Candle Vase

7 in. Ball Vase

10 in. Vase

9 in. Vase

9 in. Vase
Flared

#1469 RIDGELEIGH pattern

Ind. Cream & Sugar Tray

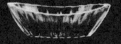
Ind. Jelly, Oval

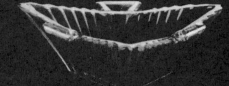
Jelly
3 Hdld.

Ind. Sugar, Oval

Ind. Cream, Oval

Sugar

Cream

Mayonnaise

Marmalade & Cover

Mustard & Cover

#1469 RIDGELEIGH pattern

Salt or Pepper & No. 57 Top

Salt or Pepper & No. 7 Top

Ind. Salt

3 oz. Oil Bottle & No. 103 P/S

OIL

VINEGAR

French Dressing Bottle & No. 100 P/S

5 in. Lemon Dish & Cover

6 in. Comport Low Foot
Flared

6 in. Comport Low Foot & Cover

#1469 RIDGELEIGH pattern

1 qt. Cocktail Shaker
No. 1 Strainer
No. 86 P/S

Ice Tub
2 Hdld.

1 pt. Decanter & No. 95 P/S

½ gal. Ice Jug

½ gal. Jug

Ice Tub Plate
2 Hdld.

#1469 RIDGELEIGH pattern

Beverage Cup

Coaster or Cocktail Rest

Cup & Saucer

2 in. Candlestick

7 in. Candelabra & Bobeche
With "A" Prisms

5 oz. Bitter Bottle and Tube

Rock & Rye Bottle & No. 104 P/S

#1469 RIDGELEIGH pattern

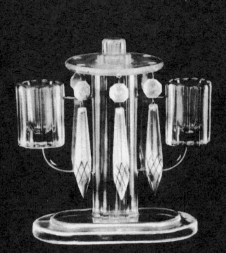

2 Lt. Candlestick
Bobeche & "A" Prisms
Consists of
1-1469—2 Lt. Candlestick
1-1469½—Bobeche
6—"A" Prisms

2 Lt. Candelabra
With "A" Prisms
Consists of
1-1469—2 Lt. Base
1-1469—2 Lt. Arm
2-1469—Bobeche
2-1469—Candleholder
2-54—Ferrules
1-51—Ferrule
20—"A" Prisms

#1469 RIDGELEIGH pattern

Ash Tray, Diamond

Ash Tray, Heart

Ash Tray, Club

Ash Tray, Spade

Ash Tray, Round

Bridge Ash Tray

Ash Tray, Square

Cigarette Holder, Square

Cigarette Holder, Round

4 oz. Cologne Bottle & No. 105 P/S

6 in. Ash Tray, Square

Oval Cigarette Box & Cover

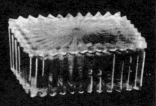

4 in. Cigarette Box & Cover
Also make 6 in.

#1469 RIDGELEIGH pattern

Goblet

Saucer Champagne

Sherbet

Oyster Cocktail

Cocktail

Wine

Claret

12 oz. Soda Ftd.
Also make 5 oz.

2½ oz. Bar

8 oz. Old Fashion

1469¾—10 oz. Tumbler

1469¾—5 oz. Soda St.
Also make 8 & 12 oz.

#1469 RIDGELEIGH pattern

5 oz. Perfume Bottle & No. 1469 P/S

Punch Cup or Custard

11 in. Punch Bowl

Orange Bowl

#1469 RIDGELEIGH pattern

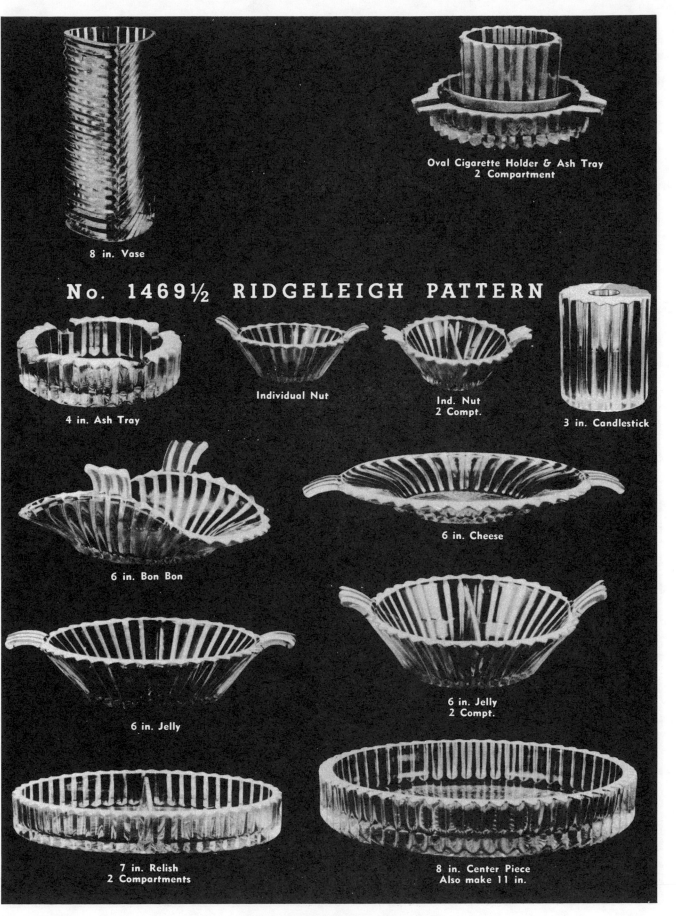

8 in. Vase

Oval Cigarette Holder & Ash Tray
2 Compartment

No. 1469½ RIDGELEIGH PATTERN

4 in. Ash Tray

Individual Nut

Ind. Nut
2 Compt.

3 in. Candlestick

6 in. Bon Bon

6 in. Cheese

6 in. Jelly

6 in. Jelly
2 Compt.

7 in. Relish
2 Compartments

8 in. Center Piece
Also make 11 in.

#1469¼ RIDGELEIGH pattern

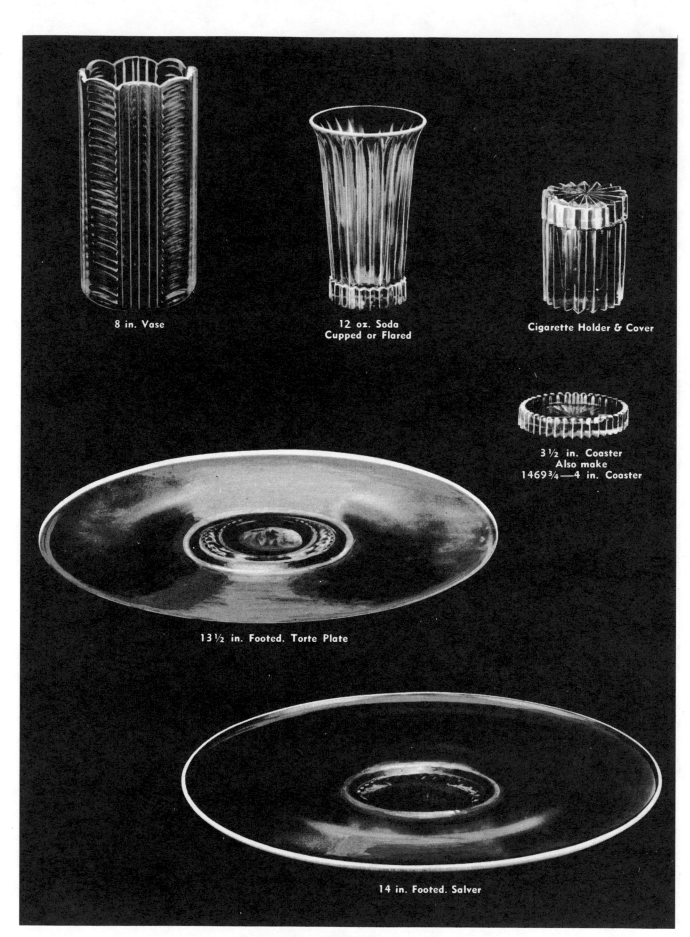

8 in. Vase

12 oz. Soda
Cupped or Flared

Cigarette Holder & Cover

3 ½ in. Coaster
Also make
1469¾—4 in. Coaster

13½ in. Footed. Torte Plate

14 in. Footed. Salver

#1469½ RIDGELEIGH pattern

5 in. Nappy

5 in. Puff Box

8 in. Plate

1 Lt. Candelabra & "A" Prisms
Consists of
1-1469½—1 Lt. Base
1-1469—Bobeche
1-1469—Candleholder
1-54—Ferrule
10—"A" Prisms

#1469½ RIDGELEIGH pattern

#4069 RIDGELEIGH - original Heisey Co. name

Dates: 1936-1939

Colors: Crystal only

Decorations: Listed with 2 etchings #482 Lines and #483 Leaf, both of which were never adopted and added to the line. Several Heisey cuttings on the full line. These stems were also decorated by Pairpoint with their Malden design, a gray cutting

Marked: No

Comments: In the first price list showing this stemware, Heisey used the name Reis-Ridgeleigh. Later catalogs and price lists use only the name Ridgeleigh. This is the blown stemware to accompany the #1469 Ridgeleigh pressed pieces. As with several other patterns, Ridgeleigh had both pressed and blown stemware available for customers. This is a delicate, blown bowl which because of its shape is easily chipped on the rim.

Imperial Reissues: No

Availability: Moderately available to scarce

8 oz. Goblet

8 oz. Luncheon Goblet

5 oz. Saucer Champagne

5 oz. Sherbet

4 oz. Oyster Cocktail

4 oz. Claret

3½ oz. Cocktail

2½ oz. Wine

2 oz. Sherry

1 oz. Cordial

5 oz. Soda
Also make 8 & 13 oz.

Finger Bowl (3335)

#4069 RIDGELEIGH pattern

#1483 STANHOPE - original Heisey Co. name

Dates: 1936-1941
Colors: Celery tray known in sahara; candlestick in experimental light blue
Decorations: Used for both cuttings and etchings by Heisey
Marked: Not usually
Comments: Named for Lady Stanhope, an English court beauty and owner of the famous Stanhope diamond. The pattern was first shown at the New York China, Glass and Housewares Show in July, 1936. A trade journal report is most interesting:

"New pressed line of stemware, dinnerware, buffet items, candelabra, decorative pieces, called 'Stanhope,' designed by Walter Von Nessen. The pressed motif is a grouping of deep swags, and a highly unusual feature is the use of colored buttons or short rods made of Plascon and inserted in the circular handles and knobs. These inserts are made in such colors as red, blue, black, yellow and ivory. All of the plates are couped and rimless, and there are two types of stemware--all pressed or with a pressed stem and blown bowl. The line may be had plain, etched, cut or with frosted swags. Interesting is news that the General Electric Co. has adopted a 'Stanhope' set for use with its coffee maker, the colors of the inserts matching the trim of the coffee maker and the tray." (August, 1936.)

Stanhope was highly thought of in the trade and won the "Modern Plastics Competition Award" in 1936 for the use of the plascon inserts. Heisey called the plastic portions "round knobs" for the small flat inserts and "T knobs" for the longer rod-like handles. These are removable and the two portions screw together. Even though the pattern was highly touted in ads and was well thought of in designer groups, it was apparently not a good seller. There seem to have been plans for some pieces, but apparently these were never made—including a cocktail shaker and a mustard. Notations in price lists indicate that the ball vase was drilled for use as a lamp base.

Patents: #101410 for plate applied for 7/29/36 and granted 9/29/36. #101900 for sugar applied for 7/29/36 and granted 11/10/36. Both patents list Walter Von Nessen as designer.
Imperial Reissues: In 1980 Imperial made the 2-handled vase in Stiegel green for the Smithsonian Institution. It is marked LIG.
Availability: Moderately available

7 in. Plate

4 ½ in. Nappy or Porringer
1 Hld.—With or without Rd. Knobs

3oz. Oil Bottle No. 106 P/S
With or without Rd. Knobs

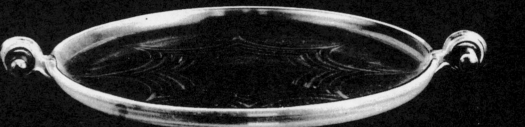

12 in. Torte Plate
2 Hld.—With or without T. Knobs

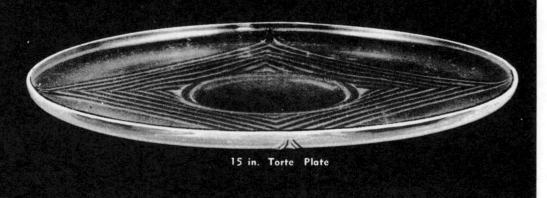

15 in. Torte Plate

#1483 STANHOPE pattern

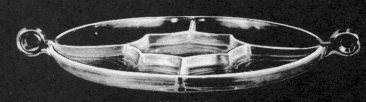

12 in. Relish
2 Hld.—5 Compt.
With or without T. Knobs

12 in. Celery Tray—2 Hld.
With or without T. Knobs

11 in. Floral Bowl—2Hld.
With or without T. Knobs

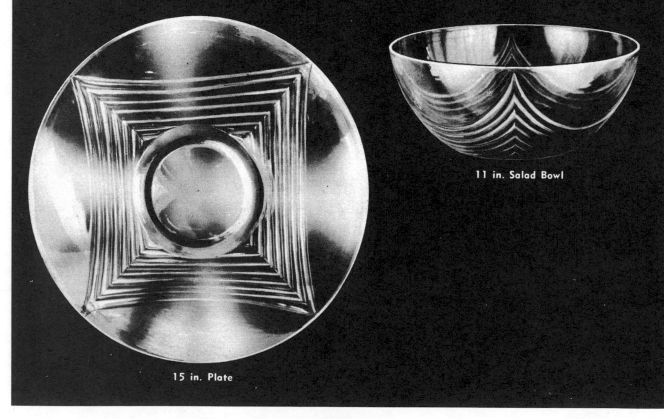

11 in. Salad Bowl

15 in. Plate

#1483 STANHOPE pattern

6 in. Mint
2 Compt.—2 Hld.
With or without Rd. Knobs

6 in. Mint—2 Hld.
With or without Rd. Knobs

Mayonnaise—2 Hld.
With or without Rd. Knobs

6 in. Jelly
3 Compt.—1 Hld.
With or without Rd. Knobs

6 in. Jelly—1 Hld.
With or without Rd. Knobs

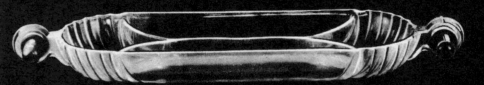

12 in. Relish
4 Compt.—2 Hld.
With or without T. Knobs

11 in. Triplex Buffet Relish—2 Hld.
With or without T. Knobs

#1483 STANHOPE pattern

Sugar—2 Hld.
With or without Rd. Knobs

Cream—1 Hld.
With or without Rd. Knobs

Cup—1 Hld.
With or without Rd. Knobs

Saucer

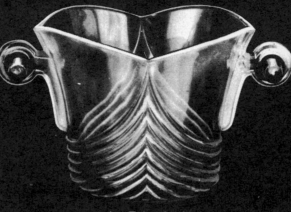

Ice Tub—2 Hld.
With or without T. Knobs

9 in. Vase—2 Hld.
With or without T. Knobs

7 in. Ball Vase

#1483 STANHOPE pattern

Salt or Pepper No. 60 Top

Individual Nut
With or without Rd Knobe

Ind. Ash Tray

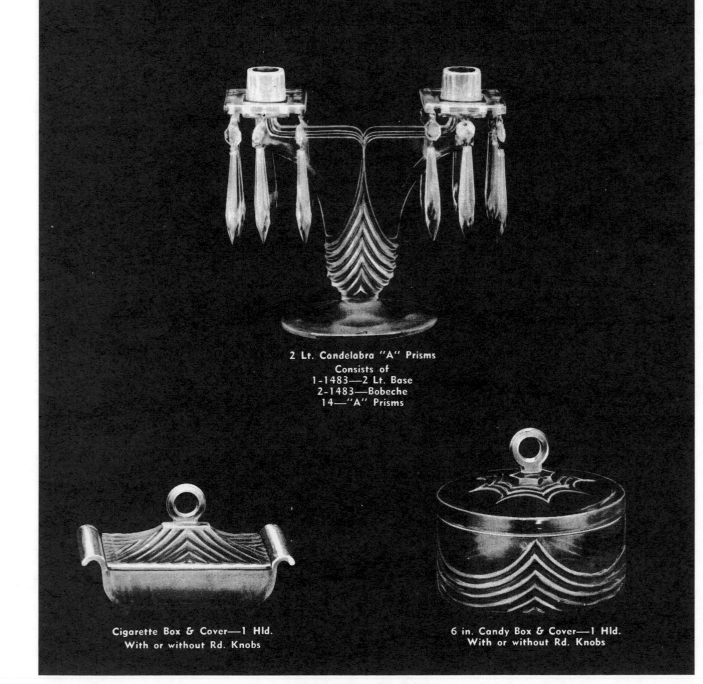

2 Lt. Candelabra "A" Prisms
Consists of
1-1483—2 Lt. Base
2-1483—Bobeche
14—"A" Prisms

Cigarette Box & Cover—1 Hld.
With or without Rd. Knobs

6 in. Candy Box & Cover—1 Hld.
With or without Rd. Knobs

#1483 STANHOPE pattern

9 oz. Goblet

5 ½ oz. Saucer Champagne

3 ½ oz. Cocktail

2 ½ oz. Wine

12 oz. Soda Ftd.

#1483 STANHOPE pattern

#4083 STANHOPE - original Heisey Co. name

Dates: 1936-1939
Colors: All crystal; crystal stem, zircon bowl; crystal stem, zircon bowl, zircon foot. All of the zircon items were discontinued by March, 1938.
Decorations: Cuttings and etchings by Heisey
Marked: No
Comments: This is the blown stem line to match the #1483 Stanhope pressed ware. The cordial was made in this pattern although not pictured. Some of the stemware was again made in 1956 in limelight but this would be indistinguishable from the earlier zircon production. Designed by Walter Von Nessen.
Imperial Reissues: No
Availability: Moderately available to scarce

4 oz. Claret

2½ oz. Wine

10 oz. Goblet

5½ oz. Saucer Champagne

3½ oz. Cocktail

Finger Bowl (4080)

5 oz. Soda
Also make 8 & 12 oz.

4 oz. Oyster Cocktail

#1485 SATURN - original Heisey Co. name

Dates: 1937-1957

Colors: Zircon. In 1956 a few items were made in dawn and limelight. Some goblets are known in an unusual yellow shade—difficult to determine whether they are stained crystal glass or a true colored glass.

Decorations: Some items used for cuttings by Heisey.

Marked: Usually

Comments: The unusual saturn optic in this line proved to be a popular innovation by the Heisey Co. In addition to the pressed Saturn pattern, Heisey used the saturn optic effectively in blown stemware in several patterns, rose bowls, jugs and many other items. In an early pattern folder, a few items (bowl and vase) are shown in what Heisey called "Wavy Line"—a combination of saturn optic and a wave optic. These items would be very unusual. The name was derived from the descriptive phrase used by Heisey for the pattern—"rings of Saturn"—referring to the optic. Other companies also produced a saturn-type optic. Duncan made their Festive pattern in colors similar to Heisey's zircon and sahara. Tiffin also produced saturn optic wares. All are similar to imported European glass. Early handled pieces have spherical knobs giving a planetary effect, while later pieces have more traditional handles. The sugar comes with or without a lid. A 7″ 2-compartment relish, handled, was listed but not pictured in catalogs. Refer to the color section for this item. The vase was also drilled for use as a lamp base. The oil was redesigned in later years to have a more modern, taller shape.

Imperial Reissues: 25 items made, possibly marked with the Diamond H. All made in crystal. The late style oil may have been made in dawn/charcoal.

Availability: Common to moderately available

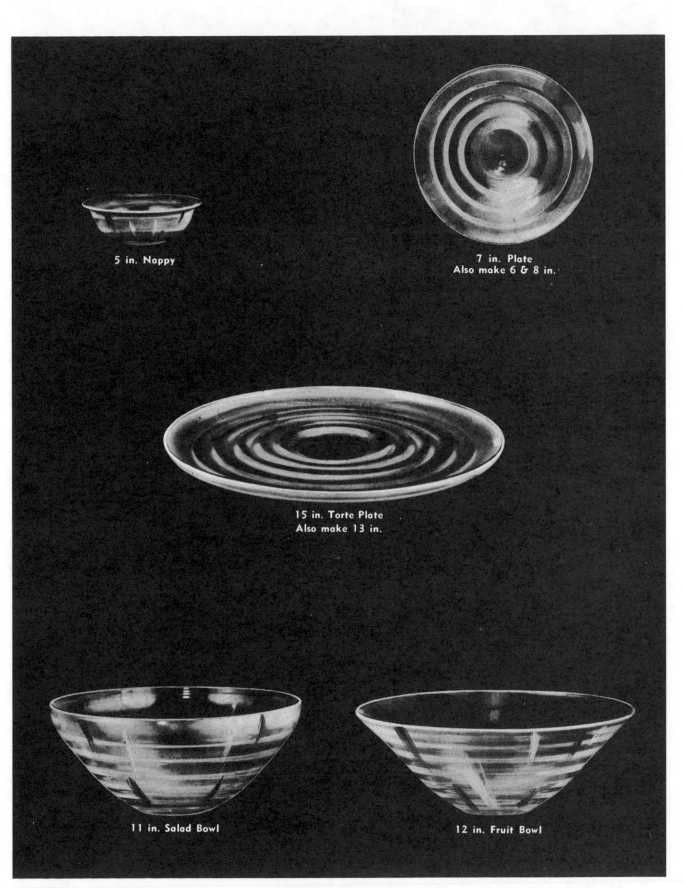

5 in. Nappy

7 in. Plate
Also make 6 & 8 in.

15 in. Torte Plate
Also make 13 in.

11 in. Salad Bowl

12 in. Fruit Bowl

#1485 SATURN pattern

Cup   Saucer

Sugar

Cream

Tid Bit Tray

5 in. Whipped Cream

Baked Apple

Mayonnaise

Violet Vase

Marmalade & Cover

8 ½ in. Vase, Flared
Also make Straight

#1485 SATURN pattern

10 oz. Goblet

6 oz. Saucer Champagne

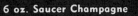

4½ oz. Sherbet
Also make 5 oz

3 oz. Cocktail

5 oz. Parfait

4 oz. Fruit Cocktail

8 oz. Old Fashion

12 oz. Soda
Also make
5 oz. Soda

10 oz. Tumbler

9 oz. Luncheon Tumbler

Finger Bowl

#1485 SATURN pattern

7 in. Comport

2 Lt. Candleblock

Mustard & Paddle Cover

2 oz. Oil & No. 1 P/S

13 in. Floral Bowl

Rose Bowl

2 Lt. Candelabra and "E" Ball Drops

#1485 SATURN pattern

#1486 COLEPORT - original Heisey Co. name

Dates: 1937-1946; reinstated mid-1948-1957
Colors: Crystal; in 1955, 2 items (the tumbler and ice tea) were made in dawn and renumbered #1487
Decorations: None. A few sodas have been found frosted all over.
Marked: Usually. Some items like the oval floral bowl are usually not marked.
Comments: A short pattern grouping. The stemware and ice bucket did not survive past 1946. In later years, Coleport was only a bar line. The stemware is difficult to find and the ice bucket would be unusual. In addition to items illustrated, price lists listed a 2-light candleblock, individual ashtray, cigarette holder, 13″ torte plate and a 10″ floral bowl, round in 1938.
Look-Alikes: Another company (possibly Federal) made several sizes of sodas in various colors—some of them similar to Heisey colors—notably dawn and amber. Another company also made sodas in a five sided version rather than the Heisey four.
Patents: #105431 for soda applied for 6/21/37 and granted 7/27/37. Ray C. Cobel listed as designer.
Imperial Reissues: 6 sizes of sodas in crystal, probably marked with the Diamond H.
Availability: Common

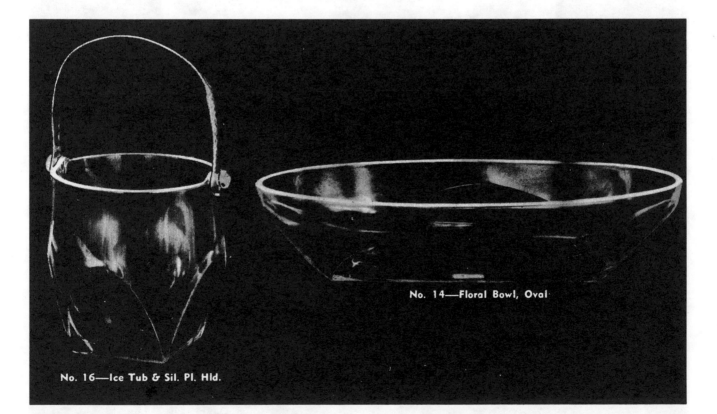

No. 16—Ice Tub & Sil. Pl. Hld.

No. 14—Floral Bowl, Oval

2 oz. Bar

7 oz. Old Fashion

8 in. Nappy
Also make 4 in.

10 oz. Tumbler

8 oz. Soda
Also make 5, 10, & 13 oz.

#1486 COLEPORT pattern

8 oz. Goblet

5½ oz. Saucer Champagne

5½ oz. Sherbet

4 oz. Oyster Cocktail

3 oz. Cocktail

2½ oz. Wine

8 oz. Soda
Also make 5, 10 & 13 oz.

7 oz. Old Fashion

10 oz. Tumbler

2 oz. Bar

#1486 COLEPORT pattern

#1488 KOHINOOR - original Heisey Co. name

Dates: 1937-1939 when only 4 items remained. Console set made again from 1941-1946

Colors: Zircon. Very scarce in sahara.

Decorations: #493 Coronation etching and several cuttings by Heisey. The candelabra were offered with many Heisey cuttings.

Marked: Usually

Comments: The pattern was designed by Walter Von Nessen. The name derives from the famous Kohinoor diamond. This diamond motif is carried throughout the pattern. It is most obvious in the candelabra. Less noticeable are the faceted bottoms of most of the other pieces. Pieces in zircon are eagerly sought by collectors. Interesting items include the 2 small ashtrays and the cigarette holder plus the candelabra.

Imperial Reissues: None

Availability: Moderately available to scarce.

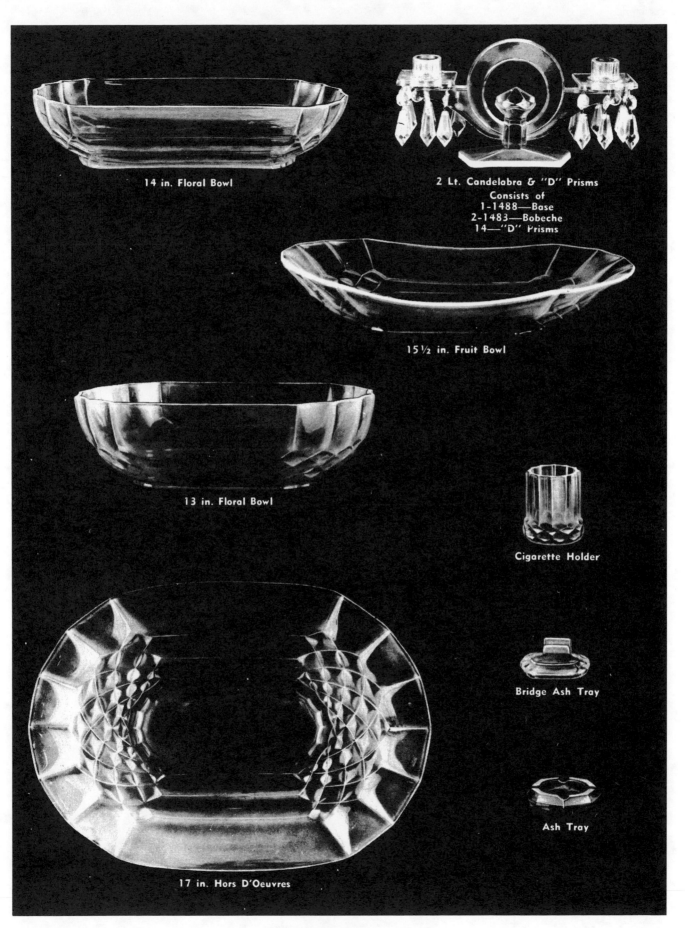

14 in. Floral Bowl

2 Lt. Candelabra & "D" Prisms
Consists of
1-1488—Base
2-1483—Bobeche
14—"D" Prisms

15½ in. Fruit Bowl

13 in. Floral Bowl

Cigarette Holder

Bridge Ash Tray

Ash Tray

17 in. Hors D'Oeuvres

#1488 KOHINOOR pattern

#4085, 4085½ KOHINOOR · original Heisey Co. name

Dates: 1937-1943

Colors: All crystal; crystal stem and foot, zircon bowl (#4085); crystal bowl, zircon base (#4085½); all zircon. A few pieces were made in experimental light blue. An old fashion with a cobalt base is known.

Decorations: Yes. #493 Coronation etching and several Heisey cuttings

Marked: No

Optic: Wide optic (discontinued by 1939) and Saturn optic

Comments: Designed by Walter Von Nessen. This is the blown stemware to accompany #1488 Kohinoor pressed ware. Heisey made effective use of the saturn optic, usually in the zircon pieces. #4085½ was used to designate footed sodas which matched the #4085 line. This numbering system was typical of Heisey and occurs in other stem lines. Other items listed in #4085½ but not illustrated include a 1¾ oz. footed bar and a 7 oz. footed old fashion, both available in wide optic and saturn optic (1938-1939). The ball vases, jug and salad bowl are shown with the Kohinoor line. When sold with Kohinoor, all had the saturn optic. In the cases of the ball vases and the jug, it is the saturn optic which makes their numbers #4085 rather than #4045 for the ball vases and #4161 for the jug. When used for cuttings, the stem was often cut and polished and notches were often added. Sometimes the available facets of the diamond were also cut and polished. Compare the illustrations with #4091 Kimberly pattern in the STEMWARE section. The patterns are very similar with Kohinoor having a straight bowl and Kimberly having a slightly flared bowl.

Imperial Reissues: None

Availability: Moderately available to scarce

9 oz. Goblet

9 oz. Goblet Low Foot

5½ oz. Sherbet

4½ oz. Claret

2½ oz. Wine

1 oz. Cordial

3 oz. Cocktail

6 oz. Rhine Wine

4½ oz. Cocktail, Tall Stem

5½ oz. Saucer
Champagne

4 oz. Oyster Cocktail

12 oz. Soda
Also make
5 & 8 oz.

4085½ 12 oz. Soda
Also make 5 & 8 oz.

Finger Bowl (3335)

6 in. Ball Vase
Also make 4, 7, & 9 in.

4085—32 oz. Jug (4161)

11 in. Salad Bowl

#4085 KOHINOOR pattern

#1495 FERN · original Heisey Co. name

Dates: 1937-1941 when 5 items remained. The candlestick was made for a longer period than most pieces—till 1953.

Colors: Zircon. A large torte plate and bowl are known in dawn

Decorations: Used for several Heisey etchings and cuttings. Sometimes found with silver overlay.

Marked: No

Comments: Designed by Walter Von Nessen. An attractive glass design. Flat pieces usually have one delicate handle with a small point to highlight the piece directly opposite the handle. The bases around each piece have delicate small borders. Zircon pieces are scarce. Some pieces were revamped and added to the #1519 Waverly line in later years. The oval floral bowl, 2 styles of mayonnaise dishes and the jello dish were treated in this manner. To make the design more in keeping with Waverly, internal swirl optic and beads around the top edges were added. When found in this manner, pieces are correctly identified as Waverly, not Fern. Notice that the creamers seem to have unusually large spouts.

Imperial Reissues: None

Availability: Moderately available

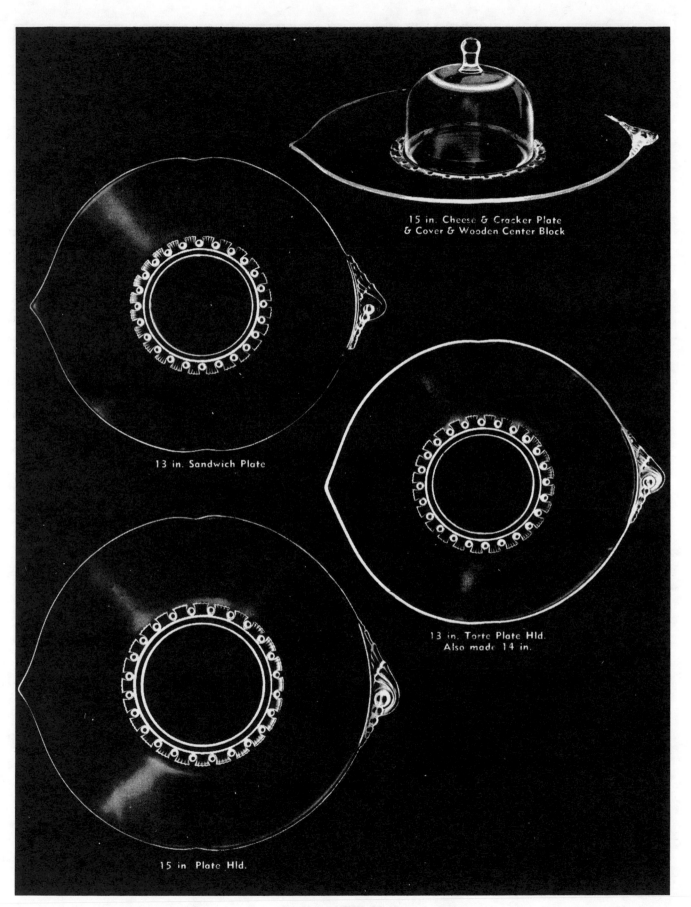

15 in. Cheese & Cracker Plate
& Cover & Wooden Center Block

13 in. Sandwich Plate

13 in. Torte Plate Hld.
Also made 14 in.

15 in. Plate Hld.

#1495 FERN pattern

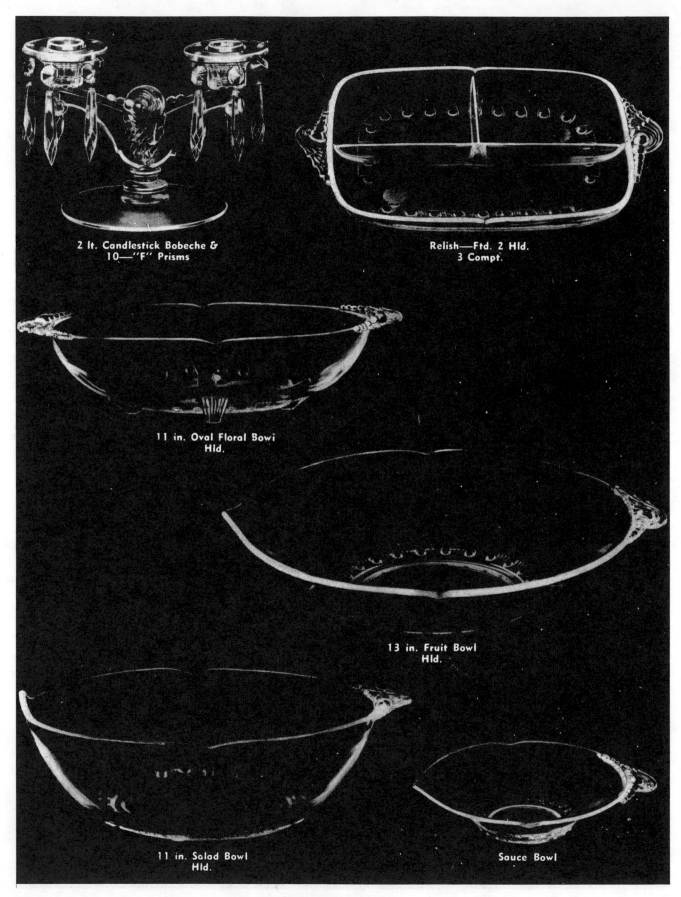

2 lt. Candlestick Bobeche &
10—"F" Prisms

Relish—Ftd. 2 Hld.
3 Compt.

11 in. Oval Floral Bowl
Hld.

13 in. Fruit Bowl
Hld.

11 in. Salad Bowl
Hld.

Sauce Bowl

#1495 FERN pattern

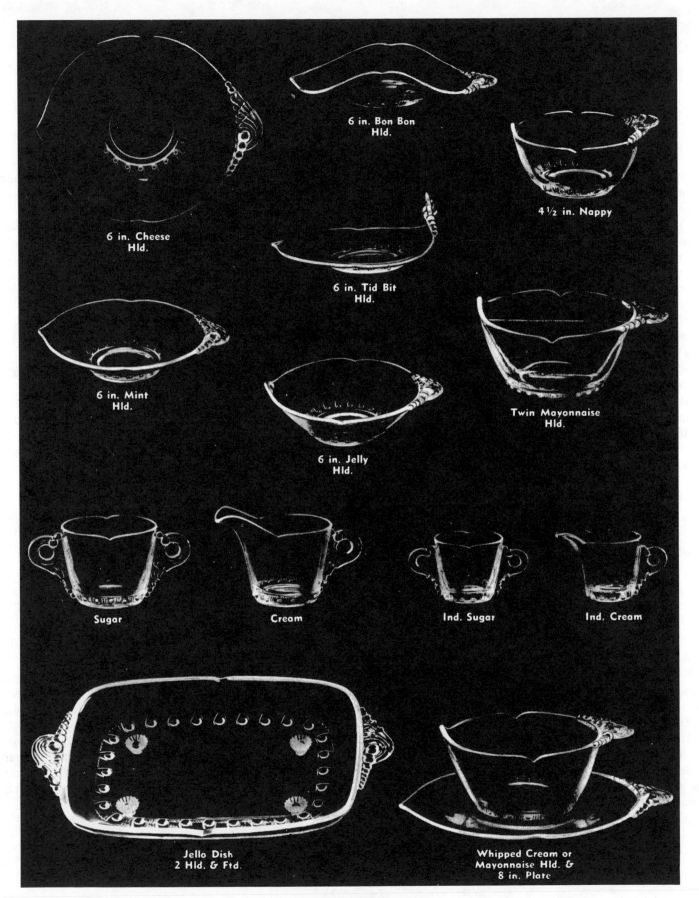

6 in. Bon Bon
Hld.

4½ in. Nappy

6 in. Cheese
Hld.

6 in. Tid Bit
Hld.

6 in. Mint
Hld.

Twin Mayonnaise
Hld.

6 in. Jelly
Hld.

Sugar

Cream

Ind. Sugar

Ind. Cream

Jello Dish
2 Hld. & Ftd.

Whipped Cream or
Mayonnaise Hld. &
8 in. Plate

#1495 FERN pattern

Stemware

During this period, stemware formed an important part of Heisey's merchandise. Heisey's stemware lines expanded and flourished after the opening of a blown ware shop circa 1914. While the company had always produced some stemware—often matching existing patterns—now stemware came into a day of its own.

From this time on, blown stemware predominated although some pressed stemware remained in vogue—notably some colonial styles. Blown ware was enhanced by decoration. At Heisey's this meant highly developed and active etching and cutting departments under the capable direction of Louise Adkins. Except for a short period during World War II, these departments remained busy until the company closed, making many of the decorations still strongly associated with Heisey: Orchid and Heisey Rose etchings; Danish Princess, Moonglo and Narcissus cuttings with myriads of others equally or less well-known.

With the employment of the Krall family about 1933, especially the famous Emil Krall, cuttings were developed to enhance stem lines on a semi-annual basis. Emil Krall was the chief designer of most of the cuttings from 1933 to the early 1940's.

Stemware was developed rapidly and decorations were designed for specific stem lines—not like many other glass companies who considered their stemware and decorations interchangeable.

Many stem lines before 1922 were of standard, universal shapes common to many glass companies. About 1922, stem lines began to be produced which were distinctive and elegant. Wabash was designed and patented by Josef Balda. Although a rather plain line, it heralded a period when stem lines became increasingly more elaborate. The fancy pressed stems such as Monte Cristo, Old Dominion, Creole and others propelled the Heisey Company to the forefront as producers of fancy stemware for the home hostess.

In a 1930 *Table Talk*, the Heisey Company said:

"In the history of the glassware industry since the establishment of A.H. Heisey & Company some 36 years ago, there are many steps in advance pioneered by Heisey.

"One of these pioneering advances was the creation of fancy pressed stems for goblets, sherbets and other stemware. The particular design for this originated by Heisey found so much favor in the industry that it is safe to say practically all manufacturers in the country are now using it.

"And while we are on the subject of stems, let us also take a look at the feet of stemware and note the fine finish and careful workmanship exemplified by them."

In 1934, Heisey introduced one of its most successful stem lines, #4044 New Era. This modern pattern (as indeed it was first named by the company) was the first of several Art Deco-inspired lines of classic simplicity.

Heisey produced all types of stemware from tiny cordials and pousse cafes to various styles of wines, champagnes, goblets and pilsners. After the repeal of Prohibition in 1933, the Heisey line fairly bloomed with various liquor glasses—each designed for its own type of beverage—from delicate cordials to large brandy snifters or beer schooners. Many of these items will be found in the BARWARE Section of the book.

The importance of stemware to the Heisey Company cannot be over-emphasized. The fancy pressed stems with their delicate blown bowls were the envy of the industry and have not been surpassed by any domestic company.

See the BARWARE and MISCELLANEOUS Sections for other stemware related items. See PATTERNS Section for #4069 Ridgeleigh, #4083 Stanhope and #4085, #4085½ Kohinoor. These blownware lines are shown with their matching pressed ware.

As additional information, the reader must be aware of the three main types of stemware produced by Heisey and how they were made.

PRESSED STEMWARE: Stemware which is entirely pressed is formed in a mold just as pressed tableware is. When making this stemware, the bowl of the goblet and also the foot are usually made as a bowl or cupped forms. After the piece is removed from the mold, a worker can hand tool the top rim of the goblet, making it either flared or cupped in, the amount entirely due to the skill and discretion of the worker. The foot is finished by flattening it out into a flat disc shape which will support the piece. Since this is also entirely done by hand, variations can occur resulting in pieces with slightly different appearances or differing heights. Because of extraordinary skill of workers, these variations occur only rarely or at least are rarely noticed. Because of the method of manufacture, a pressed stem can be marked almost anywhere. Heisey pieces are known with marks on the bottom of the foot, anywhere on the stem (sometimes more than once), on the side of the bowl or even inside the bottom of the bowl.

PULLED STEMWARE: Pulled stemware is always blown ware. The blower starts a bubble on his blow pipe then pulls the stem from the gather. This bubble with a stem is put into the paste mold where the worker blows the bubble to the final form of the piece. A small glob of glass is then stuck onto the bottom of the stem and the foot is hand formed and flattened. Close examination will show that there is a joining of two pieces of glass just above the foot where the stem joins it. Often there is a little rounded button of glass formed when the two pieces are joined. Since the piece is formed by hand, (except possibly to form the bowl shape or to add optic), it is impossible for this item to be marked with a Diamond H.

PRESSED STEM, BLOWN BOWL: Much of Heisey's production—and most of the patterns included in this book—belong in this category. In this case, both pressing and blowing are used to complete the item. This is a more exacting and time-consuming method of producing stemware but also results in the most elegant of the stems made. The bowl of the goblet is blown, a separate pressed stem portion is pressed in a mold and added to the blown bowl. Then a foot is attached by affixing a glob of glass on the bottom of the stem and forming the foot by hand. This method offers great variety both in shaping the bowl and of course, in forming many intricate variations and designs for the stem. These stemware pieces can be marked with the Diamond H but it will always be found on the pressed stem portion of the item. In no instance will a Diamond H be found on the bottom of this style of stemware or of pulled stemware. The hand forming of the foot precludes the existence of a mark. Pressed stem, blown bowl stems are often called simply "Blown Stems" by collectors but this is technically incorrect, since they are actually referring to the blown bowls of the items. The term is used to separate pressed stemware from blown stemware, but it does not distinguish between pulled stemware or pressed stem, blown bowl stemware.

#419 SUSSEX - original Heisey Co. name

Dates: 1925-1946
Colors: Moongleam, flamingo, cobalt bowls—all with crystal stems. Finger bowls and sodas are solid colors. Stemmed items were not listed in all crystal.
Decorations: Not usually decorated. Occasionally found with cuttings.
Marked: Usually. On stem beneath bowl
Comments: Goblets have been seen in green and crystal combination in handmade glass, possibly Steuben. Heisey apparently copied this pattern. Heisey items are pressed with an applied stem and foot. Sodas have a ground and polished bottom rim.
Items made include:
10 oz. goblet
8 oz. goblet
5½ oz. saucer champagne
5½ oz. sherbet
2½ oz. cocktail
5 oz. soda
8 oz. soda
12 oz. soda
Finger bowl

Imperial Reissues: None
Availability: Moderately available

#1306 COMET LEAF - name given by researchers

Dates: 1933-1935
Colors: Crystal, sahara. A few goblets are known in alexandrite.
Marked: Yes. On bottom of foot
Comments: A heavy pressed pattern. Items listed in price lists are:
9 oz. goblet
5 oz. saucer champagne
5 oz. sherbet
12 oz. soda, footed, or ice tea
No items have been reproduced. Pieces are difficult to find.

#1423 SWEET AD-O-LINE - original Heisey Co. name

Dates: 1933-1935
Colors: Crystal, moongleam, flamingo, sahara, cobalt
Marked: Yes, inside of bowl
Comments: A large, massive pressed goblet. Apparently a one-item line as only the 14 oz goblet is listed. Not reproduced and difficult to find.

#419 SUSSEX goblet and soda

#1306 COMET LEAF goblet

#1423 SWEET AD-O-LINE goblet

175

None of these items have been reproduced and all are difficult to find.

#2516 CIRCLE PAIR - name given by researchers

Dates: Ca. 1925
Colors: Moongleam, flamingo.
Marked: No. It is blown with a pulled stem and cannot be marked.
Optic: Diamond optic.
Comments: While the sodas (from which the line was developed—thus its unusual number for stemware) are found in marigold, the goblets have not been seen in this color. The sodas and even the jugs are much more easily found than the stems. See the BARWARE Section for illustrations of the sodas.

#3379 PYRAMID - name given by researchers

Dates: Ca. 1929-1933; saucer champagne listed in 1921.
Colors: Flamingo, moongleam. Not listed in crystal.
Marked: May be marked on bottom of foot.
Comments: An unusual line with triangular stems and feet. Very Art Deco in appearance. Only a few items have been seen to date. Made in diamond optic. Items listed in price lists are:
10 oz. goblet
Saucer champagne
5 oz. soda, footed
12 oz. soda, footed

#4067 (4091¼) LOREN - name given by researchers

Dates: Ca. 1935
Colors: Only crystal known
Marked: No
Comments: The only examples known are all elaborately cut or engraved. Original Heisey pattern number recently found.

#7005 DOUBLE RING - name and number given by researchers

Dates: Unknown
Colors: Unknown
Marked: Unknown
Comments: An unusual stem bearing some resemblance to the Old Dominion pattern in the stem portion. The bowl shape resembles #3361 Charlotte in appearance.

#2516 CIRCLE PAIR goblet

#3379 PYRAMID soda and saucer champagne

#4067 (4091¼) LOREN goblet

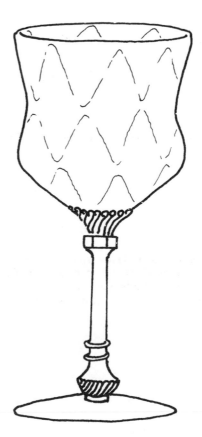

#7005 DOUBLE RING goblet

#1408 (7043) PANEL & DIAMOND POINT - name given by researchers

Dates: Ca. 1925
Colors: Crystal, moongleam
Marked: Yes, on upper stem.
Comments: A scarce stem line which has been seen with two types of treatment to the stem portion. One has a plain vertical portion while the other has small notches on each ridged surface. This may indicate that they were considered to be two lines when originally made. Original Heisey pattern number recently found.

#8005 GALAXY - name given by researchers

Dates: Ca. 1930
Colors: Moongleam, flamingo, sahara
Marked: Yes
Comments: This is a pressed stem line which is only occasionally seen.

#8021 RIB IN RING - name given by researchers

Dates: Ca. 1930
Colors: Moongleam
Marked: Yes, on upper stem
Comments: Very rare. A pressed stem. The item illustrated is probably a cocktail or sherry.

#3361 CHARLOTTE - name given by researchers

Dates: Ca. 1927
Colors: Hawthorne bowl, moongleam stem and foot. Has not been seen in crystal or any other colors.
Marked: Yes, on one panel of stem just below the hexagonal knop.
Comments: Very scarce. One set is reported. Goblets, saucer champagnes, sherbets and cocktails made. Previously known as #8034 Albemarle Variant. Original Heisey pattern number recently found.

#1408 (7043) PANEL & DIAMOND POINT goblets
note difference in stems

#8005 GALAXY goblet

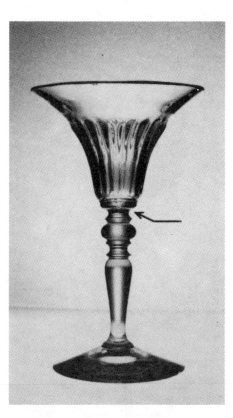

#8021 RIB IN RING sherry

#3361 CHARLOTTE saucer champagne

#3304 UNIVERSAL - original Heisey Co. name

Dates: 1917-1957

Colors: Crystal only; parfait made in amber for Fred Harvey

Optic: Plain, medium optic, wide optic

Decorations: Some pieces used for specialty etchings. Usually found undecorated

Marked: No. It is a blown stemware line with a pulled stem and cannot be marked

Comments: This pattern survived for 40 years as a good, basic stem line. Pieces were added and dropped throughout this time. Some items were listed as "discontinued for the duration" (of World War II) in 1944.

Look-Alikes: This line was a standard shape used extensively throughout the glass industry. Many companies produced lines either the same as or similar to Heisey's Universal.

Imperial Reissues: None

Availability: Common

2 oz. Sherry

1¼ oz Pony Brandy

1 oz. Cordial

1 oz. Pousse Cafe

Finger Bowl

4 oz. Oyster Cocktail (3389)

3½ oz. Cocktail Also made 3 oz.

3 oz. Burgundy

2½ oz. Creme de Menthe

2½ oz. Wine

5½ oz. Saucer Champagne

5 oz. Parfait

5½ oz. Sherbet

6 oz. Rhine Wine Also made 4 oz

4½ oz. Claret

10 oz Goblet Also made 9 & 11 oz

10 oz. Pilsner

6½ oz. Champagne

6 oz. Champagne Hollow Stem

#3304 UNIVERSAL pattern

#3311 VELVEDERE - original Heisey Co. name

Dates: 1917-1933; The sherry survived until 1956.
Colors: Crystal only
Optic: Plain, medium optic, wide optic
Decorations: Some Heisey cuttings
Marked: No. It is a blown stemware line with a pulled stem and cannot be marked.
Comments: The fruit salad bowl was made in diamond optic in moongleam and flamingo. The remainder of the line was not made in colors. Again, this is a basic plain stem line good for decorations. Note the sherry shape. It has caused some collectors confusion in the past since they assumed the existence of a complete Heisey stem line with this shape.
Look-Alikes: Again, this is a standard shape made by many companies making handmade stemware. Positive identification as Heisey is difficult unless an item is found with a known Heisey decoration.
Imperial Reissues: None
Availability: Common to moderately available

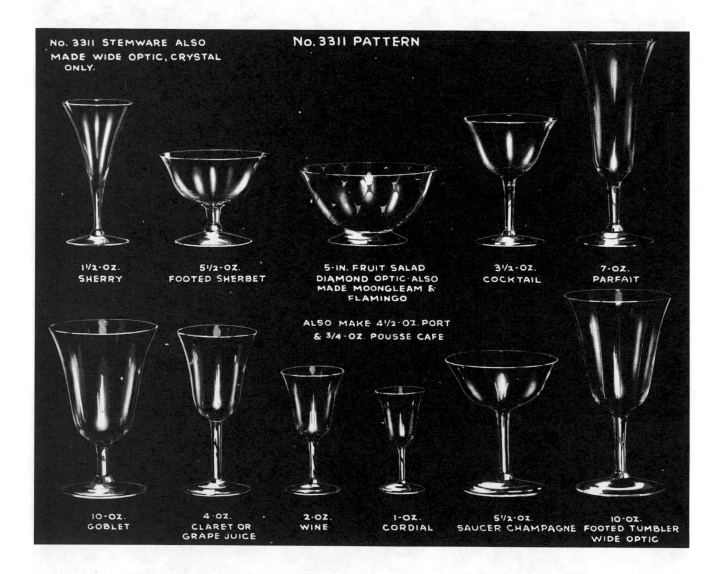

NO. 3311 STEMWARE ALSO MADE WIDE OPTIC, CRYSTAL ONLY.

NO. 3311 PATTERN

1½-OZ. SHERRY

5½-OZ. FOOTED SHERBET

5-IN. FRUIT SALAD DIAMOND OPTIC·ALSO MADE MOONGLEAM & FLAMINGO

3½-OZ. COCKTAIL

7-OZ. PARFAIT

ALSO MAKE 4½-OZ. PORT & ¾-OZ. POUSSE CAFE

10-OZ. GOBLET

4-OZ. CLARET OR GRAPE JUICE

2-OZ. WINE

1-OZ. CORDIAL

5½-OZ. SAUCER CHAMPAGNE

10-OZ. FOOTED TUMBLER WIDE OPTIC

#3312 GAYOSO - original Heisey Co. name

Dates: 1917-1933
Colors: Flamingo and marigold. Finger bowl made in moongleam; Russian coffee made with moongleam foot and handle.
Optic: Plain, medium optic, wide optic, diamond optic
Decorations: Used for etchings and some early Heisey cuttings.
Marked: No. It is a blown stemware line with a pulled stem and cannot be marked.
Comments: A good, basic stemware pattern, very attractive in colors. Scarce in marigold. The Russian coffee is eagerly sought by collectors. After collectors become familiar with Gayoso, they are easily able to distinguish it from products of other glass companies. Pay close attention to the proportions and the little flare at the tops of the pieces. Other companies made similar looking stems, but Heisey's shape is distinctive.
Imperial Reissues: None
Availability: Common to moderately available

#3316 BILTMORE - original Heisey Co. name

Dates: 1917-1929; Goblet, sherbet and almond from 1929-1935; Full line from 1935-1937
Colors: Crystal only. Individual almond comes in crystal with a moongleam foot.
Optic: Plain, medium optic, wide optic, diamond optic
Decorations: Some early Heisey etchings
Marked: No. It is a blown stemware line with a pulled stem and cannot be marked.
Comments: Another of the basic stemware patterns which the Heisey Co. produced for quite some time. Apparently styles like these were always in fashion and there was a ready market. Many of these plain stemware lines may have been sold to various decorating companies for their use. Compare this line to #3304 Universal. The shapes are quite similar. The individual almond is usually seen with diamond optic.
Look-Alikes: Many companies made stemware of this basic shape.
Imperial Reissues: None
Availability: Common to moderately available

#3316 BILTMORE individual almond

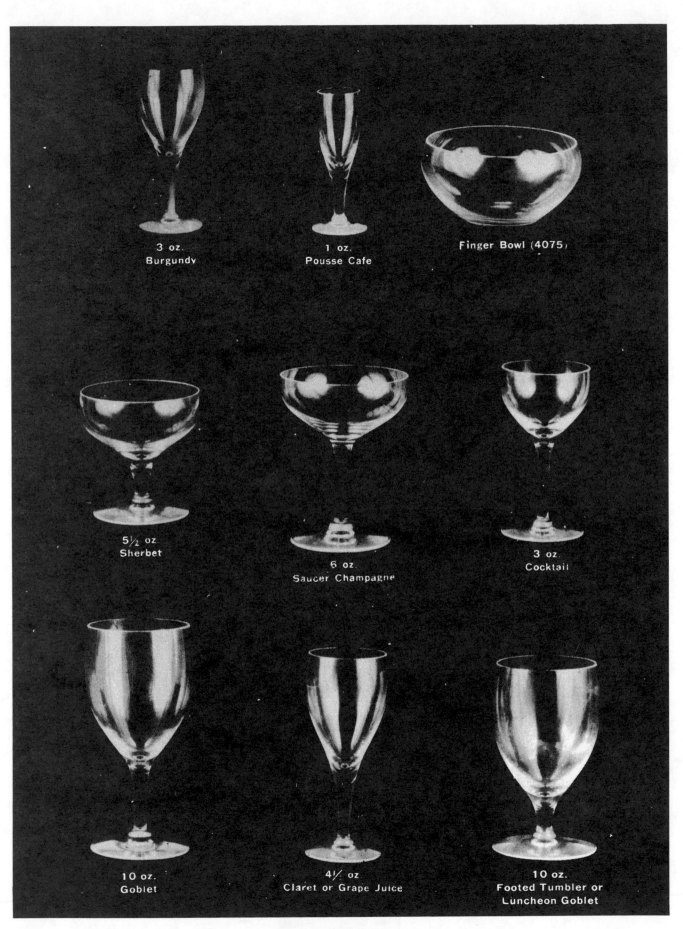

3 oz.
Burgundy

1 oz.
Pousse Cafe

Finger Bowl (4075)

5½ oz.
Sherbet

6 oz.
Saucer Champagne

3 oz.
Cocktail

10 oz.
Goblet

4½ oz.
Claret or Grape Juice

10 oz.
Footed Tumbler or
Luncheon Goblet

#3316 BILTMORE pattern

#3318, 3318½ WALDORF - original Heisey Co. name

Dates: 1917-1929; 1935-1937; cocktail made until 1956

Colors: Crystal only

Optic: Plain, medium optic, wide optic

Decorations: Used for some cuttings by Heisey. The cocktail was used for several etchings in the mid-30's. Pairpoint also decorated items with their "Baron" engraving.

Marked: No. It is a blown stemware line with a pulled stem and cannot be marked.

Comments: The bowl shape on this pattern is somewhat more distinctive than on several other of Heisey's plain stems, so it is more easily identified. Still the presence of a Heisey decoration is usually needed to be certain. Cocktails and wines were used for several of the Heisey silhouette etchings and some carvings: i.e. Tally Ho; Victory; You, Me, and Us; Bacchus; Chevy Chase and others. The #3318½ number in this case is used to identify the tall stem goblet. The rest of the line has notably shorter stems than this one item. Also note that the 4 oz. oyster cocktail shown with the line was originally from the #3389 Duquesne pattern.

Imperial Reissues: None

Availability: Moderately available

2½ oz.
Wine
Also made 2 oz.

3 oz.
Burgundy

1 oz.
Cordial

¼ oz.
Pony Brandy

Finger Bowl (4080)

6 oz.
Low Footed Sundae

5 oz.
Low Footed Sherbet

3½ oz.
Cocktail
Also made 2½ & 3 oz.

4 oz.
Oyster Cocktail (3389)

5 oz.
Low Footed Fruit Shallow

11 oz. Tall Stem Goblet
(3318½)

11 oz.
Goblet
Also made 7 & 9 oz.

4 oz.
Claret

4 oz.
Grape Juice

5 oz
Saucer Champagne

#3318 WALDORF pattern

#3324 DELAWARE - original Heisey Co. name

Dates: 1926-1935
Colors: Flamingo, hawthorne
Optic: Diamond optic, checker optic
Decorations: #173 Dover pantograph etching
Marked: No. It is a blown stemware line with a pulled stem and cannot be marked.
Comments: Strictly a stemware pattern. The distinctively shaped bowl and the slight bulge in the stem portion make it possible to identify this pattern as Heisey easily. Flamingo items are usually found with diamond optic. The hawthorne items are found in checker optic (Heisey's description). The optic gives a vague checkerboard effect when held to the light. It is quite attractive and unusual. Delaware is not common and hawthorne items are especially difficult to find. Crystal might be the most difficult of all to find.
Imperial Reissues: None
Availability: Moderately available

NO. 3324 PATTERN
DIAMOND OPTIC

NO. 3324 PATTERN MADE
CRYSTAL & FLAMINGO

FINGER BOWL

4-OZ. OYSTER
COCKTAIL

3½-OZ. COCKTAIL

4½-OZ. PARFAIT

9-OZ. GOBLET

9-OZ. LUNCHEON
GOBLET

6½-OZ. SAUCER
CHAMPAGNE

6½-OZ. SHERBET

#3325 RAMPUL - name given by researchers

Dates: 1926-1929
Colors: Flamingo, hawthorne
Optic: Diamond optic, checker optic
Decorations: None
Marked: No. It is a blown stem line with a pulled stem and cannot be marked.
Comments: A contrived name derived from the similarity of the bowl shape to the Ramshorn (#3365) pattern, but with a pulled stem - thus, Rampul. For a long time the original number of this stem was unknown, but recent research has uncovered the correct number. In this case, the hawthorne items have diamond optic while flamingo is listed with checker optic only. Thus far, all items seen conform with these descriptions from the price list. The entire pattern is difficult to find.

Items made were:
9 oz. goblet
3 oz. cocktail
6 oz. saucer champagne
6 oz. sherbet
4½ oz. oyster cocktail

Imperial Reissues: None
Availability: Scarce

#3325 RAMPUL goblet

#3333 OLD GLORY - original Heisey Co. name

Dates: 1919-1941

Colors: Hawthorne

Optic: Plain, wide optic

Decorations: Used for several Heisey etchings and cuttings. Also apparently sold in fairly large quantities to decorating companies because many unknown cuttings are found on this stemware line. Pairpoint decorated the line with their "Carol" engraving.

Marked: Yes, on stem portion immediately below bowl.

Comments: Possibly designed by Josef Balda—certainly he designed Renaissance etching which appears on the line. A rather extensive stem line, expanded to include a matching comport and tall footed grape fruit. The #3476 Temple ice teas were also sold as part of the #3333 line. Since it was apparently quite popular and remained in the line for many years, it is relatively easy to find today. It is very difficult to find in hawthorne.

Look-Alikes: There is a look-alike made by another company (unknown) which is very similar to Old Glory. Close examination shows that there is some difference at the base of the stem where the foot is attached, however, even experts almost need to compare two items side by side to tell the difference. In other words, be careful of unmarked pieces.

Imperial Reissues: None

Availability: Moderately available in crystal

2 oz. Wine   1 oz. Cordial   ¾ oz. Pousse Cafe   5½ oz. Sundae or Sherbet   4½ oz. Oyster Cocktail (3542)

3 oz. Burgundy   3 oz. Cocktail Also made 2½ oz   2 oz. Sherry   5½ oz. Saucer Champagne

9 oz. Goblet Also made 8 oz.   6 oz. Grape Juice   4½ oz. Parfait   4½ oz. Claret

#3333 OLD GLORY pattern

12 oz. Footed Ice Tea
Handled (3476)

6 in. High Footed Comport

12 oz. Footed Soda (3476)

Finger Bowl (3309)

Footed Grape Fruit

4139
Footed Grape Fruit Center

4132
Peg Grape Fruit Center

#3333 OLD GLORY pattern

#3350 WABASH - original Heisey Co. name

Dates: 1922-1947

Colors: Flamingo; moongleam foot and stem, crystal bowl; hawthorne; crystal stem and foot, marigold bowl; a few pieces known with a transitional marigold/sahara bowl and crystal stem (these items look like sahara, but react like marigold under ultraviolet light); a few goblets known with an experimental gold stem; rare in zircon bowl, crystal stem

Optic: Plain, wide optic, diamond optic

Decorations: Used for many Heisey etchings and some cuttings. Also decorated by other companies

Marked: Yes, on upper stem beneath rings

Comments: An extensive stemware line which was expanded to include both handled and non-handled ice teas, tankard jug, squat jug, comport and cover and a pressed plate. An early item produced for a short time was a tall, slim bud vase. A mayonnaise was also listed in later price lists. At first the three-pint tankard was not offered in colors. Jugs were available with a plain neck or with a band of cut flutes. The 6″ plate was made with a full ground bottom, in plain or diamond optic. Colors available were moongleam, flamingo, sahara, alexandrite and marigold. Hawthorne plates were also made in either diamond optic or checker optic. Some price lists indicate that the #3350 plate was the same as the #4182 Thin. (See PLATES Section for illustration.)

Look-Alikes: Fenton produced a pressed stemware line very similar to Wabash with a pressed diamond optic. It has been seen in colors similar to hawthorne and flamingo. Make sure items you are considering have a blown bowl and pressed stem. Most should be marked with the Diamond H.

Patents: #69434 for goblet applied for 4/29/22 and granted 2/16/26. Josef O. Balda listed as designer.

Imperial Reissues: None

Availability: Moderately available

1 oz.
Cordial

4 oz.
Oyster Cocktail

6 oz.
Sherbet

3 oz.
Cocktail

5 oz.
Parfait

4 oz.
Claret

6 oz.
Saucer Champagne

2½ oz.
Wine

10 oz.
Goblet

10 oz.
Footed Tumbler

12 oz.
Footed Soda or Ice Tea
Also made 5 & 8 oz.

12 oz. Footed Soda
Handled

#3350 WABASH pattern

4132
Peg Grape Fruit Center

4139
Footed Grape Fruit Center

3 pt Footed Jug
Squat
Also made Cut Neck

6 in.
Footed Comport and Cover

6 in.
Grape Fruit

6 in.
Plate Pressed

Finger Bowl (4071)

3 pt. Footed Tankard
Cut Neck
Also made Plain

#3350 WABASH pattern

#3355 FAIRACRE - original Heisey Co. name

Dates: 1925-1937

Colors: Moongleam stem and foot, crystal bowl; flamingo stem and foot, crystal bowl

Optic: Plain, wide optic, diamond optic

Decorations: Some etchings and possibly some cuttings by Heisey. Also cut by other decorating companies.

Marked: Yes, on stem portion just above ball.

Comments: Another rather extensive pattern line including matching ice teas and footed jug. This time a tall, footed vase was also added to the line. Handled items have handles in color in addition to the stems and feet. The 54 oz. jug is listed with moongleam foot and handle; all moongleam; all flamingo; and flamingo foot and handle. The vase is listed with moongleam foot and flamingo foot. It is also known in all flamingo. The jug was also used with the #3357 King Arthur pattern. This pattern is very similar to the #3357 King Arthur with only the bowl shape changed. Fairacre flares at the top while King Arthur is cupped. A sherbet is known with an unusual tiny, spotted optic, somewhat like checker optic, but not in squares. This is somewhat of an oddity.

Imperial Reissues: None

Availability: Moderately available.

4½ oz. Claret

2½ oz. Wine

3¾ oz. Oyster Cocktail

1 oz. Cordial

Finger Bowl (4074)

5 oz. Parfait

10 oz. Luncheon Goblet

6½ oz. Saucer Champagne

6½ oz. Sherbet

3½ oz. Cocktail

12 oz. Footed Ice Tea

12 oz. Footed Ice Tea Handled

10 oz. Goblet

54 oz. Footed Jug

#3355 FAIRACRE pattern

#8046 QUEEN GUINIVERE - name and number given by researchers

Dates: 1925

Colors: Only crystal known

Marked: Yes. On the upper stem

Comments: The name and number of this goblet have been given by researchers since the original Heisey ones are not known. The goblet was patented at the same time as #3357 King Arthur, being filed on 1/23/25 and granted 6/23/25. The patent number assigned was #67657, one number earlier than that for King Arthur. T. Clarence Heisey was listed as designer. Since it is obvious that the two stem lines were developed and patented at the same time, it is also possible that Queen Guinivere might be found in moongleam and flamingo as King Arthur is. Up to this time, only crystal has been seen, and in goblets only. It seems likely that other sizes of stemware were also made. It is known in wide optic or plain.

Imperial Reissues: None

Availability: Scarce

#8046 QUEEN GUINEVERE goblet

#3357 KING ARTHUR · original Heisey Co. name

Dates: 1925-1937

Colors: Moongleam stem and foot, crystal bowl; flamingo stem and foot, crystal bowl; all flamingo.

Optic: Plain or diamond optic.

Decorations: Used for several Heisey etchings and possibly some cuttings.

Marked: Yes, on upper stem above ball.

Comments: The companion line to #3355 Fairacre and #8046 Queen Guinivere. The bowl on King Arthur cups in while the bowl on Fairacre flares out sharply at the top. The difference between Queen Guinivere and King Arthur is in the stem. The stem on Queen Guinivere is a plain fluted stem with no knop. Often on this stem line the Diamond H is present, but very small. Close examination will often help find these tiny marks. The jug used with the King Arthur line was originally taken from the #3355 Fairacre pattern.

Patents: #67658 for goblet applied for 1/23/25 and granted 6/23/25. T. Clarence Heisey listed as designer

Imperial Reissues: None

Availability: Moderately available

2½ oz.
Wine

3½ oz.
Cocktail

1 oz.
Cordial

3¾ oz.
Oyster Cocktail

Finger Bowl (4080)

6½ oz.
Saucer Champagne

54 oz.
Footed Jug (3355)

6½ oz.
Sherbet

12 oz.
Footed Ice Tea

12 oz.
Footed Ice Tea
Handled

10 oz.
Luncheon Goblet

5 oz.
Parfait

10 oz.
Goblet

#3357 KING ARTHUR pattern

#3359 PLATEAU - name given by researchers

Dates: 1926-1937

Colors: Flamingo, marigold. The finger bowl, jug and rose bowl were made in moongleam; the jug and rose bowl were made in hawthorne. The sherbet has been seen in cobalt with a crystal foot.

Optic: Plain, diamond optic

Decorations: No

Marked: No. This is a pulled stem line and cannot be marked.

Comments: In this stem and soda line, a jug and a rose bowl were added to the line. (See VASE Section for illustration of rose bowl.) Actually the rose bowl appears more like a vase since it has a rolled edge top, but the official Heisey nomenclature was "rose bowl." Items were misidentified in the original catalog. Captions under the luncheon goblet, cocktail and saucer champagne are in error. Left to right, captions should be: 3 oz. cocktail, 6½ oz. saucer champagne and 8 oz. luncheon goblet. Pontils are ground and polished on the jug and rose bowl. Marigold items are hard to find and quite attractive. Items were made in plain (without optic) in crystal and flamingo.

Patent: #73031 for soda applied for 4/12/26 and granted 7/12/27. T. Clarence Heisey listed as designer.

Imperial Reissues: None

Availability: Moderately available

NO. 3359 PATTERN
DIAMOND OPTIC

NO. 3359 PATTERN MADE IN CRYSTAL & FLAMINGO

FINGER BOWL

4-OZ. OYSTER COCKTAIL

6½-OZ. SHERBET

9-OZ. TUMBLER

5½-OZ. SODA

8-OZ. SODA

12-OZ. SODA OR ICE TEA

NO. 3359 ROSE BOWL SHOWN ON PAGE 38

8½-OZ. GOBLET

8-OZ. LUNCHEON GOBLET

3-OZ. COCKTAIL

6½-OZ. SAUCER CHAMPAGNE

½ GAL. JUG

#3360 PENN CHARTER - original Heisey Co. name

Dates: 1926-1937   **Colors:** Flamingo, hawthorne
Optic: Wide optic; diamond optic and checker optic in flamingo; checker optic in hawthorne.
Decorations: Some cuttings by Heisey
Marked: Yes, on upper stem below swirl
Comments: A small stemware line. Similar to #3408 Jamestown and #3409 Plymouth. The difference is in the bowl shapes. Jamestown has a flared bowl, Plymouth a straight bowl and Penn Charter a bell-shaped bowl with a flared top. Penn Charter borrowed the #3381 Creole footed bar to help fill out the line. Note the very plain footed soda. The claret, footed sodas, and sherry were listed only in crystal.
Imperial Reissues: None   **Availability:** Moderately available

1½ oz.
Sherry

3 oz.
Cocktail

4 oz.
Oyster Cocktail

Finger Bowl (3309)

6 oz.
Sherbet

2½ oz.
Footed Bar (3381)

6 oz.
Saucer Champagne

10 oz.
Goblet

12 oz. Soda
Also made 5 & 8 oz.

5 oz.
Parfait

4½ oz.
Claret

203

#3362 CHARTER OAK - original Heisey Co. name

Dates: 1926-1935
Colors: Moongleam; flamingo; crystal stem, marigold bowl; all marigold; comport and goblets in hawthorne
Optic: Diamond optic
Decorations: None
Marked: Yes, on stem portion immediately beneath bowl
Comments: An unusually designed stem line featuring an acorn as the knop in the stem and unique stepped bowl. Note that the sodas and jug do not have feet but are flat. Egyptian was sometimes used as a name for this pattern, but it is improper since Charter Oak is the original Heisey name. Charter Oak is much more appropriate also, considering the acorn motif. See CANDLESTICKS Section for the matching #4262 Charter Oak water lamp.
Patents: #70754 for goblet applied for 5/25/26 and granted 8/3/26. E. Wilson Heisey listed as designer
Imperial Reissues: None
Availability: Moderately available

NO. 3362 PATTERN
DIAMOND OPTIC

NO. 3362 PATTERN MADE IN CRYSTAL,
MOONGLEAM, FLAMINGO BOWL
CRYSTAL STEM

4½-OZ. PARFAIT   3-OZ. COCKTAIL   3½ OZ. OYSTER COCKTAIL   FINGER BOWL   10-OZ. TUMBLER   12-OZ. ICE TEA

NO. 3362 JUG SHOWN ON PAGE 32

8-OZ. GOBLET   8-OZ. LUNCHEON GOBLET   7-IN. HIGH FOOTED COMPORT ALSO MAKE 6-IN-LOW FOOT   6-OZ. SHERBET   6-OZ. SAUCER CHAMPAGNE

#3365 RAMSHORN - name given by researchers

Dates: 1927-1931. Plain crystal items were offered again in 1937.
Colors: Flamingo. Fruit salad made with moongleam foot.
Optic: Plain and ramshorn optic
Decorations: Sea Nymph etching. Some cut pieces have been seen, but these may have been done by a decorating company. Known to have been cut by Newton in Bowling Green, Ohio.
Marked: Yes, on stem below wafer.
Comments: A very attractive stemware pattern, especially with the unusual ramshorn optic from which the name was taken. The optic is wide swirl which is narrower at the bottom of the item than at the top. The name causes some confusion since pieces were made both with and without the optic. Very similar to #3366 Trojan; again the difference is in the bowl shapes. The catalog page is in error when calling the 1½ oz. bar "footed" when it is obviously shown without a foot.
Patents: #77673 for goblet applied for 9/22/27 and granted 2/12/28. Ray C. Cobel listed as designer.
Imperial Reissues: None
Availability: Moderately available to scarce.

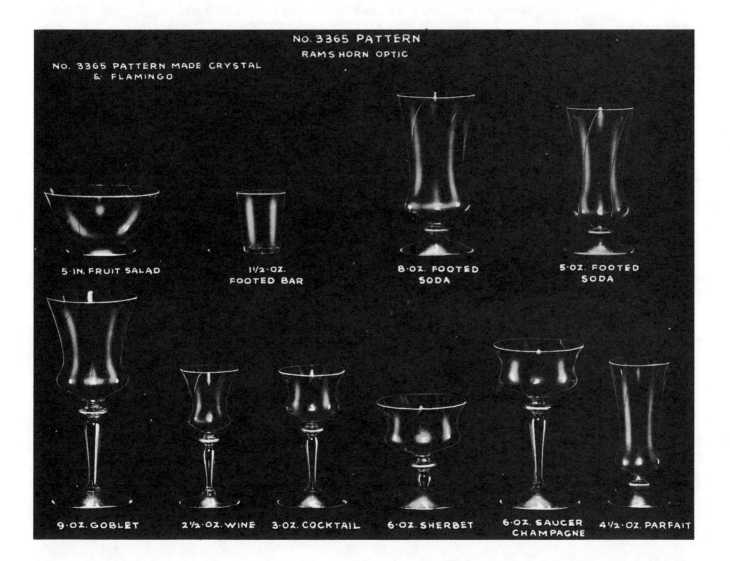

NO. 3365 PATTERN MADE CRYSTAL & FLAMINGO

NO. 3365 PATTERN
RAMSHORN OPTIC

5-IN. FRUIT SALAD | 1½-OZ. FOOTED BAR | 8-OZ. FOOTED SODA | 5-OZ. FOOTED SODA

9-OZ. GOBLET | 2½-OZ. WINE | 3-OZ. COCKTAIL | 6-OZ. SHERBET | 6-OZ. SAUCER CHAMPAGNE | 4½-OZ. PARFAIT

#3368 ALBEMARLE - original Heisey Co. name

Dates: 1928-1951; matching for cuttings until 1957.

Colors: Flamingo; moongleam stem and foot, crystal bowl; crystal stem and foot, marigold bowl; a few items in all marigold and all alexandrite; very scarce in experimental light blue.

Optic: Diamond optic

Decorations: Often seen cut. Used by Heisey for cuttings but also sold to various decorating companies.

Marked: Yes, on stem below faceted knop.

Comments: This stem line is usually easy to find in comparison with some of Heisey's other stems. It remained in the Heisey line long enough for large quantities to be made. The most popular decoration is #867 Chateau cutting. The footed comport was available in sahara and alexandrite in addition to marigold bowl, moongleam stem, and all flamingo. The captions appear to be reversed on the 3 oz. oyster cocktail and the 1½ oz. footed bar. Sometimes stained pieces are found with a gold stain or a combination of gold and blue stain. These were done by the Dominican Sisters of St. Mary's of the Springs of Columbus, Ohio. It is probable that these items were of limited production and done for their own use.

Imperial Reissues: None

Availability: Common to moderately available

3 oz.
Cocktail

2½ oz.
Wine

5 oz.
Sherbet

1 oz.
Cordial

Finger Bowl (3309)

10 oz. Footed Tumbler

3 oz.
Oyster Cocktail

7 In. High Footed Comport

1½ oz.
Footed Bar

12 oz.
Soda or Ice Tea
Also made 5 & 8 oz.

8 oz.
Goblet

4 oz.
Claret

4½ oz.
Parfait

5 oz.
Saucer Champagne

#3368 ALBEMARLE pattern

#3366 TROJAN - original Heisey Co. name

Dates: 1926-1931
Colors: Flamingo; moongleam stem and foot, crystal bowl; hawthorne
Optic: Diamond optic
Decorations: #445 Trojan etching; several cuttings have been seen on this line. Some were done by Heisey, but a great many appear to have been done by other companies, including Pairpoint.
Marked: Yes, on stem just below wafer
Comments: A tall-stemmed, nicely proportioned line. The footed sodas and bar have a very pronounced flare. Surely these were easily damaged if knocked over while in use. Heisey called both the stem line and the etching with which it was decorated, Trojan. See CANDLESTICKS Section for #4366 matching water lamp. Compare Trojan with #3365 Ramshorn.
Imperial Reissues: None
Availability: Moderately available

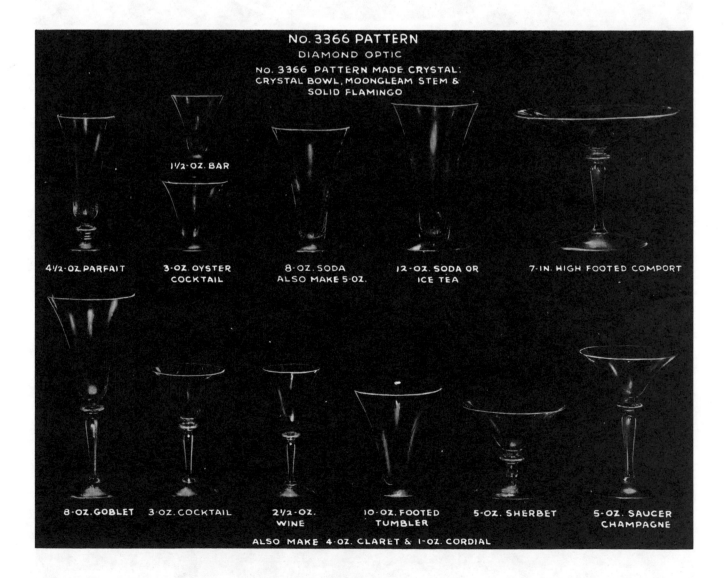

No. 3366 PATTERN
DIAMOND OPTIC
NO. 3366 PATTERN MADE CRYSTAL:
CRYSTAL BOWL, MOONGLEAM STEM &
SOLID FLAMINGO

1½-OZ. BAR

4½-OZ. PARFAIT — 3-OZ. OYSTER COCKTAIL — 8-OZ. SODA ALSO MAKE 5-OZ. — 12-OZ. SODA OR ICE TEA — 7-IN. HIGH FOOTED COMPORT

8-OZ. GOBLET — 3-OZ. COCKTAIL — 2½-OZ. WINE — 10-OZ. FOOTED TUMBLER — 5-OZ. SHERBET — 5-OZ. SAUCER CHAMPAGNE

ALSO MAKE 4-OZ. CLARET & 1-OZ. CORDIAL

#3440 PORTSMOUTH

Dates: 1924-1935
Colors: Moongleam foot, crystal stem and bowl; all flamingo. Goblet known in tangerine.
Optic: Diamond optic
Decorations: None
Marked: No. The line has a pulled stem and so cannot be marked.
Comments: A very short pattern line with only a few items made in the line. Old turn books indicate that at least a few goblets were made with flamingo bowl, moongleam foot. These would indeed be a find. It is possible that this line was not made continuously since a trade journal report refers to the pattern as being reissued from an old Heisey line.
Imperial Reissues: None
Availability: Moderately available

#3370 AFRICAN - name given by researchers

Dates: 1928-1933
Colors: Moongleam stem, crystal bowl; all flamingo
Optic: Diamond optic. Crystal available plain
Decorations: None
Marked: No
Comments: A tall, elegant stem pattern. Somewhat difficult to find. It is a relatively short pattern with only 5 stem pieces and a finger bowl listed. Crystal items were available plain or diamond optic. Colors were listed only with diamond optic. An old price list states that "#3365 (Ramshorn) or #3366 Trojan footed sodas may be used with #3370 Line."
Imperial Reissues: None
Availability: Moderately available to scarce

NO. 3440 PATTERN MADE CRYSTAL; CRYSTAL BOWL MOONGLEAM STEM; SOLID FLAMINGO.

NO. 3440 PATTERN DIAMOND OPTIC

3440-7-OZ. SHERBET

3440-7-OZ. SAUCER CHAMPAGNE

3440-3½-OZ. COCKTAIL

3440-9-OZ. GOBLET

NO. 3370 PATTERN

NO. 3370 PATTERN MADE CRYSTAL, PLAIN & DIAMOND OPTIC; CRYSTAL BOWL, MOONGLEAM STEM, & SOLID FLAMINGO, DIAMOND OPTIC

3370-8-OZ. GOBLET

3370-3-OZ. WINE

3370-4-OZ. COCKTAIL

3370-6-OZ. SHERBET

3370-6-OZ. SAUCER CHAMPAGNE

#3376 ADAM · original Heisey Co. name

Dates: 1929-1933

Colors: Flamingo

Optic: Diamond optic

Decorations: Several Heisey etchings

Marked: No. It is a pulled stem and cannot be marked.

Comments: The stems are very tall and striking in this pattern. The name "Adam" seems to have been in usage throughout the glass industry for this shape since ads for other companies indicate that they also made this shape and called it Adam. Tumblers and footed sodas have the distinctively shaped bowls of the stemmed pieces and a noticeable curve inward just above the foot. This is different from many of the Heisey footed tumblers and sodas which accompany stemware lines.

Imperial Reissues: None

Availability: Moderately available to scarce.

No. 3376 PATTERN MADE
CRYSTAL & FLAMINGO

No. 3376 PATTERN
DIAMOND OPTIC

FINGER BOWL

10-OZ. FOOTED
TUMBLER

4-OZ. OYSTER
COCKTAIL

5-OZ. FOOTED
SODA
ALSO MAKE 8-OZ.

12-OZ. FOOTED SODA
OR ICE TEA

11-OZ. GOBLET

4-OZ. CLARET

3½-OZ.
COCKTAIL

3-OZ. WINE

6-OZ. SAUCER
CHAMPAGNE

6-OZ. SHERBET

211

#3380 OLD DOMINION - original Heisey Co. name

Dates: 1930-1939. Sahara items discontinued in 1937

Colors: Moongleam bowl, crystal stem; moongleam stem, crystal bowl; flamingo; marigold bowl, crystal stem; marigold stem, crystal bowl; sahara; alexandrite. Scarce in zircon. Rare in sahara/zircon combination

Optic: Diamond optic

Decorations: Used for etchings by Heisey.

Marked: Yes, on upper stem below hexagonal knop.

Comments: A very diverse stem line as far as color variation is concerned. Usually easy to find except in the more difficult colors such as alexandrite. Two styles of goblet and saucer champagne were made: tall stem and short stem. This sometimes leads to difficulties in matching pieces.

Imperial Reissues: None

Availability: Common to moderately available

2 oz.
Bar

1 oz.
Cordial

4 oz
Oyster Cocktail

4139
Footed Grape Fruit Center

4132
Peg Grape Fruit Center

Finger Bowl (4075)

6 oz.
Saucer Champagne
Tall Stem

2½ oz.
Wine

6 oz.
Saucer Champagne
Short Stem

3 oz.
Cocktail

6 oz.
Sherbet

Footed Grape Fruit

10 oz. Goblet
Tall Stem

10 oz. Goblet
Short Stem

4 oz.
Claret

5 oz.
Parfait

12 oz.
Soda or Ice Tea
Also made 5, 8 & 16 oz

10 oz. Tumbler
Footed

#3380 OLD DOMINION pattern

#3381 CREOLE - original Heisey Co. name

Dates: 1930-1937

Colors: Alexandrite; alexandrite bowl, crystal stem and foot; sahara bowl, crystal stem and foot. NOT MADE IN ALL CRYSTAL. One printed Heisey booklet indicates that the line was available in solid sahara, but Creole was not listed in price lists in this manner.

Optic: Wide optic or diamond optic.

Decorations: None

Marked: No

Comments: An elegant stem pattern, eagerly sought in alexandrite. Actually the crystal/alexandrite combination is harder to find, with the sahara/crystal the most difficult. Since the 2½ oz. bar was also part of the #3360 Penn Charter line, it is possible that it was made in crystal. Price lists indicate that the line was available with either wide optic or diamond optic. Diamond optic seems to be the most often seen. The catalog page used here indicates that "plain" was made, but this is probably an error since price lists do not indicate it was made without optic. The goblets and saucer champagnes were made in a tall version and a short stem version. Footed sodas and tumblers have the rather unique bowl shape and thus are able to be identified even though they are never marked. A 14 oz. soda was also made.

Patents: #82151 for goblet applied for 5/16/30 and granted 9/30/30. T. Clarence Heisey listed as designer.

Imperial Reissues: None

Availability: Moderately available.

2½ oz.
Footed Bar

1 oz.
Cordial

5 oz.
Oyster Cocktail

4139
Footed Grape Fruit Center

4132
Peg Grape Fruit Center

Footed Finger Bowl

7 oz.
Saucer Champagne
Tall Stem

7 oz.
Saucer Champagne
Short Stem

2½ oz.
Wine

7 oz.
Sherbet

4 oz.
Cocktail

Footed Grape Fruit

11 oz. Goblet
Tall Stem

11 oz. Goblet
Short Stem

5 oz.
Parfait

12 oz.
Footed Soda
Also made 5 & 8 oz.

10 oz.
Footed Tumbler

#3381 CREOLE pattern

215

#3386 DIAMOND ROSE · name given by researchers

Dates: 1930-1933. Pilsners from 1933-1944

Colors: Flamingo; crystal bowl, moongleam stem and foot; moongleam bowl, crystal stem and foot; marigold bowl, crystal stem and foot; sahara. Pilsners in cobalt bowl, crystal stem and foot; sahara.

Optic: Diamond optic. Pilsners made in wide optic.

Decorations: Yes, especially #447 Empress etching

Marked: Yes, on stem just below the bowl

Comments: An unusual, short-stemmed goblet. When Heisey was introducing their Empress etching, they said: "Some people like their goblets high and some like them low . . . Both high and low goblets are to be had in the Empress Pattern by Heisey, with etching #447. The low goblet is shown here . . ." This referred to the Diamond Rose goblet, while the tall goblet was the Old Dominion pattern. The unusual large ball portion of the stem is very similar in design to the small ball on the #3389 Duquesne pattern. Both have a pressed design of flowers on the ball. The pilsners were a later addition to the line and these are the pieces seen in cobalt. The pilsners in crystal remained in the line until 1944. (See BAR-WARE Section for illustration.)
Items made were:
11 oz. (or 12 oz.) goblet
6½ oz. saucer champagne
7 oz. sherbet
cocktail
8 oz., 10 oz. & 12 oz. pilsners

Imperial Reissues: None

Availability: Scarce

#3386 DIAMOND ROSE goblet

#3389 DUQUESNE - original Heisey Co. name

Dates: 1930-1952. It was discontinued for a short time in 1942 but resurrected almost immediately.

Colors: Sahara; sahara bowl, crystal stem and foot; tangerine bowl, crystal stem and foot

Optic: Plain, wide optic.

Decorations: Used for several Heisey etchings and cuttings. The tumbler was decorated with #507 Orchid etching. Also cut by Hunt Glass of Corning, NY, among others. Engraved in "Wren" pattern by Pairpoint. Sodas engraved with Pairpoint's "Baron"

Marked: No

Comments: Due to its long life, this stem is easily found, especially in crystal. It is eagerly sought in tangerine and makes an elegant table setting in this color. The little, flower-decorated ball at the base of the stem makes it distinctive and quickly identifiable as Heisey. Compare it with the flowered ball on #3386 Diamond Rose. A variant goblet is known with a flared bowl.

Imperial Reissues: None

Availability: Common to moderately available

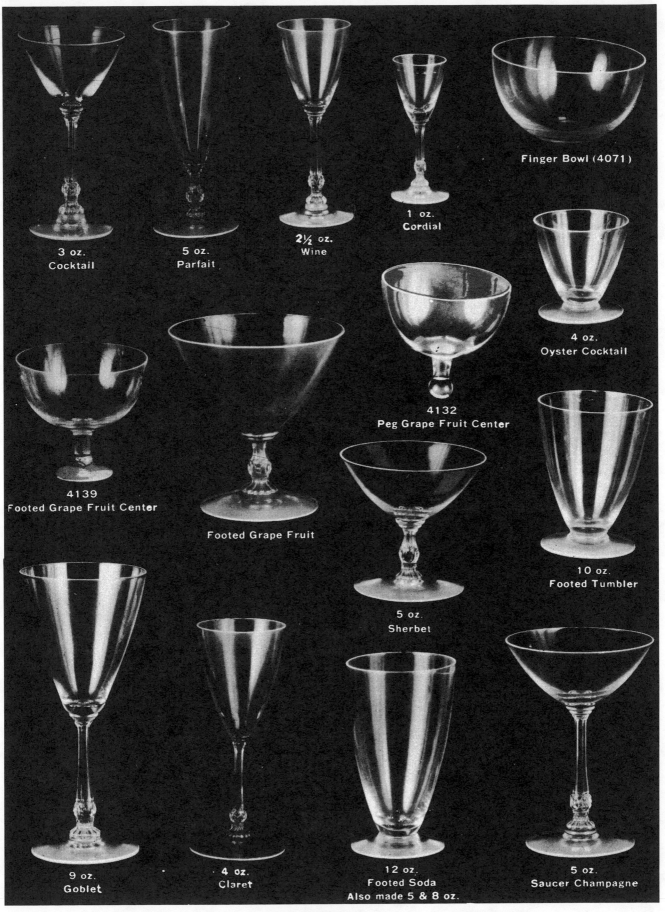

3 oz.
Cocktail

5 oz.
Parfait

2½ oz.
Wine

1 oz.
Cordial

Finger Bowl (4071)

4 oz.
Oyster Cocktail

4139
Footed Grape Fruit Center

Footed Grape Fruit

4132
Peg Grape Fruit Center

5 oz.
Sherbet

10 oz.
Footed Tumbler

9 oz.
Goblet

4 oz.
Claret

12 oz.
Footed Soda
Also made 5 & 8 oz.

5 oz.
Saucer Champagne

#3389 DUQUESNE pattern

#3390 CARCASSONNE - original Heisey Co. name

Dates: 1930-1941

Colors: Moongleam stem and foot, crystal bowl; flamingo; sahara; cobalt bowl, crystal stem and foot; alexandrite bowl, crystal stem and foot. Scarce in amber. Vase is known with a zircon bowl, crystal stem and foot. Rare in a combination of sahara and alexandrite

Optic: Wide optic

Decorations: Used for etchings and cuttings by Heisey. Some etchings were done by Lotus and possibly others. Occasionally seen with a stain applied to crystal glass—often a pale blue iridized stain. This was probably done by a lady in New England who did this type of decoration on Heisey blanks and other glass blanks.

Marked: Yes, on stem immediately below bowl.

Comments: A stem line of the popular shorter type made to give the housewife a choice of styles for her table. Even this shorter line had a tall stemmed goblet and a short stemmed goblet. The Heisey Co. seems to have preferred the tall, more elegant styles, but they marketed both types so the hostess could have the final choice. The footed bar is usually added to cordial collections by collectors. The morning after and the flagon are unusual pieces. The footed decanter is hard to find as is the vase. In at least one price list, flamingo and moongleam were listed as special order. This may explain why these two colors are more difficult to find in Carcassonne.

Imperial Reissues: None

Availability: Common to moderately available.

3 oz.
Oyster Cocktail

2½ oz.
Wine

2 oz.
Footed Bar

6 oz.
Sherbet

11 oz. Goblet
Short Stem

6 oz.
Saucer Champagne

4 oz.
Claret

3 oz.
Cocktail

12 oz.
Footed Soda or Ice Tea
Also made 5 & 8 oz.

11 oz. Goblet
Tall Stem

10½ oz.
Morning After

12 oz.
Flagon

#3390 CARCASSONNE pattern

Cigarette Holder

Footed Finger Bowl

8 in. Footed Vase

1 pt. Footed Decanter & No. 84 P/S

3 pt. Footed Jug

#3390 CARCASSONNE pattern

#3394 SAXONY - name given by researchers

Dates: 1932-1935
Colors: Sahara
Optic: Wide optic
Decorations: Used for a needle etching by Heisey. Has been seen with cuttings done by a decorating firm
Marked: No
Comments: At first glance this appears to be a variety of Carcassonne, but like so many other Heisey stems, the difference in bowl shape produces a different pattern. The stem also is different. Items are not easily found. The vase is an unusual item in the line.

Items listed in Saxony are:
12 oz. goblet, tall stem
12 oz. goblet, short stem
5½ oz. saucer champagne
5½ oz. sherbet
4 oz. oyster cocktail
3 oz. cocktail
2½ oz. wine
1 oz. cordial
5 oz. soda, ftd.
8 oz. soda, ftd.
12 oz. soda, ftd.
9″ vase, ftd
finger bowl (4074)

Imperial Reissues: None
Availability: Moderately available to scarce.

#3394 SAXONY tall goblet

#3397 GASCONY - original Heisey Co. name

Dates: 1932-1938. Floral bowl and mayonnaise were made until circa 1941.

Colors: Sahara; sahara bowl, crystal foot; tangerine bowl, crystal foot. Seen with crystal bowl, amber foot and crystal bowl with an unusual gray base. The 10″ bowl was made in cobalt. The wine and decanter in cobalt bowl, crystal foot. The decanter has been seen with crystal bowl, moongleam foot. The oval floral bowl is known in tangerine.

Optic: Wide optic—for stemware and floral bowl.

Decorations: Used for etchings and cuttings by Heisey. The 2-part mayonnaise was cut by Pairpoint in their "Boswell" gray cutting.

Marked: Yes, on underside of base. Many items are unmarked.

Comments: A low-footed stem line which was highly touted when it was new. The tomato juice set was advertised widely. Actually considering the nearness of the repeal of prohibition, this set was certainly made as a liquor set, but Heisey maintained propriety by calling it a tomato juice set. In fact, the designation of tomato juice pitcher remained in price lists even after it could have been renamed a martini pitcher. Note the saucer champagne which really looks like a sherbet. Note also the true sherbet which is the same as the finger bowl and fruit cocktail. The 10″ floral bowl was made both with and without a foot. Heisey also produced several pressed pieces to match this stem line and called them #3397 (even though this is a blown ware number.) The cream and sugar, oval floral bowl and candlestick (#138) were made in sahara. The candlestick was also made in moongleam and flamingo. Pressed items are usually marked with the Diamond H. See the MISCELLANEOUS Section for the two-compartment mayonnaise.

Imperial Reissues: None

Availability: Moderately available.

Cream

Sugar

Footed Oval Floral Bowl

5 in.
Candlestick (138)

10 in. Footed Floral Bowl
Also made without Foot

5 oz. Footed Soda
Tomato Juice or Claret

4 oz.
Oyster Cocktail

3 oz.
Cocktail

2½ oz.
Wine

6 oz. Sherbet
Fruit Cocktail or Finger Bowl

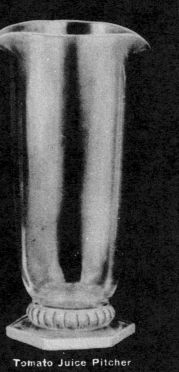

1 pt.
Footed Decanter & No. 88 P/S

Tomato Juice Pitcher
2 Lips

11 oz. Low Footed Goblet

10 oz.
Footed Tumbler

6 oz.
Saucer Champagne

12 oz. Footed Soda
Also made 10 14 & 18 oz

#3397 GASCONY pattern

#3404 SPANISH - original Heisey Co. name

Dates: 1933-1946

Colors: Sahara bowl, crystal stem; cobalt bowl, crystal stem; tangerine bowl, crystal stem. A few items are known in experimental light blue and crystal (both with crystal bowl and blue stem and with blue bowl and crystal stem). Very uncommon in amber. May have been made with cobalt stem, crystal bowl

Optic: Wide optic

Decorations: Used sparingly by Heisey for etchings. Used extensively for cuttings by Heisey, many of them quite elaborate. Also used for many special engravings by Heisey. Also cut by other decorating companies. Sometimes found with silver decor on cobalt in designs of lines and florals

Marked: Yes, on stem near base, just above lower rings

Comments: One of the most popular of the Heisey stemware patterns. Many people collect a setting in cobalt. Tangerine items range in color from a true tangerine to a deep red. Other colors are difficult to find. The line includes a tumbler, dinner bell and comport. This line had its own special "Spanish" adhesive label. When Emil Krall joined the Heisey Co. in 1932 or 1933, many of his new cuttings and engravings were developed for the Spanish stem. Florentine especially was designed to be a popularly-priced engraving simulating the old expensive copper-wheel engravings.

Look-Alikes: Duncan & Miller's Grenada stem line causes some confusion. Grenada has a faceted knop while Spanish has a puntied knop.

Imperial Reissues: None

Availability: Moderately available

3½ oz.
Cocktail

2½ oz.
Wine

1 oz.
Cordial

Finger Bowl (3335)

3½ oz.
Oyster Cocktail

12 oz.
Footed Soda

10 oz.
Footed Tumbler

5 oz.
Footed Soda

5½ oz.
Sherbet

10 oz.
Goblet

4 oz.
Claret

5½ oz.
Saucer Champagne

6 in.
Comport

#3404 SPANISH pattern

#3408, 3408½ JAMESTOWN - original Heisey Co. name

Dates: 1933-1957

Colors: Sahara. Goblet listed in moongleam, flamingo and cobalt. Mugs are found with colored handles.

Optic: Wide optic

Decorations: Used for many etchings and cuttings by Heisey. Also sold to many decorating companies as blanks.

Marked: Yes, on upper stem below swirled ball.

Comments: A common Heisey stem line, but colored items are very difficult to find. #3408½ items are footed sodas: a juice and an ice tea. Very similar to #3360 Penn Charter (bell-shaped bowl) and #3409 Plymouth (straight bowl.) Compare with these two lines. The goblet was the first piece of the line and was found listed in price lists before the other pieces. It was offered in moongleam, flamingo and cobalt. The remainder of the line was added later. An unusual item is the 9″ vase. Note that the sherry is from the #3360 Penn Charter line. Also note that the captions are reversed on the sherry and the wine. The mug is one of a series of beer mugs brought out in 1933. This mug is found with a variety of colored handles including moongleam, flamingo, tangerine, cobalt, sahara and amber. See BARWARE Section for illustrations of this mug and other beer mugs.

Imperial Reissues: None

Availability: Common

2 oz.
Wine

1½ oz.
Sherry (3360)

1 oz.
Cordial

Finger Bowl (3309)

9 oz.
Footed Tumbler

6 oz.
Sherbet

9 in.
Vase

12 oz. Beer Mug
Plain

3 oz.
Cocktail

9 oz.
Goblet

13 oz.
Footed Soda

4½ oz.
Claret

6 oz.
Saucer Champagne

#3408 JAMESTOWN pattern

#3409 PLYMOUTH - original Heisey Co. name

Dates: 1933-1937

Colors: Sahara; goblet known in cobalt

Optic: Wide optic

Decorations: Used for several etchings and at least one cutting by Heisey

Marked: Yes, on upper stem

Comments: This is the version of the Jamestown stem with the straight bowl. It is much more difficult to find than Jamestown. Compare with #3408 Jamestown and #3360 Penn Charter. The 12 oz. banquet goblet would be a magnificent piece of glass. No cordial seems to be listed with this pattern. Very difficult to find in colors.

Imperial Reissues: None

Availability: Scarce

5 oz.
Footed Soda

6 oz.
Sherbet

3 oz.
Oyster Cocktail

Finger Bowl (3335)

6 oz.
Saucer Champagne

3½ oz.
Cocktail

12 oz.
Banquet Goblet

10 oz.
Goblet

12 oz.
Footed Soda

5 oz.
Parfait

#3409 PLYMOUTH pattern

#3411 MONTE CRISTO - original Heisey Co. name

Dates: 1933-1941

Colors: Sahara listed in price lists

Optic: Wide optic

Decorations: Used extensively for both etchings and cuttings by Heisey. Often found with cuttings done by decorating companies.

Marked: No

Comments: A very popular stemware line. Compare with #3414 Marriette— the stem portion is the same while the bowl is different. Always note the footed sodas in these blownware patterns. See how difficult these would be to identify properly. Note that the oyster cocktail is the #3542 Hazelwood. The ball at the top of the stem has many raised dots, giving a thousand-eye effect to it.

Imperial Reissues: None

Availability: Common to moderately available.

3½ oz.
Cocktail

2½ oz.
Wine

1½ oz.
Sherry

1 oz.
Cordial

Finger Bowl (3309)

3 oz.
Oyster Cocktail (3542)

5 oz.
Footed Soda

7 in.
Comport

6 oz.
Sherbet

9 oz.
Goblet

4 oz.
Claret

6 oz.
Saucer Champagne

9 oz.
Footed Tumbler

12 oz.
Footed Soda

#3411 MONTE CRISTO pattern

#3414 MARRIETTE - original Heisey Co. name

Dates: 1933-1937

Colors: Crystal only

Optic: Wide optic

Decorations: Used for some cuttings and etchings by Heisey

Marked: No

Comments: The more difficult to find of the two similar stems, Monte Cristo and Marriette. Note that the sherries in the two patterns are the same. Note that the oyster cocktail is taken from the #3409 Plymouth pattern.

Imperial Reissues: None

Availability: Moderately available

1 oz.
Cordial

12 oz.
Footed Soda or Ice Tea
Also made 5 & 8 oz.

3 oz.
Oyster Cocktail (3409)

Finger Bowl (3335)

3½ oz.
Cocktail

6 oz.
Sherbet

10 oz.
Footed Tumbler

1½ oz. Sherry
Also made 3 oz.

10 oz.
Goblet

6 oz.
Saucer Champagne

3¾ oz.
Claret

2½ oz.
Wine

#3414 MARRIETTE pattern

#3416 BARBARA FRITCHIE - original Heisey Co. name

Dates: 1933-1939

Colors: Crystal only. Only the cordials are found with colored bowls

Optic: Wide optic

Decorations: Used for several etchings and cuttings by Heisey

Marked: Yes, on upper stem just below bowl.

Comments: The cordials are the only pieces of the pattern listed in colors. These were made in alexandrite, cobalt and sahara with crystal stems. Actually the cordials in colors are the size of the brandy pictured here and not the true cordial which has a taller bowl. Heisey price lists called them "cordials" however. Apparently the original cordial shown here was in the pattern for a very short time. Note the brandy snifter and the Rhine wine—both desirable pieces to the stem collector. The oyster cocktail and footed sodas originally were part of the #3409 Plymouth line. Compare the line with #4092 Kenilworth which has the same stem but a flared bowl.

Imperial Reissues: None

Availability: Moderately available to scarce

6 oz.
Saucer Champagne

¾ oz. Brandy
Tall Stem

1 oz. Cordial
Tall Stem

2½ oz.
Wine

3½ oz.
Cocktail

1½ oz. Sherry
Tall Stem

10 oz.
Footed Tumbler

18 oz.
Brandy Sniffer

6 oz.
Sherbet

Finger Bowl (3335)

3 oz.
Oyster Cocktail (3409)

10 oz.
Goblet

6 oz.
Rhine Wine

3¾ oz.
Claret

12 oz.
Footed Soda (3409)
Also made 5 oz.

10 oz. Goblet
Low Footed

#3416 BARBARA FRITCHIE pattern

#3418 SAVOY PLAZA - original Heisey Co. name

Dates: 1935-1937

Colors: Crystal only

Optic: Plain only

Decorations: Sometimes found with a satin finish (etched) stem and foot. Used for several Heisey cuttings.

Marked: Yes, on upper portion of stem near bowl.

Comments: An unusual square-footed and square-stemmed pattern line. It is difficult to find this pattern without some minor chipping on the stem. The entire pattern line is difficult to find since it was made for so short a time. Very attractive in its simplicity. Note that the bowl is straight. #3424 Admiralty is very similar but has a flared bowl.

Imperial Reissues: None

Availability: Scarce

1½ oz.
Sherry

3½ oz.
Oyster Cocktail

1 oz.
Cordial

Finger Bowl (4080)

3 oz.
Wine

6 oz.
Saucer Champagne

3½ oz.
Cocktail

10 oz.
Goblet

12 oz.
Footed Soda

5 oz.
Footed Soda

4 oz.
Claret

#3418 SAVOY PLAZA pattern

#3424 ADMIRALTY - original Heisey Co. name

Dates: 1936-1939; 1941-1943 for cuttings

Colors: Crystal only

Optic: Plain only

Decorations: Cut by Pairpoint with their "Comet" pattern, which is gray. Used for some cuttings by Heisey

Marked: Yes, on upper portion of stem near bowl

Comments: A square-footed and square-stemmed pattern line. It is hard to find these stems without some damage to the stem portion. Even though it was listed in price lists and catalogs for a longer period than Savoy Plaza, it is not much more readily available. Compare the illustrations with #3418 Savoy Plaza, which has a differently shaped bowl.

Imperial Reissues: None

Availability: Scarce

1 oz. Cordial   4½ oz. Oyster Cocktail   Finger Bowl (3309)

5 oz. Footed Soda   2 oz. Sherry   3 oz. Cocktail   2 oz. Wine

9 oz. Goblet   12 oz. Footed Soda   4½ oz. Claret   5½ oz. Saucer Champagne

#3424 ADMIRALTY pattern

#4044 NEW ERA - original Heisey Co. name

Dates: 1934-1941. Stems, celery and candlestick made again from 1944-1957
Colors: Cobalt bowl, crystal stem and foot in 1934. Candlestick known in alexandrite
Optic: Plain only
Decorations: Used for several Heisey cuttings, all very modern in appearance. Available with frosted decorations by Heisey. Found with Pairpoint "Greek Key" cutting. Pairpoint also cut their "Boswell" design (gray) on the celery and divided relish. Gold and silver decorations were done by Lotus in 1934 and possibly later.
Marked: STEMS: Yes, on wafer below bowl or on underside of foot. PRESSED WARE: Some items are marked, but most are not.
Comments: An unusual Art Deco pattern which was quite popular. The pattern number is from the stemware series of numbers, but it was used for the pressed ware as well. Several of the pieces, such as the celeries and relishes, were etched and cut by Heisey and added to cut patterns as accessory pieces. The rectangular shapes of the plates and the saucers make these quite unusual. The design was copied from a similar plate in pottery made by Jean Luce of Paris. Cup handles are also distinctive. The rye bottle was also made with a thinner style stopper than the one illustrated. Several of the pieces such as the cup, cream and sugar were used as part of the #2323 Navy line. See BARWARE Section for information on this pattern. Heisey originally called this their "Modern" line.
Patents: #92247 for goblet applied for 3/3/34 and granted 5/15/34. #92248 for plate applied for 3/3/34 and granted 5/15/34. Rodney C. Irwin listed as designer for both patents
Imperial Reissues: The 2-light candelabrum was made from 1958 to 1972 in crystal.
Availability: Common to moderately available

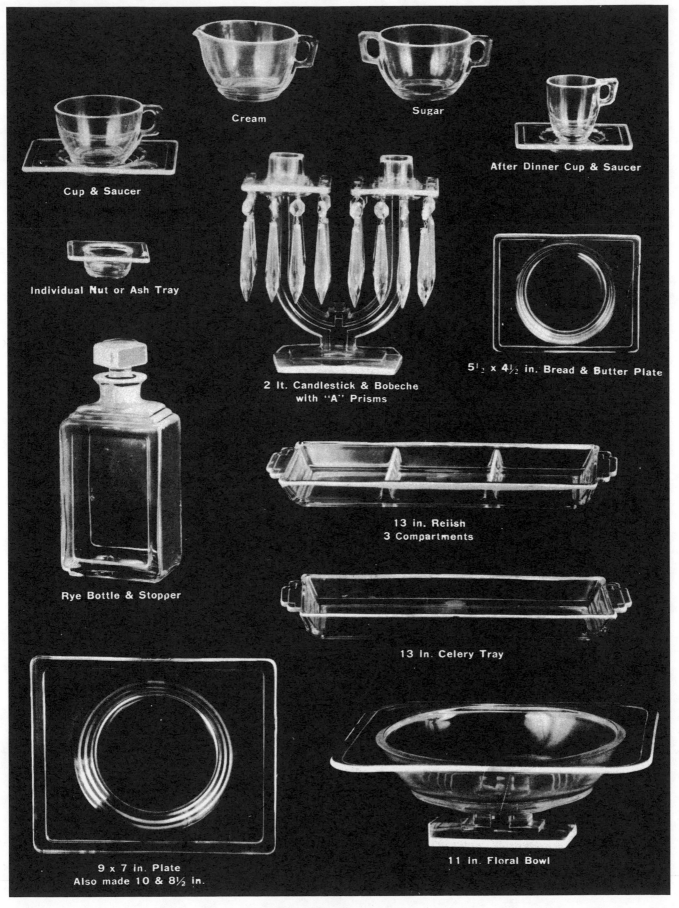

Cream

Sugar

Cup & Saucer

After Dinner Cup & Saucer

Individual Nut or Ash Tray

2 lt. Candlestick & Bobeche
with "A" Prisms

5½ x 4½ in. Bread & Butter Plate

Rye Bottle & Stopper

13 in. Reiish
3 Compartments

13 In. Celery Tray

9 x 7 in. Plate
Also made 10 & 8½ in.

11 in. Floral Bowl

#4044 NEW ERA pattern

#4054 CORONATION - original Heisey Co. name

Dates: 1935-1957

Colors: Zircon. Very few pieces are known in screen optic in dawn and limelight from circa 1955.

Optic: Usually plain. Saturn optic listed in 1937-1938. Very scarce in screen optic.

Decorations: Used for some etchings and cuttings by Heisey. Several pieces are known with special cuttings.

Marked: No

Comments: A bar line of various sizes of sodas, martini mixer, jugs and an ice tub. The footed cocktail and the tall slim jims are unusual. Most bar items were available with ½ sham but sometimes with full or double shams. Other items listed but not shown include an 8″ vase, 30 oz. small ice tankard and 10 oz. tumbler. A basket is known (probably as a whimsey and not a production item). Items are difficult to find in colors. Zircon in plain and saturn optic was listed in 1937. A flamingo item has been reported but has not been verified.

Patents: #119856 for soda applied for 2/7/40 and granted 4/9/40. T. Clarence Heisey listed as designer

Imperial Reissues: Yes. In 1982 the ice bucket was made and sold as a vase (5¾″) in "spike" optic in plum, ultra blue, sunshine yellow and crystal. They also made a 7″ vase from the cocktail shaker with "three swirl optic" (narrow optic) in the same colors. Neither item is marked.

Availability: Common

2 ½ oz. Bar
Half Sham
Also made 1 oz.

3 oz. Cocktail
Half Sham

4 oz. Cocktail Ftd.

8 oz. Old Fashion
Half Sham

11 oz. Hot Toddy
Half Sham

30 oz. Martini Mixer

14 oz. Slim Jim
Half Sham
Also made 12 oz.

8 oz. Soda
Half Sham
Also made 5, 10 & 13 oz.

28 oz. Cocktail Shaker,
No. 1 Strainer &
No. 86 P/S

½ gal. Jug

½ gal. Ice Tankard

#4054 CORONATION pattern

#4055 PARK LANE - original Heisey Co. name

Dates: 1935-1941

Colors: Crystal only

Optic: Plain only

Decorations: Used for many Heisey cuttings. Also used for "Coburn" cutting by Pairpoint.

Marked: No

Comments: An attractive stemline which was used for many desirable Heisey cuttings. It is not too easy to find since its life span of 6 years is not long. Many of the cuttings were not available for that long. The knobs at the ends of the "barbell" portion of the stems are decorated with a fine-cut motif.

Imperial Reissues: None

Availability: Moderately available to scarce

1 1/2 oz.
Sherry

2 1/2 oz.
Wine

1 oz.
Cordial

3 oz.
Cocktail

3 oz.
Oyster Cocktail

Finger Bowl (4080)

6 oz.
Sherbet

6 oz.
Saucer Champagne

10 oz.
Goblet

4 oz.
Claret

13 oz.
Footed Soda

5 oz.
Footed Soda
Also made 9 oz.

#4055 PARK LANE pattern

#4090 COVENTRY - original Heisey Co. name

Dates: 1937-1944; cordial and sherry until 1947

Colors: Zircon (discontinued by 1938)

Optic: Plain in crystal; Saturn optic in zircon

Decorations: Used for several Heisey cuttings. The sherry and cordial were offered with #507 Orchid etching.

Marked: No

Comments: This stem line is difficult to find and is especially hard to find in zircon. The Heisey Co. apparently experimented with this stem. Several goblets have been found with the bowl shapes all being different. At least 4 or 5 variant shapes have been seen to date.

Imperial Reissues: None

Availability: Moderately available to scarce

10 oz. Goblet

10 oz. Goblet
Low Foot

6 oz.
Sherbet

6 oz.
Saucer Champagne

4½ oz.
Claret

3 oz.
Cocktail

4½ oz.
Oyster Cocktail

2 oz.
Sherry

2½ oz.
Wine

1 oz.
Cordial

¾ oz.
Brandy

12 oz.
Ftd. Soda
Also made 5 oz.

Finger Bowl (4080)

#4090 COVENTRY pattern

#4091, 4091½ KIMBERLY - original Heisey Co. name

Dates: 1937-1957. Probably discontinued for 3+ years during World War II.

Colors: Zircon bowl, crystal stem and foot (for a very short period of time.)

Optic: Plain; saturn optic in zircon

Decorations: Used for many Heisey cuttings, especially the very popular Dolly Madison Rose.

Comments: A stem line making effective use of the diamond motif at the lower portion of its stem. Compare with #4085 Kohinoor. Again, the bowl shape is the major difference. Kohinoor has a perfectly straight bowl while Kimberly has a flared bowl. #4091½ items are matching footed sodas. The oyster cocktail was originally the #3542 Hazelwood. When found with cuttings, the stem and the knop are sometimes cut and polished.

Imperial Reissues: None

Availability: Moderately available

10 oz.
Goblet

10 oz.
Goblet Low Foot

5 ½ oz.
Saucer Champagne

4 ½ oz.
Claret

3 oz.
Cocktail

2 oz.
Wine

1 oz.
Cordial

4 ½ oz.
Oyster Cocktail (3542)

5 ½ oz.
Sherbet

Finger Bowl (3335)

4091 ½—12 oz.
Ftd. Soda
Also made 5 oz.

#4091 KIMBERLY pattern

#4092, 4092½ KENILWORTH - original Heisey Co. name

Dates: 1937-1941; bell made until 1944

Colors: Crystal only

Optic: Wide optic

Decorations: Used for some Heisey etchings and cuttings

Marked: Yes, on upper portion of stem beneath bowl

Comments: Very much like the #3416 Barbara Fritchie pattern—the bowl on Barbara Fritchie being straight while the bowl on Kenilworth is flared. Note that the brandy snifter, the Rhine wine, the cordial, the brandy and the sherry are all the same as the Barbara Fritchie pattern. This is not unusual in Heisey. Often items did double, triple or more duty in several pattern lines. Note the small comport which is unusual. The #4092½ items are footed sodas matching the remainder of the line.

Imperial Reissues: None

Availability: Scarce

10 oz.
Goblet

5 1/2 oz.
Saucer Champagne

3 oz.
Cocktail

4 1/2 oz.
Claret

3 oz.
Oyster Cocktail

Brandy Sniffer

6 oz.
Rhine Wine

1 oz. Cordial
Tall Stem

3/4 oz. Brandy
Tall Stem

1 1/2 oz. Sherry
Tall Stem

2 oz.
Wine

5 1/2 in.
Comport

4092 1/2—5 oz.
Ftd. Soda
Also made 12 oz.

5 1/2 oz.
Sherbet

Finger Bowl 3335

#4092 KENILWORTH pattern

#1108, 1108½ PENELOPE - name given by researchers

Dates: #1108: 1897-1938; #1108½: ca. 1917-1938
Colors: Crystal only
Marked: Yes
Comments: #1108 refers to the saucer footed version of this egg cup while #1108½ refers to the flat footed style.

#1229 BARNUM - name given by researchers

Dates: 1909-1938
Colors: Crystal only
Marked: Unknown

#394 NARROW FLUTE - original Heisey Co. description of pattern

Dates: 1909-1944
Colors: Crystal only
Marked: Probably

#1228 RINGLING - name given by researchers

Dates: 1909- ca. 1945
Colors: Crystal only
Marked: Yes, on side of bowl

#337 TOURAINE - original Heisey Co. name

Dates: 1902-1938
Colors: Crystal; an amberina shade of tangerine (very scarce)
Marked: Yes, on side of stem near foot
Comments: In 1902, the pattern consisted of many pressed tableware items including a table set, toothpick, nappies, etc. plus a full line of stemware. Very little survived beyond a few years.

#1114 ARCADE - name given by researchers

Dates: 1897-1938; Sherbet only from 1935-1944+
Colors: Crystal only
Marked: Yes
Comments: The sherbet is not shown, but is listed in price lists.

#820 FIFTH AVENUE - original Heisey Co. description

Dates: Ca. 1929- ca. 1945
Colors: Crystal only
Marked: Unknown

#414 TUDOR - original Heisey Co. name

Dates: Ca. 1925
Colors: Crystal only
Marked: Yes, on top of stem near bowl
Comments: Various stems were found in the Tudor patterns (#411, 412, 413 and 414). Care must be used when determining which pattern is being discussed. See PATTERN Section for other Tudor items.

#1464 DRAPE - name given by researchers

Dates: 1935
Colors: Crystal only
Marked: No

#1437 FLINT RIDGE - name by researchers

Dates: 1935-1937
Colors: Crystal, cobalt
Marked: Unknown

#811¾ HOFFMAN HOUSE - original Heisey Co. name

Dates: Ca. 1897-1937
Colors: Crystal, moongleam, flamingo, sahara
Marked: Yes
Comments: When first made, the Hoffman House line was extensive. Gradually it was reduced so that only this goblet or schooner as it was sometimes called, existed in the color period. It is sometimes found with several of the desirable Heisey silhouette etchings—usually sports motifs. It is scarce in colors.

No 1108—5 oz.
Saucer Footed Egg Cup

No. 1229
5½ oz. Egg Cup

No. 1108½
5 oz. Egg Cup

No. 394
Boston Egg Cup

No. 1228
4½ oz. Egg Cup

No. 337
Egg Cup

No. 1114—7 oz. High Ball
Plain or Optic

No 820
10 oz. Goblet

No. 414
8 oz. Goblet

No. 1464
Goblet

No. 1437
10 oz. Goblet

No. 811¾
17 oz. Goblet

Miscellaneous stemware

#4139, 4132

Dates: #4139: 1935-1944. #4132: 1919-1944
Colors: Crystal only known
Marked: No, these are blown and cannot be marked
Comments: These two grapefruit centers were used in conjunction with those stem lines which contained grapefruits. They were meant to be used to hold the fruit while ice was placed in the actual grapefruit.

#4052 NATIONAL - original Heisey Co. name

Dates: 1935-1957. Sodas began in 1938.
Colors: Crystal only.
Marked: No. Items are blown with a pulled stem and cannot be marked.
Optics: Usually found plain although the goblet is shown here with medium optic which was discontinued by 1938.
Comments: A standard stem line for Heisey after this time. It was expanded to include other items. Sometimes pieces are found with special etchings: i.e. Fred Harvey crests, ULC crest, and others.

#4049 OLD FITZ - name given by researchers

Dates: 1934-1943
Colors: Crystal. Amber for Fred Harvey (See discussion in HARVEY AMBER ITEMS Section for more information.)
Marked: Yes, on upper stem near bowl

#3800, 3801 TEXAS PINK - name given by researchers

Dates: #3800: 1917-1937. #3801: 1917-1943
Colors: #3800 crystal only. #3801 crystal and amber for Fred Harvey
Marked: No. Items are blown with pulled stems and cannot be marked
Optics: Plain or diamond optic
Comments: These two grapefruits or comports are the same except for the height of the stem. #3800 is high footed while #3081 is low footed.

Miscellaneous stemware

Ashtrays

As with most other items made throughout the color period, ashtrays suddenly bloomed with color. Many new designs were brought out and many old ones began to appear in the new colors. Most of the Heisey ashtrays are marked with the Diamond H, but many have not been seen with the mark. Often the bottoms are ground and polished and the finishing is fine. On items like the #355, #439, #440 and #364, the entire bottom is ground and polished leaving a glistening surface.

Usually the ashtrays are not found with decorations, but some of them are occasionally found with cuttings or stains. The #439 has been seen cut and signed "Hawkes"; the #1186 individual is often seen cut and monogrammed. This was probably done by Heisey and also by decorating companies. The #1187 ash receiver has been seen with an amber stain and sterling silver decoration. The #1401 Empress ashtray was cut with several different cuttings by Heisey and also used for special engravings. The #361 ashtray and cigarette container has been seen with silver overlay. The #1180 has been seen with enameled decoration. Of course, many other variations could be found, especially if the ashtrays were sold to decorating firms.

See also the PATTERN SECTION for ashtrays in specific patterns such as #1469 Ridgeleigh, #1483 Stanhope, #1488 Kohinoor and others.

Information about the introduction dates and color availability is often fragmentary about ashtrays, so this data should be viewed with caution.

#356 WHITE OWL - name given by researchers
Dates: 1917-1938
Colors: Crystal only
Marked: Yes

#357 DUCK - collectors' popular name
Dates: Ca. 1928-1933
Colors: Crystal, moongleam, flamingo, marigold.
Marked: Yes

#358 SOLITAIRE - name given by researchers
Dates: Ca. 1928-1938
Colors: Crystal, moongleam, flamingo, marigold, sahara
Marked: Not usually

#359 CHESTERFIELD - name given by researchers
Dates: Ca. 1928- ca. 1945
Colors: Crystal, moongleam, flamingo
Marked: Yes

#360 WINSTON - name given by researchers
Dates: Ca. 1928-1939
Colors: Crystal, moongleam, flamingo
Marked: Yes, on top of the match holder

#363 WINGS - name given by researchers
Dates: Ca. 1928-1933
Colors: Crystal, moongleam, flamingo, marigold
Marked: No

#361 IRWIN - name given by researchers
Dates: 1928-1935
Colors: Crystal, moongleam, flamingo, marigold, sahara
Marked: Yes
Comments: Patent #77602 applied for 11/19/28 and granted 1/29/29. Rodney C. Irwin listed as designer.

#365 RHOMBIC - name given by researchers
Dates: Ca. 1928-1944
Colors: Crystal, moongleam, flamingo
Marked: No
Comments: Usually has a full ground and polished bottom

#366 SALEM - name given by researchers
Dates: Ca. 1928-1939
Colors: Crystal, moongleam, flamingo
Marked: Unknown

#439 FATIMA - name given by researchers
Dates: 1923-1937
Colors: Crystal, moongleam
Marked: No
Comments: Usually has a full ground and polished bottom

#440 FACET - name given by researchers
Dates: Ca. 1923-1933
Colors: Crystal
Marked: Sometimes

#442 MALTESE CROSS - name given by researchers
Dates: 1927-1938
Colors: Crystal, moongleam, flamingo
Marked: Yes

#600 OLD GOLD - name given by researchers
Dates: Ca. 1927-1945
Colors: Crystal. An example has been seen in purple
Marked: Yes

#1179 BOW TIE - collectors' popular name
Dates: Ca. 1927-1933
Colors: Crystal, moongleam, flamingo
Marked: No

#1180 TREFOIL - name given by researchers
Dates: 1924+
Colors: Crystal, moongleam, flamingo
Marked: Some are marked on the stem

#1186 YEOMAN - original Heisey Co. name

Dates: Ca. 1927-1944
Colors: Crystal, moongleam, flamingo, sahara, hawthorne, amber
Marked: Not usually
Comments: There are look-alikes made by other companies, including Cambridge. The Heisey ashtray should be fully ground and polished on the bottom. This tray was used for promotional advertising when Wilson Heisey was running as a candidate for director of the national Chamber of Commerce and examples of this ashtray are sometimes found with the legend "Heisey for Director" in the bottom. See also #1286 and #1386.

#1187 YEOMAN - original Heisey Co. name

Dates: Ca. 1927-1933
Colors: Crystal, moongleam
Marked: Yes
Comments: This is a two piece combination ash receiver.

#1200 YEOMAN - original Heisey Co. name

Dates: Ca. 1927-1933
Colors: Crystal, moongleam, flamingo, hawthorne, marigold
Marked: No
Comments: This was sold as part of the #1184 Yeoman bridge smoking set which consists of a handled tray and 8 individual ashtrays. (See PATTERN Section for an illustration of the set.)

#1286 CUPID & PSYCHE

Dates: 1927-1933
Colors: Crystal, moongleam, flamingo
Marked: No
Comments: The design is molded into the base of the #1186 individual ashtray and then is frosted (etched). Grinding and polishing the bottom results in just the design being frosted.

#1386 IRISH SETTER

Dates: 1927-1933
Colors: Crystal, moongleam, flamingo
Marked: No
Comments: Made in the same manner as #1236. (See above)

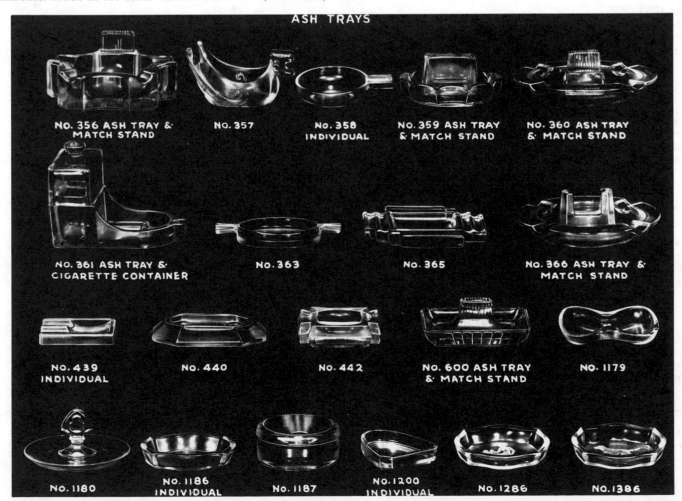

ASH TRAYS

NO. 356 ASH TRAY & MATCH STAND
NO. 357
NO. 358 INDIVIDUAL
NO. 359 ASH TRAY & MATCH STAND
NO. 360 ASH TRAY & MATCH STAND

NO. 361 ASH TRAY & CIGARETTE CONTAINER
NO. 363
NO. 365
NO. 366 ASH TRAY & MATCH STAND

NO. 439 INDIVIDUAL
NO. 440
NO. 442
NO. 600 ASH TRAY & MATCH STAND
NO. 1179

NO. 1180
NO. 1186 INDIVIDUAL
NO. 1187
NO. 1200 INDIVIDUAL
NO. 1286
NO. 1386

See previous entries in this section for: #358, #439, #1186, #356, #365, #366, #359, #360 and #600 ashtrays.

#1454 DIAMOND POINT - name given by researchers

Dates: 1935-1944+
Colors: Crystal only
Marked: Yes
Comments: Often seen with a tiny plate and sold as a set. Actually the small plate is an individual jelly according to Heisey price lists. See MISCELLANEOUS Section for illustration. Also made in a top hat match holder.

#4044 NEW ERA - original Heisey Co. name

Dates: 1934-1941
Colors: Crystal only
Marked: No
Comments: See STEMWARE Section for remainder of pattern.

#355 QUATOR - name given by researchers

Dates: Ca. 1906-1938
Colors: Crystal, experimental light blue
Marked: Yes
Comments: This became the #1435 ashtray which was widely used for cuttings and etchings by Heisey in later years. #1435 has a plain bottom rather than a star bottom. #355 should be ground and polished on the bottom while #1435 is only fire polished. See PATTERN Section for other items in the pattern.

#1425 VICTORIAN - original Heisey Co. name

Dates: 1933-1953
Colors: Crystal, sahara, cobalt
Marked: Yes
Comments: See PATTERN Section for remainder of pattern.

#1424 LUCKY STRIKE - name given by researchers

Dates: 1933-1938
Colors: Crystal only
Marked: No
Comments: There is a look-alike made by Fostoria. The Fostoria ashtray sometimes has a star or other pressed design in the bottom. The Heisey one is plain. Heisey also made a cigarette box in this pattern. (Illustration not available)

#1404 OLD SANDWICH - original Heisey Co. name

Dates: 1931+
Colors: Crystal, moongleam, flamingo, sahara, cobalt
Marked: Yes
Comments: Crystal and cobalt items are relatively easy to find, sahara is somewhat more difficult. Flamingo and moongleam items are difficult to find. Heisey price lists always called this item an ashtray, even though many people today call it a butter pat or a salt dip. Both of these names are incorrect.

#1184 YEOMAN - original Heisey Co. name

Dates: Ca. 1919+
Colors: Crystal, moongleam, flamingo, sahara
Marked: Unknown
Comments: See PATTERN Section for remainder of pattern.

#1401 EMPRESS - original Heisey Co. name

Dates: 1930-1938
Colors: Crystal, moongleam, flamingo, sahara, cobalt, alexandrite
Marked: Yes
Comments: Sometimes found with cuttings, occasionally elaborate ones. See PATTERN Section for remainder of pattern.

#353 MEDIUM FLAT PANEL - name given by researchers

Dates: 1909-1935+
Colors: Crystal, flamingo
Marked: Yes, on top of match holder

No. 358
Individual Ash Tray

No. 1454
Individual Ash Tray

No. 4044
Individual Ash Tray or Nut

No. 355
Individual Ash Tray

No. 1425
Individual Cigarette
Holder & Ash Tray

No. 1424
Bridge Ash Tray

No. 1404
Individual Ash Tray F/P

No. 439
Individual Cigarette
Ash Tray (Cut)

No. 1184
Cigarette Box Ash Tray & Cover

No. 1401
Ash Tray

No. 353
Match Stand Ash Tray

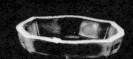
No. 1186
Individual Ash Tray

No. 1469
4 In. Ash Tray F/P

No. 1469
Square Ash Tray

No. 1469
Oval Cigarette Holder
& Ash Tray
2 Compartments

No. 1469
Round Ash Tray

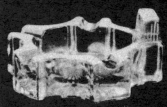
No. 356
Match Stand Ash Tray

No. 365
Ash Tray

No. 366
Match Stand Ash Tray
(Bk. Match)

No. 359
Match Stand Ash Tray
(Bk. Match)

No. 360
Match Stand Ash Tray
(Bk. Match)

No. 1201
Match Stand Ash Tray

No. 364
Square Ash Tray

No 600
Match Stand Ash Tray

Ash trays

#1469½ RIDGELEIGH - original Heisey Co. name

Dates: 1935-1944
Colors: Crystal only
Marked: Yes
Comments: See PATTERN Section for remainder of pattern.

#1469 RIDGELEIGH - original HEISEY Co. name

Dates: 1935-1944
Colors: Crystal only
Marked: Yes
Comments: See PATTERN Section for remainder of pattern.

#1469¼ RIDGELEIGH - original Heisey Co. name

Dates: 1935-1944
Colors: Crystal only
Marked: Yes
Comments: This is a two-piece combination. The small cigarette holder is a separate piece, fitting into one of the compartments in the ashtray. See PATTERN Section for remainder of pattern.

#1469 RIDGELEIGH - original Heisey Co. name

Dates: 1935-1944
Colors: Crystal, sahara and zircon
Marked: Yes
Comments: Note that the captions for the round and square ashtrays are reversed. See PATTERN Section for remainder of pattern. Imperial made this ashtray in heather and charcoal marked with the Diamond H.

#1201 PHILIP MORRIS - name given by researchers

Dates: Ca. 1933-1938
Colors: Crystal, moongleam, flamingo, experimental light blue
Marked: Yes, in center of match holder

#364 PEDESTAL - name given by researchers

Dates: 1930-1938
Colors: Crystal, moongleam, flamingo
Marked: Yes

#441 GRAPE LEAF SQUARE - name given by researchers

Dates: 1927-1933
Colors: Crystal, moongleam, flamingo, hawthorne
Marked: No
Comments: This was Heisey's attempt to make a glass similar to Lalique according to Paul Fairall who was in charge of shipping and selling out remaining stock after Heisey closed. In fact, Lalique did make a glass item almost like this piece. The Heisey item is frosted with highlights polished clear. The bottom is ground and polished.

#441 GRAPE LEAF SQUARE ashtray

Barware

Barware comprised an important area of sales for the Heisey Company, especially after the repeal of Prohibition in 1933. The company marketed full stemware lines (including various sizes of liquor glasses) and a few decanters throughout the Prohibition era, but the quantities and styles of these items were greatly expanded after repeal. For a more indepth discussion of this period, see the chapter on Prohibition and Changing Glassware Styles in the text portion of the book.

Blown decanters were made in various sizes and styles in almost all of the Heisey colors. While some were made only in crystal, others like the #4027 Christos came in a wide array of colors and combinations of crystal and colors. Some decanters were used for cuttings and etchings and these are quite desirable.

Beer mugs also were made in various styles and colors. Again, these were often decorated—usually with some of the sports motif silhouette etchings which were very popular items in Heisey's line.

Various sodas and tumblers are also included in this section since much of their sales appeal was for use as sets with different decanters or jugs. Most of these sodas and tumblers are not marked since they are blown. Many are difficult to identify as Heisey since they are of standard shapes made by many glass companies.

Other pieces which would fall in this category are found in the PATTERN Section (particularly #1404 Old Sandwich, #1405 Ipswich and #1425 Victorian) and in the MISCELLANEOUS Section, which contains the #417 Double Rib & Panel cocktail carafe, #367 Prism Band decanter, #1115 Bradbury bitters, #4163 Whaley pretzel jar, #3417 Adkins bitters, and #4225 Cobel cocktail shaker.

Decanters

#4026 SPENCER - name given by researchers

Dates: 1924-1939
Colors: Crystal, moongleam, flamingo. Also crystal bottle with colored stoppers
Marked: No

#2401 OAKWOOD - name given by researchers

Dates: 1917-1939
Colors: Crystal only
Marked: No. See a later page in this section for the matching sodas

#3417 ADKINS - name given by researchers

Dates: 1934-1939
Colors: Crystal only
Marked: No
Comments: See matching soda later in this section. See MISCELLANEOUS Section for bitters bottle.

#3397 GASCONY - original Heisey Co. name

Dates: 1932-1937
Colors: Crystal; sahara; cobalt with crystal foot & stopper; tangerine with crystal foot & stopper; crystal with moongleam foot & stopper
Marked: May be on base
Comments: See STEMWARE Section for remainder of pattern.

#4027 CHRISTOS - name given by researchers

Dates: 1925-1944
Colors: Crystal; crystal with moongleam foot & stopper; flamingo; crystal with flamingo foot & stopper; sahara; alexandrite; cobalt with crystal foot and stopper
Marked: No
Comments: Sometimes found with cuttings and silver decorations added by other companies. Usually made diamond optic, but sometimes made plain

#3390 CARCASSONNE - original Heisey Co. name

Dates: 1930-1941
Colors: Crystal; crystal with moongleam foot & stopper; flamingo; sahara; alexandrite with crystal foot & stopper; cobalt with crystal foot & stopper
Marked: No
Comments: See STEMWARE Section for remainder of pattern.

#4036 MARSHALL - name given by researchers

Dates: 1935-1946
Colors: Crystal only
Marked: No
Comments: Made later without a foot as #4036½. The #101 pressed stopper was designed for this bottle by Walter Von Nessen to complement the bottle shape. Prior to this it was sold with a faceted, pointed stopper. Used for some Heisey cuttings.

#4033 MALONEY - name given by researchers

Dates: 1935-1938
Colors: Crystal only
Marked: No
Comments: Used for several liquor carvings by Heisey: "Scotch", "Rye", and others.

#4035 BETHEL - name given by researchers

Dates: 1935-1953
Colors: Crystal only
Marked: No
Comments: Used by Heisey for some cuttings, etchings and carvings. Also cut by other companies. Sometimes found with silver overlay. Compare with #4037 shown earlier.

#4028 ROBINSON - name given by researchers

Dates: 1925-1944; bitters bottle from 1947-1955
Colors: Crystal, moongleam, flamingo
Marked: No
Comments: Available with #48 or #81 stoppers.

#4040 RYAN - name given by researchers

Dates: 1936-1938
Colors: Crystal only
Marked: No
Comments: Made in 1½ oz. and 2 oz. sizes either plain or with cut flutes.

#4038 DE KUYPEUR - name given by researchers

Dates: 1936-1937
Colors: Crystal only
Marked: No

#4039 MARTIN - name given by researchers

Dates: 1936-1939
Colors: Crystal only
Marked: No
Comments: Used for several Heisey cuttings.

#4037 CLARENCE - name given by researchers

Dates: 1936-1938
Colors: Crystal only
Marked: No
Comments: Used for several Heisey cuttings.

#4224 STEEPLECHASE - name given by researchers

Dates: 1931-1935
Colors: Moongleam, flamingo, sahara—usually in combination with crystal
Marked: No
Comments: Although it was not listed in all crystal in price lists, a crystal cocktail has been seen. This is a pattern with the foot usually etched (or frosted) giving the piece a Lalique style. A trade journal account stated: ". . . As a matter of fact, the cocktail itself, when inverted, would serve as an English egg cup. This base part is treated with a matt finish in the Lalique style and is quite effective."

#4224 STEEPLECHASE 3 oz. cocktail, cocktail shaker

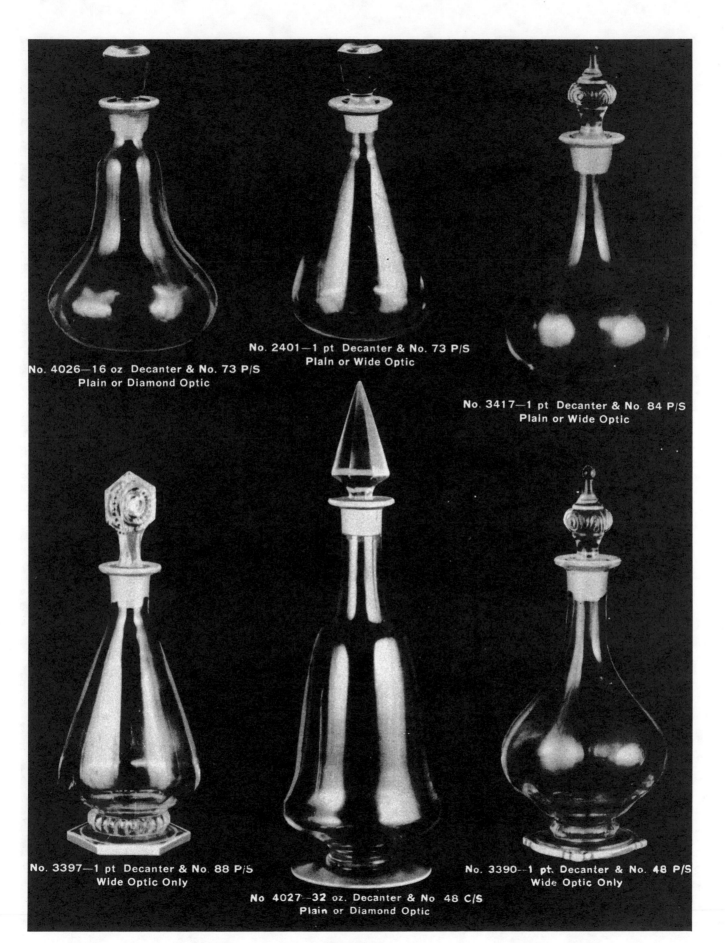

No. 4026—16 oz. Decanter & No. 73 P/S
Plain or Diamond Optic

No. 2401—1 pt. Decanter & No. 73 P/S
Plain or Wide Optic

No. 3417—1 pt. Decanter & No. 84 P/S
Plain or Wide Optic

No. 3397—1 pt. Decanter & No. 88 P/S
Wide Optic Only

No. 4027—32 oz. Decanter & No. 48 C/S
Plain or Diamond Optic

No. 3390—1 pt. Decanter & No. 48 P/S
Wide Optic Only

Decanters

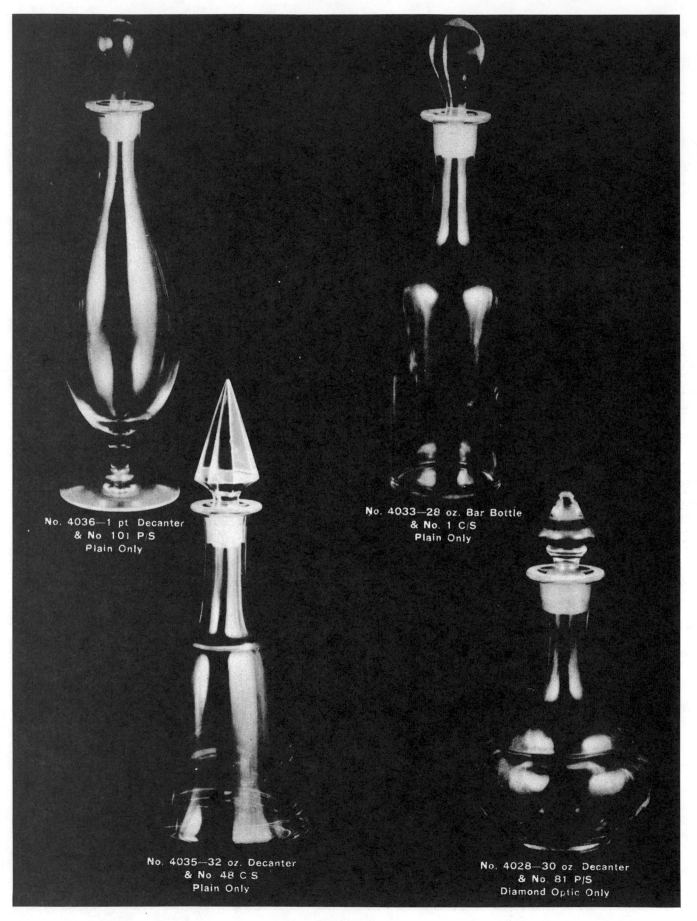

No. 4036—1 pt Decanter
& No 101 P/S
Plain Only

No. 4033—28 oz. Bar Bottle
& No. 1 C/S
Plain Only

No. 4035—32 oz. Decanter
& No. 48 C/S
Plain Only

No. 4028—30 oz Decanter
& No. 81 P/S
Diamond Optic Only

Decanters

No. 4040—2 oz.
Individual Decanter
Plain Only
Also made 1½ oz.

No. 4038
Cordial Bottle & No. 73 P/S
Plain Only

No. 4039—9 oz.
Decanter & No. 10 P/S
Wide Optic Only

No. 4037—32 oz.
Decanter & No. 2 C/S
Plain Only

Decanters

Beer Mugs
See Color Plate for many mugs in colors.

#1426 CLOVER ROPE - name given by researchers

Dates: 1933-1935
Colors: Crystal, sahara, cobalt
Marked: Yes

#1434 TOM & JERRY - original Heisey Co. description

Dates: 1933-1935
Colors: Crystal, sahara
Marked: Yes
Comments: Note the similarity of the handle to the handles of #1401 Empress pieces.

#3405 COYLE - name given by researchers

Dates: 1933-1937
Colors: Crystal, moongleam, flamingo, sahara, alexandrite, tangerine
Marked: No
Comments: Made in 12 oz. size. Colors are usually in combination with crystal.

#3406 THRAN - name given by researchers

Dates: 1933-1937
Colors: Crystal, moongleam, flamingo, sahara, alexandrite, tangerine, cobalt
Marked: No
Comments: Made in 12 oz. size. Colors are usually in combination with crystal.

#3407 OVERDORF - name given by researchers

Dates: 1933-1937
Colors: Crystal, moongleam, flamingo, sahara, cobalt, tangerine
Marked: No
Comments: Made in 16 oz. size. In cobalt, this mug has been seen with a cobalt body, crystal handle and with cobalt handle, crystal body. Again, colors are usually in combination with crystal. Two handle styles are also known.

NOTE: Much as it might be unbelievable to today's collectors, a notation in an old Heisey price list says that mugs with colored handles were priced the same as crystal mugs!

#3476 TEMPLE - name given by researchers

Dates: 1919-1937
Colors: Crystal only
Marked: No. It has a blown bowl with an applied foot and cannot be marked
Comments: Made plain and wide optic. Also made with and without handle. It is similar in shape to ice teas made by other companies, especially Fostoria. Heisey used the soda for many of their etchings and some cuttings.

#2516 CIRCLE PAIR - name given by researchers

Dates: 1924-1937
Colors: Crystal, moongleam, flamingo
Marked: No. It has a blown bowl with a pulled stem and cannot be marked
Comments: While sodas are sometimes found in marigold, it is unknown whether the ice tea or goblet were made in this color. See sections on VASES , JUGS and STEMWARE for matching items.

#3408 JAMESTOWN - original Heisey Co. name

Dates: 1933-1946; 1948-1953 in crystal
Colors: Crystal bowl with colored handles: moongleam, flamingo, sahara, cobalt, tangerine, amber
Marked: No
Comments: Used for some etchings by the Heisey Co. See STEMWARE Section for remainder of pattern.

#4163 WHALEY - name given by researchers

Dates: 1933-1944
Colors: Crystal bowl with colored handles: Moongleam, flamingo, sahara, cobalt, red
Marked: Yes
Comments: Frequently found with the silhouette sports etchings by Heisey. See JUGS Section and MISCELLANEOUS Section for pretzel jar. Made in 12 oz. and 16 oz. sizes.

#3386 DIAMOND ROSE - name given by researchers

Dates: 1933-1944. Only the 12 oz. was made after 1938.
Colors: Crystal; cobalt bowl, crystal stem & foot; sahara
Marked: Yes, on stem just below bowl.
Comments: Made in 8 oz., 10 oz. and 12 oz sizes. See STEMWARE Section for discussion of the pattern.

#4044 NEW ERA - original Heisey Co. name

Dates: 1934-1944; 1947-1955
Colors: Crystal; crystal foot, cobalt bowl
Marked: No
Comments: Made in 8 oz., 10 oz., and 12 oz. sizes. Occasionally found with Tally Ho silhouette etching. See STEMWARE Section for remainder of pattern.

#3420 MILWAUKEE - name given by researchers

Dates: 1933-1944
Colors: Crystal only
Marked: No
Comments: Made in 8 oz., 10 oz. and 12 oz. sizes.

#3304 UNIVERSAL - original Heisey Co. name

Dates: 1935-1944
Colors: Crystal only
Marked: No
Comments: See STEMWARE Section for remainder of pattern.

#1426 Clover Rope

#1434 Tom & Jerry

#3405 Coyle

#3406 Thran

#3407 Overdorf

#3407 Overdorf

No. 3476—12 oz. Soda
Footed and Handled
Plain or Wide Optic

No. 2516—12 oz. Soda
Footed
Diamond Optic Only

No. 3476—12 oz. Soda
Footed
Plain or Wide Optic

No. 3408—12 oz. Beer Mug
Plain Only

No. 4163—12 oz. Beer Mug
Pressed
Also made 16 oz.
Plain Only

No. 3386—8 oz. Pilsner
Also made 10 & 12 oz.

No. 4044—12 oz. Pilsner
Also made 8 & 10 oz.
Plain Only

No. 3420—10 oz. Pilsner
Also made 8 & 12 oz
Plain Only

No. 3304—10 oz. Pilsner
Plain Only

Footed and handled sodas, beer mugs and pilsners

Luncheon Goblets and Sodas

#3373 MORNING GLORY - name given by researchers

Dates: Ca. 1929-1933
Colors: Flamingo; moongleam foot, crystal bowl. NOT LISTED IN ALL CRYSTAL.
Marked: Yes, on narrow stem portion
Comments: Difficult to find. The #4206 Optic Tooth jug complements these nicely.

#3478 CONE - name given by researchers

Dates: 1924-1933
Colors: Crystal only
Marked: Yes, on stem portion near bowl
Comments: Sometimes found with a floral cutting.

#3482 MONO-RING - name given by researchers

Dates: 1925-1933
Colors: Crystal; crystal bowl, moongleam foot
Marked: No

#3373 MORNING GLORY luncheon goblet

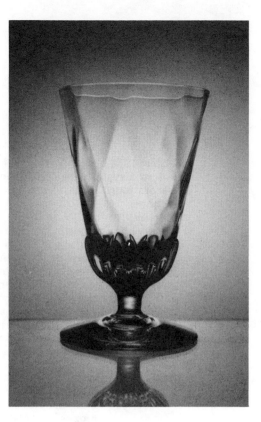

#3478 CONE

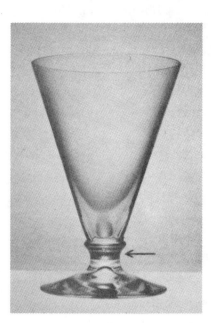

#3482 MONO-RING

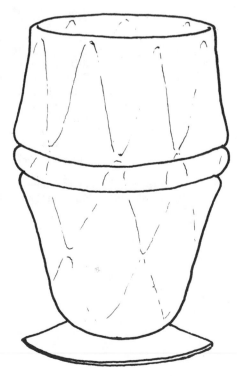

#2323 NAVY - original Heisey Co. name

Dates: 1934-1941
Colors: Crystal with cobalt bases
Decorations: Some sodas occasionally found with some Heisey silhouette etchings
Marked: No
Comments: Primarily a bar line of various sodas. For a short time in 1937-1938 a cup, saucer, sugar and cream were also offered. The cup, saucer, cream and sugar are the same as the items in New Era (#4044), but with cobalt bases. Several plates were offered. Contemporary trade journal accounts state that plates were made with cobalt centers and crystal rims and also with cobalt rims and crystal centers. Those known have had only cobalt centers. It is uncertain if the other variety was ever made. Much of this pattern was made for Victor V. Clad. The items in the pattern were taken from existing lines and had cobalt bases added. Sodas were available either plain or wide optic with ½ shams. Numbers in parentheses indicate the original pattern lines from which the pieces were taken.

Items made were:
2 oz. bar (#2052)
5 oz. soda (#2401)
6 oz. soda (#2351)
6 oz. old fashion (#2401)
7 oz. soda (#2506)
8 oz. soda (#2351)
8 oz. old fashion (#2401)
8 oz. toddy (#2351)
10 oz. soda (#2351)
12 oz. soda (#2351)
13 oz. soda (#2351)
6 in. plate (#1184)
7 in. plate (#1184)
8 in. plate (#1184)
bouillon plate (#1184)
cup (#1247)
saucer (#1247)
cream (#1247)
sugar (#1247)

Imperial Reissues: None
Availability: Moderately available to scarce

#2323 NAVY saucer, cup, and tall soda.

#2323 NAVY bar glasses—one with normal sham and one with double sham.

#2351 NEWTON - name given by researchers

Dates: 1917-1957
Colors: Crystal

> 8 oz. straight, light:
> moongleam - d/o
> flamingo - plain, d/o
> marigold - plain, d/o
> sahara - d/o
> hawthorne - d/o, checker optic
> 10 oz. straight, light:
> moongleam - d/o
> flamingo - plain, d/o
> marigold - plain, d/o
> 12 oz. straight, light:
> moongleam - d/o, w/o
> flamingo - plain, d/o, w/o
> marigold - plain, d/o
> sahara - d/o, w/o
> hawthorne - d/o, checker optic

Marked: No
Comments: Made in a complete range of sizes from 1½ oz. to 18 oz. Made plain, wide optic, diamond optic, or checker optic. Made with a variety of shams: regular, ½, and full. Full sham was discontinued in 1938. Occasionally made with various cut flutes and spikes around bottom. Used for many early etchings and some early cuttings by Heisey. Often used for monograms. Not all sizes were made for the entire length of time. Notice that the decanter was also used with the #2401 line. A very common shape which every blown ware company produced, thus making it very difficult to identify sodas unless they are decorated with a Heisey decoration.
Imperial Reissues: Imperial made the 8 oz. old fashion, sham, and the 12 oz. ice tea from May, 1958 until January, 1961.
Availability: Common

No. 2351—2 oz. Bar
Half Sham (2052)

No. 2351—2 oz. Bar
Full Sham (2052)
Also made 1½ & 2½ oz.

No. 2351—2 oz. Bar
Regular (2052)

No. 2351—6 oz. Toddy
Half Sham
Also made Full Sham

No. 2351—1 pt. Decanter
& No. 73 P/S (2401)

No. 2351—8 oz. Toddy
Full Sham
Also made Half Sham

No. 2351—10 oz. Soda
Straight—Half Sham

No. 2351—10 oz. Soda
Straight—Full Sham
Also made 3, 4, 4½, 5, 5½,
6, 7, 8, 9, 10½, 11, 11½,
12, 13, 14, 15, 16 & 18 oz.

No. 2351—1.0 oz. Soda
Straight—Regular

#2351 pattern

#2401 OAKWOOD - name given by researchers

Dates: 1917-1946

Colors: Crystal
        5 oz. soda, light:
           flamingo - d/o
           hawthorne - d/o, checker optic
        5½ oz. soda, taper, light:
           flamingo - d/o
           moongleam - d/o
           sahara - d/o

Marked: No

Comments: Made in a complete range of sizes from 1½ oz. to 18 oz. Made plain, wide optic, diamond optic, or checker optic. Occasionally made with various cut flutes and spikes around bottom. Used for many early etchings and some cuttings by Heisey. Often used for monograms. The decanter was also used with the #2351 line. A very common shape which every blown ware company produced, thus making it very difficult to identify sodas unless they are decorated with a Heisey decoration.

Imperial Reissues: No

Availability: Common

8 oz. Taper Soda
Regular

6 oz. Old Fashion Cocktail
Half Sham
Also made Full Sham

4 oz. Footed Whiskey
Regular
Also made Half Sham or Full Sham

3 oz. Taper Bar
Regular (2051)

3 oz. Taper Bar
Half Sham (2051)

1 pt. Decanter & No. 73 P/S

3 oz. Taper Bar
Full Sham (2051)
Also made 1½, 2, 2½ & 3½ oz.

8 oz. Taper Soda
Half Sham

8 oz. Taper Soda
Full Sham
Also made 4, 4½, 5, 5½ 6, 7, 9, 10, 10½,
11, 11½, 12, 13, 14, 15, 16 & 18 oz.

8 oz. Old Fashion Cocktail
Full Sham
Also made Half Sham

#2401

Sodas

#2451

Dates: 1917-1938. Bar made until 1939
Colors: Crystal only
Marked: No

#2852

Dates: 1917-1938
Colors: Crystal only
Marked: No

#3422

Dates: 1936-1941
Colors: Crystal only
Marked: No

#2516 CIRCLE PAIR - name given by researchers

Dates: 1924-1937
Colors: Crystal, moongleam, flamingo, marigold, sahara
Marked: No
Comments: See JUGS Section for matching pitcher. Footed soda is shown elsewhere in this section.

#2512

Dates: 1917-1938
Colors: Crystal only
Marked: No

#3417 ADKINS - name given by researchers

Dates: 1934-1937
Colors: Crystal only
Marked: No
Comments: See decanter earlier in this section. See MISCELLANEOUS Section for matching bitters bottle.

#2352

Dates: 1917-1937
Colors: Crystal only
Marked: No

#2351X NEWTON - name given by researchers

Dates: 1936-1946
Colors: Crystal only
Marked: No
Comments: See remainder of pattern earlier in this section.

#2405

Dates: 1936-1944
Colors: Crystal only
Marked: No
Comments: Made plain and wide optic. Listed as early as 1925 as a soda for B & O Railroad.

No. 2451—10 oz. Soda
Flared Edge Light
Also made 7, 8, 11, 12, 15 & 18 oz
Plain or Wide Optic

No. 2852 10 oz. Soda
Bell
Also made 7, 9, 11 & 12 oz
Plain or Wide Optic

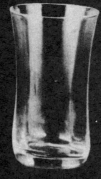

No. 3422—12 oz. Soda
Concave
Plain Only

No. 2516—8 oz. Soda
Straight
Also made 5 & 12 oz
Diamond Optic Only

No. 2512—12 oz. Soda
Touraine
Also made 4, 5, 6, 7, 8, 9 & 10 oz.
Plain or Wide Optic

No. 3417—10 oz. Soda
Touraine
Also made 5, 8 & 12 oz
Wide Optic Only

No. 2352—10 oz. Soda
Straight—Light
Also made 4, 5, 6, 7, 8, 9 & 12 oz.
Plain or Wide Optic

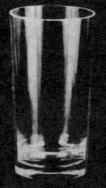

No. 2351X—10 oz. Soda
Straight Light Half Sham
Plain or Wide Optic

No. 2405—14 oz. Soda
Half Sham
Also made Regular and Full Sham
Plain or Wide Optic

Sodas

#3481 GLENFORD - name given by researchers

Dates: 1925-1937
Colors: Crystal; moongleam foot, crystal bowl; flamingo; hawthorne; flamingo foot, crystal bowl; moongleam foot, flamingo bowl
Marked: No
Comments: A blown soda line. Very difficult to find in the moongleam/flamingo combination. Usually it is diamond optic, in hawthorne it is checker optic. Occasionally found with swirl or wide optic.

#3480 KOORS - name given by researchers

Dates: 1925-1937
Colors: Crystal; moongleam foot, crystal bowl; flamingo; hawthorne
Marked: No
Comments: Usually found with diamond optic, although it is scarce in swirl optic (made in 1925). See JUGS and VASES Sections for matching items. Checker optic in hawthorne.

#3405 ALIBI - name given by researchers

Dates: 1926-1943
Colors: Crystal; moongleam foot, crystal bowl
Marked: No
Comments: Sometimes found with the special Chicken Chase etching and also used for several silhouette etchings by Heisey.

#3542 HAZELWOOD - name given by researchers

Dates: 1919-1944
Colors: Crystal, flamingo, hawthorne, sahara, zircon
Marked: No
Comments: Used with various stemware lines as a complementary item. Zircon items were made in saturn optic.

#3428 BRITTANY - name given by researchers

Dates: Ca. 1936-1946
Colors: Crystal only
Marked: No

#3419 COGNAC - name given by researchers

Dates: 1935-1944; 1951-1953.
Colors: Crystal; amber for Fred Harvey (for large brandy)
Marked: No
Comments: Made in a Rhine wine for a few years (1935-1938) and in a pony brandy in 1951-1953.

#3421 AVIGNON - name given by researchers

Dates: 1936-1937
Colors: Crystal only
Marked: No

No. 3481—1½ oz.
Footed Bar
Diamond Optic Only

No. 3480—1½ oz.
Footed Bar
Diamond Optic Only

No. 3481—3 oz.
Cocktail
Diamond Optic Only

No. 3480—3 oz.
Cocktail
Diamond Optic Only

No. 3405—3 oz.
Cocktail
Wide Optic Only

No. 3542—4½ oz
Oyster Cocktail
Plain or Wide Optic

No. 3428—3½ oz.
Cocktail
Plain Only

No. 3481—8½ oz
Footed Soda
Diamond Optic Only

No. 3419—22 oz.
Brandy Sniffer
Plain Only

No. 3421—5 oz.
French Champagne
Wide Optic Only

No. 3481—12 oz
Footed Soda
Diamond Optic Only

No. 3480—5 oz.
Footed Soda
Diamond Optic Only

No. 3480—8½ oz.
Footed Soda
Diamond Optic Only
Also made 12 oz.

No. 3481—5 oz.
Footed Soda
Diamond Optic Only

Miscellaneous stemware

Tumblers

#2451, #2516 - See descriptions earlier in this section.

#2502

Dates: 1917-1939
Colors: Crystal only
Marked: No
Comments: Handled sodas were made until 1928.

#2506

Dates: 1917-1946
Colors: Crystal only
Marked: No
Comments: Made plain or wide optic.

#2930 PLAIN & FANCY - name given by researchers

Dates: 1917-1946
Colors: Crystal; 9 oz. d/o in moongleam, flamingo, marigold; 10 oz. d/o in moongleam, flamingo, marigold, hawthorne, sahara. Hawthorne in checker optic.
Marked: No
Comments: Widely used for etchings and cuttings by Heisey. Made in 9 oz. and 10 oz. sizes. Made plain, diamond optic, wide optic, and in hawthorne, checker optic.

#2931

Dates: 1917-1938
Colors: Crystal only
Marked: No

#3004

Dates: 1925-1933
Colors: Crystal only
Marked: No

#3359 PLATEAU - name given by researchers

Dates: 1926-1933
Colors: Crystal, flamingo, marigold
Marked: No
Comments: See STEMWARE & VASES Sections for matching items.

#3362 CHARTER OAK - original Heisey Co. name

Dates: 1926-1936. Tumbler, jug, finger bowl and compote were made slightly longer
Colors: Crystal, moongleam, flamingo, marigold
Marked: No
Comments: See STEMWARE Section for remainder of line.

#3517

Dates: 1927-1936
Colors: Crystal, moongleam, flamingo
Marked: No

TUMBLERS

NO. 2451-10-OZ.

NO. 2502-10-OZ.

NO. 2506-7-OZ.
WIDE OPTIC
ALSO MADE PLAIN

NO. 2516-10-OZ.
DIAMOND OPTIC
CRYSTAL, MOON
GLEAM, FLAMINGO

NO. 2930-10-OZ.
ALSO MAKE 9-OZ.

NO. 2930-10-OZ.
WIDE OPTIC

MADE IN CRYSTAL, MOONGLEAM,
FLAMINGO AND SAHARA

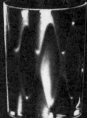

NO. 2930-10-OZ.
DIAMOND OPTIC
ALSO MAKE 9-OZ.

NO. 2931-10-OZ.

NO. 3004-10-OZ.

NO. 3359-9-OZ.
DIAMOND OPTIC
CRYSTAL-FLAMINGO

NO. 3362-10-OZ.
DIAMOND OPTIC
CRYSTAL
MOONGLEAM &
FLAMINGO

NO. 3517-9-OZ.

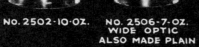

#7007 ANGULAR CRISS CROSS tumbler

285

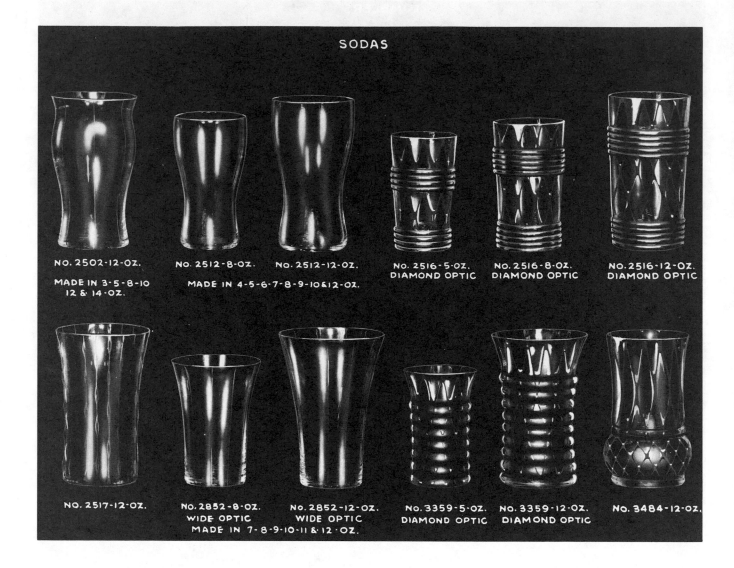

SODAS

NO. 2502-12-OZ.
MADE IN 3-5-8-10 12 & 14-OZ.

NO. 2512-8-OZ.
MADE IN 4-5-6-7-8-9-10&12-OZ.

NO. 2512-12-OZ.

NO. 2516-5-OZ.
DIAMOND OPTIC

NO. 2516-8-OZ.
DIAMOND OPTIC

NO. 2516-12-OZ.
DIAMOND OPTIC

NO. 2517-12-OZ.

NO. 2852-8-OZ.
WIDE OPTIC
MADE IN 7-8-9-10-11 & 12-OZ.

NO. 2852-12-OZ.
WIDE OPTIC

NO. 3359-5-OZ.
DIAMOND OPTIC

NO. 3359-12-OZ.
DIAMOND OPTIC

NO. 3484-12-OZ.

#2512, #2516, #2852 - See descriptions earlier in this section

#2517 TEARDROP - name given by researchers

Dates: 1925-1930
Colors: Crystal, moongleam, flamingo, hawthorne
Marked: No
Comments: See JUGS & VASES Sections for matching items.

#3484 DONNA - name given by researchers

Dates: 1929-1957
Colors: Crystal, moongleam, flamingo, marigold
Marked: No
Comments: In later years, the crystal soda and jug (without optic) were used for Orchid etching. In colors, it is usually diamond optic.

#7007 ANGULAR CRISS CROSS - name given by researchers

Dates: Unknown. Probably ca. 1925.
Colors: Only flamingo known. Has not been seen in crystal
Marked: Yes
Comments: Somewhat similar to an old Heisey pattern of nappies and plates, #361 Criss Cross, but the pattern is slightly different. Original number and name not known.

286

Baskets

There are many collectors of glass baskets making these Heisey items very desirable. As with other specialized fields, there are also Heisey collectors who specialize in Heisey baskets.

The Heisey Company began producing baskets circa 1912 and first called them "basket vases". Eventually the word vase was dropped and they referred to them simply as baskets. A few were designated as fruit baskets although baskets were generally meant to be flower containers.

Most Heisey baskets found are in crystal but some remained in vogue during the color period. While Heisey made other baskets, the ones included in this section are those which are found in colors. The easiest basket to find in color is the #417 in either flamingo or moongleam.

Sizes of baskets refer to the measurement across the widest part of the opening. Most baskets are marked with the Diamond H.

None of these baskets have been reproduced.

#458 PICKET - name given by researchers

Dates: Ca. 1915-1933
Colors: Crystal only
Marked: Yes

#459 ROUND COLONIAL - name given by researchers

Dates: 1915-1933
Colors: Crystal only
Marked: Yes
Comments: Used for some Heisey cuttings and etchings. Often found with decorations done by other companies. Patent #47 applied for 6/3/15 and granted 8/17/15—Arthur J. Sanford, designer. Made in 7″ and 8″ sizes.

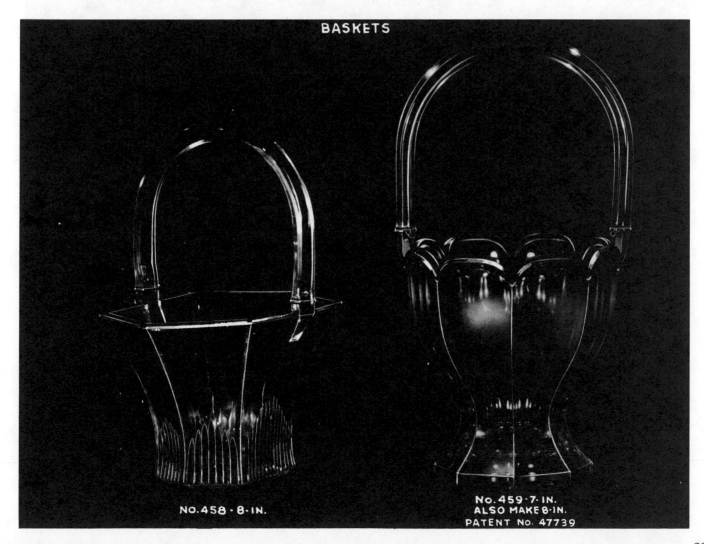

BASKETS

NO. 458 · 8 · IN.

NO. 459 · 7 · IN.
ALSO MAKE 8 · IN.
PATENT NO. 47739

#461 BANDED PICKET - name given by researchers

Dates: Ca. 1915-1933
Colors: Crystal, moongleam, flamingo, hawthorne
Marked: Yes
Comments: Used for a few cuttings by Heisey.

#462 PLAIN HEXAGON - name given by researchers

Dates: Ca. 1915-1933
Colors: Crystal only
Marked: Yes
Comments: Used for a few Heisey cuttings.

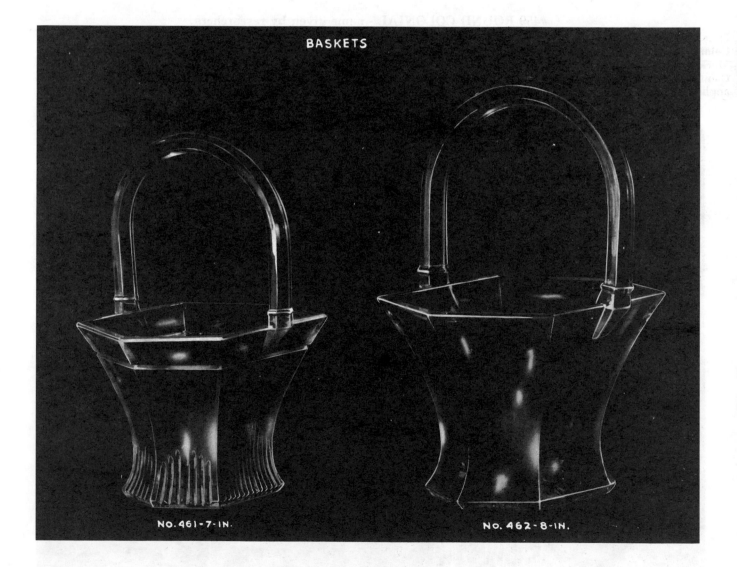

BASKETS

NO. 461-7-IN.　　　　NO. 462-8-IN.

#463 BONNET - name given by researchers

Dates: Ca. 1915-1933
Colors: Crystal, flamingo
Marked: Yes

#467 HELMET - name given by researchers

Dates: 1917-1933
Colors: Crystal, moongleam, flamingo.
Marked: Yes
Comments: Patent #51308 applied for 6/30/17 and granted 9/25/17, Arthur J. Sanford, designer. Used for some Heisey cuttings.

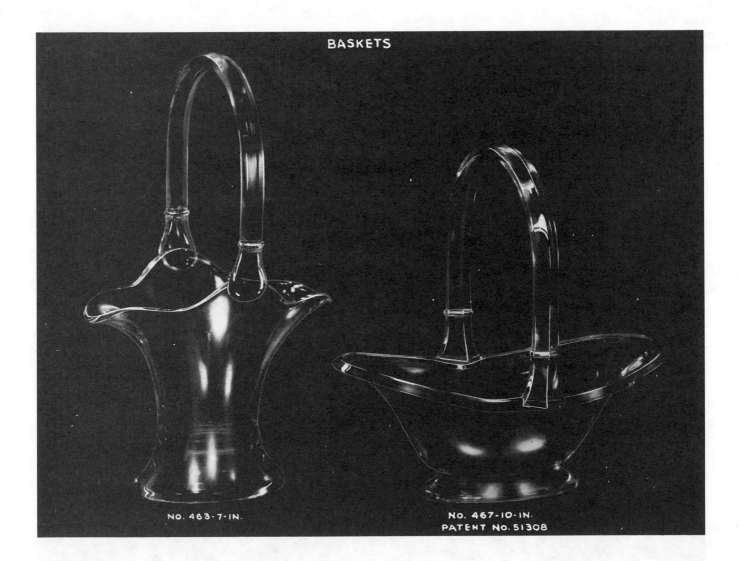

BASKETS

NO. 463-7-IN.

NO. 467-10-IN.
PATENT No. 51308

#500 OCTAGON - name given by researchers

Dates: Ca. 1928-1935
Colors: Crystal, moongleam, flamingo, marigold
Marked: Yes
Comments: A tiny basket which is difficult to find. Marigold is scarce.

#417 DOUBLE RIB & PANEL - name given by researchers

Dates: Ca. 1923-1935
Colors: Crystal, moongleam, flamingo, hawthorne
Marked: Yes
Comments: This basket is probably easier to find in color than in crystal. Hawthorne is especially desirable. The Diamond H is often faint and difficult to see.

#465 RECESSED PANEL - name given by researchers

Dates: 1915-1933
Colors: Crystal only
Marked: Yes
Comments: Patent #47736 applied for 3/1/15 and granted 8/17/15. Designed by Arthur J. Sanford. Made in 7″, 8″ and 9″ sizes. Used for several Heisey etchings, usually florals and some satin finish and combinations.

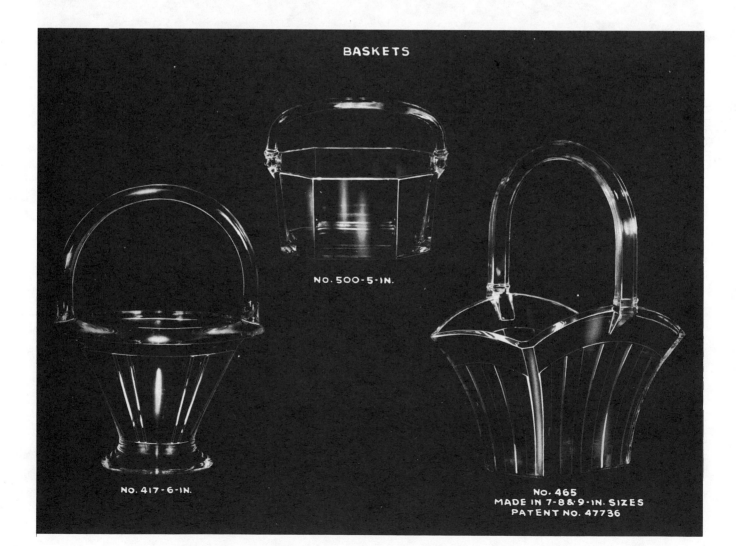

BASKETS

NO. 500-5-IN.

NO. 417-6-IN.

NO. 465
MADE IN 7-8 & 9-IN. SIZES
PATENT NO. 47736

Candlesticks

Candlesticks had always been an important part of Heisey's line and this certainly continued to be true during the color years.

Color, of course, was a dominant aspect differentiating these candlesticks from those produced in the colonial period or in the later years. In fact, many of these candlesticks are actually more difficult to find in crystal than in color, although now, as then, they are generally more sought after in color.

A number of style trends dominated this period. The years between 1921 and 1925 were a transitional period, with candlesticks such as the #100 Centennial, which were reminiscent of the earlier tall colonial styles with their heavy puntied bases, continued to be made. Very few of them were offered in color and the newer candlesticks are easily distinguishable from them by the absence of such bases.

In 1925, a series of reproduction candlesticks was offered, beginning with the #109 Petticoat Dolphin, the #110 Sandwich Dolphin and the #111 Cherub. In the 1930's, a number of other candlesticks were also issued which were inspired by early American glass patterns.

Most typical of the middle period candlesticks, however, was the series which began with the #112 Mercury in 1926. Small, informal candlesticks were by far the most popular styles during these years.

In 1926, Heisey issued the #116 Oak Leaf candlestick with an accompanying floral bowl. By 1929, such console sets had become very popular and many of the candlesticks issued after this date had matching bowls.

In 1928, three styles of water lamps were introduced. Although not in production for a very long period of time, these lamps are occasionally found today.

A final style trend began in 1934 with the #4044 New Era pattern and continued from 1935 to 1937 with such patterns as #1469 Ridgeleigh, #1483 Stanhope and #1485 Saturn, all strongly influenced by the Art Deco, or Art Moderne, movement.

Many candlesticks from this period were used, both by Heisey and by other decorating companies, as blanks for cutting and etching. Both Hawkes and Pairpoint used Heisey blanks during this period, including the #301 candelabra. Honesdale gold decorations have been seen on the #520 candlelamp and the Lotus Glass Company also offered gold decorations, silver overlay and various cuttings and etchings on Heisey blanks. Amber stain is sometimes found on the #300 candelabra and candlelamp and lavender stain was also applied by a decorating company to the #109 Petticoat Dolphin candlestick. Candlesticks were so popular for use by decorating companies that it would be impossible to list all of them. It is also not unusual to find a pair of Heisey candlesticks with a bowl from another company or vice versa, both with a cutting or etching applied by still another firm.

Tom Felt
Bob O'Grady

#1 GEORGIAN - name given by researchers

Dates: Ca. 1900-1931
Colors: Crystal, flamingo
Marked: Occasionally, in the constriction beneath the candleholder
Comments: The 9″ size only has been reported in flamingo, but is very rare. This candlestick was a copy of an old cut glass design. A pressed copy was also made by the Paden City Glass Manufacturing Company, in crystal and various colors, but will have a star pressed in the base.

#2 OLD WILLIAMSBURG - original Heisey Co. name

Dates: Ca. 1903-1957
Colors: Crystal, moongleam
Marked: Yes, at the top of the column
Comments: A single turn was made in moongleam of the 7″ size only. Imperial Glass produced this stick in crystal from 1958 to 1983. They also produced it in several colors: blue haze, nut brown, verde, ruby, antique blue, amber and emerald green.

#5 PATRICIAN - name given by researchers

Dates: Ca. 1904-1933
Colors: Crystal only. A one-light candelabrum was made in moongleam
Marked: Sometimes, at the neck
Comments: Patent #37213 applied for 10/8/04 and granted 11/8/04. A. H. Heisey listed as designer.

#16 CLASSIC - name given by researchers

Dates: Ca. 1906-1931
Colors: Crystal only
Marked: Sometimes, at the top of the column.

#20 SHEFFIELD - name given by researchers

Dates: Ca. 1907-1931
Colors: Crystal; crystal with moongleam candleholder.
Marked: Not usually.
Comments: In September, 1925, a single turn of the 9″ size only was made in the crystal-moongleam combination. This was probably an experiment, with no more than 69 pairs produced.

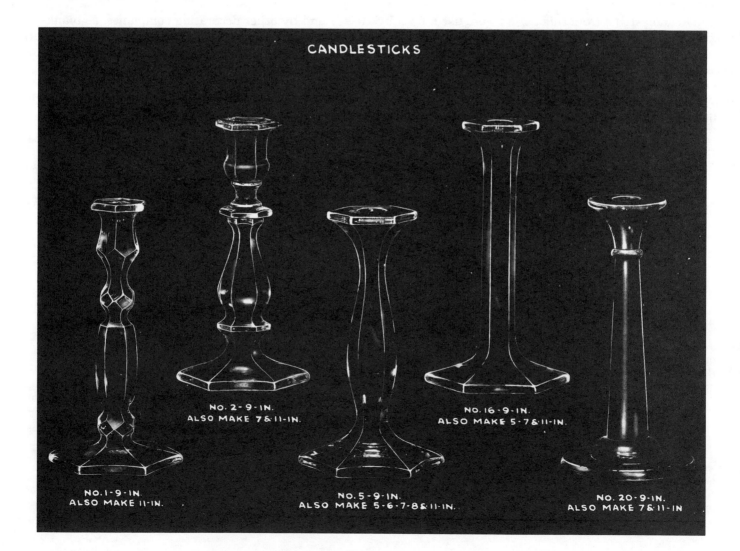

CANDLESTICKS

NO. 1 - 9 - IN.
ALSO MAKE 11-IN.

NO. 2 - 9 - IN.
ALSO MAKE 7 & 11-IN.

NO. 5 - 9 - IN.
ALSO MAKE 5 - 6 - 7 - 8 & 11-IN.

NO. 16 - 9 - IN.
ALSO MAKE 5 - 7 & 11-IN.

NO. 20 - 9 - IN.
ALSO MAKE 7 & 11-IN

#99 LITTLE SQUATTER - **name given by researchers**
Dates: June 1922-1944
Colors: Crystal, moongleam, flamingo
Marked: Yes, on bottom.

#70 OCTAGON - **name given by researchers**
Dates: Ca. 1917-1929
Colors: Crystal only
Marked: Yes, at the top of the column on the candleholder

#71 OVAL - original Heisey Co. description

Dates: July 1921-1929
Colors: Crystal only
Marked: Yes, at the constriction of the neck

#100 CENTENNIAL - name given by researchers

Dates: Ca. 1921-1929
Colors: Crystal, vaseline, moongleam, flamingo
Marked: Yes, in the contriction at the top of the column
Comments: Patent #68997 applied for 3/17/23 and granted 12/8/25. T. Clarence Heisey listed as designer. Only the 6″ size was made in vaseline, probably on an experimental basis.

#33 SKIRTED PANEL - name given by researchers

Dates: Ca. 1910-1929
Colors: Crystal only
Marked: Yes, at the top of the skirt just under the candleholder

#101 SIMPLICITY - name given by researchers

Dates: March 1922-1929
Colors: Crystal only
Marked: Yes, at the top of the column

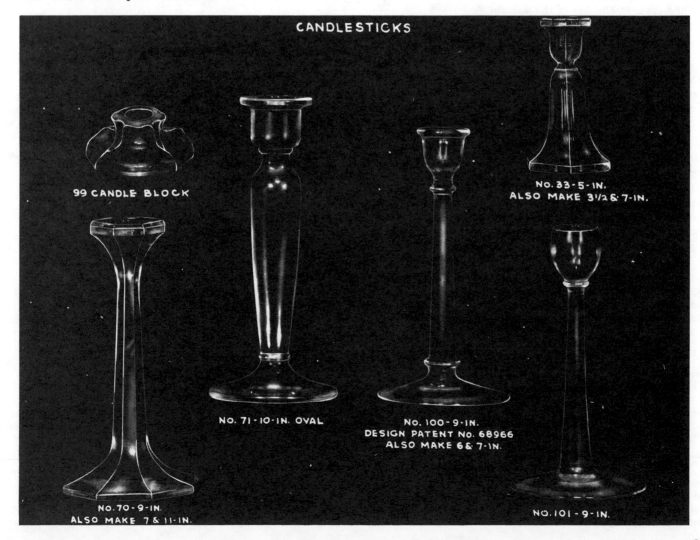

CANDLESTICKS

99 CANDLE BLOCK

NO. 71-10-IN. OVAL

NO. 100-9-IN.
DESIGN PATENT No. 68966
ALSO MAKE 6 & 7-IN.

NO. 33-5-IN.
ALSO MAKE 3½ & 7-IN.

NO.70-9-IN.
ALSO MAKE 7 & 11-IN.

NO.101-9-IN.

293

#103 CUPPED SAUCER - name given by researchers
Dates: April 1922-1929
Colors: Crystal, flamingo
Marked: Sometimes, on the bottom

#106 INVERTED SAUCER - name given by researchers
Dates: January 1925-1929
Colors: Crystal, moongleam, flamingo
Marked: Sometimes, on the bottom or in the constriction of the candleholder.

#104 BERTHA - name given by researchers
Dates: January 1924-1929
Colors: Crystal, moongleam, flamingo
Marked: Yes, at the top of the column

#102 BALLSTEM - name given by researchers
Dates: 1922-1929
Colors: Crystal only
Marked: Yes, at the top of the column
Comments: Similar candlesticks were also made in color by Cambridge and New Martinsville.

#105 PEMBROKE - name given by researchers
Dates: Ca. 1924-1934
Colors: Crystal, moongleam, flamingo
Marked: Yes, in the constriction of the neck
Comments: Usually found with prisms.

#107 WELLINGTON - name given by researchers
Dates: January 1925-1930
Colors: Crystal, moongleam, flamingo
Marked: Yes, at the top of the column

#108 THREE-RING - name given by researchers
Dates: February 1925-1929
Colors: Crystal only
Marked: Yes, at the top of the column

#109 PETTICOAT DOLPHIN - name given by researchers
Dates: August 1925-1935
Colors: Crystal, moongleam, flamingo, sahara, cobalt
Marked: No
Comments: Although attributed to Sandwich by Heisey, this candlestick is actually a reproduction of an earlier design originally made by the Northwood Company or its successor, the Dugan Glass Company of Indiana, Pa. Found both with the skirt flattened out (as shown) or with the skirt cupped.

#113 MARS - name given by researchers
Dates: 1926-1933
Colors: Crystal, moongleam, flamingo, hawthorne, marigold, sahara
Marked: Sometimes, at the bottom of the candleholder just above the top ring
Comments: Patent #70879 applied for 4/23/26 and granted 8/24/26. T. Clarence Heisey listed as designer.

#112 MERCURY - name given by researchers
Dates: January 1926-1957 (3″ size); Ca. 1927-1930 (9″ size)
Colors: Crystal, moongleam, flamingo, hawthorne, sahara. Rare in opalescent gold
Marked: Yes, in the constriction at the top of the stem (3″ size) and at the top of the column (9″ size).
Comments: Patent #70558 applied for 3/23/26 and granted 7/13/26. T. Clarence Heisey listed as designer. 9″ size was available only in crystal, moongleam and flamingo. Made by Imperial Glass in crystal from 1958 to 1964. (3″ size)

#110 SANDWICH DOLPHIN - name given by researchers
Dates: October 1925-1935
Colors: Crystal, moongleam, flamingo, sahara, cobalt, zircon, amber
Marked: No
Comments: Reproduction of a candlestick originally made by the Boston and Sandwich Glass Company. Many other companies also made dolphin candlesticks. This candlestick was offered electrified by the Ideal Cut Glass Company of Canastota, New York

#111 CHERUB - name given by researchers
Dates: October 1926-1929
Colors: Crystal, moongleam, flamingo
Marked: No
Comments: Probably a reproduction of a 19th century American or French candlestick. Frequently found with a satin finish.

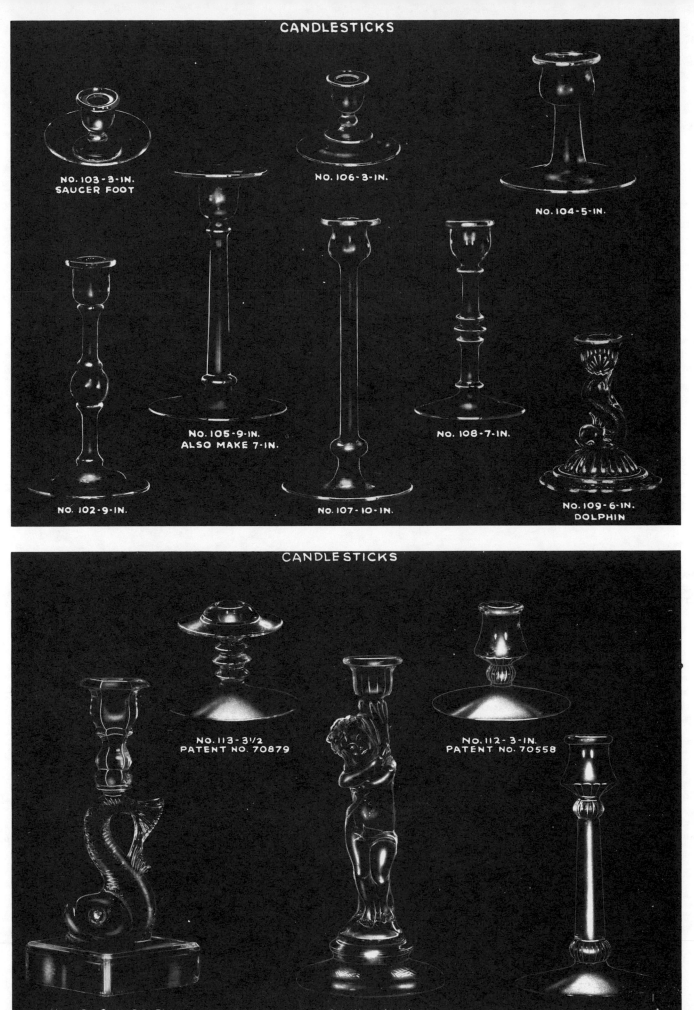

CANDLESTICKS

NO. 103 - 3 - IN.
SAUCER FOOT

NO. 106 - 3 - IN.

NO. 104 - 5 - IN.

NO. 105 - 9 - IN.
ALSO MAKE 7-IN.

NO. 108 - 7 - IN.

NO. 102 - 9 - IN.

NO. 107 - 10 - IN.

NO. 109 - 6 - IN.
DOLPHIN

CANDLESTICKS

NO. 113 - 3 1/2
PATENT NO. 70879

NO. 112 - 3 - IN.
PATENT NO. 70558

NO. 110 - 10 - IN. DOLPHIN

NO. 111 - 11 1/2 - IN.
MADE PLAIN & ETCHED

NO. 112 - 9 - IN.
PATENT NO. 70558

295

#114 PLUTO - name given by researchers

Dates: May 1926-1931
Colors: Crystal, moongleam, flamingo, hawthorne, marigold
Marked: Sometimes, at the top of the column.

#116 OAK LEAF - name given by researchers

Dates: August 1926-1929
Colors: Crystal; crystal top with moongleam foot; flamingo; flamingo top with crystal foot; hawthorne
Marked: Sometimes, in the constriction just above the base
Comments: Patent #74012 applied for 1/7/27 and granted 12/6/27. T. Clarence Heisey listed as designer. Frequently found with the oak leaf portion frosted. See FLORAL BOWLS Section for matching bowl.

#118 MISS MUFFET - name given by researchers

Dates: August 1926-1930
Colors: Crystal, moongleam, flamingo. Rare in opalescent gold
Marked: Sometimes, on the bottom.
Comments: Available with diamond optic on the base.

#120 OVERLAPPING SWIRL - name given by researchers

Dates: Ca. 1927-1931
Colors: Crystal, moongleam, flamingo, hawthorne
Marked: Sometimes, on the bottom

#122 ZIG ZAG - name given by researchers

Dates: Ca. 1927-1929
Colors: Crystal, moongleam, flamingo, hawthorne
Marked: Yes, on the side under the turned down edge

#117 BAMBOO - name given by researchers

Dates: Ca. 1927-1929
Colors: Crystal top with moongleam foot; moongleam top with crystal foot; crystal top with flamingo foot; flamingo top with crystal foot
Marked: Yes, at top of column
Comments: A floral bowl which may match was made. It is similar to a Tudor bowl, but with segments, making it look like bamboo.

#121 PINWHEEL - name given by researchers

Dates: Ca. 1927-1929
Colors: Crystal, moongleam, flamingo, hawthorne
Marked: Yes, on the side under the turned down edge

#123 MERCURY (INSERT) - name given by researchers

Dates: Ca. 1927-1929
Colors: Crystal, moongleam, flamingo, hawthorne
Marked: Yes, in the middle on the bottom
Comments: Same design as the #112 candlestick, modified to fit inside the #15 flower block.

#126 TROPHY - name given by researchers

Dates: Ca. 1928-1929
Colors: Crystal, moongleam, flamingo
Marked: Yes, at the bottom of the column

#125 LEAF DESIGN - original Heisey Co. description

Dates: 1928-1929; 1939-1941
Colors: Crystal, moongleam, flamingo
Marked: Not usually

#129 TRICORN - name given by researchers

Dates: June 1929-1936
Colors: Crystal, moongleam foot with crystal arms, moongleam, flamingo, marigold
Marked: Yes, just above the acorn between two of the arms

#130 ACORN - name given by researchers

Dates: Ca. 1929
Colors: Crystal, moongleam, flamingo. Hawthorne reported
Marked: Not usually

#127 TWIST STEM - name given by researchers

Dates: Ca. 1929
Colors: Crystal, moongleam, flamingo
Marked: Not usually

#128 LIBERTY - name given by researchers

Dates: Ca. 1928-1929
Colors: Crystal, moongleam, flamingo, marigold.
Marked: Yes, at the bottom of the column.
Comments: Also available in a 6″ height.

#132 SUNBURST - name given by researchers

Dates: Ca. 1929-1936
Colors: Crystal, moongleam, flamingo, marigold
Marked: Yes, under the candleholder on the top portion of the column
Comments: There is a variant of this candlestick which has the panels on the foot of the candlestick as well as on the top portion.

#600 SQUARE-HANDLED - name given by researchers

Dates: October 1924-1936; May 1939-1945
Colors: Crystal only
Marked: Yes, at the bottom of the candleholder just above the saucer foot.

#1205 RAINDROP - name given by researchers

Dates: Ca. 1929
Colors: Crystal, moongleam, flamingo
Marked: Yes, on the side under the turned down edge.
Comments: See FLORAL BOWLS Section for matching floral bowl.

#1231 RIBBED OCTAGON - name given by researchers

Dates: Ca. 1929-1933
Colors: Crystal, moongleam, flamingo
Marked: Yes, on the side under the turned down edge.
Comments: See PATTERN Section for remainder of pattern.

#1252 TWIST - name given by researchers

Dates: Ca. 1929-1933
Colors: Crystal, moongleam, flamingo, marigold
Marked: Yes, on the side under the turned down edge
Comments: See PATTERN Section for remainder of pattern

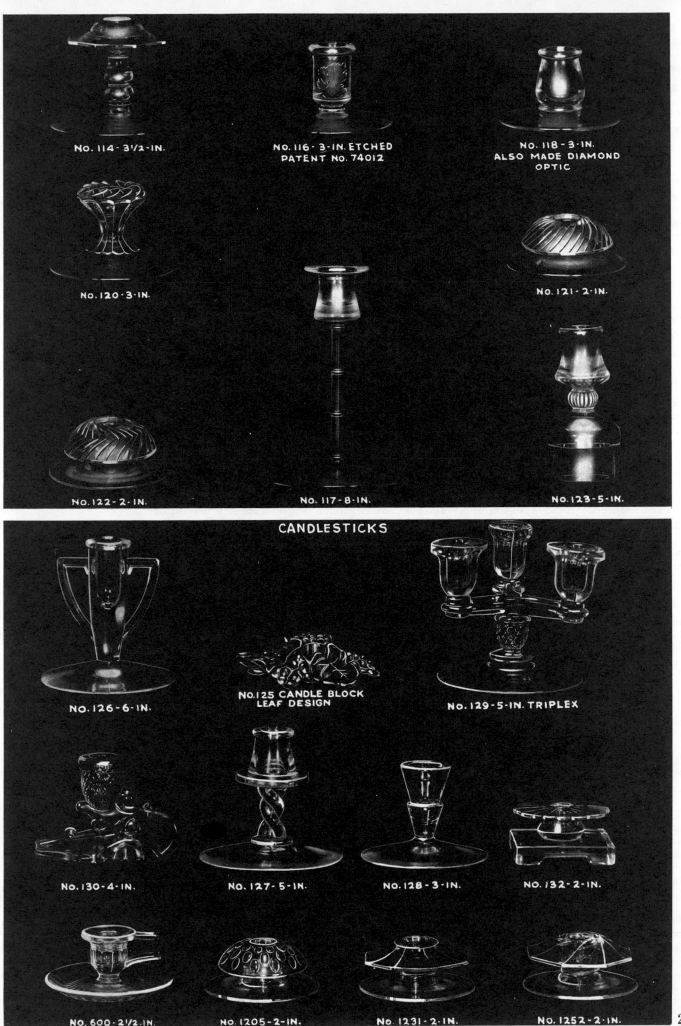

NO. 114 - 3 1/2 - IN.

NO. 116 - 3 - IN. ETCHED
PATENT No. 74012

NO. 118 - 3 - IN.
ALSO MADE DIAMOND
OPTIC

NO. 120 - 3 - IN.

NO. 121 - 2 - IN.

NO. 122 - 2 - IN.

NO. 117 - 8 - IN.

NO. 123 - 5 - IN.

CANDLESTICKS

NO. 126 - 6 - IN.

NO. 125 CANDLE BLOCK
LEAF DESIGN

NO. 129 - 5 - IN. TRIPLEX

NO. 130 - 4 - IN.

NO. 127 - 5 - IN.

NO. 128 - 3 - IN.

NO. 132 - 2 - IN.

NO. 600 - 2 1/2 - IN.

NO. 1205 - 2 - IN.

NO. 1231 - 2 - IN.

NO. 1252 - 2 - IN.

299

#112, #99, #600, #132 and #109-see information earlier in this section.

#1472 PARALLEL QUARTER - name given by researchers
Dates: June 1935-1942
Colors: Crystal only
Marked: Not usually
Comments: See FLORAL BOWLS Section for matching bowl.

#1469½ RIDGELEIGH - original Heisey Co. name
Dates: Ca. 1935-1941
Colors: Crystal only
Marked: No
Comments: See PATTERN Section

#1401 EMPRESS footed, 2 handled - original Heisey Co. name
Dates: March 1932-1936
Colors: Crystal, moongleam, flamingo, sahara
Marked: Yes, on the bottom
Comments: Reissued in 1938 with a wide optic added to the inside of the rim and a flared rim, as part of the #1509 Queen Ann pattern. See PATTERN Section for remainder of pattern.

#1404 OLD SANDWICH - original Heisey Co. name
Dates: September 1931-1937
Colors: Crystal, moongleam, flamingo, sahara, cobalt.
Marked: Yes, on the underside in the center of the base.
Comments: See PATTERN Section for remainder of pattern.

#1401 EMPRESS toed candlestick - original Heisey Co. name
Dates: Ca. 1929-1935
Colors: Crystal, moongleam, flamingo, alexandrite, sahara
Marked: Yes, on the back of one of the feet
Comments: See PATTERN Section for remainder of pattern. Reproduced by Imperial Glass in 1981 in sunshine yellow (similar to sahara) for Collectors Guild. These items are marked with a CG in a circle on the bulbous bottom portion of the candlestick.

#1405 IPSWICH 6″ candlestick - original Heisey Co. name
Dates: June 1932-1936
Colors: Crystal, moongleam, flamingo, sahara
Marked: Yes, at the bottom of the column just above the base
Comments: See PATTERN Section for remainder of pattern.

#2 OLD WILLIAMSBURG - original Heisey Co. name
Dates: Ca. 1903-1957
Colors: Crystal, moongleam
Marked: Yes, at the top of the column
Comments: A single turn was made in moongleam of the 7″ size only. Imperial Glass produced this stick in crystal from 1958 until 1983. They also produced it in several colors: blue haze, nut brown, verde, ruby, antique blue and amber.

#135 EMPRESS - original Heisey Co. name
Dates: Ca. 1929-1937
Colors: Crystal, moongleam, flamingo, marigold, alexandrite, sahara, cobalt
Marked: Sometimes
Comments: There is a matching floral bowl in the FLORAL BOWL Section. Originally this was just a console set, but the candlestick was later added to the Empress line.

#133 SWAN HANDLED - name given by researchers
Dates: Ca. 1929-1936
Colors: Crystal, moongleam, flamingo, marigold, alexandrite, sahara
Marked: Not usually
Comments: There is a matching floral bowl

#21 ARISTOCRAT - name given by researchers
Dates: Ca. 1907-1935
Colors: Crystal only
Marked: Yes, on the candleholder just above the column.
Comments: Patent #41590 applied for 3/4/10 and granted 7/18/11. Andrew J. Sanford listed as designer. This candlestick was made in a variety of sizes and also was used as the base for several electric lamps by Heisey. Lamp bases are occasionally found in moongleam and flamingo.

No. 1472
3 in. Candlestick

No. 1469½ Candlestick
Cut Top and Bottom

No. 112—3 in. Candlestick
Pat. No. 70558

No. 99 Candlestick

No. 600
2½ in. Handled Candlestick
Saucer Footed

No. 132 2 in. Candlestick

No. 1401
Footed Candlestick

No. 1404
6 in. Candlestick

No. 109 Candlestick

No. 1401
6 In. Toed Candlestick

No. 1405
6 In. Candlestick

No. 2—7 in. Candlestick
Puntied Bottom
Also made 9 In.

No. 135—6 in. Candlestick

No. 133 6 in. Candlestick

No. 21 7 in. Candlestick
Puntied Bottom   Cut Top
Also made 9 in

Candlesticks

#129 - See information on earlier page in this section

#134 TRIDENT - name given by researchers

Dates: Ca. 1929-1957
Colors: Crystal; moongleam; moongleam foot with crystal arms; flamingo; marigold; alexandrite; alexandrite foot with sahara arms; sahara; sahara arms with moongleam foot; tangerine arms with crystal foot; dawn foot with crystal arms; crystal foot with experimental light blue arms.
Marked: Sometimes, just above the foot.
Comments: Most of the two-color combinations were experimental. This was a popular blank for decorations and was offered by Heisey with 80 different production cuttings and 18 etchings. Made in crystal by Imperial Glass from 1958 to 1971. There is a matching floral bowl.

#1428 WARWICK 2-light - original Heisey Co. name

Dates: Ca. 1933-1950
Colors: Crystal, moongleam, flamingo, sahara, cobalt
Marked: Sometimes, on the top center of the base.
Comments: See PATTERN Section for remainder of pattern. Made by Imperial Glass in verde and heather.

#141 EDNA - name given by researchers

Dates: Ca. 1933-1936
Colors: Crystal, moongleam, flamingo, sahara, cobalt
Marked: Yes, just below the center of the curved candleholder on the upper portion of the base.
Comments: Marked "Pat. Applied For." However, patent records indicate that the application for a similar design was approved in the name of Willard L. Morrison of Chicago instead. Required the use of a U-shaped candle.

#31 JACK-BE-NIMBLE - name given by researchers

Dates: Ca. 1908-1944
Colors: Crystal, moongleam, flamingo, sahara
Marked: Yes, on the bottom
Comments: A similar toy candlestick was also made by the Westmoreland Glass Company. The handle on the Westmoreland candlestick touches the candleholder portion, whereas the handle of the Heisey toy stands away from it. Imperial Glass reproduced this candleholder in 1981 in crystal, unmarked.

#1471 EMPIRE - original Heisey Co. name

Dates: June 1935-1937
Colors: Crystal only
Marked: Not usually
Comments: A removable center plug could be placed in the center candleholder to convert this candlestick from a 3-light to a 2-light.

#1433 THUMBPRINT AND PANEL - name given by researchers

Dates: Ca. 1935-1937
Colors: Crystal, moongleam, flamingo, sahara, cobalt
Marked: Sometimes, in the constriction under the finial
Comments: See FLORAL BOWLS and MISCELLANEOUS Sections for matching items.

#4044 NEW ERA - original Heisey Co. name

Dates: Ca. 1934-1957
Colors: Crystal, alexandrite
Marked: No
Comments: Designed by Rodney Irwin. See STEMWARE Section for remainder of pattern. Available with and without bobeches and prisms. Imperial Glass reproduced the candlestick in crystal from 1958 to 1972, unmarked.

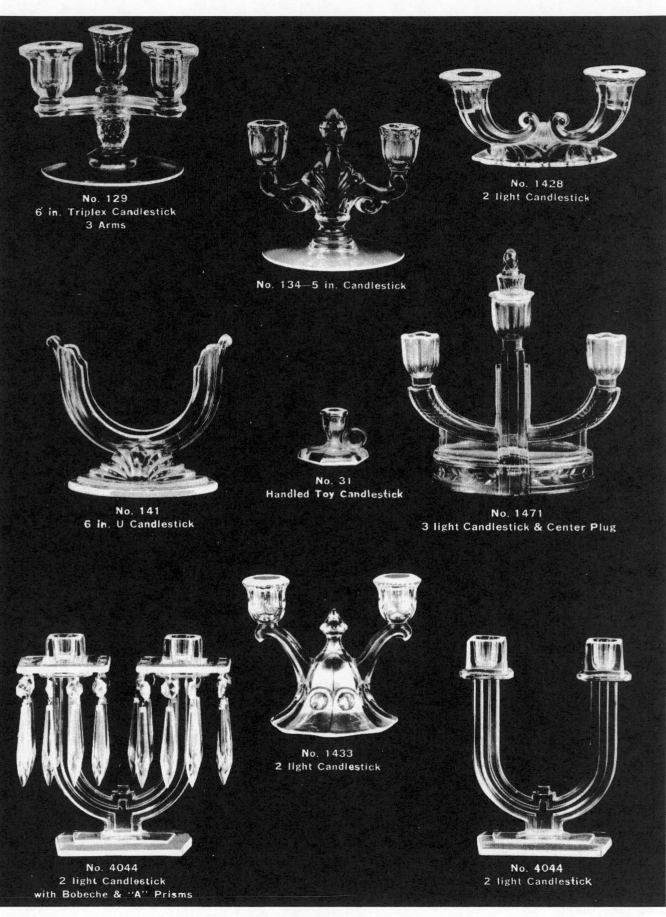

No. 129
6 in. Triplex Candlestick
3 Arms

No. 134—5 in. Candlestick

No. 1428
2 light Candlestick

No. 141
6 in. U Candlestick

No. 31
Handled Toy Candlestick

No. 1471
3 light Candlestick & Center Plug

No. 4044
2 light Candlestick
with Bobeche & "A" Prisms

No. 1433
2 light Candlestick

No. 4044
2 light Candlestick

Candlesticks

#1445 GRAPE CLUSTER 1-light - name given by researchers

Dates: Ca. 1935-1944
Colors: Crystal, cobalt
Marked: Yes, at the bottom just above the base.
Comments: See FLORAL BOWLS Section for matching bowl.

#140 CROCUS - name given by researchers

Dates: Ca. 1933-1936
Colors: Crystal, moongleam, flamingo, sahara, cobalt
Marked: Yes, at the bottom of the column just above the base.

#1445 GRAPE CLUSTER 2-light - name given by researchers

Dates: Ca. 1935-1944
Colors: Crystal, alexandrite, sahara, cobalt
Marked: Yes, at the bottom just above the foot.
Comments: See FLORAL BOWLS Section for matching bowl.

#142 CASCADE - name given by researchers

Dates: Ca. 1933-1957
Colors: Crystal, sahara, cobalt
Marked: Not usually
Comments: Very popular as a blank for decorations. Heisey offered 46 production cuttings and 8 etchings on this candlestick. Imperial Glass reproduced this candlestick in crystal from 1958 to 1979, unmarked.

#1425 VICTORIAN - original Heisey Co. name

Dates: Ca. 1933-1937; 1951
Colors: Crystal, sahara, cobalt
Marked: Yes, in the center of the underside of the skirted base
Comments: See PATTERN Section for remainder of pattern.

#1447 ROCOCO - original Heisey Co. name

Dates: Ca. 1933-1938
Colors: Crystal, sahara
Marked: Yes, at the bottom just above the base
Comments: See PATTERN Section for remainder of pattern.

#136 TRIPLEX - name given by researchers

Dates: January 1931-1936
Colors: Crystal, moongleam, flamingo, sahara, cobalt
Marked: Not usually.

#110 - See information earlier in this section.

#300 OLD WILLIAMSBURG 2-light candelabrum - original Heisey Co. name

Dates: Ca. 1901-1944
Colors: Crystal, sahara
Marked: Not usually

#300 OLD WILLIAMSBURG 1-light candelabrum - original Heisey Co. name

Dates: Ca. 1901-1957
Colors: Crystal, sahara
Marked: Yes, at the top of the column
Comments: The 12″ height only was made in sahara. Imperial Glass reproduced this candelabrum in crystal from 1958 to 1979.

#300 OLD WILLIAMSBURG 3-light candelabrum - original Heisey Co. name

Dates: Ca. 1901-1944; 1957
Colors: Crystal, sahara
Marked: Sometimes, at the top of the column.

No. 140
7 in. 2 light Candlestick

No. 1445
1 light Candlestick

No. 1445
2 light Candlestick

No. 142
3 light Candlestick

No. 110 Candlestick

No. 1425
2 light Candlestick

No. 1447
2 light Candlestick

No. 136
Triplex Candlestick

No. 1445
1 light Candlestick
with No. 6 Bobeche & "A" Prisms

Candlesticks

No 300—Two Light Candelabrum
Consists of:
1—No. 300—Two Light Base
1—No. 300—Two Light Arm
2—No. 300—Bobeche
2—No. 300—Candleholders
2—No. 51—Ferrules
2—No. 54—Ferrules
20—"A" Prisms
or
20—4 in. "C" Prisms
(Height 16 in.—Spread 14 in.)

No. 300
No. 0—One Light Candelabrum
Consists of:
1—No. 0—One Light Base
1—No. 300—Bobeche
1—No. 300—Candleholder
1—No. 54—Ferrule
10—"A" Prisms
or
10—4 in. "C" Prisms
(Height 10 in.)

No. 1—One Light Candelabrum
Consists of:
1—No. 1—One Light Base
1—No. 300—Bobeche
1—No. 300—Candleholder
1—No. 54—Ferrule
10—"A" Prisms
or
10—4 in. "C" Prisms
(Height 12 in.)

#300 pattern candelabra

No. 300—Three Light Candelabrum
Consists of:
1—No. 300—Three Light Base
1—No. 300—Three Light Arm
3—No. 300—Bobeche
1—No. 6—Bobeche
3—No. 300—Candleholders
1—No. 51—Ferrule
3—No. 54—Ferrules
52—"A" Prisms
or
40—"A" Prisms & 12—5½ in. "C" Prisms
(Height 21 in.—Spread 14 in.)

#300 pattern candelabrum

#301 OLD WILLIAMSBURG (short base) - original Heisey Co. name

Dates: August, 1924-1957
Colors: Crystal, alexandrite, sahara, cobalt
Marked: Occasionally, in the constriction of the base.
Comments: Imperial Glass reproduced the 2-light in crystal from 1958 to 1976. It also reproduced the 3-light from 1958 to 1981 in crystal. Both styles were engraved with Pairpoint's "Harwich" design.

No. 301   Two Light Candelabrum
Consists of:
1 No. 301 Two Light Base
1 No. 300 Two Light Arm
2 No. 300 Bobeche
2 No. 300 Candleholders
1 No. 51 Ferrule
2 No. 54 Ferrules
20 "A" Prisms
or
20—4 in. "C" Prisms
(Height 10½ in.)

No. 301—Three Light Candelabrum
Consists of:
1—No. 301—Three Light Base
1—No. 300—Three Light Arm
3—No. 300—Bobeche
3—No. 300—Candleholders
1—No. 51—Ferrule
3—No. 54—Ferrules
30—4 in. "C" Prisms
or
30—"A" Prisms
(Height 10½ in.—Spread 13 in.)

#101 SHELF SUPPORT

Dates: Ca. 1915-1933+
Colors: Crystal only
Marked: May be marked on top
Comments: A very basic, standard shape made by other companies as well as Heisey. Many are seen in yellowish, poor quality glass.

#520 INNOVATION - name given by researchers

Dates: Ca. 1928-1929
Colors: Crystal only
Marked: Yes, in the constriction at the bottom of the stopper
Comments: Patent #1761200 applied for 1/30/28 and granted 6/3/30. E. Wilson Heisey listed as designer. Made in two parts: the stopper held the candle, while the well could be filled with colored water or sand.

#300 OLD WILLIAMSBURG candle lamp - original Heisey Co. name

Dates: Ca. 1901-1916; 1924-1955
Colors: Crystal only
Marked: Sometimes, at the top of the column

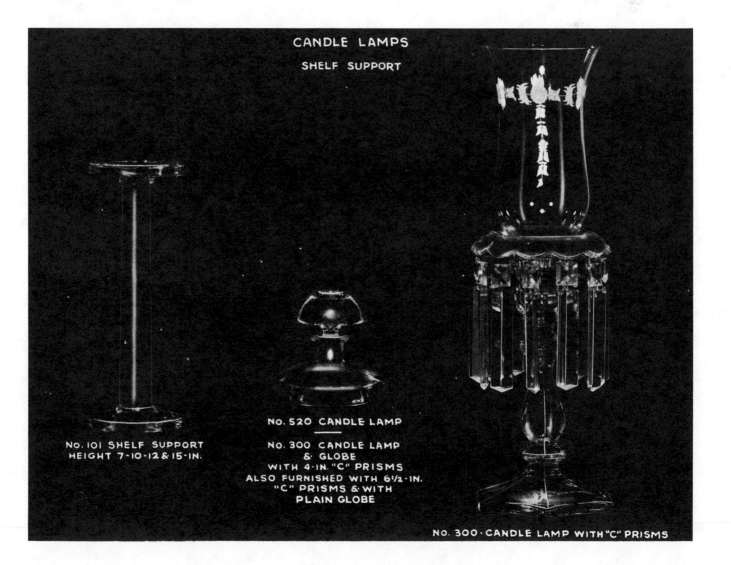

CANDLE LAMPS
SHELF SUPPORT

NO. 101 SHELF SUPPORT
HEIGHT 7-10-12 & 15-IN.

NO. 520 CANDLE LAMP

NO. 300 CANDLE LAMP
& GLOBE
WITH 4-IN. "C" PRISMS
ALSO FURNISHED WITH 6½-IN.
"C" PRISMS & WITH
PLAIN GLOBE

NO. 300 · CANDLE LAMP WITH "C" PRISMS

#402 GOTHIC - name given by researchers

Dates: December 1932-1936
Colors: Crystal, sahara, crystal with cobalt foot, cobalt with crystal foot
Marked: Sometimes, on the center point between the arms.

#401 OLD WILLIAMSBURG - original Heisey Co. name

Dates: Ca. 1929-1944
Colors: Crystal only
Marked: Sometimes, at the top of the column

#400 OLD WILLIAMSBURG - original Heisey Co. name

Dates: Ca. 1929-1944
Colors: Crystal only
Marked: Sometimes, at the top of the column.

No. 402—Two Light Candelabrum
Consists of:
1—No. 402—Two Light Base
2—No. 402—Bobeche
20—"A" Prisms
or
20—4 in. "C" Prisms
(Height 11 in.—Spread 13 In.)

No 401—One Light Candelabrum
Consists of:
1—No. 300—No. 1—One Light Base
1—No. 7—Bobeche
1—No. 300—Candleholder
1—No. 51—Ferrule
12—"A" Prisms
or
12—4 in. "C" Prisms
or
12—5½ in. "C" Prisms
(Height 13 in.)

No. 400—One Light Candelabrum
Consists of:
1—No. 300—No. 1—One Light Base
1—No. 7—Bobeche
1—No. 300—Bobeche
1—Center Post
1—No. 300—Candleholder
1—No. 51—Ferrule
1—No. 54—Ferrule
22—"A" Prisms
or
10—"A" Prisms & 12—4 in. "C" Prisms
(Height 22 in.)

#400-401 & 402 pattern candelabra

Water Lamps

In 1928, the *POTTERY, GLASS AND BRASS SALESMAN* reported that Heisey's New York showroom was displaying a number of new items, including water lamps. These were a novelty item consisting of a blown lamp base to which electrical fittings and a shade were affixed. The idea was that the lamp base could be filled with water which would magnify and accentuate the optic design in the glass while giving stability to the lamp. These lamps were made in a number of different patterns, although some which have been seen were probably "one of a kind" whimseys or presentation pieces. All of these lamps were produced from molds which were already in existence for vases, comports or pitchers in their various patterns. The lamps seem not to have met with much success and were probably all discontinued by late 1931.

#4206 OPTIC TOOTH - name given by researchers

Dates: Ca. 1928-1931
Colors: Crystal; crystal with moongleam foot; flamingo
Marked: No

#4262 CHARTER OAK - name given by researchers

Dates: Ca. 1928-1931
Colors: Crystal, moongleam, flamingo
Marked: Yes, at the top of the stem
Comments: The same design as Heisey's #3362 stemware, from which the name was taken.

#4366 TROJAN - name given by researchers

Dates: Ca. 1929
Colors: Crystal, moongleam foot with crystal bowl, flamingo
Marked: Yes, at top of stem
Comments: Same design as Heisey's #3366 stemware, from which the name was taken.

WATER LAMPS
DIAMOND OPTIC

ALL LAMPS SOLD WITH, OR WITHOUT, FIXTURES
IN CRYSTAL, MOONGLEAM FOOT-CRYSTAL BOWL, AND ALL FLAMINGO

4206 - HEIGHT 12-IN.
ALSO MAKE 8 & 10-IN. HIGH

4262 - HEIGHT 10-IN.

4366 - HEIGHT 9-IN.

#1183 REVERE - original Heisey Co. name
Dates: 1933-1937
Colors: Crystal, sahara
Marked: Yes, at bottom of each column
Comments: The four candleholders screw into the flat base. Occasionally found with cuttings.

#1183 REVERE - original Heisey Co. name
Dates: 1926-1927
Colors: Crystal, moongleam
Marked: Yes, on bottom
Comments: A two-piece combination able to be used as a vase or a candlestick or as both at the same time. The insert has 4 holes in it to accommodate flower stems. The insert was only made in crystal. Occasionally found with a cutting. Available with a variety of prisms from Heisey including cobalt and amethyst prisms (imported).

#8040 EVA MAE - name given by researchers
Dates: Unknown. Circa 1925 (because of colors available)
Colors: Crystal, moongleam, flamingo
Marked: Yes, at the top of the column just beneath knob
Comments: Original number not known.

#1183 REVERE candle vase with insert

#1183 REVERE 4-light candleblock

#8040 EVA MAE candlestick

313

Colognes

Collectors searching for Heisey colognes often have a difficult time finding examples. Collectors also often add other ladies' dresser items such as hair receivers, powder jars, trays, pin trays and the like. In the color period, the colognes were often sold with puff boxes as boudoir sets.

Most Heisey colognes shown here are marked although the #4034 and #4035 are not. Colognes in colors are quite attractive and the diamond optic added to some makes them absolutely glisten.

The long stoppers shown are difficult to find without damage to their tips and are usually not marked.

If the colognes have been filled with cologne or perfume for a long period, they are often cloudy. The chemicals from the perfumes seem to discolor glass much as water or salt does.

Several of the colognes are found with various decorations: enamels, gold, silver or colored stains. Some cutting companies, such as Hawkes, used the colognes for their designs. Sometimes these are found with their signatures.

Even though some of the small sizes such as ¼ oz. or ½ oz. would seem to be better called perfumes, the Heisey Company consistently called all these bottles "colognes" from the smallest to the largest.

See PATTERN Section for photograph of the #1405 Ipswich cologne

#4034 SEVEN CIRCLE - name given by researchers
Dates: Ca. 1929-1933
Colors: Crystal, moongleam, flamingo
Marked: No
Comments: Made in ¾ oz. with #69 stopper.

#4035 SEVEN OCTAGON - name given by researchers
Dates: Ca. 1929-1933
Colors: Crystal, moongleam, flamingo
Marked: No
Comments: Made in ¾ oz. with #69 or Duck stopper. This cologne differs from #4034 because it has eight sides while the #4034 is round.

#485 , #487 HEXAGON STEM - name given by researchers
Dates: #485: Ca. 1920-Ca. 1935; #487: Ca. 1920-1933.
Colors: Crystal, moongleam, flamingo
Marked: Yes, on bottom of foot
Comments: Made in ½ oz., 1 oz., 1¾ oz. and 3½ oz. sizes. #485 has a #64 stopper while #487 has a #63 stopper, otherwise they are identical. See the MISCELLANEOUS Section for #485 with a #71 peg stopper.

#515 TAPER - name given by researchers

Dates: Ca. 1922-1933
Colors: Crystal, moongleam, flamingo. ¼ oz. also made in hawthorne.
Marked: Yes, on bottom of body just above foot.
Comments: Made in ¼ oz. and 1 oz. sizes in diamond optic or plain.

#516 FAIRACRE - name given by researchers

Dates: Ca. 1922-1933
Colors: Crystal, moongleam, flamingo, hawthorne
Marked: Sometimes marked on bottom
Comments: Made in 1 oz. size only with diamond optic. Also listed as made plain, although this is more difficult to find. The name is taken from Heisey's #3355 Fairacre stemware, which is very similar to the stem on this cologne.

#517 CIRCLE PAIR - name given by researchers

Dates: Ca. 1922-1933
Colors: Crystal, moongleam, flamingo.
Marked: Unknown
Comments: Made in ¼ oz. size in diamond optic. Name is taken from the name given to the #2516 Circle Pair soda line, which the cologne closely resembles.

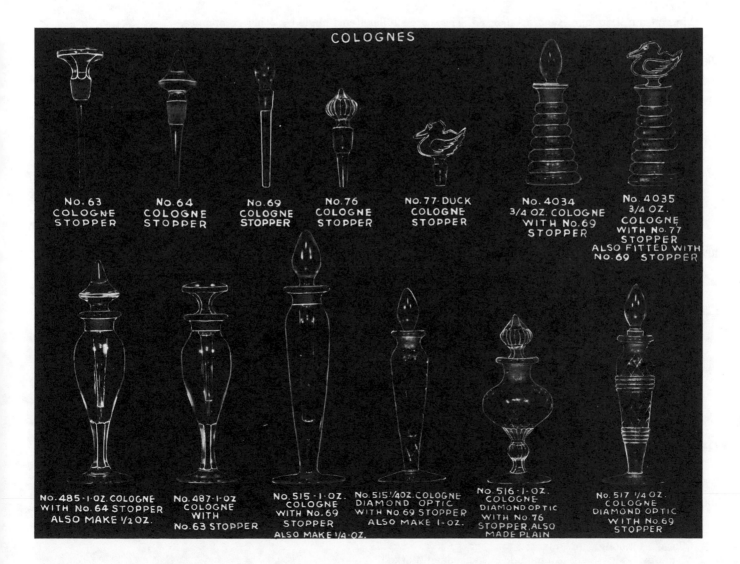

COLOGNES

NO. 63 COLOGNE STOPPER

NO. 64 COLOGNE STOPPER

NO. 69 COLOGNE STOPPER

NO. 76 COLOGNE STOPPER

NO. 77 - DUCK COLOGNE STOPPER

NO. 4034 3/4 OZ. COLOGNE WITH NO. 69 STOPPER

NO. 4035 3/4 OZ. COLOGNE WITH NO. 77 STOPPER ALSO FITTED WITH NO. 69 STOPPER

NO. 485 - 1 OZ. COLOGNE WITH NO. 64 STOPPER ALSO MAKE 1/2 OZ.

NO. 487 - 1 OZ. COLOGNE WITH NO. 63 STOPPER

NO. 515 - 1 OZ. COLOGNE WITH NO. 69 STOPPER ALSO MAKE 1/4 OZ.

NO. 515 1/4 OZ. COLOGNE DIAMOND OPTIC WITH NO. 69 STOPPER ALSO MAKE 1 - OZ.

NO. 516 - 1 OZ. COLOGNE DIAMOND OPTIC WITH NO. 76 STOPPER. ALSO MADE PLAIN

NO. 517 1/4 OZ. COLOGNE DIAMOND OPTIC WITH NO. 69 STOPPER

Colonial Pieces in Color

Colonial patterns are usually described as simple, plain items with panels, flutes and scallops as their main design elements. Since the great interest in colonial patterned glass was during the early 1900's and teens, most of these simple lines had been discontinued before Heisey's color period began. There was always a continuing market for some colonial pieces, however, and Heisey marketed a colonial line until it closed in 1957.

There is no one colonial pattern which was made in color. Often several pieces of a pattern were made in various colors, but these seem to be limited. The usual colors found in colonials are moongleam and flamingo, but even these are scarce. Occasionally items are found in sahara, zircon and vaseline. Pieces in tangerine and cobalt should be considered scarce. In one price list, Heisey offered four sizes of a colonial stem line (#359) in alexandrite, but these are also very difficult to find.

Very few colored colonial items were actually listed in the price lists, but several pieces have been found by collectors. A very unusual tangerine pilsner was recently found. Zircon humidors in #352 Flat Panel pattern are occasionally found. These usually bear the impression of "Benson and Hedges" along with a patent date and were undoubtedly a special order item for this tobacco company.

Also included in this section are several pieces of #350 Pinwheel and Fan. Although this pattern is not a colonial, being rather a copy of cut glass, it is included to complete this section. Other colonial pieces may be found in the PATTERN Section.

Many of the items were not listed in price lists in colors, so dating would only be guesswork. Consequently, that entry has been dropped. All items were also made in crystal.

#150 BANDED FLUTE - name given by researchers
10″ tray - moongleam, flamingo - marked

#299 TODDY
Moongleam, flamingo, sahara - marked. There are similar items made by other companies.

#300 PEERLESS - adaptation of Heisey description of pattern
Low footed tumbler - moongleam, flamingo - marked
4½ oz. low footed sherbet, shallow - flamingo - marked
8 oz. schoppen - flamingo - marked

#300½ PEERLESS
2 oz. bar, flared - moongleam, flamingo - marked
2 oz. bar - moongleam, flamingo - marked
#2 water bottle - sahara - not marked
8 oz. tumbler - moongleam, flamingo - marked
11″ vase - flamingo - marked (not illustrated)

#302 PEERLESS
12 oz. ice tea - flamingo - marked

#339 CONTINENTAL - original Heisey Co. name
Water bottle - flamingo - rarely marked

#341 PURITAN - original Heisey Co. name
½ gal. tankard - flamingo - marked
3 oz. low sherbet - flamingo - marked
Custard - flamingo - marked

#341½ PURITAN
1 pint squat jug - crystal with moongleam handle - marked

#350 PINWHEEL AND FAN - name given by researchers
Punch bowl - moongleam - marked
Tumbler - unusual shade of yellow - marked
Custard - moongleam - marked
4″ nappy - odd shade of moongleam, vaseline - marked
8″ nappy - moongleam, flamingo, vaseline, marigold - marked

#351 PRISCILLA - original Heisey Co. name

4 oz. ale - flamingo - marked
12 oz. ale - moongleam, flamingo, sahara, cobalt - marked
14 oz. ale - tangerine - marked

#352 FLAT PANEL - name given by researchers

French dressing bottle - flamingo; crystal bottle, moongleam stopper; crystal bottle, flamingo stopper - unmarked
Cigar jar - moongleam, zircon - marked
Lavender jar - moongleam, flamingo - marked
Finger bowl - flamingo - marked

#353 MEDIUM FLAT PANEL - name given by researchers

8″ vase - flamingo, hawthorne, vaseline - marked
12″ ice cream or candy tray - flamingo - marked
Toothbrush holder - moongleam - marked
Individual almond (#393) - moongleam, flamingo, sahara, hawthorne - sometimes marked
Large almond - moongleam, flamingo, hawthorne - marked

#354 WIDE FLAT PANEL - name given by researchers

Stack set (individual cream, sugar and butter) - flamingo - marked
Individual butter - flamingo, sahara - marked
Hotel cream & sugar, oval, footed - moongleam, flamingo, sahara, hawthorne - marked
16 oz. sanitary syrup - moongleam - marked and usually patent date of May 9, 1909 in bottom in circular pattern

#393 NARROW FLUTE - original Heisey Co. description of pattern

Bitters bottle - cobalt - usually unmarked
Individual salt - moongleam flamingo - sometimes marked
Banana split - flamingo - marked
Individual cream - moongleam, flamingo, sahara, experimental light blue - marked
Individual sugar - moongleam, flamingo, marigold - marked
Salt shaker - moongleam, flamingo - usually not marked

#394 NARROW FLUTE - original Heisey Co. description of pattern

Domino sugar - moongleam, flamingo, sahara - marked
12″ celery tray - moongleam, flamingo - marked
12″ combination relish, 3-part - moongleam, flamingo - marked

#433 GRECIAN BORDER - original Heisey Co. description of pattern

21″ punch bowl plate - flamingo - marked
15″ punch bowl and foot - flamingo - marked
4½ oz. custard - flamingo - marked

#465 RECESSED PANEL - name given by researchers

½ lb. candy jar and cover - moongleam, vaseline - marked

#473 NARROW FLUTE WITH RIM - name given by researchers

Low footed compote - vaseline - marked
Small oval plate - vaseline - marked (not illustrated)
NOTE: See PATTERN Section for other items in the pattern.

#468 OCTAGON WITH RIM - name given by researchers

12″ celery - moongleam, flamingo - marked

#527 TAPER - name given by researchers

4½ oz. soda, diamond optic - moongleam,
flamingo, sahara - marked

#588

3 oz. soda - flamingo, amber - marked

#603

5 oz. soda, diamond optic - flamingo - marked
12 oz. soda, diamond optic - flamingo - marked

#1112

4½ oz. sherbet, diamond optic - flamingo - probably marked

#1216

4½ in. nappy, star bottom, cupped - amber - marked
Roman punch, narrow optic - amber - marked

317

Colonial Pieces in Color

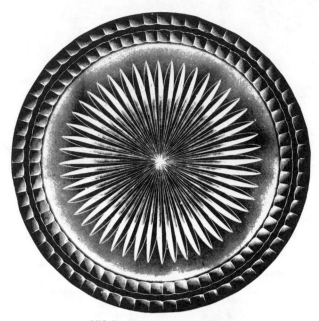

150 BANDED FLUTE tray

299 toddy

300 PEERLESS
low footed tumbler

300 sherbet

300 schoppen

PEERLESS

300½
bar, flared

300½
bar

300½ tumbler

300½ PEERLESS
#2 water bottle

#302 PEERLESS
ice tea

#339 CONTINENTAL
water bottle

#341 PURITAN
tankard

#341 PURITAN
sherbet

#341 PURITAN
custard

#341½ PURITAN
squat jug

#350 PINWHEEL & FAN

4" nappy

custard

tumbler

punch bowl and foot

8" nappy

#351 PRISCILLA

4 oz. ale   12 oz. ale

#352 FLAT PANEL
French dressing
bottle

#352 FLAT PANEL
cigar jar

#352 lavender jar   #352 finger bowl

#353 MEDIUM FLAT PANEL
individual almond   large almond

#353 MEDIUM FLAT PANEL

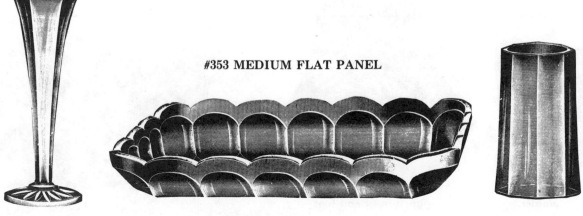

8″ vase   12″ ice cream or candy tray   toothbrush
holder

320

#354 WIDE FLAT PANEL

stack set   hotel sugar   hotel cream   16 oz. sanitary syrup

#393 NARROW FLUTE

individual sugar   individual cream

salt

bitters
bottle

individual
salt

banana split

#394 NARROW FLUTE domino sugar

#394 NARROW FLUTE celery tray

#465 RECESSED PANEL
½ lb. covered candy jar

#433 21" punch bowl plate

#433 GRECIAN BORDER
punch bowl and foot

#433 custard

#473 NARROW FLUTE WITH RIM
low footed comport

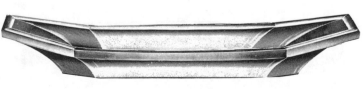

#468 OCTAGON WITH RIM
celery tray

#527 TAPER
4½ oz. soda

#588
3 oz. soda

#603
5 oz. soda

#603
12 oz. soda

#1112 4½ oz. sherbet

1216 PLAIN
nappy

1216 ROMAN PUNCH

Colonial Pieces in Alexandrite

#300 PEERLESS - original description of pattern
 Low footed tumbler

#341½ PURITAN - original Heisey Co. name
 Finger bowl

#359 COLONIAL stemware - original Heisey Co. description
 7 oz. goblet
 4 oz. saucer champagne
 3 oz. cocktail
 2 oz. sherbet

#373 OLD WILLIAMSBURG - original Heisey Co. name
 Goblet

#517
 1 quart jug

#1000
 Marmalade and cover

#1150 COLONIAL STAR - name given by researchers
 7″ plate

NOTE: All items except the #300 Peerless and #373 goblets were listed in a price list. The #517 jug was only found as a handwritten notation.

Colonial Pieces in Alexandrite

#300 PEERLESS
low footed tumbler

#341½ PURITAN
finger bowl

#373 OLD WILLIAMSBURG
goblet

goblet

saucer champagne

cocktail

sherbet

#359 COLONIAL stemware

#517 jug

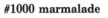

#1000 marmalade

#1150 COLONIAL STAR
7″ plate

Creams and Sugars

Every major Heisey pattern had at least one size cream and sugar set. Many had a variety of sizes usually referred to as the hotel or individual. A number of these sugars are pictured with lids but were sold with or without them.

About 1915 Heisey seemed to branch out with several sets of miscellaneous creams and sugars. Many were very plain and have been found decorated with silver overlay, enameling, acid etchings or wheel cuttings. Some of these were cut in the Heisey factory but most were sold to decorating companies such as Honesdale and Lotus.

Even though many creams and sugars are labeled in catalogs as "hotel", this does not mean that they were made exclusively for hotel use. The term seems to be a manner of identification for the company - usually an indication of a moderate size.

Cream and sugar sets from #1020 to #1180 seem to have been made for the extra market decorating companies provided. These plain styles were probably good selling gift items and easily blended with other pattern lines and also accented fine china and linens.

Some of these sets were eventually adopted into other lines (such as the #1023 set into the #1184 Yeoman line), but most continued to be just a cream and sugar set with no other matching pieces.

See the MISCELLANEOUS Section for #1189, #354 and #4222 creams and sugars. Also see the PATTERN Section and the COLONIAL PIECES IN COLOR Section.

Eileen and George Schamel

#414 TUDOR - original Heisey Co. name

Dates: Ca. 1925-1935
Colors: Crystal only
Marked: Yes
Comments: No matching cream was listed in price lists. Uncommon.

#479 PETAL - name given by researchers

Dates: Ca. 1927-1937
Colors: Crystal, moongleam, flamingo, sahara, hawthorne
Marked: Usually, on side of stem
Comments: Crystal sets are more difficult to find than some of the other colors. The handled jelly was made in 1919. The sugar has also been seen with a notched lid, making it a marmalade. To date, no matching sugar lid has been seen.

#1020 PHYLLIS - name given by researchers

Dates: 1920-1933
Colors: Crystal, moongleam, flamingo, vaseline
Marked: Yes
Comments: Often has a patent date of 8/30/21 in base along with Diamond H. Patent #58832 applied for 11/18/20 and granted 8/30/21. Designed by A. J. Sanford. Made plain or wide optic. Moongleam is found both in the early deep green shade and in a lighter shade.

#1021 CHRISTINE - name given by researchers

Dates: Ca. 1921-1933
Colors: Crystal only
Marked: Yes. Lid is also marked.
Comments: Often found cut or with silver overlay or enamel decorations.

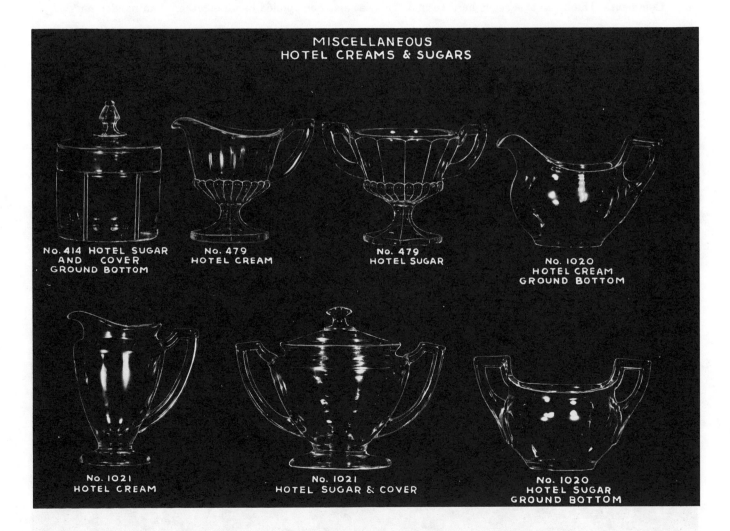

MISCELLANEOUS
HOTEL CREAMS & SUGARS

No. 414 HOTEL SUGAR AND COVER GROUND BOTTOM

No. 479 HOTEL CREAM

No. 479 HOTEL SUGAR

No. 1020 HOTEL CREAM GROUND BOTTOM

No. 1021 HOTEL CREAM

No. 1021 HOTEL SUGAR & COVER

No. 1020 HOTEL SUGAR GROUND BOTTOM

#1022 HARDING - name given by researchers

Dates: Ca. 1921-1933
Colors: Crystal only
Marked: Yes. Lid is also marked.
Comments: Somewhat difficult to find.

#1024 EILEEN - name given by researchers

Dates: Ca. 1922-1933
Colors: Crystal only
Marked: Yes
Comments: Somewhat difficult to find. Often seen with cuttings or silver overlay.

#1025 SHARON - name given by researchers

Dates: Ca. 1922-1933
Colors: Crystal only
Marked: Yes
Comments: Usually found cut or with silver overlay.

#1180 DEBRA - name given by researchers

Dates: Ca. 1919-1935
Colors: Crystal only
Marked: Yes
Comments: The lid to this set is hard to find. This set also has applied handles rather than molded ones.

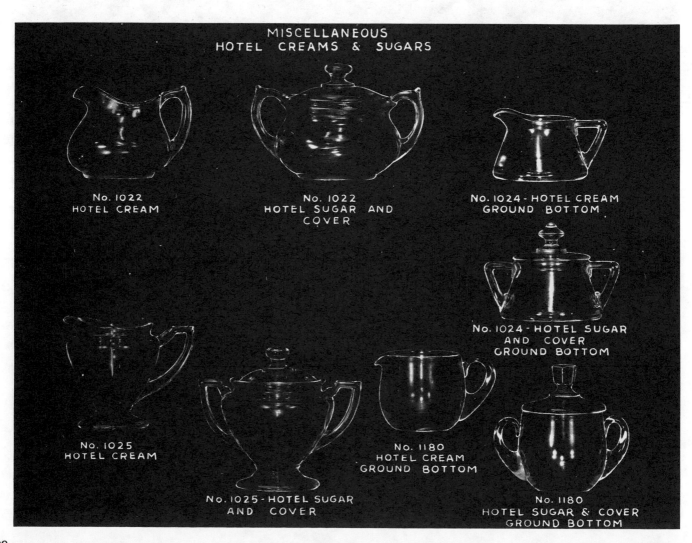

MISCELLANEOUS
HOTEL CREAMS & SUGARS

No. 1022
HOTEL CREAM

No. 1022
HOTEL SUGAR AND
COVER

No. 1024 - HOTEL CREAM
GROUND BOTTOM

No. 1024 - HOTEL SUGAR
AND COVER
GROUND BOTTOM

No. 1025
HOTEL CREAM

No. 1025 - HOTEL SUGAR
AND COVER

No. 1180
HOTEL CREAM
GROUND BOTTOM

No. 1180
HOTEL SUGAR & COVER
GROUND BOTTOM

#360 CORBY - name given by researchers
Dates: 1922-1929; 1933-1935 (for colors)
Colors: Crystal, moongleam, flamingo, sahara
Marked: Yes. Lid is also marked.
Comments: Not common. Colors were listed in only one price list. (Illustration not available)

#1403 HALF CIRCLE - name given by researchers
Dates: 1930-1935
Colors: Crystal, moongleam, flamingo, sahara
Marked: Yes
Comments: An individual set and difficult to find. Sahara is most common.

#1001 CASWELL - name given by researchers
Dates: Ca. 1925-1933
Colors: Crystal, flamingo, crystal body with moongleam foot & handle
Marked: No
Comments: An unusual set, possibly made as a waffle set: sugar sifter and syrup. Made in diamond optic.

1403 HALF CIRCLE individual sugar & cream

1001 CASWELL sugar sifter and cream

Finger Bowls

These small bowls were made to accompany stemware lines. Usually the shape of the finger bowl matches the shape of the goblet bowl in the corresponding stem line.

Standard shapes such as #3335, #3309, #4071, #4075 and #4080 were used with many stemware lines.

Many of these bowls were made in colors and various optics. Since most are not marked with the Diamond H, recognition of the shape is important. The only bowl shown which may be found marked is the #3397 Gascony.

Most of these bowls are also shown in the STEMWARE Section along with their corresponding stemware lines.

#3309 PETITE - original Heisey Co. name
Dates: 1917 +
Colors: Crystal, moongleam, flamingo, marigold

#3311 VELVEDERE - original Heisey Co. name
Dates: 1917+
Colors: Crystal only

#3312 GAYOSO - original Heisey Co. name
Dates: 1917+
Colors: Crystal, moongleam, flamingo, marigold

#3317 DRAKE - name given by researchers
Dates: 1917+
Colors: Crystal, flamingo

#3359 PLATEAU - name given by researchers
Dates: 1926-1937
Colors: Crystal, moongleam, flamingo, marigold

#3481 GLENFORD - name given by researchers
Dates: 1925-1937
Colors: Crystal, moongleam, flamingo

#4071
Dates: 1917+
Colors: Crystal, moongleam, flamingo, marigold, sahara, tangerine

#4072
Dates: 1917-1937
Colors: Crystal only

#4074
Dates: 1917-1937
Colors: Crystal, moongleam, flamingo

#4075
Dates: 1917+
Colors: Crystal, moongleam, flamingo, marigold, sahara, alexandrite

#4079
Dates: 1917-1937
Colors: Crystal only

#4080
Dates: 1917+
Colors: Crystal, moongleam, flamingo. Zircon in saturn optic.

#3335 LADY LEG - name given by researchers
Dates: 1919+
Colors: Crystal, sahara, cobalt. Zircon in saturn optic.

#3308 BOB WHITE - original Heisey Co. name
Dates: 1917+
Colors: Crystal only

See STEMWARE Section for finger bowls matching other stemware lines. (#3390, #3381, #3397 and #3362)

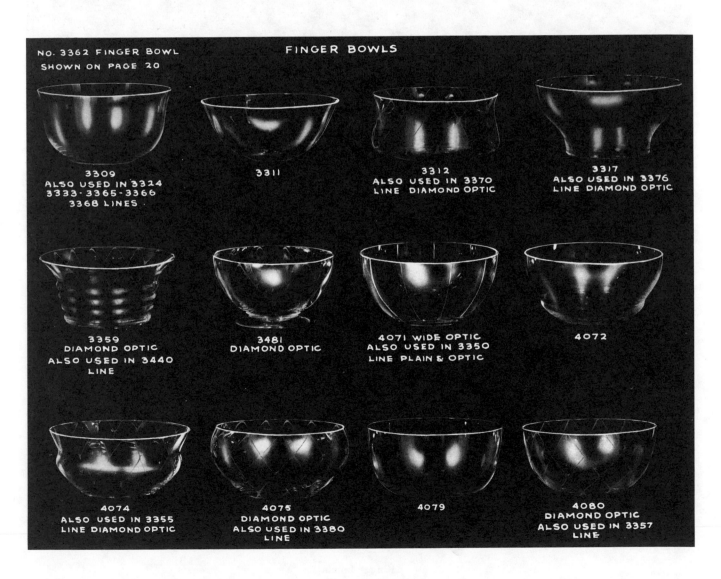

FINGER BOWLS

NO. 3362 FINGER BOWL SHOWN ON PAGE 20

3309
ALSO USED IN 3324
3333-3365-3366
3368 LINES

3311

3312
ALSO USED IN 3370
LINE DIAMOND OPTIC

3317
ALSO USED IN 3376
LINE DIAMOND OPTIC

3359
DIAMOND OPTIC
ALSO USED IN 3440
LINE

3481
DIAMOND OPTIC

4071 WIDE OPTIC
ALSO USED IN 3350
LINE PLAIN & OPTIC

4072

4074
ALSO USED IN 3355
LINE DIAMOND OPTIC

4075
DIAMOND OPTIC
ALSO USED IN 3380
LINE

4079

4080
DIAMOND OPTIC
ALSO USED IN 3357
LINE

No. 3390
Wide Optic Only

No. 3381
Wide Optic or Diamond Optic

No. 3397
Wide Optic Only

No. 3311
Plain or Wide Optic

No. 4080
Plain, Wide Optic or Diamond Optic

No. 4071
Plain or Diamond Optic

No. 3309
Plain, Wide Optic or Diamond Optic

No. 4074
Plain, Wide Optic or Diamond Optic

No. 3312
Plain or Wide Optic

No. 3362
Diamond Optic Only

No. 3335
Plain or Wide Optic

No. 4075
Plain, Wide Optic or Diamond Optic

No. 3308
Plain or Wide Optic

Finger bowls

Floral Bowls and Plateaus

The late 1920's and early 1930's created a demand for a new decorative arrangement—the console set. Composed of a floral bowl and candlesticks, these sets became very popular during this time.

In the past flowers were displayed in vases—usually tall vases. Apparently styles changed and floral arrangements took on a new, lower look which required the use of a flatter holder—the floral bowl. This may have occured with the advent of smaller, more intimate dinners where conversation could include everyone at the table, not just persons seated on either side.

Candlesticks had been popular for many years and good sellers for the company. The first floral bowls seem to have been just that—bowls with no matching candlesticks, although they were combined with candlesticks which blended well in design. The next step seems to have been matching candlesticks to the shapes of floral bowls, and we have low candlesticks with tooled rims which match the bowl shapes. Next came the console set in which the candlestick seems to have been designed first and the floral bowl which carries motifs found on the candlestick. This seems to be the case with types such as the #1445 Grape Cluster set.

After the time when console sets were brought out as separate items, no major Heisey tableware line was made without candlesticks and at least one style of floral bowl for use as a console set. Often the lines had several styles of both candlesticks and floral bowls so the lady of the home could choose the styles she preferred.

See the MISCELLANEOUS Section for #1201 floral bowl. Also see the section of FLOWER BLOCKS for the flower frogs used in floral bowls.

#9, #10, #11 GIBSON GIRL - name given by researchers

Dates: 1923-1933
Colors: Crystal, moongleam, flamingo, hawthorne
Marked: Yes
Comments: Used for some cuttings by Heisey. Compare with #45. Patent #75653 applied for 3/23/22 and granted 6/26/28. A. J. Sanford listed as designer.

#12, #13, #14 FLAT RIM - name given by researchers

Dates: 1923-1933
Colors: Crystal, moongleam, flamingo
Marked: Yes

#45 FOOTED GIBSON GIRL - name given by researchers

Dates: Ca. 1925-1933
Colors: Crystal, moongleam, flamingo
Marked: Should be.

#116 OAK LEAF - collectors' popular name

Dates: 1926-1933
Colors: Crystal, moongleam, flamingo, hawthorne
Marked: Yes
Comments: See CANDLESTICKS Section for matching candlestick.

#1194 PAUL REVERE & #1195 PAUL REVERE, OPTIC - names given by researchers

Dates: 1923-1933
Colors: Crystal, moongleam, flamingo
Marked: Not usually, but base is
Comments: #1195 was described as a "floral tray" and "new" in a 1926 turn book entry. Here the #1195 is illustrated on the separate base.

#1202 PANELED OCTAGON - name given by researchers

Dates: Ca. 1924-1935
Colors: Crystal, moongleam, flamingo. 11″ size made in hawthorne
Marked: Not usually, but base is
Comments: The base is a separate piece from the bowl.

#1203 FLAT PANELED OCTAGON - name given by researchers

Dates: Ca. 1924-1933
Colors: Crystal, moongleam, flamingo, hawthorne
Marked: Not usually, but base is
Comments: Illustrated here with a separate base.

#1204 SWIRL - name given by researchers

Dates: Ca. 1924-1933
Colors: Crystal, moongleam, flamingo
Marked: Yes

#1205 RAINDROP - name given by researchers

Dates: Ca. 1924-1933
Colors: Crystal, moongleam, flamingo
Marked: Yes
Comments: See CANDLESTICKS Section for matching candlestick.

#1206 SWIRL AND RAINDROP - name given by researchers

Dates: Ca. 1924-1933
Colors: Crystal, moongleam, flamingo
Marked: Yes

#1252 TWIST 12″ round floral bowl - name given by researchers

Dates: 1928-1937
Colors: Crystal, moongleam, flamingo, marigold, sahara, alexandrite
Marked: Yes
Comments: See PATTERN Section and CANDLESTICKS Section for matching items.

#1401 EMPRESS 8½″ footed floral bowl - original Heisey Co. name

Dates: 1930-1938
Colors: Crystal, moongleam, flamingo, sahara
Marked: Yes
Comments: See PATTERN Section and CANDLESTICKS Section for matching items.

#1252 TWIST 8″ round nasturtium bowl - name given by researchers

Dates: 1928-1937
Colors: Crystal, moongleam, flamingo, marigold, sahara, alexandrite
Marked: Yes
Comments: See PATTERN Section and CANDLESTICKS Section for matching items. These two floral bowls are some of the few items in Twist made in alexandrite.

#135 EMPRESS

Dates: 1930-1938
Colors: Crystal, moongleam, flamingo, sahara
Marked: Yes
Comments: The name is derived from the candlestick which was added to the #1401 Empress line but retained the number 135. See the CANDLESTICKS Section for the matching candlestick. Made as a console set only. Pairpoint engraved their "Bingham" pattern on this bowl.

#134 TRIDENT - name given by researchers

Dates: 1930-1938
Colors: Crystal, moongleam, flamingo, sahara, alexandrite
Marked: Probably not
Comments: The name is taken from the one given to the candlestick (see CANDLESTICKS Section for illustration.) Made only as a console set.

#1401 EMPRESS 7½″ footed nasturtium bowl - original Heisey Co. name

Dates: 1930-1938
Colors: Crystal, moongleam, flamingo, sahara
Marked: May be on the back of one of the dolphin feet
Comments: See CANDLESTICKS and PATTERN Section for matching items. Probably made from the same mold as the 10″ floral bowl, but it is cupped rather than flared.

#1429 PRISTINE - name given by researchers

Dates: 1933-1938
Colors: Crystal, moongleam, sahara, cobalt
Marked: Yes

#1440 ARCH - name given by researchers

Dates: Ca. 1934-1937
Colors: Crystal, sahara, cobalt
Marked: Yes
Comments: Note the six small feet. Compare the design with the #1417 Arch tumbler in the MISCELLANEOUS Section.

#1425 VICTORIAN 10½" floral bowl - original Heisey Co. name

Dates: 1933-1939
Colors: Crystal, sahara, cobalt
Marked: Should be
Comments: See PATTERN and CANDLESTICKS Section for matching items. Notice that the bowl did not remain in the line as long as some of the sodas.

#1445 GRAPE CLUSTER - name given by researchers

Dates: Ca. 1934 -ca. 1945
Colors: Crystal, moongleam, sahara, cobalt. Rare in a zircon shade.
Marked: Yes
Comments: See the CANDLESTICKS Section for matching 1 and 2 light candlesticks. While the 2-light is known in alexandrite, there is no report of a floral bowl in this color. The zircon bowl seen is an odd shade. Made as a console set only. Sometimes used for cuttings.

#1433 THUMBPRINT AND PANEL - name given by researchers

Dates: 1934-1937
Colors: Crystal, moongleam, flamingo, sahara, cobalt
Marked: No
Comments: See CANDLESTICKS and MISCELLANEOUS Sections for other items in this pattern. This is a very short pattern composed of the console set, vase and a cheese and cracker. Its design is taken from old early American glass, possibly Sandwich.

#1428 WARWICK 11" horn of plenty floral bowl - original Heisey Co. name

Dates: 1933-1941
Colors: Crystal, sahara, cobalt
Marked: Probably
Comments: Other pieces in Warwick are known in flamingo and moongleam so this piece might also be found in these colors. See PATTERN and CANDLESTICKS Sections for other items.

#3397 GASCONY 10" footed floral bowl, 10" floral bowl, no foot - original Heisey Co. name

Dates: 1932-1941
Colors: Crystal; sahara; cobalt bowl, crystal base; tangerine bowl, crystal base. Possibly the bowl with no foot was made in the solid colors.
Marked: Footed bowl may be marked on base
Comments: See the STEMWARE Section for other items in pattern.

#4044 NEW ERA 11" floral bowl - original Heisey Co. name

Dates: 1934-1941
Colors: Crystal only
Marked: Not usually
Comments: See STEMWARE Section for matching items. Also see CANDLESTICKS Section. Sometimes seen with frosted designs.

#1472 PARALLEL QUARTER - name given by researchers

Dates: 1935-1944
Colors: Crystal only
Marked: No
Comments: See CANDLESTICKS Section for the matching candlestick. The floral bowl was made in a 9" and a 12" size. The console set was etched by Heisey and is sometimes seen with a cutting done by a decorating company. Made as a console set only.

#1447 ROCOCO 12" oval floral bowl - original Heisey Co. name

Dates: 1935-1938
Colors: Crystal, sahara
Marked: Should be
Comments: See CANDLESTICKS and PATTERN Section for matching items.

#1471 EMPIRE - original Heisey Co. name

Dates: 1935-1938
Colors: Crystal only
Marked: Unknown
Comments: See the CANDLESTICKS Section for matching candlestick. Made as a console set only. Sometimes used for cuttings by Heisey.

#3397 GASCONY oval footed floral bowl - original Heisey Co. name

Dates: 1932-1938
Colors: Crystal, sahara, tangerine
Marked: Yes
Comments: See STEMWARE Section for other items.

#50 ADENA - name given by researchers

Dates: Ca. 1929-1933
Colors: Crystal, moongleam, flamingo
Marked: Yes
Comments: This floral bowl was made in a 7″ size and a 9″ bowl, rolled edge. The bottom has three raised bars to hold one of the flat top Heisey flower frogs.

#133 SWAN HANDLED - name given by researchers

Dates: Late 1929-1937
Colors: Crystal, moongleam, flamingo, sahara
Marked: No, but the matching floral block is
Comments: See the CANDLESTICKS Section for the matching candlestick. This bowl is quite large. Compare it with the same item in the #1469 Ridgeleigh pattern in the PATTERN Section. Made as a console set only. Used for some Heisey cuttings. Possibly made in alexandrite and marigold.

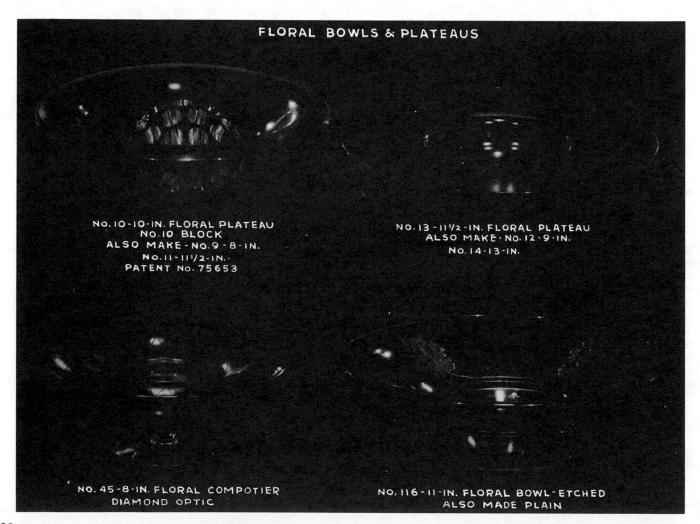

FLORAL BOWLS & PLATEAUS

NO. 10-10-IN. FLORAL PLATEAU
NO. 10 BLOCK
ALSO MAKE - NO. 9 - 8 - IN.
NO. 11 - 11½ - IN. -
PATENT No. 75653

NO. 13 - 11½ - IN. FLORAL PLATEAU
ALSO MAKE - NO. 12 - 9 - IN.
NO. 14 - 13 - IN.

NO. 45 - 8 - IN. FLORAL COMPOTIER
DIAMOND OPTIC

NO. 116 - 11 - IN. FLORAL BOWL - ETCHED
ALSO MADE PLAIN

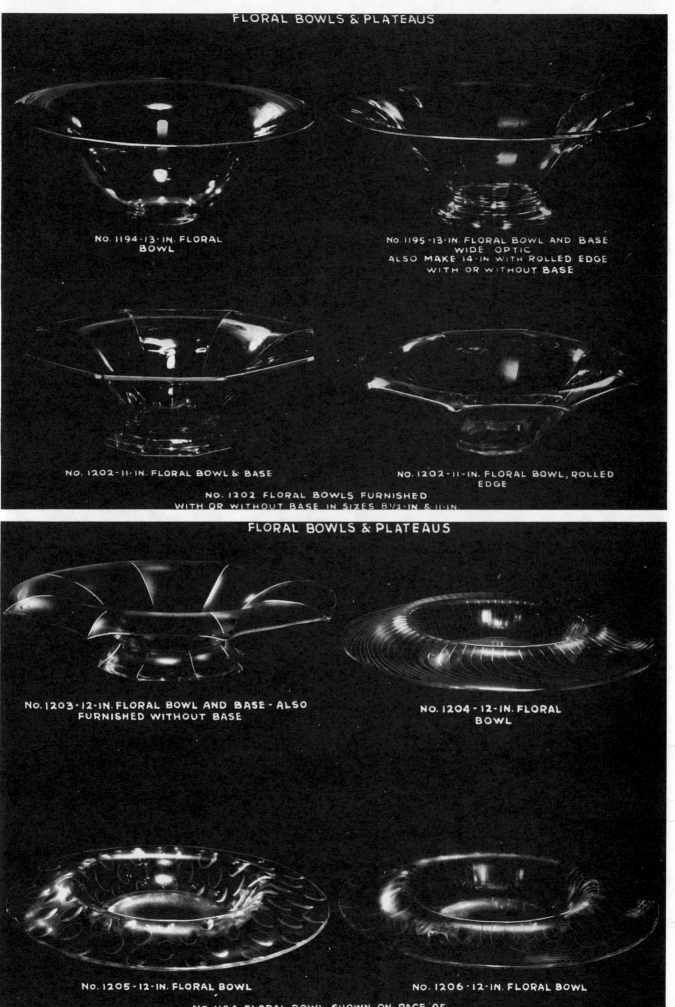

NO. 1194-13-IN. FLORAL
BOWL

NO. 1195-13-IN. FLORAL BOWL AND BASE
WIDE OPTIC
ALSO MAKE 14-IN WITH ROLLED EDGE
WITH OR WITHOUT BASE

NO. 1202-11-IN. FLORAL BOWL & BASE

NO. 1202-11-IN. FLORAL BOWL, ROLLED
EDGE

NO. 1202 FLORAL BOWLS FURNISHED
WITH OR WITHOUT BASE IN SIZES 8½-IN & 11-IN.

NO. 1203-12-IN. FLORAL BOWL AND BASE - ALSO
FURNISHED WITHOUT BASE

NO. 1204-12-IN. FLORAL
BOWL

NO. 1205-12-IN. FLORAL BOWL

NO. 1206-12-IN. FLORAL BOWL

NO. 1184 FLORAL BOWL SHOWN ON PAGE 95
NO. 1252 FLORAL BOWL SHOWN ON PAGE 105

No. 1252
12 in. Round Floral Bowl

No. 1401
8½ in. Footed Floral Bowl

No. 1252
8 in. Round Nasturtium Bowl

No. 135
12½ in. Round Floral Bowl

No. 134
14 in. Oval Floral Bowl
Ground Bottom

No. 1401
7½ in. Footed Nasturtium Bowl

Floral bowls

No. 1440
Floral Bowl

No. 1429
Oval Floral Bowl

No. 1425
10½ in. Floral Bowl

No. 1445
Oval Floral Bowl

No. 1428
11 in. Horn of plenty Floral Bowl

No. 1433
11 in Floral Bowl

Floral bowls

No. 3397
10 in. Footed Floral Bowl

No. 4044
11 in. Floral Bowl

No. 3397
10 in. Floral Bowl
No Foot

No. 1472
12 in. Floral Bowl
Also made 9 in.

No. 1447
12 in. Oval Floral Bowl

No. 1471
12 in. Oval Floral Bowl

No. 3397
Oval Footed Floral Bowl

Floral bowls

#50 ADENA floral bowl, shown with #2 floral block

#133 SWAN HANDLED floral bowl with cutting.

Flower Blocks

With the development of lower containers for flower arrangements, the need for flower blocks became apparent. Now that flowers were displayed in shallow bowls, the sides of the container no longer supported the flower stems as they had in vases. A block or support was needed to keep the stems vertically in place to make pleasing arrangements.

The Heisey Company produced several different types of floral blocks for use in floral bowls—often in several sizes and colors. The most interesting are the two figural blocks—the Duck and the Kingfisher.

Most of the floral blocks, especially the flat and mushroom top ones, are not marked with the Diamond H. Other companies made floral blocks similar to Heisey's mushroom top ones.

#1, #2, #3

Dates: Ca. 1914-ca.1933
Colors: Crystal, moongleam, flamingo. #2 was the only size listed in colors
Marked: No
Comments: Often used with the #50 Adena floral bowl. All have ground and polished tops.

#9, #10, #11

Dates: 1923-1938. #9 and #10 continued to 1939
Colors: Crystal, moongleam, flamingo. #10 and #11 also in hawthorne
Marked: No
Comments: Similar to other companies' floral blocks. Heisey's has 6 small feet on bottom and holes do not go through the block. There is a small ledge around the top rim. Dimensions on each block are:
#9: 3″ wide x 2″ high with 7 holes
#10: 4½″ wide x 2¾″ high with 19 holes
#11: 5″ wide x 3″ high with 19 holes

#501 FOGG - name given by researchers

Dates: Ca. 1929-1933
Colors: Crystal, moongleam, flamingo, marigold
Marked: Yes
Comments: See the #1469 Ridgeleigh pattern for a similar floral box. Sometimes the box is found without the matching two floral blocks.

#14 KINGFISHER - collectors' popular name

Dates: Ca. 1927-1933
Colors: Crystal, moongleam, flamingo, hawthorne
Marked: Yes. On plain portion between the bird's feet.
Comments: This flower frog is made in one piece while the Duck is a two-piece block.

#15

Dates: Ca. 1927-1933
Colors: Crystal, moongleam, flamingo, hawthorne
Marked: Usually not
Comments: Used as the holder for the Duck insert and the #123 Mercury candlestick insert.

#15 DUCK - collectors' popular name

Dates: 1927-1933
Colors: Crystal, moongleam, flamingo, hawthorne
Marked: No
Comments: Patent #73280 applied for 5/3/27 and granted 8/23/27. Ray C. Cobel listed as designer.

#17

Dates: 1930-1938
Colors: Crystal, moongleam, flamingo, sahara
Marked: Yes
Comments: Made for use in the #133 Swan Handled floral bowl and the #1469 Ridgeleigh swan handled bowl. The block has 16 small feet or supports and 14 holes.

Dates: 1930-1938
Colors: Crystal, moongleam, flamingo, sahara
Marked: No
Comments: Made for use in the #134 Trident floral bowl.

#19, #20, #21

Dates: Ca. 1930-1938
Colors: Crystal, moongleam, flamingo, sahara
Marked: No
Comments: Similar to flower blocks made by many other companies. Heisey's have no feet and are relatively flat on the bottom, the holes go completely through and there is no central hole in the blocks. There is also a small ledge around the top diameter. Dimensions of the blocks are:
#19: 3″ wide x 2″ high with 6 holes
#20: 4½″ wide x 2¾″ high with 18 holes
#21: 5½″ wide x 3″ high with 19 holes

#22

Dates: 1931-1938
Colors: Crystal, moongleam, flamingo, sahara
Marked: No
Comments: Made for use in the #1404 Old Sandwich oval floral bowl.

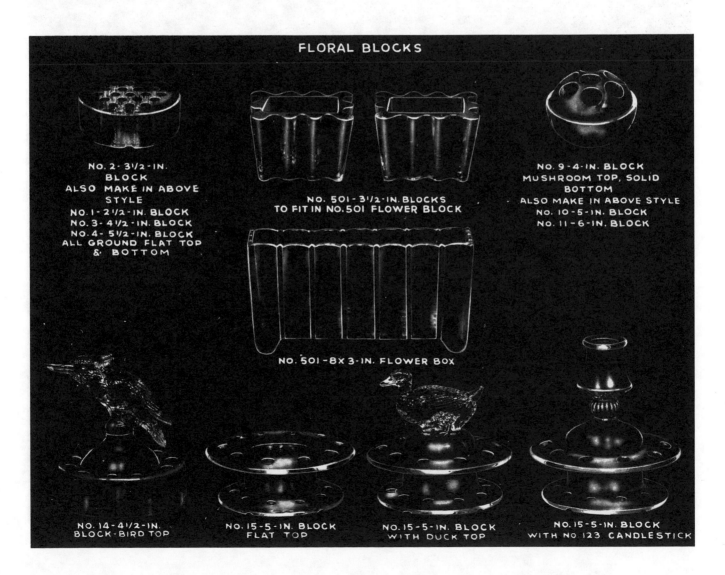

FLORAL BLOCKS

NO. 2 - 3½-IN. BLOCK ALSO MAKE IN ABOVE STYLE
NO. 1 - 2½-IN. BLOCK
NO. 3 - 4½-IN. BLOCK
NO. 4 - 5½-IN. BLOCK
ALL GROUND FLAT TOP & BOTTOM

NO. 501 - 3½-IN. BLOCKS TO FIT IN NO. 501 FLOWER BLOCK

NO. 9 - 4-IN. BLOCK MUSHROOM TOP, SOLID BOTTOM
ALSO MAKE IN ABOVE STYLE
NO. 10 - 5-IN. BLOCK
NO. 11 - 6-IN. BLOCK

NO. 501 - 8 X 3-IN. FLOWER BOX

NO. 14 - 4½-IN. BLOCK - BIRD TOP

NO. 15 - 5-IN. BLOCK FLAT TOP

NO. 15 - 5-IN. BLOCK WITH DUCK TOP

NO. 15 - 5-IN. BLOCK WITH NO. 123 CANDLESTICK

No. 19—4 in. Block
Mushroom Top Holes Thru

No. 21—6 in. Block
Mushroom Top Holes Thru

No. 20—5 in. Block
Mushroom Top Holes Thru

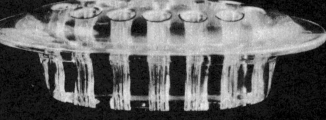

No. 18—9 in. Block
(134 Bowl) Holes Thru

No. 17—10 in. Block
(1469 Bowl) Holes Thru

No. 22—6 in. Block
(1404 Oval Bowl) Holes Thru

Flower blocks

Harvey Amber Items

The Fred Harvey Restaurants, in conjunction with the Santa Fe Railroad, had a long-standing association with the Heisey Company. Former workers remember that there were standing orders to be filled for the restaurants so that when work was slow on other orders, often pieces were made for the Harvey chain.

Beginning in 1933 (and possibly before this), Fred Harvey ordered much of the glass used in the Harvey House restaurants from Heisey. Harvey had the monopoly for dining service on the Santa Fe and also had various restaurants along the line. The Harvey connection with Heisey continued until the company closed, according to orders and price quotes from the late 1950's.

Most of the glass ordered by the Harvey Houses was in crystal—sometimes etched either with the "FH" crest or the Santa Fe crest.

However, a significant amount of the glass ordered was in amber, but this is difficult to find today. Harvey also used the same items in crystal. The shade of amber usually found in these pieces is pale in comparison to Heisey's Sultana—giving rise to the collectors' term "Harvey Amber" when referring to these items. Not all Harvey items were in this pale shade though, since several pieces are known in a dark amber.

Pieces known to have been made in amber for Fred Harvey include the following:

    *#12 SMALL EIGHT FLUTE salt & pepper
    *#201 HARVEY COLONIAL 8 oz. tumbler
    #300 PEERLESS individual decanter
    #337 TOURAINE (all pieces in narrow optic)
        goblet
        parfait
        *5 oz. juice
    *#337½ TOURAINE 4½ oz. sherbet, narrow optic
    #352 FLAT PANEL 4 oz. oil
    #353 MEDIUM FLAT PANEL
        *1 qt. Hall Boy jug
        *10" Hall Boy tray
        *10 oz. footed soda
    *#398 HOPEWELL 5" nappy
    *#586 HARVEY HOUSE 12 oz. soda or ice tea, narrow optic
    #1106 handleless custard, narrow optic
    *#1125 STARBURST 7½" plate
    #1184 YEOMAN
        *6¼" plate
        8" plate
    *#1217 finger bowl
    #1509 QUEEN ANN triplex relish
    #3304 UNIVERSAL parfait
    #3419 COGNAC brandy inhaler
    #3801 TEXAS PINK low comport
    #4049 OLD FITZ hot whiskey
    *#4059 ALLEN water bottle, plain
    *#4165 SHAW 3 pt. jug, no handle

While all of the above items are known in amber, the Harvey chain also ordered many, many more items in crystal—mainly in stemware, sodas and various plain pieces suitable for restaurant service.

*These items were included in a handwritten list dated 1951 indicating production in "Lead Amber."

Harvey Amber Items

#12 salt

#201 tumbler

#300 individual
decanter

#337 goblet

#337 parfait

#337½ sherbet

#352 oil

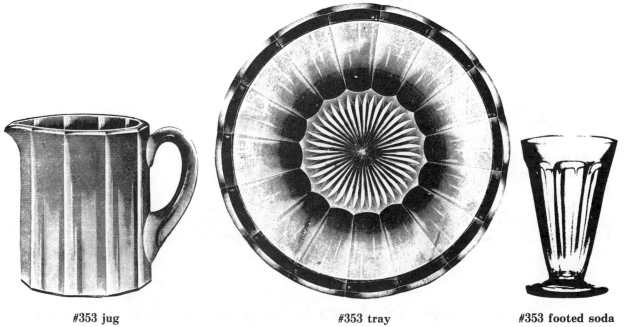

#353 jug

#353 tray

#353 footed soda

346

Harvey Amber Items

#398 nappy

#586 soda

#1106 custard

#1125 plate

#1217 finger bowl

#1509 triplex relish

#3304 parfait

#3419 brandy inhaler

#3801 low comport

#4049 hot whiskey

#4059 water bottle

See PATTERN Section for #1184 YEOMAN Plates and JUGS Section for #4165 jug

Jugs

Many stemware lines had matching jugs or pitchers. These effectively completed the set. Some of the earlier stem lines also had handled ice teas (or lemonades) and the jugs made quite attractive lemonade sets with these pieces.

Other jugs were made to match sodas and thus were sold as water sets. Still others were simply standard shaped jugs which were sold with various plain stems or sodas.

Many of the jugs shown in this section are blown and have diamond optic, which greatly adds to their beauty. Some of the jugs, especially when made to match moongleam tableware had crystal bodies with applied moongleam handles and possibly feet.

Often the pitchers were used for decorations—both etchings and cuttings by Heisey and other companies. The #4165 Shaw pitcher was made specifically to be held in a metal holder—a rather unusual idea.

Some of the jugs were made in a wide range of sizes and for long periods of time. Standard shapes are always in style.

Jugs made in major patterns or in stemware lines are also illustrated in the PATTERN and STEMWARE Sections.

#2517 TEARDROP - name given by researchers

Dates: 1925-1930
Colors: Crystal; moongleam handle, crystal body; flamingo; hawthorne
Marked: No
Comments: See BARWARE Section for soda and VASES Section for matching vase.

#3350 WABASH - original Heisey Co. name

Dates: 1922-1939
Colors: Crystal; moongleam foot & handle; flamingo foot & handle; marigold; flamingo; hawthorne
Marked: Yes
Comments: See STEMWARE Section for remainder of pattern.

#2516 CIRCLE PAIR - name given by researchers

Dates: 1924-1933
Colors: Crystal; moongleam handle, crystal body; flamingo; flamingo handle, crystal body
Marked: No
Comments: See STEMWARE, BARWARE, and VASES Sections for matching items.

#3350 WABASH - original Heisey Co. name

Dates: 1922-1939
Colors: Crystal; moongleam foot & handle, crystal body; flamingo
Marked: Yes
Comments: See STEMWARE Section for remainder of pattern.

#4161 - See #4085 KOHINOOR in PATTERN Section

#4165 SHAW - name given by researchers

Dates: 1924-1946
Colors: Crystal, amber for Fred Harvey, cobalt
Marked: No
Comments: Made to be used with a metal handle with collars around the top and bottom to hold the glass. Made plain or wide optic. Similar jugs were made by other companies.

#4164 GALLAGHER - name given by researchers

Dates: 1919-1957
Colors: Crystal, moongleam, flamingo, hawthorne, marigold, alexandrite, sahara
Marked: No
Comments: Made in plain, wide optic or diamond optic. Also available with or without cut flutes on neck. Heisey stated it was made to be used with #3333 Old Glory, #3350 Wabash, #3357 King Arthur, and #3380 Old Dominion stemware patterns. In later years it was made with an ice lip. Sometimes found with Heisey decorations.

#4163 WHALEY - name given by researchers

Dates: 1919-1953
Colors: Crystal only
Marked: No
Comments: Heisey used this jug for several silhouette etchings and cuttings. Made plain and in 108 oz. size in saturn optic. In later years the 54 oz. size was made with an ice lip. See BARWARE and MISCELLANEOUS Sections for other items in this pattern.

#4166 BALDA - name given by researchers

Dates: 1921-1937
Colors: Crystal only
Marked: No
Comments: Patent #66258 applied for 2/15/22 and granted 12/23/24. Josef O. Balda, designer.

#4206 OPTIC TOOTH - name given by researchers

Dates: 1925-1933
Colors: Moongleam foot, crystal body; flamingo; hawthorne body with moongleam foot.
Marked: No
Comments: Has not been seen in all crystal. Possibly made in all hawthorne. See BARWARE and CANDLESTICK Sections for matching items.

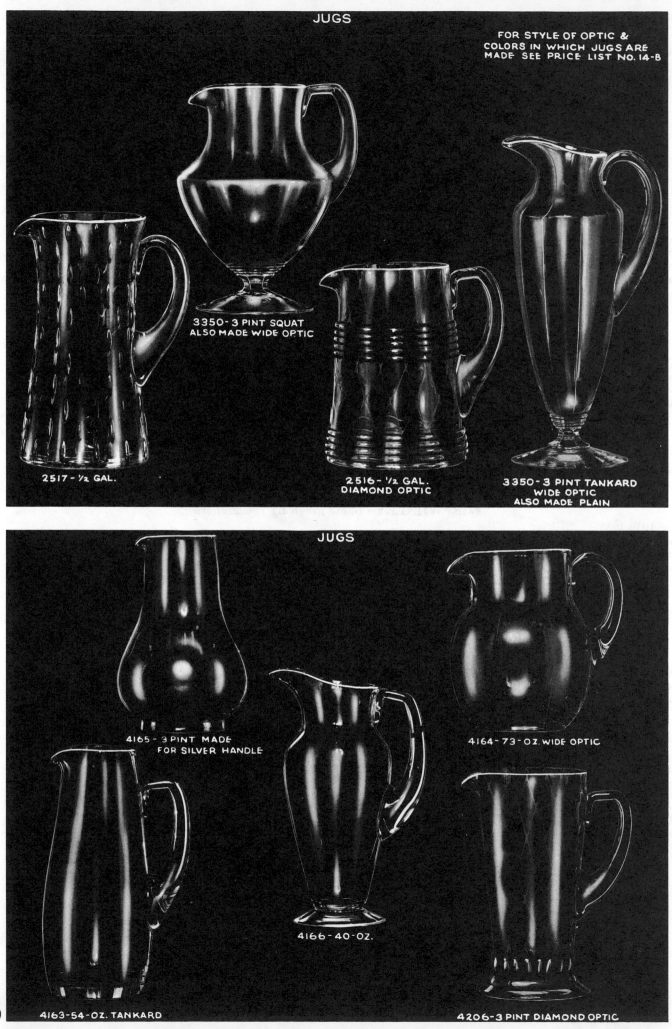

JUGS

FOR STYLE OF OPTIC &
COLORS IN WHICH JUGS ARE
MADE SEE PRICE LIST NO. 14-B

3350-3 PINT SQUAT
ALSO MADE WIDE OPTIC

2517 - ½ GAL.

2516 - ½ GAL.
DIAMOND OPTIC

3350 - 3 PINT TANKARD
WIDE OPTIC
ALSO MADE PLAIN

JUGS

4165 - 3 PINT MADE
FOR SILVER HANDLE

4164 - 73 - OZ. WIDE OPTIC

4166 - 40 - OZ.

4163 - 54 - OZ. TANKARD

4206 - 3 PINT DIAMOND OPTIC

350

#3484 DONNA - name given by researchers

Dates: 1925-1937; 1944-1957 in plain crystal for decoration
Colors: Crystal, moongleam, flamingo, marigold
Marked: No
Comments: Used by Heisey for some cuttings and for #507 Orchid etching. See BARWARE Section for matching soda. Colored items are usually found in diamond optic. Later production was in crystal only, usually without optic.

#4157 STEELE - name given by researchers

Dates: 1917-1937
Colors: Crystal only
Marked: No
Comments: See VASES Section for matching vase. Made in several sizes.

#3485 IRENE - name given by researchers

Dates: 1935-1937
Colors: Crystal, moongleam, flamingo, sahara
Marked: No
Comments: Heisey also made a vase in this pattern.

#4159 CLASSIC - name given by researchers

Dates: 1917-1939; 1948-1957
Colors: Crystal only
Marked: No
Comments: In 1937, a hand written note said "4159 jug, ribbon handle and extra heavy." Made with ice lip after 1948 in 8, 14, 21, 31, 54 and 63 oz. sizes.

#3480 KOORS - name given by researchers

Dates: 1925-1937
Colors: Crystal; moongleam; moongleam foot & handle; flamingo; flamingo foot & handle; hawthorne
Marked: No
Comments: See BARWARE and VASES Sections for matching items.

#4164, #4165, #4163 and #4166 - See discussion previously in this section.

#3805

Dates: 1921-1938
Colors: Crystal, moongleam, flamingo
Marked: No
Comments: Made to be used with the #4164 jug.

No. 3484—½ gal. Jug
Plain or Diamond Optic

No. 4157—1 pt. Jug
Plain or Wide Optic
Also made 1 qt , 3 pt. & ½ gal.

No. 4163—54 oz.
Tankard
Plain or Wide Optic

No. 3485—3 pt. Jug
Wide Optic Only

No. 4159—65 oz.
Tankard
Plain or Wide Optic

No. 3480—3 pt. Jug
Footed
Diamond Optic Only

Jugs

No. 4164—73 oz. Jug
Plain, Wide Optic or Diamond Optic
· Also made Cut Neck

No. 3805 Jug Cover
Diamond Optic Only

No. 4165—3 pt Jug
No Handle
Plain or Wide Optic

No. 4163—108 oz Tankard
Plain or Wide Optic

No. 4166—40 oz. Jug
Footed
Pat No 66258
Plain or Wide Optic

Jugs

Plates

Beginning in 1924, the Heisey Company designed and produced a great variety of plates. The 8″ size plate seems to have been the most popular. Many plates began with this size and some of the more successful had other sizes added later. Occasionally small bowls were also made to match the plates, such as in #1223 Fluted Border and #1233 Pressed Diamond.

The entire series of numbers from #1220 to #1254 is given to new plates designed from 1924 to 1938. Included in this series are three patterns which were developed from plate designs and became relatively major patterns: #1229 Octagon, #1231 Ribbed Octagon and #1252 Twist.

Several of the plates are Heisey's copies of old Sandwich glass designs - the Beehive, the Eagle, and the Sandwich Star being the most typical. Also included in a proposed booklet of the period showing Sandwich Glass copies were the Stippled Diamond plate and another which is believed to be the #8071 Sandwich Hairpin. See the text portion of the book for more information on Sandwich-inspired designs by Heisey.

Also see the MISCELLANEOUS Section for other plates. Most patterns included in the PATTERN Section also had their matching plates.

#416 HERRINGBONE - name given by researchers

Dates: Ca. 1929-1933
Colors: Crystal, moongleam, flamingo, hawthorne
Marked: Probably
Comments: The matching bowl from this plate was used as a top on some of the #109 Petticoat Dolphin comports.

#1125 STARBURST - name given by researchers

Dates: 1910-1935; 1939-1941
Colors: Crystal, amber for Fred Harvey
Marked: Yes, in center bottom

#1150 COLONIAL STAR - name given by researchers

Dates: 1908-1957. Became part of #341 Old Williamsburg after 1939
Colors: Crystal, alexandrite
Marked: Yes, in center bottom
Comments: Made in plain or narrow optic. See also COLONIAL PIECES IN COLOR Section.

#1128 PLAIN JANE - name given by researchers

Dates: 1917-1933
Colors: Crystal only
Marked: Unknown

#1130 HEISEY STAR - name given by researchers

Dates: 1922-1933
Colors: Crystal only
Marked: Unknown

#1218 SIMPLICITY - name given by researchers

Dates: 1910-1933
Colors: Crystal only
Marked: Unknown

#1219 SIMPLICITY WITH STAR - name given by researchers

Dates: 1909-1937
Colors: Crystal only
Marked: Probably

#1220 TWELVE SCALLOP - name given by researchers

Dates: 1924-1933
Colors: Crystal only
Marked: Unknown
Comments: Heisey's description of the plate was "scalloped edge."

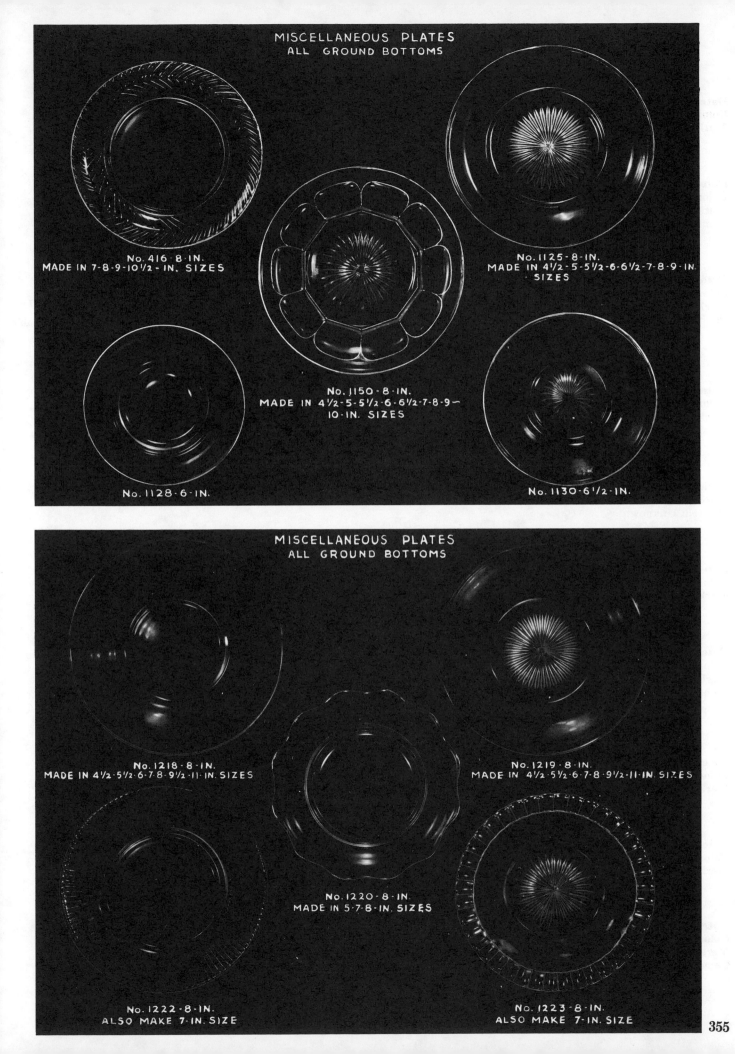

MISCELLANEOUS PLATES
ALL GROUND BOTTOMS

No. 416 · 8 · IN.
MADE IN 7-8-9-10½ - IN. SIZES

No. 1125 · 8 · IN.
MADE IN 4½-5-5½-6-6½-7-8-9-IN.
SIZES

No. 1150 · 8 · IN.
MADE IN 4½-5-5½-6-6½-7-8-9—
10 · IN. SIZES

No. 1128 · 6 · IN.

No. 1130 · 6½ · IN.

MISCELLANEOUS PLATES
ALL GROUND BOTTOMS

No. 1218 · 8 · IN.
MADE IN 4½-5½-6-7-8-9½-11-IN. SIZES

No. 1219 · 8 · IN.
MADE IN 4½-5½-6-7-8-9½-11-IN. SIZES

No. 1220 · 8 · IN.
MADE IN 5-7-8-IN. SIZES

No. 1222 · 8 · IN.
ALSO MAKE 7-IN. SIZE

No. 1223 · 8 · IN.
ALSO MAKE 7-IN. SIZE

#1222 FINE PLEAT - name given by researchers

Dates: 1924-1933
Colors: Crystal only
Marked: Yes, on center bottom

#1223 FLUTED BORDER - name given by researchers

Dates: 1924-1935
Colors: Crystal, moongleam, flamingo
Marked: Yes
Comments: Often found with a marigold-colored stain. See page later in this section for matching items.

#1224 HEXAGON SIX - name given by researchers

Dates: 1924-1935
Colors: Crystal, moongleam, flamingo
Marked: Not usually
Comments: Original Heisey price lists refer to this as "hexagon." See the MISCELLANEOUS Section for the matching salad bowl. Made plain or diamond optic.

#1225 RIDGE AND STAR - name given by researchers

Dates: 1924-1935
Colors: Crystal, moongleam, flamingo, hawthorne
Marked: Yes
Comments: Used on the #109 Petticoat Dolphin candlestick to make a comport.

#1226 RIDGE BORDER - name given by researchers

Dates: 1924-1933
Colors: Crystal only
Marked: Unknown

#1227 PINWHEEL - name given by researchers

Dates: 1924-1933
Colors: Crystal only
Marked: Unknown

#1228 SWIRL - name given by researchers

Dates: 1924-1933
Colors: Crystal, moongleam, hawthorne and probably flamingo
Marked: Yes
Comments: See later page in MISCELLANEOUS section for the baked apple and plate. "Marcel Wave" is a descriptive term used by Heisey and refers to the ruffled edge which is hand tooled on some plates.

#1230 FLUTED BORDER WITH RIB - name given by researchers

Dates: 1924-1933
Colors: Crystal only
Marked: Usually

#1232 SPOKE - name given by researchers

Dates: 1925-1933
Colors: Crystal, moongleam, flamingo
Marked: Yes

#1233 PRESSED DIAMOND - name given by researchers

Dates: 1925-1933
Colors: Crystal, flamingo, hawthorne
Marked: Yes
Comments: See page later in this section for the baked apple and cereal dish.

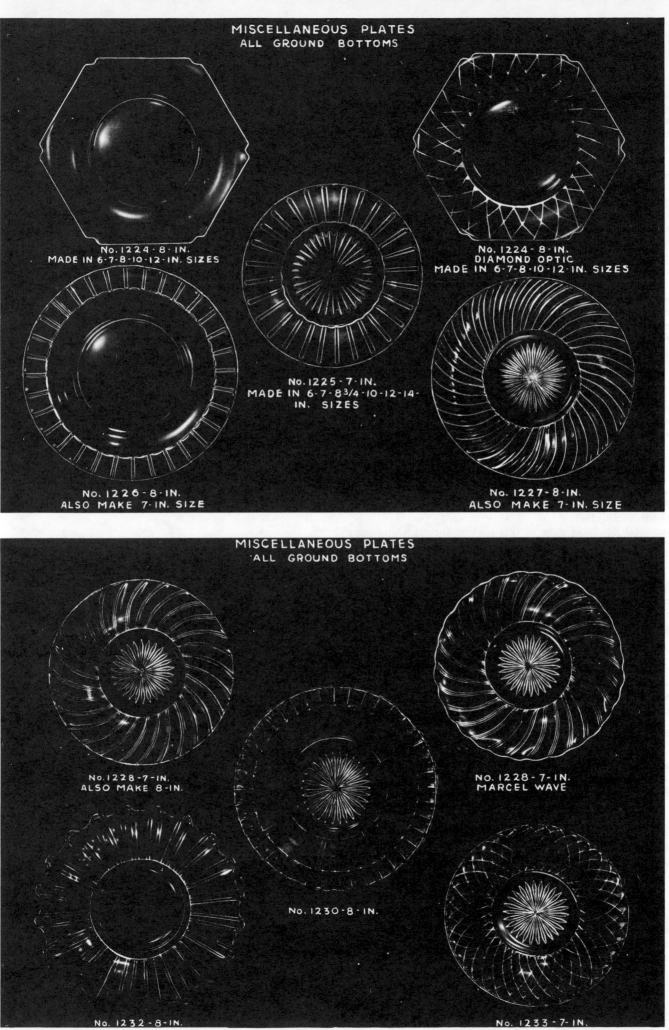

MISCELLANEOUS PLATES
ALL GROUND BOTTOMS

No. 1224-8-IN.
MADE IN 6-7-8-10-12-IN. SIZES

No. 1224-8-IN.
DIAMOND OPTIC
MADE IN 6-7-8-10-12-IN. SIZES

No. 1225-7-IN.
MADE IN 6-7-8¾-10-12-14-IN. SIZES

No. 1226-8-IN.
ALSO MAKE 7-IN. SIZE

No. 1227-8-IN.
ALSO MAKE 7-IN. SIZE

MISCELLANEOUS PLATES
ALL GROUND BOTTOMS

No. 1228-7-IN.
ALSO MAKE 8-IN.

No. 1228-7-IN.
MARCEL WAVE

No. 1230-8-IN.

No. 1232-8-IN.

No. 1233-7-IN.

357

#1238 BEEHIVE - collectors' popular name

Dates: 1925-ca.1939
Colors: Crystal, moongleam, flamingo, hawthorne, sahara, zircon
Marked: No
Comments: This is one of several original Sandwich designs which the Heisey Company copied in 1925. See the discussion of the SANDWICH REPRODUCTIONS in the text portion of the book. Not all sizes were made in all colors.

#1241 OCTAGON SPIRAL - name given by researchers

Dates: Ca. 1925-1933
Colors: Crystal, moongleam, flamingo
Marked: Unknown
Comments: See later page in this section for matching nappy.

#1245 SPIRAL - name given by researchers

Dates: Ca. 1926-1935
Colors: Crystal, moongleam, flamingo
Marked: Probably
Comments: Called "spiral flute" in catalogs. A high-footed comport was also made in moongleam and flamingo - an illustration of this was not found.

#1242 OCTAGON SQUARE - name given by researchers

Dates: Ca. 1925-1935
Colors: Crystal, moongleam, flamingo
Marked: Not usually

#1243 STEPPED OCTAGON - name given by researchers

Dates: Ca. 1925-1935
Colors: Crystal, moongleam, flamingo
Marked: Sometimes
Comments: See later page in this section for matching nappy.

#1246 ACORN AND LEAVES - name given by researchers

Dates: Ca. 1926-1933
Colors: Crystal, moongleam, flamingo, hawthorne
Marked: No
Comments: The original Heisey description of this plate in price lists was "Oak Leaf."

#1248 PLAIN - name given by researchers

Dates: 1926-1933
Colors: Crystal only
Marked: Unknown

#1249 REVERSE SPIRAL - name given by researchers

Dates: Ca. 1926-1933
Colors: Crystal, moongleam, flamingo, hawthorne
Marked: Yes, above ground rim toward the center of the plate

#1250 WIDE RIM PLAIN - name given by researchers

Dates: Ca. 1926-1933
Colors: Crystal, moongleam, flamingo
Marked: Unknown

#1251 UNIQUE - name given by researchers

Dates: Ca. 1926-1933
Colors: Crystal only
Marked: Unknown

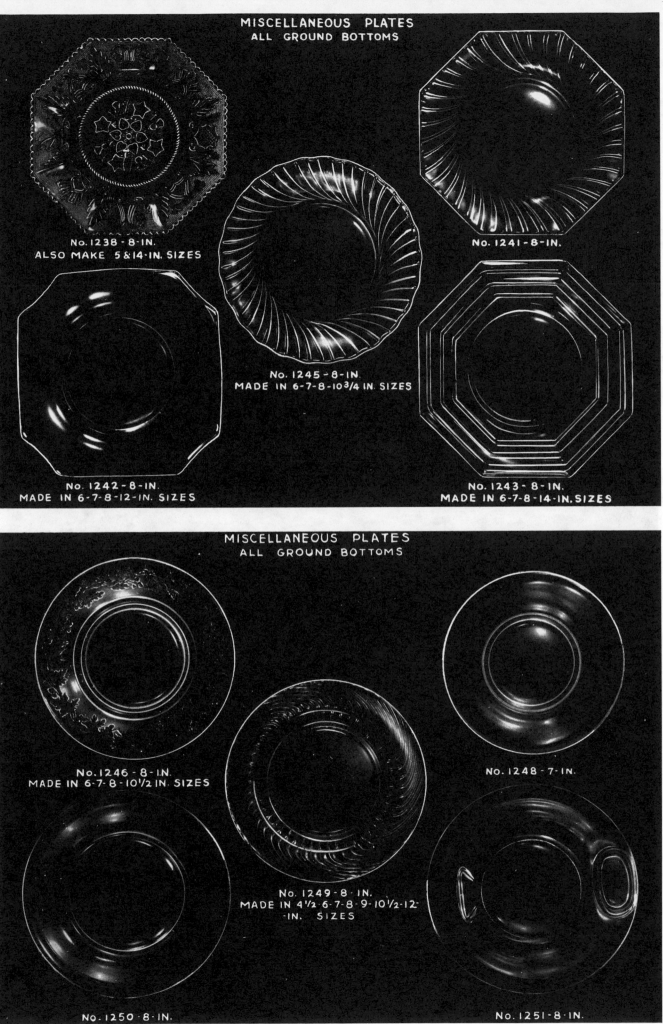

MISCELLANEOUS PLATES
ALL GROUND BOTTOMS

No. 1238 - 8 - IN.
ALSO MAKE 5 & 14 - IN. SIZES

No. 1241 - 8 - IN.

No. 1245 - 8 - IN.
MADE IN 6 - 7 - 8 - 10¾ IN. SIZES

No. 1242 - 8 - IN.
MADE IN 6 - 7 - 8 - 12 - IN. SIZES

No. 1243 - 8 - IN.
MADE IN 6 - 7 - 8 - 14 - IN. SIZES

MISCELLANEOUS PLATES
ALL GROUND BOTTOMS

No. 1246 - 8 - IN.
MADE IN 6 - 7 - 8 - 10½ IN. SIZES

No. 1248 - 7 - IN.

No. 1249 - 8 - IN.
MADE IN 4½ - 6 - 7 - 8 - 9 - 10½ - 12 - IN. SIZES

No. 1250 - 8 - IN.

No. 1251 - 8 - IN.

359

#4182 THIN - name given by researchers

Dates: 1919-ca.1945
Colors: Plain-sahara, wide optic-crystal, diamond optic-crystal, moongleam, flamingo, marigold, hawthorne, alexandrite, sahara
Marked: No
Comments: A plate widely used to match various stemware lines, so it is found in a wide variety of colors. It was also used for many cuttings and etchings.

#4183 NARROW RIM PLAIN - name given by researchers

Dates: Ca. 1929-1933
Colors: Crystal only
Marked: No

#4184 SIX SCALLOP - name given by researchers

Dates: Ca. 1929-1933
Colors: Crystal only
Marked: No
Comments: Used for a few Heisey cuttings

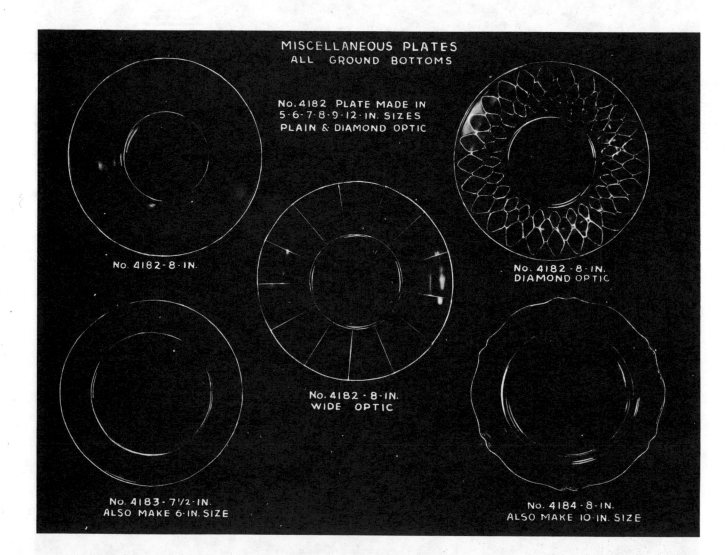

#1222, #1223 Liners - See MISCELLANEOUS Section for descriptions.

#1223, #1233, #1241, #1243 - See discussion earlier in this section.

#1253 LEAF EDGE - name given by researchers
Dates: 1928-1933
Colors: Crystal, moongleam, flamingo, marigold
Marked: No
Comments: A very heavy plate - almost a shallow dish in appearance.

#1254 CONCENTRIC RINGS - name given by researchers
Dates: 1928-1933
Colors: Crystal, moongleam, flamingo, marigold. Cobalt reported
Marked: Unknown

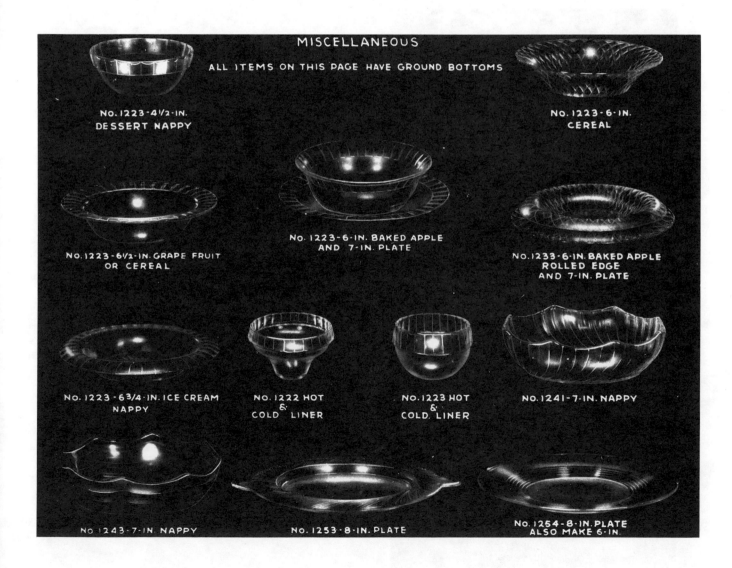

MISCELLANEOUS

ALL ITEMS ON THIS PAGE HAVE GROUND BOTTOMS

NO. 1223-4½-IN. DESSERT NAPPY

NO. 1223-6-IN. CEREAL

NO. 1223-6½-IN. GRAPE FRUIT OR CEREAL

NO. 1223-6-IN. BAKED APPLE AND 7-IN. PLATE

NO. 1233-6-IN. BAKED APPLE ROLLED EDGE AND 7-IN. PLATE

NO. 1223-6¾-IN. ICE CREAM NAPPY

NO. 1222 HOT & COLD LINER

NO. 1223 HOT & COLD LINER

NO. 1241-7-IN. NAPPY

NO. 1243-7-IN. NAPPY

NO. 1253-8-IN. PLATE

NO. 1254-8-IN. PLATE ALSO MAKE 6-IN.

#1234 STIPPLED DIAMOND - name given by researchers

Dates: 1925-1933
Colors: Crystal, moongleam, flamingo
Marked: Yes
Comments: This plate was included in a small hand-drawn brochure being developed for the Sandwich Glass Reproductions by Heisey, but it does not seem to be an actual Sandwich copy.

#1236 EAGLE - collectors' popular name

Dates: 1925-1933; 1937-1941
Colors: Crystal, moongleam, cobalt
Marked: No. Some collectors think there is a Diamond H in the middle of the plate near the eagle, but this really seems to be a mold flaw rather than part of a diamond.
Comments: Another of the Sandwich Reproductions by Heisey.

#1237 SANDWICH STAR - name given by researchers

Dates: 1925-ca.1929
Colors: Crystal, moongleam
Marked: No
Comments: Another of the Sandwich Reproductions by Heisey.

#1234 STIPPLED DIAMOND plate

#1236 EAGLE plate

#1237 SANDWICH STAR plate

#1406 FLEUR DE LIS - original Heisey description

Dates: 1932-1935
Colors: Crystal, moongleam, flamingo, sahara
Marked: Yes
Comments: Two versions of this plate were made, round and square. The square version is found with small teardrops below the fleur de lis which caused collectors to think that there were two different patterns. Actually, the Heisey Co. used the same number for both plates—#1406. Fleur de lis was the descriptive reference to the plate used in an early trade journal report. Other names for the plate include Beestinger and Fleur de Lis and Teardrop (for the square version.) Imperial Glass reproduced a nappy in this pattern in pink satin in 1981. It is marked LIG.

#7093 BEADED ARROW - name given by researchers

Dates: Unknown—probably about 1925
Colors: Crystal only known
Marked: Yes, in the patterned area near the interior rim
Comments: Original factory number and data not known.

#7026 HEART AND DRAPE - name given by researchers

Dates: Unknown—probably about 1925
Colors: Moongleam and flamingo known
Marked: Yes
Comments: Original factory number and data not known.

#1406 FLEUR DE LIS plates, square and round versions. Note the small teardrops on the square version.

#7093 BEADED ARROW plate   **#7026 HEART AND DRAPE plate**

#1239 KATHIE - name given by researchers

Dates: Unknown—probably about 1925
Colors: Crystal known
Marked: Yes
Comments: Original factory data not known.

#1480 FAN RIB - name given by researchers

Dates: Ca. 1935
Colors: Crystal known
Marked: No
Comments: Made in various plates and bowls by Heisey. Imperial made a one-piece chip and dip (never made by Heisey) in crystal and cobalt from 1959-1962. Some Heisey pieces have been seen with frosted fans.

#1432 CACTUS - popular collectors' name

Dates: Ca. 1934
Colors: Cobalt known
Marked: Yes
Comments: Original factory data not known. The design appears on the back of the plate. Photograph not available.

#8071 SANDWICH HAIRPIN - name given by researchers

Dates: Ca. 1925
Colors: Only crystal known
Marked: No
Comments: A drawing (very vague) was found in the hand-done Sandwich brochure being prepared by the Heisey Co.—it may be this plate which was being illustrated. Original factory number and data are not known. Several of these plates have been found in the Newark, Ohio, area—some with original Heisey labels. Photograph not available.

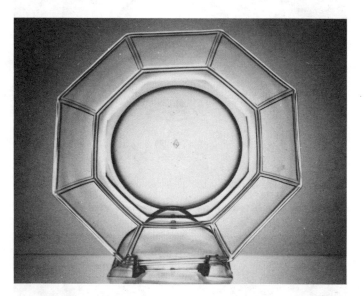

#1239 KATHIE plate

#1480 FAN RIB plate

Salts and Peppers

Salts and peppers are popular with today's Heisey collectors because great variety is available without sacrifice of display space.

Many of the salts are not marked and so hunting them is a challenge. Even if marked, the mark is often faint and so is overlooked. Salts in colors are usually difficult to find—moongleam and flamingo are easiest to locate. Hawthorne, marigold and alexandrite shakers are difficult to find. Zircon and amber are harder to locate and tangerine and cobalt are almost impossible.

Collectors seem to prefer original Heisey-type tops with their salts and peppers, but many do not demand tops if the shakers are uncommon enough. Glass tops (which were also made at Heisey's) usually make the salts more valuable, especially in colors to match the shakers. The combination glass and metal sanitary tops are also considered somewhat more desirable than plain metal tops.

See the PATTERN Section for salts and peppers in various patterns such as Empress, Old Sandwich, Victorian, etc.

#27 TALL SIX PANEL - name given by researchers

Dates: 1912-1941
Colors: Crystal only
Marked: Unknown. Probably marked on opposite panels at the top.

#29 SHORT DOUBLE PANEL - name given by researchers

Dates: 1913-1935
Colors: Crystal only
Marked: Yes, usually twice on opposite panels at the top

#30 TALL DOUBLE PANEL - name given by researchers

Dates: 1913-1935
Colors: Crystal, flamingo
Marked: Yes, usually twice on tops of opposite panels

#42 ELEGANCE - name given by researchers

Dates: 1924-1953
Colors: Crystal, flamingo, marigold, sahara, moongleam foot
Marked: No
Comments: Used fairly extensively for cuttings and etchings by Heisey. Glass tops were made in colors to match the shaker. Heisey also made a very similar shaker which is taller and marked on the side. This shaker is an unknown number and data is unavailable for it.

#44 DETROIT - name given by researchers

Dates: 1924-1933
Colors: Crystal only
Marked: Unknown

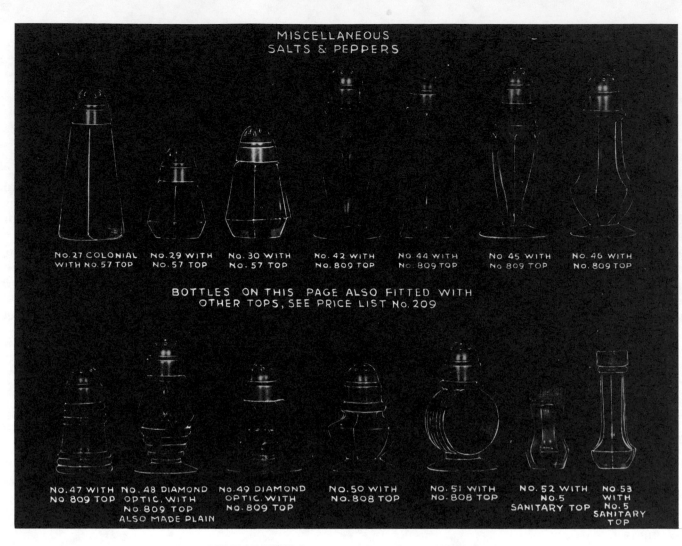

MISCELLANEOUS
SALTS & PEPPERS

NO. 27 COLONIAL WITH NO. 57 TOP   NO. 29 WITH NO. 57 TOP   NO. 30 WITH NO. 57 TOP   NO. 42 WITH NO. 809 TOP   NO. 44 WITH NO. 809 TOP   NO 45 WITH NO 809 TOP   NO. 46 WITH NO. 809 TOP

BOTTLES ON THIS PAGE ALSO FITTED WITH
OTHER TOPS, SEE PRICE LIST No. 209

NO. 47 WITH NO. 809 TOP   NO. 48 DIAMOND OPTIC, WITH NO. 809 TOP ALSO MADE PLAIN   NO. 49 DIAMOND OPTIC. WITH NO. 809 TOP   NO. 50 WITH NO. 808 TOP   NO. 51 WITH NO. 808 TOP   NO. 52 WITH NO. 5 SANITARY TOP   NO. 53 WITH NO. 5 SANITARY TOP

#45 PALMYRA - name given by researchers

Dates: 1924-1933
Colors: Crystal only
Marked: Unknown

#46 CHESHIRE - name given by researchers

Dates: 1924-1933
Colors: Crystal; moongleam; flamingo; moongleam foot, crystal body
Marked: Yes, at top of one panel
Comments: Patent #66566 applied for 11/20/24 and granted 2/10/25. T. Clarence Heisey listed as designer.

#47 SPOOL - name given by researchers

Dates: 1925-1933
Colors: Crystal, moongleam, flamingo
Marked: No

#48 KOORS - name given by researchers

Dates: 1927-1939
Colors: Crystal; moongleam; flamingo; moongleam foot, crystal body; flamingo foot, crystal body
Marked: No
Comments: Made plain or diamond optic. Patent #73431 applied for 5/11/27 and granted 9/13/27. T. Clarence Heisey listed as designer.

#49 YORKSHIRE - name given by researchers

Dates: 1927-1933
Colors: Crystal; moongleam; flamingo; hawthorne; moongleam foot, crystal body; flamingo foot, crystal body
Marked: No
Comments: Two patents were held on this shaker.
    1. Plain: #73032 applied for 4/15/27 and granted 7/12/27.
    2. Diamond Optic: #73377 applied for 6/17/27 and granted 8/30/27.   T. Clarence Heisey listed as designer on both.

#50 LOUISIANA - name given by researchers

Dates: Ca. 1927-1933
Colors: Crystal, moongleam, flamingo
Marked: No

#51 DRUM - name given by researchers

Dates: Ca. 1927-1933
Colors: Crystal; moongleam; flamingo; moongleam foot, crystal body
Marked: No

#52 SHORT INDIVIDUAL - name given by researchers

Dates: 1927-ca. 1937
Colors: Crystal, moongleam, flamingo, hawthorne, sahara
Marked: Yes, on one panel near top
Comments: Glass tops were made in colors and should match the shaker. Colored shakers with crystal tops were probably matched up later. This tiny shaker is sometimes confused with #429 Plain Panel Recess, but #429 is a much larger shaker.

#53 TALL INDIVIDUAL - name given by researchers

Dates: 1929-ca.1937
Colors: Crystal, moongleam, flamingo
Marked: Possibly on bottom
Comments: As for #52

#12 SMALL EIGHT FLUTE - original Heisey Co. description

Dates: 1908-1955
Colors: Crystal, moongleam, flamingo, sahara, cobalt, amber for Fred Harvey
Marked: Yes, on top of one of the flutes. Later ones may be marked on the bottom. Many appear never to have been marked.
Comments: This style of shaker is very common and was made by many companies. If you cannot be sure, it is best to buy only marked shakers, even though there were probably many thousands made without the Diamond H.

#23 SHORT PANEL - name given by researchers

Dates: 1912-ca.1946
Colors: Crystal, moongleam, flamingo, sahara
Marked: Yes, on top of two opposite panels
Comments: This shaker has eight panels. Patent #42411 applied for 1/18/12 and granted 4/30/12. A.J. Sanford listed as designer. This is another commonly used shape by many companies. Again, it is best to buy marked shakers to be certain you have genuine Heisey ones. This is true of #24 and #25 also.

#24 MEDIUM PANEL - name given by researchers

Dates: 1912-1955
Colors: Crystal, moongleam, flamingo, sahara, amber, cobalt
Marked: Yes, on top of two opposite panels. Later ones are marked on the outside bottom
Comments: Same as for #23 above (including patent data)

#27, #42, #48, #52 - See data earlier in this section.

#25 TALL PANEL - name given by researchers

Dates: 1912-1955
Colors: Crystal only
Marked: Yes, on top of two opposite panels. Sometimes marked on bottom.
Comments: This shaker has eight panels. Patent #42411 applied for 1/18/12 and granted 4/30/12. A.J. Sanford listed as designer. This is a standard shape used by many companies. Again, it is best to buy marked shakers to be certain you have genuine Heisey ones. See also #23 and #24.

#54 TWIST - name given by researchers

Dates: 1929-1937
Colors: Crystal, moongleam, flamingo, sahara, marigold
Marked: Yes, on bottom
Comments: Also listed as part of #1252 Twist pattern. (See PATTERN Section). This was the original Twist shaker; the footed Twist shaker was listed as new in November, 1930.

No. 12 Salt or Pepper
No. 60 Metal Top

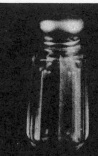

No. 12 Salt or Pepper
No. 336 Chromium Plated Top

No. 12 Salt or Pepper
No. 4 Glass Top

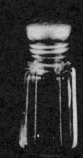

No. 12 Salt or Pepper
No. AA Silver Plated Top

No. 12 Salt or Pepper
No. 682-2 Salt Proof Top

No. 23 Blown Salt or Pepper
No. 7 Glass Top

No. 23 Blown Salt or Pepper
No. 57 Metal Top

No. 23 Blown Salt or Pepper
No. 657 Salt Proof Top

No. 24 Blown Salt or Pepper
No. 7 Glass Top

No. 24 Blown Salt or Pepper
No. 57 Metal Top

No. 24 Blown Salt or Pepper
No. 657 Salt Proof Top

Miscellaneous salts or peppers

No. 25
Blown Salt or Pepper
No. 57 Metal Top

No. 25
Blown Salt or Pepper
No. 657 Salt Proof Top

No. 27
Blown Salt or Pepper
No. 57 Metal Top

No. 27
Blown Salt or Pepper
No. 657 Salt Proof Top

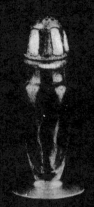

No. 42
Blown Salt or Pepper
No. 7 Glass Top

No. 42
Blown Salt or Pepper
No. 57 Metal Top

No. 42
Blown Salt or Pepper
No. 657 Salt Proof Top

No. 48
Blown Salt or Pepper
No. 7 Glass Top

No. 48
Blown Salt or Pepper
No. 57 Metal Top

No. 48
Blown Salt or Pepper
No. 657 Salt Proof Top

No 54
Blown Salt or Pepper
No 7 Glass Top

No. 52
Blown Salt or Pepper
No. 5 Glass Top
For All Other Salts or Peppers See Lines

No. 54
Blown Salt or Pepper
No. 57 Metal Top

No. 54
Blown Salt or Pepper
No. 657 Salt Proof Top

Miscellaneous salts or peppers

Vases

Heisey produced a large number of vases during this color period. Primarily they were blown and thus are not marked with the Diamond H. Still, identification of most poses few problems as the shapes and colors used by Heisey are easily identifiable.

Vases were made in all sizes—some tiny and delicate to hold flowers at individual table settings, such as the six favor vases. Others were large and massive. One of Heisey's most popular items was the #4045 Ball vase, which was made in various sizes and colors.

Often vases were made in one form and then tooled into various styles, resulting in several shapes from one basic piece such as the #516 series. Sometimes vases were made from the jug or pitcher mold with the handle left off. (Or maybe more accurately, the jug was made from the vase mold!) Regardless, several of these are apparent from the pictures such as the #4159 Classic vase, the #4206 Optic Tooth vase and others. A mention in factory literature is made of a #4225 vase—probably made from the cocktail shaker mold.

A few vases were not listed in all crystal—making them some of the few items Heisey made only in colors. Many of the vases were made in diamond optic to heighten the brilliance of the glass. The company did not give names to these vases so most of the names used here have been given recently.

See the section of FLORAL BOWLS AND PLATEAUS for related items and also see the MISCELLANEOUS Section for the #1413 Cathedral, #1420 Tulip, #1421 Hi-Lo and #1433 Thumbprint and Panel vases. Vases belonging to pattern groups are found in the PATTERN Section.

#4203 EMOGENE - name given by researchers

Dates: 1924-1937
Colors: Crystal, moongleam, flamingo, hawthorne
Marked: No

#2516 CIRCLE PAIR - name given by researchers

Dates: 1929-1933
Colors: Crystal, moongleam, flamingo
Marked: No
Comments: See BARWARE and JUGS Sections for matching items.

#4202 BAMBOO - collectors' popular name

Dates: 1924-1943
Colors: Crystal, moongleam, flamingo
Marked: No

#3359 PLATEAU - name given by researchers

Dates: 1926-1937
Colors: Crystal, moongleam, flamingo, hawthorne, marigold
Marked: No
Comments: Usually has a ground and polished pontil. See STEMWARE Section for remainder of pattern.

#4157 STEELE - name given by researchers

Dates: Ca. 1925-1939
Colors: Crystal; moongleam; flamingo; sahara; hawthorne. Known in tangerine with opaque yellow rim; also known in an opaque tangerine/yellow slag.
Marked: No
Comments: See JUGS Section for matching pitcher. The two tangerine varieties are quite rare.

#4191 OLYMPIA - name given by researchers

Dates: 1919-1944+
Colors: Crystal; crystal body, moongleam foot
Marked: Yes, on stem portion above foot
Comments: Heisey used this vase for some cuttings and etchings. It was made in several sizes: 4″, 6″, 8″, 10″ and 12″.

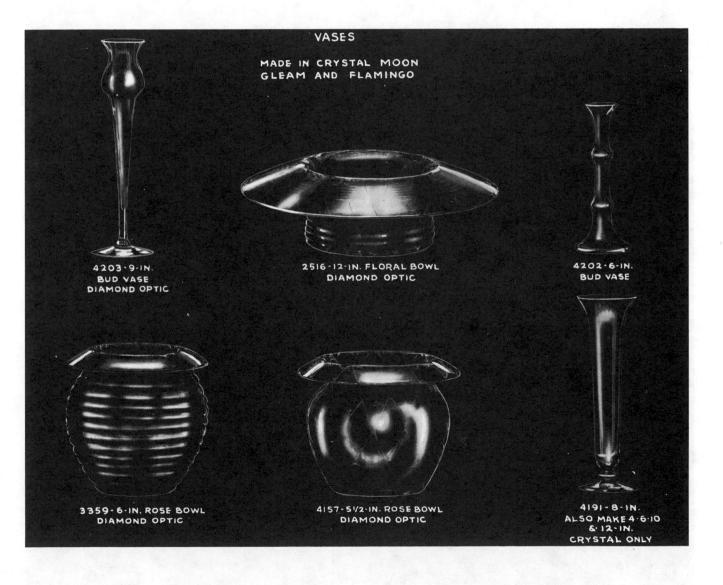

VASES

MADE IN CRYSTAL MOON GLEAM AND FLAMINGO

4203-9-IN. BUD VASE DIAMOND OPTIC

2516-12-IN. FLORAL BOWL DIAMOND OPTIC

4202-6-IN. BUD VASE

3359-6-IN. ROSE BOWL DIAMOND OPTIC

4157-5½-IN. ROSE BOWL DIAMOND OPTIC

4191-8-IN. ALSO MAKE 4-6-10 & 12-IN. CRYSTAL ONLY

#4204 JOYCE - name given by researchers

Dates: 1925-1933
Colors: Crystal, moongleam, flamingo, marigold, hawthorne
Marked: No

#4205 VALLI - name given by researchers

Dates: Ca. 1925-1944+
Colors: Crystal, moongleam, flamingo, marigold, hawthorne
Marked: May be on stem portion

#4206 OPTIC TOOTH - name given by researchers

Dates: Ca. 1925-1937
Colors: Crystal; moongleam foot, crystal bowl; moongleam foot, hawthorne bowl; hawthorne; marigold; flamingo
Marked: No
Comments: Made in 8", 10" and 12" sizes, usually diamond optic. Rod Irwin's description of the vase was "claw foot." See the CANDLESTICKS and JUGS Sections for matching items. Footed sodas or ice teas were also made.

#4207 MODERNE - name given by researchers

Dates: Ca. 1925-1933
Colors: Crystal, moongleam, flamingo, marigold
Marked: No

#4209 OVAL - original Heisey Co. description

Dates: Ca. 1925-1937
Colors: Crystal, moongleam, flamingo, marigold, sahara
Marked: No
Comments: Used for #1 Sport etching by Heisey.

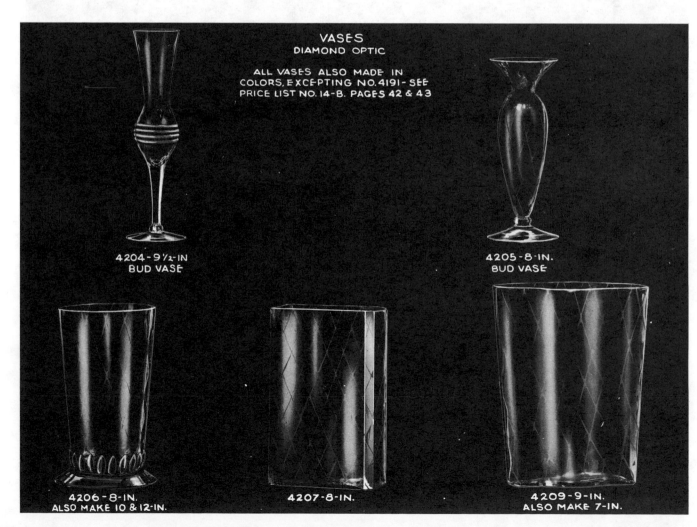

#4214 ELAINE - name given by researchers
Dates: Ca. 1925-1937
Colors: Crystal, moongleam, flamingo, sahara
Marked: No
Comments: Made in diamond optic or swirl optic

#4215 DOROTHY - name given by researchers
Dates: Ca. 1925-1937
Colors: Crystal, moongleam, flamingo
Marked: No

#4217 FRANCES - name given by researchers
Dates: Ca. 1925-1937
Colors: Crystal, moongleam, flamingo, marigold
Marked: No
Comments: Made in 4½″ and 7″ sizes.

#4211 LILAC - name given by researchers
Dates: 1925-1933
Colors: Crystal, moongleam, flamingo, marigold
Marked: No

#4216 OCTAGON - original Heisey Co. description
Dates: Ca. 1925-1939
Colors: Crystal, moongleam, flamingo, sahara, alexandrite
Marked: No

#4218 MARILYN - name given by researchers
Dates: 1925-1933
Colors: Crystal, moongleam, flamingo
Marked: No

#4219 LUCILE - name given by researchers
Dates: 1925-1933
Colors: Crystal, moongleam, flamingo
Marked: No

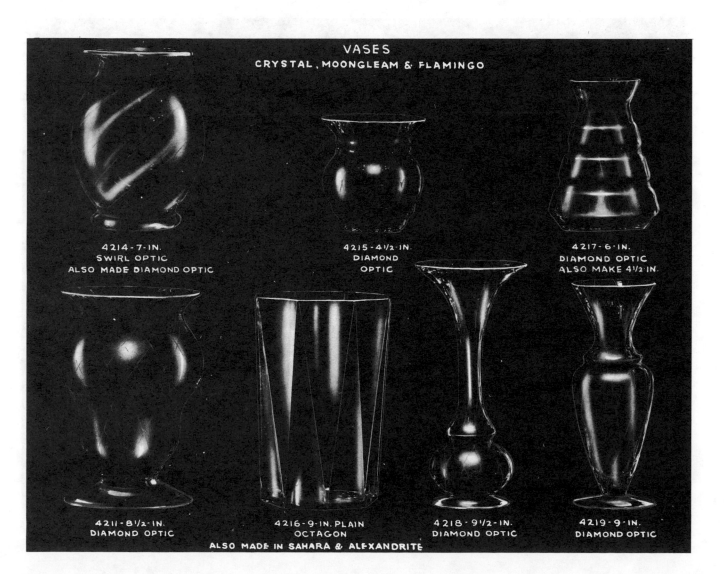

VASES
CRYSTAL, MOONGLEAM & FLAMINGO

4214 - 7 - IN.
SWIRL OPTIC
ALSO MADE DIAMOND OPTIC

4215 - 4½ - IN.
DIAMOND
OPTIC

4217 - 6 - IN.
DIAMOND OPTIC
ALSO MAKE 4½ - IN.

4211 - 8½ - IN.
DIAMOND OPTIC

4216 - 9 - IN. PLAIN
OCTAGON
ALSO MADE IN SAHARA & ALEXANDRITE

4218 - 9½ - IN.
DIAMOND OPTIC

4219 - 9 - IN.
DIAMOND OPTIC

#516/1, #516/2, #516/3

Dates: Ca. 1927-1933
Colors: Moongleam, flamingo, hawthorne. NOT LISTED IN CRYSTAL.
Marked: No
Comments: All shapes were made from the same mold—just hand-tooled differently.

#3480 KOORS - name given by researchers

Dates: Ca. 1919-1933
Colors: Moongleam, flamingo. NOT LISTED IN CRYSTAL.
Marked: No
Comments: See BARWARE Section for matching sodas and JUGS Section for pitcher.

#2517 TEARDROP - name given by researchers

Dates: Ca. 1927-1930
Colors: Moongleam, flamingo. NOT LISTED IN CRYSTAL
Marked: No
Comments: Hawthorne is possible since other pieces in the pattern are known in this color. See BARWARE and JUGS Sections for matching pieces. A very limited line. The floral bowl is made from the same mold as the vase.

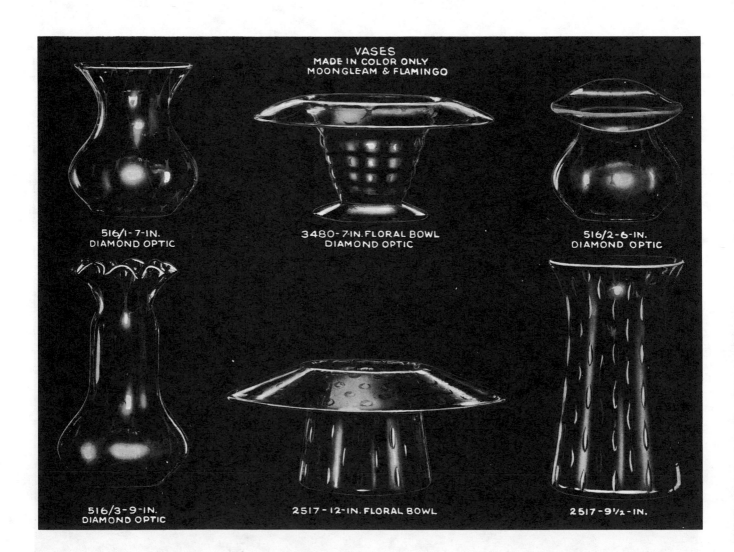

VASES
MADE IN COLOR ONLY
MOONGLEAM & FLAMINGO

516/1-7-IN.
DIAMOND OPTIC

3480-7-IN. FLORAL BOWL
DIAMOND OPTIC

516/2-6-IN.
DIAMOND OPTIC

516/3-9-IN.
DIAMOND OPTIC

2517-12-IN. FLORAL BOWL

2517-9½-IN.

#4209 - See discussion earlier in this section.

#4160/1 ELLEN - name given by researchers
Dates: 1929-1933
Colors: Moongleam, flamingo. NOT LISTED IN CRYSTAL.
Marked: No
Comments: A jug was also made in #4160.

#4159/1 CLASSIC - name given by researchers
Dates: 1929-1933
Colors: Moongleam, flamingo, hawthorne. NOT LISTED IN CRYSTAL
Marked: No
Comments: Has a ground and polished pontil. See JUGS Section for matching pitcher.

#4196 RHODA - name given by researchers
Dates: 1919-1933
Colors: Moongleam foot, crystal body; all flamingo. NOT LISTED IN CRYSTAL.
Marked: Yes, on stem

VASES
MADE IN COLOR ONLY

ALL VASES ON THIS PAGE
ARE MADE DIAMOND OPTIC ONLY

4160/1- 7-IN.
MOONGLEAM-FLAMINGO

4209-9-IN. WITH
NO.I-SPORT ETCHING
CRYSTAL-MOONGLEAM-FLAMINGO

4159/1-9-IN.
MOONGLEAM-FLAMINGO

4196-10-IN.
MOONGLEAM FOOT-ALL
FLAMINGO

#4162/1, #4162/2, #4162/3, #4162/4 GENIE - name given by researchers

Dates: 1929-1933
Colors: Moongleam, flamingo. NOT LISTED IN CRYSTAL
Marked: No

#3355 FAIRACRE - original Heisey Co. name

Dates: 1925-1937
Colors: Moongleam foot, flamingo foot, all flamingo. NOT LISTED IN ALL CRYSTAL.
Marked: Yes
Comments: See STEMWARE Section for remainder of pattern.

#4191, #4157, #4202 listed previously in this section.

#4045 BALL - original Heisey Co. description

Dates: 1936-1953
Colors: Crystal, moongleam, flamingo, alexandrite, sahara, cobalt, zircon (in saturn optic), tangerine
Marked: No
Comments: Made in wide optic in colors except zircon which was made in saturn optic. Crystal was available in either wide optic or saturn optic. Only saturn optic vases were available after 1944. One hand-written reference is known of a 9″ cobalt vase, plain. Made in 3″, 4″, 6″ 7″ 9″ and 12″ sizes. A few 2″ vases are known, primarily in cobalt. Used for some etchings, carvings and cuttings by Heisey. This type of vase was made by other companies. Variations are usually in the number of optics and the weight of the vases—Heisey's are often heavier. Occasionally the vases are found with special Heisey cuttings and engravings—usually on crystal and rarely on zircon. In 1982 Imperial Glass made the 4″ vase in a narrow spiral optic in plum, ultra blue, sunshine yellow and crystal. They also made the 9″ in "spike optic", which is similar to wide optic, but has 18 optics, many more than the original Heisey vase. The 9″ vase was made in plum, ultra blue, sunshine yellow, emerald and crystal. A few 9″ vases were made in emerald and blue satin with no optic.

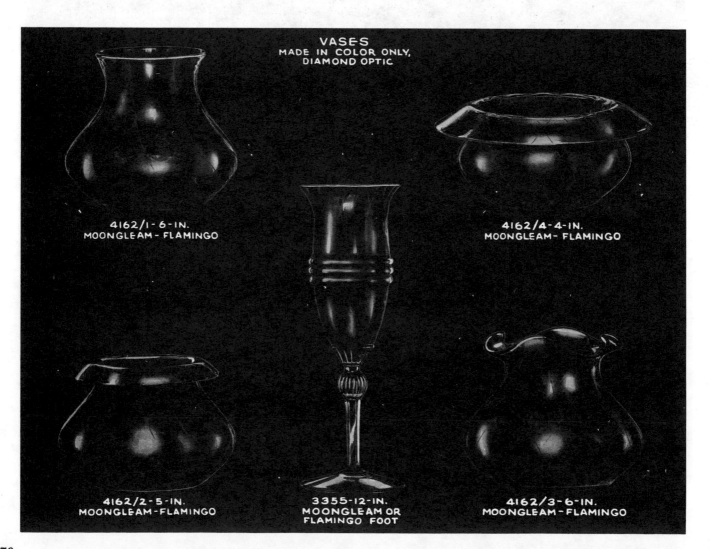

No. 4191—8 in. Footed Vase
Plain Only
Also made 4, 6, 10 & 12 in.

No. 4157—5½ in. Rose Bowl
Diamond Optic

No. 4202—6 in. Bud Vase
Plain Only

No. 4045—9 in. Ball Vase
Also made 4, 6 7 & 12 in.
Wide Optic Only

No. 4057—10 in. Vase
Plain Only

Miscellaneous vases

#4057 CECELIA - name given by researchers

Dates: 1936-1957
Colors: Crystal, zircon (ca. 1936) and limelight (ca. 1956). Rare in amber and dawn.
Marked: No
Comments: Made saturn optic or plain. Made in 5″, 7″ 9″ and 10½″ sizes. Widely used by Heisey for special, elaborate cuttings and engravings. Also sometimes found with Heisey carvings. Occasionally found with #507 Orchid etching.

#4217, #4215, #4216 and #4214 - See discussions earlier in this section.

#4227, #4228, #4229, #4230, #4231, #4232 favor vases

Dates: 1933-1944. #4227, #4230, #4231 discontinued in 1943.
Colors: Crystal, moongleam, flamingo, sahara, cobalt, tangerine.
Marked: No
Comments: All shapes were made in all colors. Always listed as diamond optic in price lists. There are look-alikes in a light weight glass, often with no optic which were made by Dunbar. Unusual in swirl optic.

#4224 IVY - original description

Dates: 1932-1937
Colors: Crystal, moongleam, flamingo, sahara, cobalt
Marked: No
Comments: Several of these have been seen in varying shades of a tangerine color, but this color was not listed in Heisey price lists and is considered doubtful by some experts. Even though the catalog caption states "plain only", authentic items known all have wide optic.

#4222 HORSESHOE - name given by researchers

Dates: 1931-1937
Colors: Crystal, moongleam, sahara
Marked: No
Comments: A matching cream and sugar were also made (see MISCELLANEOUS Section). Creams and sugars are known in flamingo so the vase might be found in this color too. The base is ground and polished. Used for #5009 Diana carving by Heisey.

#4223 SWIRL - name given by researchers

Dates: 1931-1939
Colors: Crystal, moongleam, sahara, cobalt
Marked: No
Comments: Possibly flamingo was also made. Made plain or diamond optic.

#4220 JANICE - name given by researchers

Dates: 1930-1939
Colors: Crystal, moongleam, flamingo, sahara, alexandrite. Experimental in tangerine, cobalt and gold ruby.
Marked: No
Comments: Sometimes used for cuttings and etchings by Heisey. Made in swirl optic. Very rare in gold ruby. Made in 4½″ and 7″ sizes. Imperial Glass made the 4½″ vase in "draped optic" in plum, sunshine yellow, ultra blue, crystal, lemon frost satin, pink satin, emerald, ultra blue satin and possibly other colors.

No. 4227
Favor Vase
Diamond Optic

No. 4228
Favor Vase
Diamond Optic

No. 4229
Favor Vase
Diamond Optic

No. 4230
Favor Vase
Diamond Optic

No. 4231
Favor Vase
Diamond Optic

No. 4232
Favor Vase
Diamond Optic

No. 4217—6 in. Vase
Diamond Optic Only

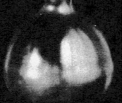

No. 4224
Ivy Vase
Plain Only

No. 4222—6 in. Vase
Plain Only

No. 4215—4½ in. Vase
Diamond Optic Only

No. 4220—7 in. Vase
Swirl Optic Only
Also made 4½ in.

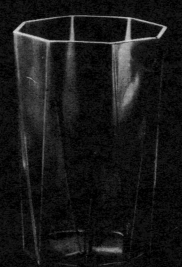

No. 4223—12 in. Vase
Plain Only

No. 4216—9 in. Vase
Octagon
Plain Only

No. 4214—7 in. Vase
Swirl or Diamond Optic

Miscellaneous vases

379

Miscellaneous

Every book needs a miscellaneous section to tie up loose ends and include information not easily included elsewhere. The Heisey catalogs were no exception to this and thus every one had a section with miscellaneous items shown. Sometimes these were just that, such things as ladles, muddlers, odd nappies and other items which had few or no matching pieces to make a complete pattern. Other items included might be left over items from a major pattern which was going out of fashion and thus had only a few popular pieces remaining in the line. This is shown by items from the #417 Double Rib & Panel pattern and the #1170 Pleat and Panel pattern. Also sometimes, pieces were added to a major pattern, but were too late to be included with the pattern. Such is the case with the #1404 Old Sandwich pilsner.

Included in this section are some major sellers and important pieces from the Heisey line. Be sure to give this section full attention as many interesting and scarce items are shown here.

#2 three-part liner

Dates: Ca. 1929
Colors: Crystal, marigold. Possibly moongleam and flamingo
Marked: Yes

#6 mayonnaise ladle

Dates: 1917-ca.1935
Colors: Crystal, moongleam, flamingo, hawthorne, sahara, alexandrite
Marked: Yes
Comments: Very similar to ladles made by other companies. See the first page in alexandrite in the COLOR SECTION for illustration.

#10 CARTER inkwell & cover - name given by researchers

Dates: Ca. 1929-1933
Colors: Crystal only
Marked: Yes
Comments: This item is similar to two other patterns. The base is very like the #99 candleblock, while the finial is the same as the stopper for the #1170 Pleat and Panel oil

#10 OAK LEAF coaster

Dates: Ca. 1925
Colors: Crystal, moongleam, flamingo, hawthorne, sahara
Marked: No
Comments: The main motif is similar to the design of the leaf in the edge of the Beehive plate. A variant in crystal is known without the panels in the edge of the coaster.

#500 milk bottle top

Dates: Unknown. Only referred to in a handwritten notation.
Colors: Crystal. Others could be found
Marked: No
Comments: These small items were made from the bottoms of small stemware items and ground to fit into a milk bottle. Although occasionally found, authentic ones are not easy to find. The one shown is made from a Kimberly stem, but other stem lines were sometimes used. Late note: A mold was recently found for this item listed as "#500 cover". It is similar to the Kimberly Stem shown but is pressed and has 4 crossed lines under the base.

#2 Three-part liner

#10 CARTER inkwell & cover

#10 OAK LEAF coaster

#500 Milk bottle top

#1010 DECAGON - name given by researchers

Dates: Ca. 1933-1935
Colors: Crystal, moongleam, flamingo
Marked: Yes
Comments: The piece has eight main panels with two tiny panels where the handles are located.

#7089 CLOVERLEAF snack plate - name and number given by researchers

Dates: Unknown
Colors: Flamingo known. Others, especially crystal and moongleam are possible.
Marked: Yes

#1245/3970 comport

Dates: Unknown
Colors: Flamingo and moongleam in combination with crystal
Marked: Yes
Comments: A piece made from the old #3970 comport stem with the #1245 plate attached. Probably made about the same time as the Petticoat dolphin comports (ca. 1925).

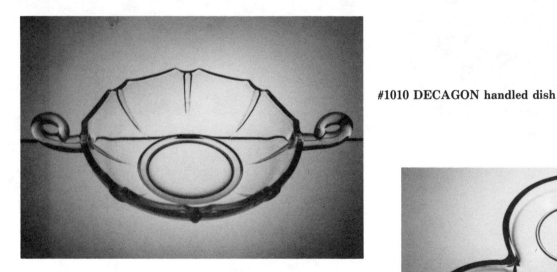

#1010 DECAGON handled dish

#7089 CLOVERLEAF snack plate

#1245/3970 comport

382

#1180 BRAZIL - name given by researchers

Dates: Ca. 1919-1933
Colors: Crystal, moongleam, flamingo
Marked: Yes

#1189 YEOMAN 13″ celery - original Heisey Co. name

Dates: 1921-1937
Colors: Crystal, moongleam, flamingo
Marked: Yes
Comments: Patent #65870 applied for 2/8/21 and granted 10/28/24. Designed by Arthur J. Sanford.

#1186 YEOMAN cup & saucer - original Heisey Co. name

Dates: Ca. 1929-1937
Colors: Crystal, moongleam, flamingo
Marked: Yes
Comments: This style of Yeoman cup has the rounded handle rather than the angular one sometimes seen. See PATTERN Section for other #1184 Yeoman items.

#1183 REVERE parfait - original Heisey Co. name

Dates: 1913-1935
Colors: Crystal only
Marked: Should be

#1185 YEOMAN 12″ celery - original Heisey Co. name

Dates: 1922-1937
Colors: Crystal, moongleam, flamingo
Marked: Yes
Comments: Made plain or diamond optic. A 10½″ handled sandwich in plain was also made in moongleam and flamingo; in diamond optic it was made in hawthorne.

#1186 YEOMAN 7″ high footed comport - original Heisey Co. name

Dates: Ca. 1922-1933
Colors: Crystal, moongleam, flamingo, hawthorne
Marked: Yes, at top of stem

#1183 REVERE 6″ comport - original Heisey Co. name

Dates: Ca. 1927+
Colors: Crystal, moongleam, flamingo, hawthorne
Marked: Yes, at top of stem

#1181 cheese & cracker
   Dates: Ca. 1923-1933
   Colors: Crystal only
   Marked: Should be

#1186 YEOMAN 6″ comport, deep - original Heisey Co. name
   Dates: 1922-1935
   Colors: Crystal, moongleam, flamingo, sahara
   Marked: Yes, at top of stem
   Comments: Made plain or diamond optic.

MISCELLANEOUS

NO. 1180 INDIVIDUAL NUT
GROUND BOTTOM

NO. 1189-13-IN. CELERY TRAY- GROUND OR FIRE
POLISHED BOTTOM- PATENT NO. 65870
ALSO MAKE 9-IN.
NO. 1189-13-IN. PICKLE & OLIVE LIKE CELERY TRAY
WITH TWO COMPARTMENTS

NO. 1186 CUP & SAUCER
DIAMOND OPTIC
ALSO MADE PLAIN

NO. 1183-5-OZ.
PARFAIT OPTIC
ALSO MADE PLAIN

NO. 1185-12-IN. CELERY TRAY- GROUND BOTTOM
ALSO MADE DIAMOND OPTIC
MADE WITH FIRE POLISHED BOTTOM
PLAIN ONLY

NO. 1186-7-IN.
HIGH FOOTED COMPORT
SHALLOW-DIAMOND OPTIC

NO. 1183-6-IN. COMPORT
SWIRL OPTIC

NO. 1181 CHEESE & CRACKER
GROUND BOTTOM

NO. 1186-6-IN.
HIGH FOOTED COMPORT DEEP
DIAMOND OPTIC-ALSO MADE PLAIN

#1191 LOBE - name given by researchers

Dates: Ca. 1927-1933; pickle & olive only from 1933-1937
Colors: Crystal, moongleam, flamingo, hawthorne
Marked: Pickle & olive—no, Handled spice—may be marked on handle
Comments: The spice dish was also made without a handle. Pairpoint used the pickle & olive and the spice dish for their Wilton, Graham and Kentwood engravings.

#1194 PENTAGON - name given by researchers

Dates: 1923-1933
Colors: Crystal, moongleam, flamingo
Marked: Sometimes

#1193 INSIDE SCALLOP - name given by researchers

Dates: 1923-1933
Colors: Crystal, moongleam, flamingo, vaseline
Marked: Yes
Comments: Various sizes of nappies were also made in this pattern. These nappies are occasionally found in vaseline.

#1187 YEOMAN 13″ tray - original Heisey Co. name

Dates: 1922-1933
Colors: Crystal only
Marked: Unknown

#1201 LAVERNE - name given by researchers

Dates: 1924-1933
Colors: Crystal, moongleam, flamingo, vaseline
Marked: Usually

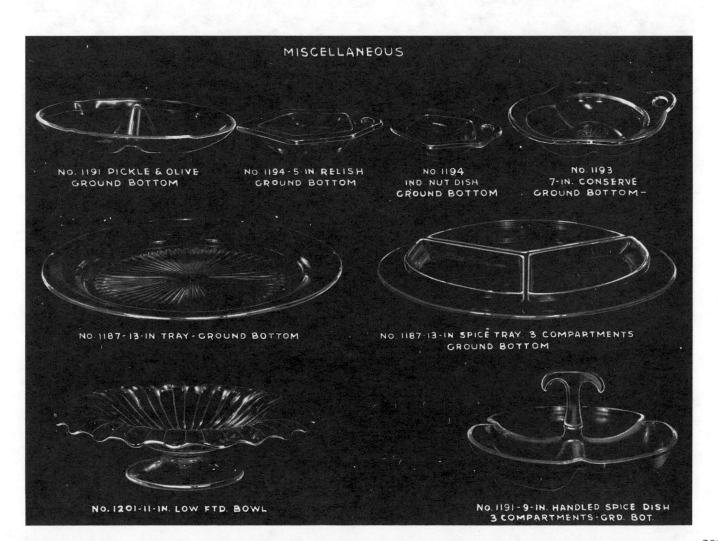

MISCELLANEOUS

NO. 1191 PICKLE & OLIVE GROUND BOTTOM

NO. 1194-5-IN RELISH GROUND BOTTOM

NO. 1194 IND NUT DISH GROUND BOTTOM

NO. 1193 7-IN. CONSERVE GROUND BOTTOM—

NO. 1187-13-IN TRAY-GROUND BOTTOM

NO. 1187-13-IN SPICE TRAY, 3 COMPARTMENTS GROUND BOTTOM

NO. 1201-11-IN. LOW FTD. BOWL

NO. 1191-9-IN. HANDLED SPICE DISH 3 COMPARTMENTS-GRD. BOT.

#1210 FROG handled cheese dish
Dates: Ca. 1929-1933
Colors: Crystal, moongleam, flamingo, marigold
Marked: No

#1210 bon bon
Dates: Ca. 1929-1933
Colors: Crystal, moongleam, flamingo, marigold
Marked: No

#1210 relish
Dates: Ca. 1929-1933
Colors: Crystal, moongleam, flamingo, marigold
Marked: No

#1210 duplex confection tray
Dates: Ca. 1929-1933
Colors: Crystal, moongleam, flamingo
Marked: No

#1216 PLAIN - name given by researchers
Dates: 1909-1933
Colors: Crystal only
Marked: Yes

#1221 STAR CENTER - name given by researchers
Dates: 1913-1935
Colors: Crystal only
Marked: Usually

#1228, #1224 - See PLATES Section for information

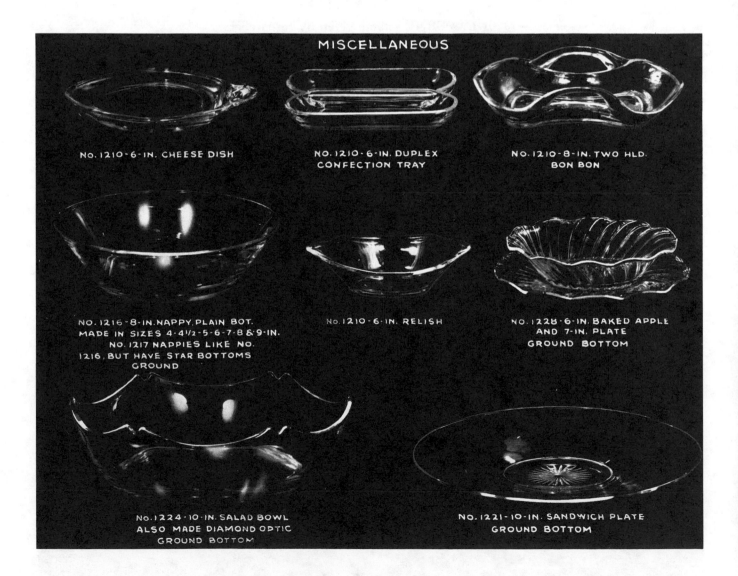

MISCELLANEOUS

NO. 1210-6-IN. CHEESE DISH

NO. 1210-6-IN. DUPLEX
CONFECTION TRAY

NO. 1210-8-IN. TWO HLD.
BON BON

NO. 1216-8-IN. NAPPY, PLAIN BOT.
MADE IN SIZES 4-4½-5-6-7-8 & 9-IN.
NO. 1217 NAPPIES LIKE NO.
1216, BUT HAVE STAR BOTTOMS
GROUND

NO. 1210-6-IN. RELISH

NO. 1228-6-IN. BAKED APPLE
AND 7-IN. PLATE
GROUND BOTTOM

NO. 1224-10-IN. SALAD BOWL
ALSO MADE DIAMOND OPTIC
GROUND BOTTOM

NO. 1221-10-IN. SANDWICH PLATE
GROUND BOTTOM

#1150, #1219, #4182 - See PLATES Section for information

#406 COARSE RIB - See PATTERN Section for information

#372 McGRADY - name given by researchers

Dates: Ca. 1929-1948
Colors: Crystal, moongleam, flamingo, sahara
Marked: Yes, on side of spout
Comments: Made in 5 oz., 7 oz. and 12 oz. sizes.

#398 HOPEWELL - name given by researchers

Dates: 1909-1957. In later years was listed as part of #1183 Revere
Colors: Crystal only. 5″ nappy in amber for Fred Harvey
Marked: Yes
Comments: Widely used for decorations by Heisey and other companies.

#1458 COURTHOUSE - name given by researchers

Dates: Ca. 1935-ca. 1938; 1953-1955
Colors: Crystal only
Marked: No
Comments: In 1953 the plate was made with a well to hold either a #5082 Mid-Century cocktail or a #1503 Crystolite tea cup and it was called a snack or cocktail plate.

#1101 STICH - name given by researchers

Dates: Ca. 1897-ca. 1945
Colors: Crystal. In diamond optic it was made in moongleam and flamingo
Marked: Yes

#1242 finger bowl

Dates: Ca. 1909-1944
Colors: Crystal, moongleam, flamingo
Marked: Should be

#1212 CRIM - name given by researchers

Dates: 1909-1944
Colors: Crystal only
Marked: Should be

#2 grape fruit center, peg

Dates: 1913-1944
Colors: Crystal only
Marked: No

#3 grape fruit center, footed

Dates: 1913-1944
Colors: Crystal only
Marked: No

#5 mustard spoon

Dates: 1916-1944
Colors: Crystal, moongleam, flamingo, sahara, marigold
Marked: Yes, near top of handle

#2 salad fork & spoon

Dates: 1913-1944
Colors: Crystal only
Marked: Usually
Comments: Another variety was made without the beads on the handles. The fork and spoon were used for some Heisey cuttings, including #812 Sweet Briar.

#2 mustard spoon

Dates: 1913-1936
Colors: Crystal only
Marked: Yes

#1 mustard spoon

Dates: 1908-1936
Colors: Crystal only
Marked: Yes, near top of handle

387

No. 1150—6 in. Colonial Plate
Star Bottom Ground
Also made 4½, 5, 5½, 6½,
7, 8, 9 & 10 in.

No. 1219—6 in. Plain Plate
Star Bottom Ground
Also made 4½, 5½, 7, 8, 9½ & 11 In.

No. 406—4½ in. Nappy
Also made 4, 5, 6, 7, 8 & 9 in.

No. 372—5 oz. Sanitary Syrup
Chromium Plated Top or Nickel Plated Top
Also made 7 & 12 oz.

No. 398—4 in. Nappy
Also made 3½, 4½, 5, 5½,
6, 7, 8 & 9 in.

No. 1458—8 in. Plate

No. 4182—7 in. Plate
Plain or Diamond Optic
Also made 6 & 8 in.

Miscellaneous syrups, nappies & plates

No. 1101—5 oz. Custard
Plain or Diamond Optic

No. 1242 Finger Bowl
Plain or Diamond Optic

No. 1212—4 oz. Custard

MISCELLANEOUS ITEMS

No. 2 Peg Grape Fruit Center

No. 3 Footed Grape Fruit Center

No. 5 Mustard Spoon

No. 2 Mustard Spoon

No. 2 Salad Fork

No. 2 Salad Spoon

No. 1 Mustard Spoon

Miscellaneous custards & finger bowls

#10 mustard paddle
Dates: 1936-1944
Colors: Crystal only
Marked: No

#7 mayonnaise ladle
Dates: Ca. 1933-1957
Colors: Crystal, moongleam, flamingo, sahara
Marked: No

#10 muddler, small
Dates: 1935-1944; 1949-1956
Colors: Crystal, moongleam, flamingo, sahara, cobalt
Marked: No

#11 muddler, large
Dates: 1935-1937
Colors: Crystal
Marked: No

#300½ #1 PEERLESS - original Heisey Co. name
Dates: 1899-1944
Colors: Crystal only
Marked: No

#339 CONTINENTAL - original Heisey Co. name
Dates: 1903-1944
Colors: Crystal, flamingo
Marked: Not usually. Sometimes on top of the bulge on opposite panels

#300½ #2 PEERLESS - original Heisey Co. name
Dates: 1899-1939
Colors: Crystal, sahara
Marked: No

#354 WIDE FLAT PANEL - name given by researchers
Dates: Ca. 1913-ca. 1937
Colors: Crystal, flamingo. Butter pat also made in sahara
Marked: Yes, all three pieces.
Comments: Known as a "stack set" since all three pieces stack together for use on a tray or in a restaurant. See COLONIAL PIECES IN COLOR Section for other pieces.

#417 DOUBLE RIB & PANEL cocktail carafe - name given by researchers
Dates: 1935-1937
Colors: Crystal only
Marked: Unknown

#367 PRISM BAND - name given by researchers
Dates: 1915-1957. After 1939 it was part of #341 Old Williamsburg
Colors: Crystal, moongleam, flamingo
Marked: Sometimes, on side of neck
Comments: Probably a copy of an old Boston & Sandwich piece. Stoppers are usually crystal.

#417 DOUBLE RIB & PANEL mustard - name given by researchers
Dates: 1923-1937
Colors: Crystal, moongleam, flamingo, hawthorne
Marked: Yes
Comments: See BASKETS Section for matching basket.

#394 NARROW FLUTE chow chow - Heisey description of pattern
Dates: 1909-ca. 1939
Colors: Crystal only
Marked: Yes

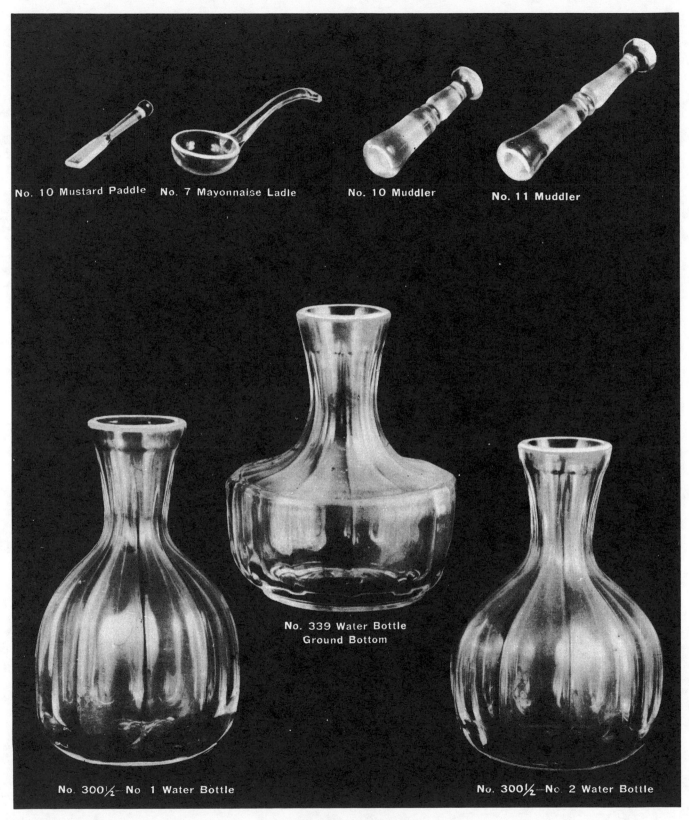

No. 10 Mustard Paddle   No. 7 Mayonnaise Ladle   No. 10 Muddler   No. 11 Muddler

No. 339 Water Bottle
Ground Bottom

No. 300½ — No. 1 Water Bottle   No. 300½ — No. 2 Water Bottle

Miscellaneous items

No. 354 Individual Sugar

No. 354 Individual Cream

No. 354 Individual Butter

No. 417 Cocktail Carafe

No. 367—1 pt. Decanter & No. 48 C/S
Also made with No. 48 P/S

No. 417 Mustard & Cover

No 394 —4½ in. Chow Chow

Miscellaneous items

392

No. 1115
Bitters Bottle & Short Tube

No. 479
Footed Hotel Sugar

No. 479
Footed Hotel Cream

No. 485
1 oz. Cologne
& No. 71 Peg Stopper

No. 473
3½ in. Salad Nut Dish

No. 1170
10 in. Spice Tray
5 Compartments

No. 485
9 in. Beverage Bowl

No. 485
14 in. Beverage Bowl Plate

No. 1170
3 pt. Ice Jug

#1115 BRADBURY bitters bottle - name given by researchers
Dates: 1897-1938+
Colors: Crystal only
Marked: No

#479 - See CREAMS & SUGARS Section
#485 - See COLOGNE Section
#473, #1170 - See PATTERN Section

#485 DUNHAM - name given by researchers
Dates: 1935-1957, as part of #1183 Revere
Colors: Crystal only
Marked: Probably not
Comments: Made in a combination beverage bowl and
underplate. Used for several cuttings
by Heisey.

#1185, #1189, #1186 - See discussion earlier in this section

#1189 YEOMAN cream & sugar - original Heisey Co. name

Dates: Ca. 1933-1937
Colors: Crystal, moongleam, flamingo, sahara
Marked: No
Comments: A pottery set has been seen in an old ad - either these were copied from Heisey or Heisey copied the ceramic set.

#1222 hot & cold liner

Dates: Ca. 1937-1956
Colors: Crystal
Marked: Yes
Comments: Patent #104175 applied for 2/24/37 and granted 4/30/37. C.S. Whipple listed as designer.

#1224 hot & cold liner

Dates: 1937-1956
Colors: Crystal, moongleam, sahara
Marked: Yes. Sometimes unmarked

#1223 hot & cold liner

Dates: Ca. 1937-1956
Colors: Crystal
Marked: Yes

#1413 CATHEDRAL - name given by researchers

Dates: 1932-1944. Flared only after 1939
Colors: Crystal, moongleam, flamingo, sahara, cobalt. Straight and flared were made in alexandrite
Marked: Not usually
Comments: The shape most often seen is the flared version of the handleless vase. Imperial Glass has made the flared vase in their rose pink for Collectors' Guild. These are marked with a CG in a circle on the base. The flared Cathedral vase was used by Heisey for many cuttings and some etchings. Pairpoint also decorated the vase with their Boswell engraving.

#1404 OLD SANDWICH - original Heisey Co. name

Dates: 1931-1944
Colors: Crystal, sahara
Marked: Unknown
Comments: See PATTERN Section for remainder of pattern.

No 1185
12 in. Celery Tray
Plain or Diamond Optic
Ground Bottom or Fire Polish

No. 1224
Hot & Cold Liner

No. 1189
Individual Sugar & Cover

No. 1222
Hot & Cold Liner

No 1186
Cup & Saucer
Plain or Diamond Optic

No. 1189
Individual Cream

No 1223
Hot & Cold Liner

No. 1189
9 in. Celery Tray
Ground Bottom
Also made 13 in.

No. 1413
Straight Vase
Stuck Handles

No. 1404
8 oz. Pilsner

No. 1413
Straight Vase
Also made Flared

Miscellaneous items

#1417 ARCH - name given by researchers

Dates: 1933-1939
Colors: Crystal, moongleam, flamingo, sahara, cobalt, amber (in 1938). The variation with toes is known in crystal and tangerine
Marked: Yes
Comments: The first style of this tumbler had four small "toes" around the base. Apparently these were quite fragile, since the mold was soon changed to eliminate these toes. Compare design with the #1440 floral bowl in the FLORAL BOWLS Section.

#1454 DIAMOND POINT - name given by researchers

Dates: 1935-1944+
Colors: Crystal only
Marked: Yes
Comments: See ASH TRAY Section for the ash tray. The top hat match holder was made only in crystal by Heisey and has a rolled brim. Imperial Glass made the hat in its carnival glass, "Aurora Jewels," which is a blue carnival and the hat has a flat brim. The original Heisey hat is unmarked.

#1460 FLAME - name given by researchers

Dates: 1935-1944+
Colors: Crystal, cobalt
Marked: Yes

#1433 THUMBPRINT & PANEL - name given by researchers

Dates: 1934-1937
Colors: Crystal, moongleam, flamingo, sahara, cobalt. The cheese & cracker was made in sahara and cobalt.
Marked: No
Comments: See CANDLESTICK and FLORAL BOWLS Sections for matching pieces. A very limited line, but usually of excellent quality glass. A copy of a old flint glass pattern.

#1421 HI LO - name given by researchers

Dates: 1933-1937
Colors: Crystal, moongleam, flamingo, sahara, cobalt
Marked: Sometimes

#1430 ARISTOCRAT - name given by researchers

Dates: 1933-1937
Colors: Crystal, moongleam, sahara, cobalt. Rare in tangerine
Marked: Yes
Comments: Note the plain and beaded lids shown on the catalog illustration. These candy jars were frequently used for special cuttings and also for regular cuttings by Heisey. Made both with a tall stem and a low stem. The ball in the stem portion resembles the one found on #3404 Spanish stemware.

#1420 TULIP - name given by researchers

Dates: 1933-1937
Colors: Crystal, moongleam, flamingo, sahara, cobalt
Marked: Yes, on bottom
Comments: This vase is probably most often seen in cobalt and the factory evidently had some of these for sale near the time it closed in 1957. The vase is difficult to find in crystal.

#1466 STAR - name given by researchers

Dates: 1935-1953
Colors: Crystal only
Marked: No
Comments: Rather frequently used for cuttings and etchings by Heisey.

No. 1417
9 oz. Straight Footed Tumbler
Also made Cupped

No. 1454
2½ In. Individual Jelly

No. 1460
Footed Tumbler

No. 1433
8½ in. Vase

No. 1421
8 in. Footed & Handled Vase

No. 1430
½ lb. Low Footed Candy Jar & Cover

No. 1420
9 in. Footed Vase

No. 1430
½ lb. High Footed Candy Jar & Cover

No. 1466
5 Compartment Relish

No. 1433
Cheese & Cracker

Miscellaneous items

#1473 BUTTRESS - original Heisey Co. name

Dates: 1935-1938
Colors: Crystal only
Marked: Yes
Comments: Used for some cuttings and a few etchings by Heisey. The various pieces were meant to be used in different ways for floral arrangements. All pieces could be used or only a few. The corners were usually grouped around one of the centerpieces.

#2000 bobeche

Dates: Ca. 1935-1937
Colors: Crystal only
Marked: Unknown

#1479 BECKMAN - name given by researchers

Dates: 1935-ca. 1945
Colors: Crystal only
Marked: Unknown

#4163 WHALEY pretzel jar - name given by researchers

Dates: 1933-1938
Colors: Crystal, sahara
Marked: Yes
Comments: Used for several silhouette etchings by Heisey. Sometimes found decorated by outside firms. See discussion of the piece in the text under "Prohibition. . ."

#4163 WHALEY beer mug - name given by researchers

Dates: 1933-ca.1945
Colors: Crystal. Handles in moongleam, flamingo, sahara, cobalt, tangerine, red
Marked: Yes
Comments: Made in 12 oz. and 16 oz. sizes. Used for many of the silhouette etchings with sports motifs by Heisey. Also used for some special etchings. Mugs with colored handles are difficult to find. See JUGS section for matching pitcher.

#3397 - See discussion in STEMWARE Section

#1476 MORSE torte plate - name given by researchers

Dates: 1935-1937
Colors: Crystal. Cobalt reported
Marked: Unknown
Comments: Difficult to find. Sometimes used with the Pumpkin punch bowl.

No. 1473
Medium Center Piece

No. 1473
Large Center Piece

No. 1473
Corner Center Piece

No. 2000
Bobeche Candleholder

No. 1479—4½ oz. Optic Sherbet

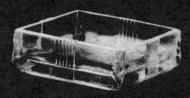

No. 1473
Small Center Piece

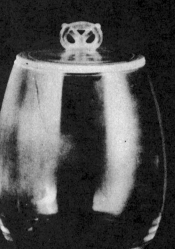

No. 4163—12 oz. Beer Mug
Also made 16 oz.

No. 3397
2 Compartment Mayonnaise

No. 4163
Pretzel Jar & Cover

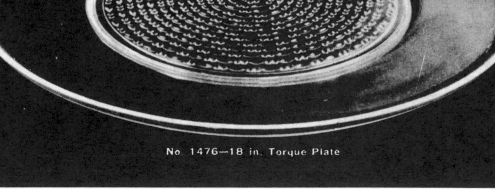

No. 1476—18 in. Torque Plate

Miscellaneous items

399

#4056 CAESAR salad bowl - name given by researchers

Dates: 1935-1956
Colors: Crystal
Marked: No
Comments: Made in a 9″ and 11″ size. Walter Von Nessen designed this bowl from the #4045 ball vase as an item to be in a special display in the Metropolitan Museum. This bowl was used for several decorations by Heisey and is sometimes found with elaborate special cuttings.

#4266 custard

Dates: 1917-1943
Colors: Crystal only
Marked: No

#4058 PUMPKIN - original Heisey Co. name

Dates: 1935-1944
Colors: Crystal. Cobalt reported
Marked: No
Comments: Difficult to find with the matching lid. Infrequently used for some Heisey cuttings.

#4059 ALLEN water bottle - name given by researchers

Dates: 1917-ca. 1945
Colors: Crystal. Amber for Fred Harvey
Marked: No
Comments: A rare example is known in crystal with cobalt stripes.

#4061 McPEEK water bottle - name given by researchers

Dates: 1917-1933; 1936-1938
Colors: Crystal only
Marked: No

#3417 ADKINS bitters bottle - name given by researchers

Dates: 1934-1935
Colors: Crystal only
Marked: No
Comments: Used for some etchings and cuttings by Heisey. Heisey also made a 7″ comport in diamond optic with this number. See also the BARWARE Section for matching sodas.

#4044 NEW ERA - See discussion in STEMWARE Section

#3806 mushroom cover

Dates: 1919-1944
Colors: Crystal only
Marked: No

#4056 FRYE water bottle - name given by researchers

Dates: 1917-1938
Colors: Crystal only
Marked: No

#4057 SCHNAIDT water bottle - name given by researchers

Dates: 1917-1939
Colors: Crystal, moongleam, flamingo
Marked: No
Comments: A turn book entry in 1930 indicated some water bottles were made "s/o - green". This probably means swirl optic since saturn optic had not yet been introduced by Heisey.

#4121 GLENN - name given by researchers

Dates: 1917-1946
Colors: Crystal only
Marked: No
Comments: Sometimes used for cuttings and etchings by Heisey, including #507 Orchid.

#4122 WEAVER - name given by researchers

Dates: 1917-1928; 1934-1937
Colors: Crystal only
Marked: No
Comments: Sometimes used for early cuttings by Heisey.

#4002 AQUA CALIENTE - original Heisey Co. description

Dates: 1933-1944; 1948-1953 in crystal
Colors: Crystal, moongleam, flamingo, sahara, cobalt
Marked: Yes, on stem below bowl
Comments: Used by Heisey for some cuttings and etchings. In colors, it was sold as a set with the #4225 Cobel cocktail shaker. Often confused with Heisey's #5024 Oxford pattern.

#4225 COBEL - name given by researchers

Dates: 1932-1957
Colors: 1 quart - crystal, moongleam, flamingo, sahara, cobalt & rare in experimental red. 1 pt., 2 qt. and Rock & Rye made only in crystal
Marked: No
Comments: Named for Ray C. Cobel, who designed the mold. Patent #1,966,611 applied for 12/19/31 and granted 7/17/34. Also made in 1-pint and 2-quart sizes. The pint shaker is similar in appearance but has tapering sides. Notice the Rock & Rye bottle, which is not often seen. This cocktail shaker was widely used by Heisey for cuttings and etchings. It is often seen with animal stoppers, especially the Rooster Head and the Horse Head. Other stoppers sometimes used were the Large Horse Head, the Rams Head, and the Girls Head. Other companies also decorated the cocktail shaker, especially with cuttings and sometimes silver overlay or even rattan handles. Cobalt shakers are sometimes seen with silver overlay. Imperial Glass continued to make the 1-quart shaker until 1968. It also made the 1-pint and 2-quart shakers until 1961.

#4182 - See PLATES Section for discussion

#4222 HORSESHOE - name given by researchers

Dates: 1931-1937
Colors: Crystal, moongleam, flamingo, sahara, crystal with moongleam handles.
Marked: No
Comments: Heisey also made a vase in this pattern. Pieces are usually ground and polished on the bottoms. See VASES Section.

#2 BARNES - name given by researchers

Dates: 1936-1937
Colors: Crystal only
Marked: No

#1 PAULSON - name given by researchers

Dates: 1936-1937
Colors: Crystal only
Marked: No

#4042 REYNOLDS - name given by researchers

Dates: 1919-1937
Colors: Crystal, moongleam, flamingo
Marked: No

No. 4056—11 in.
Salad Bowl
Plain Only

No. 4266—5 oz.
Custard
Plain Only

No 4058—5 oz.
Custard
Wide Optic Only

No. 4058
Punch Bowl & Cover
Wide Optic Only

Miscellaneous items

No. 4059—42 oz.
Water Bottle
Plain or Diamond Optic

No. 4061
Water Bottle
Wide Optic Only

No. 3417—6 oz.
Bitter Bottle & Tube
Plain Only

No. 4044—28 oz.
Rock & Rye & No. 93 P/S
Plain Only

No. 3806—4½ in.
Mushroom Cover
Plain Only

No. 4056—38 oz.
Water Bottle
Plain or Wide Optic

No. 4057—40 oz.
Water Bottle
Plain or Wide Optic

Miscellaneous items

403

No. 4121
Marmalade & Cover
Plain or Diamond Optic

No. 4122
Marmalade & Cover
Plain or Diamond Optic

No. 4002
Agua Caliente Coffee or Cocktail
Plain Only

No. 4182—7 in. Plate
Plain or Wide Optic
Also made 6 & 8 in.

No. 4225—1 qt.
Cocktail Shaker
No. 1 Strainer
No. 86 P/S
Plain Only
Also made 2 qt.

No. 4225—1 qt.
Rock & Rye Bottle
& No. 86 P/S
Plain Only

No. 4222
Sugar
Plain Only

No. 4222
Cream
Plain Only

Miscellaneous items

No. 2
Oil Bottle & No. 97 P/S
Plain Only

No. 1
Oil Bottle & No. 98 P/S
Plain Only

No. 4042—6 oz.
Oil Bottle & No. 62 C/S
Plain or Wide Optic

Oil bottles

Numerical Index

Numbers in bold indicate pages in color section.

Alphabetical Index

Numbers in bold indicate pages in color section.

413

Heisey Price Guide

Prices given are for known colors for each piece listed. Often price ranges are not given for extreme color rarities. These so seldom reach the market that true values are almost impossible to establish. Unusual colors are mentioned in the text and some are shown in the color section. Reasonable beginning values are given for these pieces. (e.g. $500.00+)

Prices are for pieces in perfect or near perfect condition. Major damage (such as large chips, cracks, scratches, cloudiness or other imperfections) usually reduces the price considerably.

Prices for candlesticks and salts and peppers are given for pairs unless otherwise indicated.

Price ranges were established by having eleven regional study clubs of HCA submit reports. These were tallied and should result in an accurate national average. Prices do vary considerably from one geographical area to another.

Decorations such as etchings, cuttings and engravings usually add to the value of items.

Clubs whose members participated in the pricing are: 1. BAY STATE HCC - Massachusetts; 2. GOLDEN GATE HCC - San Francisco Area, California; 3. HEISEY CLUB OF CALIFORNIA - Los Angeles Area, California; 4. HCC OF MICHIGAN - Michigan; 5. HEISEY COLLECTORS OF TEXAS - Texas; 6. HEISEY HERITAGE SOCIETY - New Jersey, Pennsylvania; 7. LONG ISLAND HCC - New York; 8. NATIONAL CAPITAL HCC - Washington D.C. Area; 9. NORTHWEST HCC - Washington, Oregon; 10. SOUTHERN ILLINOIS DIAMOND H SEEKERS - Illinois; 11. WESTERN RESERVE HEISEY CLUB - Ohio

Price Guide for Color Pages of
The Collector's Encyclopedia of Heisey Glass 1925-1938

Page 33: VASELINE

Row 1:
3345 MARY N VIRG goblet	375.00
473 NARROW FLUTE WITH RIM 5" footed almond	175.00
353 MEDIUM FLAT PANEL vase	350.00
341½ PURITAN jug	850.00+

Row 2:
350 PINWHEEL & FAN large nappy	450.00
1020 PHYLLIS cream & sugar	400.00 pr
465 RECESSED PANEL covered candy	600.00
1184 YEOMAN oval preserve	150.00

Row 3:
1193 INSIDE SCALLOP large nappy	225.00
351 PRISCILLA extra high footed shallow bowl	1250.00+
1201 LAVERNE floral bowl	250.00

Page 34: MOONGLEAM

Row 1:
367 PRISM BAND decanter	300.00
1408 PANEL & DIAMOND POINT goblet	350.00+
465 RECESSED PANEL covered candy	600.00
1252 TWIST oil & stopper	90.00
3386 DIAMOND ROSE goblet	90.00
3480 KOORS 2 hdld vase	175.00+

Row 2:
1020 PHYLLIS cream & sugar	80.00 pr
125 LEAF DESIGN candlestick	175.00 pr

Row 3:
4045 BALL vase 6"	350.00
4224 STEEPLECHASE cocktail mixer	350.00
4224 STEEPLECHASE cocktail	100.00
352 FLAT PANEL lavender jar/sterling overlay	250.00
8040 EVA MAE candlestick	250.00 pr

Row 4:
411 TUDOR luncheon goblet	45.00
1406 FLEUR DE LIS plate	90.00
1200 YEOMAN indiv ash tray	20.00
1184 YEOMAN hdld bon bon	40.00
1413 CATHEDRAL vase with Arctic etching	225.00
50 ADENA floral bowl with frog	75.00

Page 35: MOONGLEAM

Row 1:
1428 WARWICK vase	325.00
1405 IPSWICH covered candy	275.00
1183 REVERE candlevase	350.00 pr
solid block	40.00+
1404 OLD SANDWICH ice lip pitcher	140.00

Row 2:
141 EDNA candlestick	600.00 pr
500 OCTAGON sugar & cream, moongleam hdl	70.00 pr
473 NARROW FLUTE WITH RIM 2 compartment relish	35.00
4215 DOROTHY vase, diamond optic	60.00

Row 3:
1401 EMPRESS pitcher (no feet)	250.00
1401 EMPRESS oil - moongleam foot & stopper	100.00
1401½ EMPRESS plate	50.00
300½ PEERLESS tumbler	75.00
353 MEDIUM FLAT PANEL toothbrush holder	100.00

Row 4:
1445 GRAPE CLUSTER floral bowl	200.00
4224 IVY vase with Arctic etching	185.00
416/109 HERRINGBONE/PETTICOAT DOLPHIN compote	225.00
1170 PLEAT AND PANEL goblet	35.00
1170 PLEAT AND PANEL high footed compotier & cover	85.00

Page 36: FLAMINGO

Row 1:
353 MEDIUM FLAT PANEL vase	130.00
300½ PEERLESS bar	75.00
300 PEERLESS low ftd goblet	100.00
300 PEERLESS sherbet	75.00
341 PURITAN tankard	250.00
300½ PEERLESS tumbler	75.00
351 PRISCILLA ftd ale	60.00
341 PURITAN sherbet	75.00

Row 2:
1184 YEOMAN cigarette ash tray	85.00
14 KINGFISHER floral block	250.00
1001 CASWELL sugar sifter & cream	110.00 pr
1252 TWIST oil & stopper	65.00
1184 YEOMAN bridge smoking set	80.00

Row 3:
7007 ANGULAR CRISS CROSS tumbler	80.00
1201 PHILIP MORRIS match stand/ash tray	45.00
130 ACORN candlestick	250.00 pr
1403 HALF CIRCLE indiv cream & sugar	110.00
433 GRECIAN BORDER punch cup	45.00

Row 4:
463 BONNET basket	225.00
412 TUDOR ftd tankard	150.00
412 TUDOR ftd ice tea	35.00
3355 FAIRACRE vase	95.00
2517 TEARDROP pitcher	250.00

416

Page 37: FLAMINGO
Row 1:
7089 CLOVERLEAF snack plate	50.00
1433 THUMBPRINT & PANEL vase	195.00
1428 WARWICK 1 lt candlestick	300.00 pr
1420 TULIP vase	400.00
1404 OLD SANDWICH popcorn bowl	225.00

Row 2:
500 OCTAGON variety tray	90.00
1405 IPSWICH covered candy	250.00
1184 YEOMAN crescent salad plate	30.00
1010 DECAGON relish	40.00

Row 3:
136 TRIPLEX candlestick	200.00 pr
516/3 vase	65.00
111 CHERUB candlestick	750.00 pr
1225/109 RIDGE & STAR/PETTICOAT DOLPHIN comport	175.00
325 PILLOWS water bottle	275.00+

Page 38: HAWTHORNE
Row 1:
1191 LOBE hdld spice dish	95.00
406 COARSE RIB low ftd jelly	50.00
15 DUCK with floral block	275.00
1170 PLEAT & PANEL spice tray	125.00+

Row 2:
121 PINWHEEL candlestick	75.00 pr
4203 EMOGENE vase	95.00
3480 KOORS Pitcher	200.00
1186 YEOMAN indiv ash tray	60.00
479 PETAL sugar & cream	130.00 pr

Row 3:
417 DOUBLE RIB & PANEL basket	250.00
354 WIDE FLAT PANEL ftd hotel cream & sugar	150.00 pr
461 BANDED PICKET basket	350.00
1186 YEOMAN puff box & cover	125.00

Page 39: MARIGOLD
Row 1:
355 QUATOR cream & sugar	150.00 pr
393 NARROW FLUTE indiv sugar	100.00
1229 OCTAGON ftd mayonnaise d/o	40.00
500 OCTAGON nappy	45.00

Row 2:
501 FOGG floral box	175.00
1401 EMPRESS salt	350.00 + pr
357 DUCK ash tray	500.00+
500 OCTAGON basket	300.00
1252 TWIST CREAM soup	45.00

Row 3:
1210 FROG hdld cheese plate	425.00
411 TUDOR ftd grapefruit	80.00
350 PINWHEEL & FAN nappy	250.00
361 IRWIN ash tray/cigarette container	175.00

Row 4:
128 LIBERTY candlestick	200.00 pr
3368 ALBEMARLE goblet (crystal stem)	90.00
1252 TWIST goblet	50.00
1252 TWIST cocktail	30.00
1252 TWIST saucer champagne	40.00
1252 TWIST high ftd compote	100.00

Page 40: SAHARA
Row 1:
140 CROCUS candlestick	300.00 pr
1447 ROCOCO candlestick	600.00 pr
3397 GASCONY sugar & cream	160.00 pr
3485 IRENE jug	300.00

Row 2:
1483 STANHOPE celery tray	250.00
1447 ROCOCO sugar & cream	160.00 pr
1401 EMPRESS tumbler, dolphin foot	110.00

Row 3:
1189 YEOMAN indiv cream & covered sugar	180.00 pr
1184 YEOMAN mustard & cover	110.00
1184 YEOMAN indiv cream	45.00
1415 TWENTIETH CENTURY cereal bowl	60.00
1469 RIDGELEIGH cigarette box & cover	70.00

| 1469 RIDGELEIGH round cigarette holder | 45.00 |

Row 4:
1445 GRAPE CLUSTER 2 lt candlestick	750.00 pr
1405 IPSWICH oil & stopper	150.00
1252 TWIST French dressing & stopper	90.00
1430 ARISTOCRAT tall covered candy	325.00
4223 SWIRL vase	250.00
4225 COBEL cocktail shaker, Chintz etching	450.00

Page 41: ALEXANDRITE
Row 1:
3381 CREOLE goblet	195.00
3381 CREOLE saucer champagne	150.00
3381 CREOLE ftd soda	125.00
1150 COLONIAL STAR plate	200.00
3416 BARBARA FRITCHIE cordial	400.00
3405 COYLE beer mug	1500.00+

Row 2:
3381 CREOLE finger bowl	75.00
3381 CREOLE cordial	350.00
3381 CREOLE wine	165.00
1184 YEOMAN candy box bottom, etched & cut	500.00+
1000 marmalade & cover	400.00+
1401 EMPRESS ASH TRAY	225.00

Row 3:
1401 EMPRESS cup & saucer	120.00
6 mayonnaise ladle	100.00
1401 EMPRESS mayonnaise	175.00
miniature candlesticks, full cut	500.00+ ea.
1401 EMPRESS cream soup & underplate	90.00

Row 4:
300 PEERLESS low ftd goblet	500.00+
4027 CHRISTOS decanter	1500.00
373 OLD WILLIAMSBURG goblet	600.00+
1306 COMET LEAF goblet	600.00+
301 OLD WILLIAMSBURG 2 light candelabrum	1750.00 ea
135 EMPRESS candlestick	450.00 pr

Page 42: ALEXANDRITE
Row 1:
3390 CARCASSONNE flagon	200.00
3390 CARCASSONNE bar	150.00
3390 CARCASSONNE tall goblet	125.00
3390 CARCASSONNE short goblet	125.00
3390 CARCASSONNE cocktail	90.00
3390 CARCASSONNE whimsey pitcher	1000.00+
3390 CARCASSONNE saucer champagne	100.00
3390 CARCASSONNE jug	1500.00

Row 2:
4044 NEW ERA candlestick	1200.00 pr
4045 BALL vase, 12"	1250.00+
3368 ALBEMARLE goblet	225.00

Row 3:
1428 WARWICK vase	650.00+
1252 TWIST ice bucket	275.00
1413 CATHEDRAL flared vase	350.00

Page 43: AMBER
Row 1:
3404 SPANISH saucer champagne	600.00+
3397 GASCONY goblet	600.00+
1186 YEOMAN indiv ash tray	90.00+
3390 CARCASSONNE saucer champagne	650.00+
201 HARVEY COLONIAL tumbler	50.00
353 MEDIUM FLAT PANEL ftd soda	75.00

Row 2:
1170 PLEAT & PANEL oil & stopper	500.00+
337½ TOURAINE sherbet	35.00
586 soda	35.00
586 juice	35.00
588 soda	45.00
1404 OLD SANDWICH beer mug	500.00

417

Row 3:	337 TOURAINE parfait	65.00
	4049 OLD FITZ hot whiskey	90.00
	1125 STARBURST plate	35.00
	337 TOURAINE goblet	75.00
	1417 ARCH tumbler	115.00
Row 4:	353 MEDIUM FLAT PANEL tray	150.00
	4165 SHAW jug, cut	250.00
	353 MEDIUM FLAT PANEL jug	300.00

Page 44: COBALT

Row 1:	1405 IPSWICH candlevase, crystal insert	850.00 pr
	1433 THUMBPRINT & PANEL 2 lt candlestick	375.00 pr
	1433 THUMBPRINT & PANEL vase	250.00
	4224 IVY vase	250.00
Row 2:	4044 NEW ERA goblet	200.00
	3390 CARCASSONNE ftd soda	70.00
	3397 GASCONY decanter & stopper	500.00
	3397 GASCONY ftd floral bowl	650.00
Row 3:	1428 WARWICK floral bowl	325.00
	1413 CATHEDRAL 2 hdld vase	350.00
	1440 ARCH floral bowl	450.00

Page 45: COBALT

Row 1:	1404 OLD SANDWICH decanter	325.00
	393 NARROW FLUTE bitters bottle	350.00
	3359 PLATEAU sherbet	275.00+
	142 CASCADE candlestick	600.00 pr
Row 2:	1421 HI LO vase	325.00
	1533 WAMPUM floral bowl	1200.00+
	1425 VICTORIAN cream & sugar	500.00 pr
	1445 GRAPE CLUSTER 1 lt candlestick	1150.00 pr
	10 muddler	125.00
Row 3:	4225 COBEL cocktail shaker	500.00
	110 SANDWICH DOLPHIN candlestick	2000.00 pr
	4165 SHAW jug	300.00
	bottle/vase (experimental)	350.00+

Page 46: TANGERINE

Row 1:	3404 SPANISH goblet	550.00
	3404 SPANISH saucer champagne	550.00
	3404 SPANISH cocktail	350.00
	bottle/vase (experimental)	1000.00+
	3389 DUQUESNE oyster cocktail	200.00
	3389 DUQUESNE wine	275.00
	3389 DUQUESNE parfait	225.00
Row 2:	3397 GASCONY oval floral bowl	850.00+
	1401 EMPRESS cream & sugar	900.00 pr
	1401 EMPRESS salt	400.00 pr
	4230 favor vase	600.00
	3389 DUQUESNE finger bowl	100.00
Row 3:	134 TRIDENT candlestick	750.00+
	1417 ARCH tumbler with toes	600.00+
	1401 EMPRESS cup & saucer	600.00+
	3397 GASCONY soda (2)	250.00 ea
	3397 GASCONY wine	250.00
	3397 GASCONY saucer champagne	250.00
	3397 GASCONY goblet	250.00
Row 4:	1404 OLD SANDWICH plate	600.00+
	1404 OLD SANDWICH oyster cocktail	500.00+
	1404 OLD SANDWICH soda	600.00+
	1401 EMPRESS 2 hdld sandwich plate	400.00+
	1401 EMPRESS 8" square plate	135.00
	Diamond H advertising sign	250.00

Page 47: ZIRCON

Row 1:	4085 KOHINOOR soda	80.00
	4085 KOHINOOR goblet	90.00
	1495 FERN 3 compartment relish	125.00
	1404 OLD SANDWICH soda	600.00+
	3390 CARCASSONNE vase, saturn optic	650.00+
Row 2:	4090 COVENTRY goblet	150.00
	4083 STANHOPE saucer champagne	70.00
	4083 STANHOPE goblet	80.00
	4083 STANHOPE wine	85.00
	1469 RIDGELEIGH oval floral bowl	175.00
Row 3:	1496 MAHABAR cigarette box & cover	175.00
	1496 MAHABAR square ash tray	70.00
	1485 SATURN cocktail	80.00
	1485 SATURN saucer champagne	70.00
	1485 SATURN mustard & paddle cover	250.00
	1485 SATURN violet vase	125.00
Row 4:	1495 FERN candlestick	750.00 pr
	1485 SATURN 2 light candleblock	400.00 pr
	352 FLAT PANEL cigar jar & cover	600.00
	4085 BALL vase, saturn optic	175.00

Page 48: ZIRCON - ODD SHADES

Back:	1445 GRAPE CLUSTER floral bowl	1000.00+
	110 SANDWICH DOLPHIN candlestick	3000.00 pr
Middle:	1401 EMPRESS triplex relish	200.00+
	1425 VICTORIAN 3 compartment relish	700.00
	1469 RIDGELEIGH 1 light candlestick	150.00 pr
Front:	1401 EMPRESS bon bon	100.00+
	1485 SATURN 2 compartment relish	175.00

Page 49: BI-COLORED ITEMS

Back:	4206 OPTIC TOOTH vase, hawthorne/moongleam	350.00
Middle:	134 TRIDENT candlestick, sahara/alexandrite	750.00 pr
	3361 CHARLOTTE saucer champagne, hawthorne/moongleam	350.00+
	3361 CHARLOTTE goblet, hawthorne/moongleam	600.00+
Front:	3481 GLENFORD tumbler, flamingo/moongleam	200.00

EXPERIMENTAL LIGHT BLUE

Back:	1483 STANHOPE candelabrum	3000.00+ pr
Middle:	134 TRIDENT candlestick	3000.00+ pr
	3404 SPANISH sherbet	500.00+
	3324 DELAWARE goblet	600.00+
	4085 KOHINOOR low goblet	600.00+
Front:	393 NARROW FLUTE individual cream	500.00+
	355 QUATOR individual ash tray	500.00+

Page 50: COBALT

Back:	4059 ALLEN water bottle, crystal with blue stripes	1500.00+
	4223 SWIRL vase	450.00+
Middle:	2323 NAVY bar	90.00
	2323 NAVY tall soda	65.00
	2323 NAVY saucer	60.00+
	419 SUSSEX goblet	160.00
Front:	2323 NAVY plate	125.00
	2323 NAVY cup	135.00

TANGERINE VARIATIONS

Back:	4157 STEELE rose bowl, opaque	1250.00+
	8066 LARSON bottle/vase	1250.00+
Front:	337 TOURAINE sherbet	500.00+
	1229 OCTAGON mayonnaise d/o	600.00+
	1252 TWIST plate	550.00+

Page 51:	**GOBLETS**	
Row 1:	3362 CHARTER OAK, marigold bowl, crystal stem	60.00
	3362 CHARTER OAK, moongleam	40.00
	3362 CHARTER OAK, flamingo	40.00
	3362 CHARTER OAK, hawthorne	110.00
	3324 DELAWARE, hawthorne	80.00
	3324 DELAWARE, flamingo	50.00
	3386 DIAMOND ROSE, moongleam bowl	90.00
	4044 NEW ERA cobalt bowl	200.00
Row 2:	3350 WABASH, sahara bowl	150.00+
	3350 WABASH cocktail, zircon bowl	150.00+
	3350 WABASH, flamingo	35.00
	3350 WABASH, experimental gold stem	200.00+
	3350 WABASH, moongleam stem	35.00
	3350 WABASH, hawthorne (2)	75.00 ea
Row 3:	3397 GASCONY, tangerine bowl	400.00
	3397 GASCONY sahara, etched	125.00
	3357 KING ARTHUR, flamingo stem, cut	50.00
	3357 KING ARTHUR, moongleam stem	40.00
	3357 KING ARTHUR cocktail, moongleam stem	30.00
	3357 KING ARTHUR, flamingo, etched	45.00
	3373 MORNING GLORY, flamingo	100.00
	3379 PYRAMID saucer champagne, flamingo	50.00
Row 4:	3333 OLD GLORY, hawthorne	75.00
	3389 DUQUESNE, sahara	65.00
	3320 RITZ, moongleam foot, etched	60.00
	3390 CARCASSONNE low ftd, moongleam foot	50.00
	4083 STANHOPE, zircon bowl & foot	80.00
	4085 KOHINOOR footed soda, all zircon	90.00
	4090 COVENTRY, zircon	150.00
	4085 KOHINOOR, zircon bowl	90.00
Page 52:	**GOBLETS**	
Row 1:	3381 CREOLE, alexandrite bowl	175.00
	3381 CREOLE, sahara bowl	150.00
	3381 CREOLE, all alexandrite	195.00
	3370 AFRICAN, flamingo	50.00
	3370 AFRICAN, moongleam stem	50.00
	3366 TROJAN, flamingo	50.00
	3366 TROJAN, hawthorne	75.00
	3365 RAMSHORN, flamingo	60.00
Row 2:	3361 CHARLOTTE, hawthorne bowl, moongleam stem & foot	600.00+
	3325 RAMPUL, hawthorne	100.00
	3390 CARCASSONNE sahara, etched	55.00
	3390 CARCASSONNE, alexandrite bowl	125.00
	3390 CARCASSONNE, cobalt bowl	100.00
	3360 PENN CHARTER, flamingo	60.00
	3360 PENN CHARTER, hawthorne	70.00
Row 3:	3312 GAYOSO, flamingo	25.00
	2516 CIRCLE PAIR, moongleam	55.00
	3359 PLATEAU, flamingo	35.00
	3376 ADAM, flamingo	60.00
	3404 SPANISH, sahara bowl	325.00
	3404 SPANISH, tangerine bowl (2)	550.00 ea
	3404 SPANISH, cobalt bowl	120.00
Row 4:	3368 ALBEMARLE, marigold bowl	90.00
	3368 ALBEMARLE, alexandrite	225.00
	3368 ALBEMARLE, moongleam stem	50.00
	3380 OLD DOMINION short stem, sahara, etched	60.00
	3380 OLD DOMINION short stem, flamingo	45.00
	3380 OLD DOMINION tall stem, moongleam bowl	45.00
	3380 OLD DOMINION tall stem, moongleam stem	40.00

Page 53:	**BEER MUGS**	
Row 1:	1404 OLD SANDWICH 18 oz, cobalt	400.00
	1404 OLD SANDWICH 18 oz, sahara	175.00
	1404 OLD SANDWICH 18 oz, moongleam	300.00
	1404 OLD SANDWICH 18 oz, crystal	70.00
	1404 OLD SANDWICH 18 oz, amber	500.00
	1404 OLD SANDWICH 18 oz, flamingo	500.00
Row 2:	1404 OLD SANDWICH 14 oz, crystal	55.00
	1404 OLD SANDWICH 12 oz, sahara	150.00
	1404 OLD SANDWICH 12 oz, flamingo	325.00
	1404 OLD SANDWICH 12 oz, crystal	35.00
	1404 OLD SANDWICH 12 oz, moongleam	310.00
Row 3:	3405 COYLE, alexandrite	1500.00+
	3408 JAMESTOWN, sahara handle	140.00
	3408 JAMESTOWN, tangerine handle	325.00+
	3408 JAMESTOWN, moongleam handle	140.00
	3408 JAMESTOWN, cobalt handle	200.00
Row 4:	4163 WHALEY, sahara handle, etched	220.00
	4163 WHALEY, flamingo handle	350.00+
	4163 WHALEY, moongleam handle	175.00
	4163 WHALEY, red handle, etched	650.00+
	4163 WHALEY, cobalt handle, etched	220.00
Row 5:	3407 OVERDORF, cobalt with crystal handle	300.00+
	3407 OVERDORF, crystal with cobalt handle	250.00+
	412 TUDOR, sahara	140.00
	1434 TOM & JERRY	150.00
	1426 CLOVER ROPE, sahara	400.00+
	1426 CLOVER ROPE, cobalt	500.00+
Page 54:	**COLONIAL PIECES IN COLOR**	
Back:	393 NARROW FLUTE banana split, flamingo	65.00
	353 MEDIUM FLAT PANEL ice cream or candy tray, flamingo	175.00
Middle:	300 PEERLESS low footed goblet, flamingo	100.00
	300 PEERLESS sherbet, flamingo	75.00
	372 McGRADY sanitary syrup, sahara	75.00
	300½ PEERLESS bar, flamingo	75.00
	300 PEERLESS schoppen, flamingo	65.00
	351 PRISCILLA ale, flamingo	65.00
Front:	341 PURITAN sherbet, flamingo	75.00
	394 NARROW FLUTE domino sugar, sahara	100.00
	300½ PEERLESS tumbler, moongleam	85.00
Page 55:	**ASH TRAYS**	
Back:	364 RHOMBIC, moongleam	60.00
	361 IRWIN, flamingo	95.00
	411 TUDOR, moongleam	100.00
	357 DUCK, flamingo	165.00
Middle:	363 WINGS, moongleam	40.00
	1488 KOHINOOR bridge, zircon	85.00
	442 MALTESE CROSS, flamingo	35.00
	1187 YEOMAN, amber stain with silver overlay	60.00
	1180 TREFOIL, moongleam	40.00
Front:	1488 KOHINOOR, zircon	80.00
	1425 VICTORIAN, sahara	60.00
	439 FATIMA, moongleam	35.00
	1186 YEOMAN, hawthorne	60.00
	358 SOLITAIRE, marigold (gold variant)	60.00
	COLOGNES	
Back:	517 CIRCLE PAIR, flamingo	110.00
	515 TAPER, hawthorne	150.00
	515 TAPER, flamingo	100.00

516 FAIRACRE variant, moongleam applied crystal foot	200.00+	
487 HEXAGON STEM, amber stain, gold decor	95.00+	

Front:
4035 SEVEN OCTAGON, moongleam	155.00
1405 IPSWICH, crystal	150.00
4034 SEVEN CIRCLE, flamingo	140.00
4035 SEVEN OCTAGON, flamingo	155.00
1186 YEOMAN puff box & cover, hawthorne	125.00
516 FAIRACRE, moongleam	175.00
516 FAIRACRE, flamingo	160.00
485 HEXAGON STEM, moongleam	125.00

Page 56: Decorations on Heisey by Other Companies
Back:
1229 OCTAGON cheese plate, enamel & cut	50.00
4209 OVAL vase, marigold stain	60.00
352 FLAT PANEL lavender jar, moongleam with silver overlay	450.00
353 MEDIUM FLAT PANEL vase, enamel decor	50.00

Middle:
411 TUDOR cigarette jar, amber stain & silver overlay	75.00+
1223 FLUTED BORDER nappy, marigold stain	40.00
1184 YEOMAN covered candy, enamel & gold decor	60.00
485 DUNHAM nappy, enamel decor by Charleton	30.00

Front:
4035 SEVEN OCTAGON cologne, lavender iridized	125.00
353 MEDIUM FLAT PANEL ash tray, amber stain with engraving	50.00
468 OCTAGON WITH RIM celery, enamel & gold	40.00
341½ OLD WILLIAMSBURG compote, yellow & blue iridized	50.00

Page 56 Salts and peppers--(priced per pair)
Back:
1404 OLD SANDWICH, sahara	95.00
1404 OLD SANDWICH, flamingo	65.00
1404 OLD SANDWICH, moongleam	95.00
12 SMALL EIGHT FLUTE, flamingo	50.00
12 SMALL EIGHT FLUTE, moongleam	60.00
42 ELEGANCE, flamingo	65.00
46 CHESHIRE, flamingo	80.00

Middle:
1401 EMPRESS, moongleam foot	100.00
1401 EMPRESS, marigold	250.00+
1401 EMPRESS, sahara	100.00
1401 EMPRESS, tangerine	400.00
1252 (54) TWIST, sahara	80.00
1252 (54) TWIST, moongleam	70.00
1252 TWIST, sahara	125.00
53 TALL INDIVIDUAL, moongleam	60.00
53 TALL INDIVIDUAL, flamingo	60.00
12 SMALL EIGHT FLUTE, amber	125.00
51 DRUM, moongleam foot	110.00
48 KOORS, flamingo	65.00

Front:
23 SHORT PANEL, sahara	50.00
23 SHORT PANEL, moongleam	45.00
1469½ RIDGELEIGH, amber	350.00
49 YORKSHIRE, moongleam foot	75.00
49 YORKSHIRE, flamingo	85.00
47 SPOOL, moongleam	90.00

Page 57: CIGARETTE SETS
Back:
1496 MAHABAR cigarette box, sahara	75.00
1469 RIDGELEIGH round cigarette holder, sahara	45.00
1469 RIDGELEIGH square ash tray, sahara	35.00

Middle:
1496 MAHABAR square ash tray, sahara	40.00

1496 MAHABAR cigarette box, zircon	175.00
1469 RIDGELEIGH round cigarette holder, zircon	80.00

Front:
1496 MAHABAR round ash tray, zircon	50.00
1496 MAHABAR square ash tray, zircon	50.00
1469 RIDGELEIGH cigarette box, sahara	70.00

Left to Right: DOLPHIN COMPORTS
109 PETTICOAT DOLPHIN lamp, flamingo	350.00+
416/109 HERRINGBONE/PETTICOAT DOLPHIN, moongleam & crystal	250.00
1225/109 RIDGE & STAR/PETIICOAT DOLPHIN, flamingo & crystal	200.00
1185/109 YEOMAN/PETTICOAT DOLPHIN, flamingo with gold decor	200.00

Page 58: VASES
Back:
2516 TEARDROP, hawthorne	125.00
4026 SPENCER decanter, moongleam	130.00
21 ARISTOCRAT candelabrum, moongleam	500.00+

Front:
4215 DOROTHY, moongleam	60.00
4162/4 GENIE, moongleam	65.00
4205 VALLI, flamingo	65.00

Back:
516/1, hawthorne	100.00
4207 MODERNE, moongleam	80.00
3485 IRENE, flamingo	200.00

Front:
4196 RHODA, flamingo, cut	125.00
133 SWAN HANDLED floral bowl & block, sahara, cut	450.00
4204 JOYCE, flamingo	60.00

Page 59: FAVOR VASES AND BASKETS
Favor Vases:
Back:
4232, cobalt	150.00
4229, moongleam	300.00
4227, flamingo	325.00

Front:
4231, sahara	200.00
4230, tangerine	600.00
4228, crystal	80.00

BASKETS
Back:
461 BANDED PICKET, hawthorne	350.00
463 BONNET, flamingo	250.00

Front:
417 DOUBLE RIB & PANEL, moongleam	125.00
500 OCTAGON, marigold	300.00

Page 60: MISCELLANEOUS GOBLETS AND TUMBLERS
GOBLETS:
Back:
1423 SWEET AD O LINE, crystal	200.00
8005 GALAXY, flamingo	60.00
3386 DIAMOND ROSE, flamingo	75.00

Middle:
3373 MORNING GLORY, flamingo	100.00
3394 SAXONY, crystal	40.00

Front:
419 SUSSEX, moongleam	75.00
3379 PYRAMID saucer champagne, flamingo	50.00

TUMBLERS & SODAS:
Back:
1417 ARCH, cobalt	95.00
3484 DONNA, moongleam	30.00

Middle:
2516 CIRCLE PAIR soda, marigold	50.00

Front:
1485 SATURN, zircon	60.00
299 toddy, sahara	40.00
3362 CHARTER OAK, flamingo	25.00

Page 61:	TABLE SETTINGS	
	MOONGLEAM: All items are 1404	
	OLD SANDWICH pattern	
Back:	sherbet	20.00
	plate	25.00
	comport	80.00
	salt & pepper	95.00 pr
	soda or ice tea	25.00
	ice lip pitcher	150.00
Front:	indiv ash tray	45.00
	sundae & plate	45.00
	saucer champagne	45.00
	FLAMINGO:	
Back:	516/3 vase	60.00
	3355 FAIRACRE vase	95.00
	3312 GAYOSO Russian coffee	30.00
	3312 GAYOSO goblet	25.00
	3350 WABASH compote & cover	85.00
Front:	1186 YEOMAN cup & saucer	35.00
	1184 YEOMAN dinner plate	45.00
	52 SHORT INDIVIDUAL salt & pepper	50.00 pr
Page 62:	TABLE SETTINGS	
	MARIGOLD: All items are in 1252	
	TWIST pattern	
Back:	oyster cocktail	30.00
	saucer champagne	40.00
	goblet	50.00
Middle:	indiv bon bon	50.00
	cup	
	saucer	50.00 set
Front:	dinner plate	60.00
	salad plate	27.00
	cream soup	40.00
COBALT:		
Back:	1430 ARISTOCRAT low ftd candy	300.00
	301 OLD WILLIAMSBURG 3 lt	
	candelabrum	1750.00 ea
Middle:	1183 (1184) REVERE indiv salt	200.00
	3404 SPANISH oyster cocktail	80.00
	3404 SPANISH cocktail	125.00
	3404 SPANISH goblet	120.00
Front:	1401 EMPRESS dinner plate (crystal)	75.00
	1401 EMPRESS salad plate	55.00
SAHARA: All items in 1447 ROCOCO pattern		
Back:	cigarette box	130.00
	five-part relish	175.00
	ftd cheese	95.00
Front:	sugar & cream	200.00 pr
	SAHARA:	
Back:	1405 IPSWICH ftd juice	30.00
	1405 IPSWICH ftd ice tea	25.00
	1231 RIBBED OCTAGON rum pot	950.00
Front:	1405 IPSWICH oil	150.00
	1405 IPSWICH salad plate	20.00
Page 63:	TABLE SETTINGS	
	HAWTHORNE:	
Back:	15 DUCK flower block	275.00
	417 DOUBLE RIB & PANEL basket	250.00
	3366 TROJAN saucer champagne	60.00
	3366 TROJAN wine	75.00
	3366 TROJAN goblet	75.00
Front:	52 SHORT INDIVIDUAL salt & pepper	90.00 pr
	1184 YEOMAN dinner plate	60.00

	1184 YEOMAN salad plate	20.00
	1184 YEOMAN cup & saucer	45.00
	1229 OCTAGON indiv nut dish	60.00
	ALEXANDRITE:	
Back:	4220 JANICE vase	400.00
	4045 BALL vase, Mermaids etch	1000.00+
	1445 GRAPE cluster 2 lt candlestick	1500.00 pr
Middle:	1401 EMPRESS salt & pepper	250.00 pr
	3381 CREOLE finger bowl	85.00
	1401 EMPRESS indiv nut	125.00
	3381 CREOLE cordial	350.00
	3381 CREOLE goblet	195.00
	1401 EMPRESS cup & saucer	120.00
Front:	1401 EMPRESS dinner plate	200.00
	1401 EMPRESS salad plate	40.00
	1401 EMPRESS cream soup	140.00
Page 64:	TABLE SETTINGS	
	TANGERINE:	
Back:	4045 BALL vase	1500.00+
	3404 SPANISH goblet	550.00
	3404 SPANISH cocktail	350.00
	3404 SPANISH saucer champagne	550.00
	1401 EMPRESS cup & saucer	600.00+
Front:	1401 EMPRESS dinner plate (crystal)	75.00
	1401 EMPRESS salad plate	135.00
	ZIRCON:	
Back:	1485 SATURN wine	85.00
	1485 SATURN goblet	80.00
	4085 (4161) KOHINOOR jug	250.00
Middle:	1485 SATURN covered mustard	250.00
	1485 SATURN parfait	60.00
	1485 SATURN oyster cocktail	40.00
	1485 SATURN oil & stopper	250.00
Front:	1485 SATURN salad plate	40.00
	1485 SATURN sherbet	40.00
	1485 SATURN cup & saucer	75.00
	LAMPS:	
	4206 OPTIC TOOTH, flamingo-engraved	
	by Emil Krall	1750.00+
	21 ARISTOCRAT electro portable, early	
	moongleam	1200.00 ea
	DECANTERS:	
	4027 CHRISTOS, sahara	250.00
	4027 CHRISTOS, moongleam	250.00
	4027 CHRISTOS, cobalt	450.00
	4027 CHRISTOS, alexandrite	1500.00
	3380 OLD DOMINION wine, alexandrite (2)	135.00 ea
	3380 OLD DOMINION wine, flamingo (2)	40.00 ea
	3380 OLD DOMINION wine, sahara (2)	60.00 ea

General Price Guide

Page 66:   #355 QUATOR Pattern

	crystal	moongleam	flamingo	sahara	marigold
ftd sugar or bon bon	15.00	35.00	35.00	45.00	75.00
ftd cream	15.00	35.00	35.00	45.00	75.00
indiv cream	30.00				
24 oz Sanitary syrup	80.00				
indiv sugar	30.00				
hotel cream	25.00				
hotel sugar	25.00				

Page 67:   #406 COARSE RIB Pattern

	crystal	moongleam	flamingo	hawthorne
8 oz tumbler	15.00	45.00		
hotel cream	15.00	35.00	35.00	50.00
hotel sugar & cover	20.00	35.00	35.00	60.00
4½″ nappy	10.00	15.00	15.00	
8 oz soda	15.00			
9″ nappy	25.00			
12 oz ice tea	18.00			

Page 68:   #407 COARSE RIB Pattern

	crystal	moongleam	flamingo	hawthorne	marigold
mustard & cover	35.00				
8″ plate	10.00	15.00	15.00	25.00	50.00
6″ preserve	15.00				
5″ 2 hdld jelly	20.00				
6″ pickle tray	15.00	25.00	20.00		
custard	12.00				
5″ lemon dish & cover	25.00				
9″ celery tray	15.00	30.00	25.00		
4½″ nappy	10.00				
9″ nappy	25.00				

	crystal	moongleam	flamingo	hawthorne
indiv cream	20.00			
indiv sugar	20.00			
finger bowl	10.00			
6 oz oil	40.00			
hotel cream	20.00			
hotel sugar & cover	25.00			
5″ low foot jelly	15.00	30.00	25.00	50.00
pickle jar & cover	45.00			
ice tub	65.00		85.00	
5″ high foot jelly	25.00	50.00	45.00	

Page 69:

	crystal	moongleam
8 oz tumbler, straight	15.00	
6½ oz sherbet	10.00	
5½ oz saucer champagne	15.00	
3 pt tankard	75.00	
8 oz goblet	20.00	40.00
½ gal jug	65.00	

Page 70:   #411 TUDOR Pattern (Rib & Panel)

	crystal	moongleam hdl	hawthorne
hotel cream	20.00	30.00	50.00
8″ plate	10.00	18.00	
hotel sugar & cover	25.00	35.00	55.00
12″ celery tray	25.00		
7″ pickle tray	20.00		
8″ nappy	25.00		
10″ fruit dish	35.00		

Page 71:

	crystal	moongleam	flamingo	hawthorne
2 hdld bon bon	15.00	25.00		35.00
6″ 2 hdld cheese	15.00	25.00		35.00
5″ 2 hdld jelly	15.00	25.00		35.00
6″ 2 hdld mint	15.00	25.00		35.00
5″ lemon dish & cover	25.00	45.00	40.00	
7″ marmalade	20.00			
4½″ nut bowl	25.00			
6½″ preserve	20.00			
5″ ftd preserve & cover	30.00	40.00		80.00
20″ punch bowl with foot	200.00			
4½ oz custard	12.00			

422

#411 TUDOR Pattern (Rib & Panel) (continued)

Page 72:	crystal	moongleam	hawthorne
5 oz sherbet	12.00		
4 oz oyster cocktail	12.00		
finger bowl	12.00		
5″ high ftd jelly	25.00	35.00	60.00
8 oz goblet	20.00	35.00	
5½ oz saucer champagne	15.00		
3 oz wine	18.00		
4 oz parfait	18.00		
7 oz luncheon goblet	20.00	45.00	

	crystal	moongleam hdl	moongleam	hawthorne	flamingo
cigarette jar & ash tray	55.00		100.00	150.00	
8 oz tumbler	12.00				
2½ oz bar tumbler	15.00				
4½ oz orange juice glass	10.00				
12 oz soda	12.00		30.00		
water bottle	50.00				
8″ vase	40.00				
½ gal jug*	70.00	95.00			65.00

*also made with a cover

Page 73:	crystal	moongleam	hawthorne	marigold	sahara
salt & pepper, pr	35.00				
grape fruit center	15.00				
mustard & cover	35.00				
indiv almond	25.00				
6½″ grape fruit	15.00				
mayonnaise & plate	40.00	60.00	80.00		
sugar dispenser	30.00				95.00
6 oz oil	45.00				
5″ ftd grape fruit	15.00			80.00	

NOT ILLUSTRATED:

	crystal	moongleam	hawthorne	sahara/ crys hdl
12½″ floral bowl, ftd	35.00	60.00		
5½″ plate	10.00	15.00	20.00	
7″ plate	10.00	15.00		
mug (412)	50.00			140.00

#412 TUDOR Pattern (Rib & Panel)

	crystal	flamingo
8 oz tumbler	12.00	
8″ ftd banana split	25.00	
12 oz hand & ftd ice tea	20.00	35.00
7½ oz goblet	20.00	
6 oz saucer champagne	15.00	
5 oz sherbet	15.00	
4½ oz parfait	20.00	

NOT ILLUSTRATED:
tankard, ftd   75.00   150.00 (See Flamingo in Color Section)

Page 74:	crystal
hotel sugar & cover	30.00
finger bowl	10.00

	crystal	moongleam	flamingo	hawthorne
cigarette box & cover	40.00	85.00	80.00	150.00
8 oz goblet	20.00			
6 oz saucer champagne	18.00			
5½ oz sherbet	15.00			

Page 75:   #413 TUDOR Stemware

	crystal
6 oz saucer champagne	15.00
8 oz goblet	20.00
5½ oz low ftd sherbet	10.00
10 oz heavy goblet	20.00
10½ oz ftd soda	15.00

Page 76:   #473 NARROW FLUTE WITH RIM Pattern

	crystal	moongleam	flamingo	hawthorne	vaseline
6″ pickle tray	15.00		20.00		
3½″ salted nut dish (475)	20.00	35.00	25.00	50.00	
5″ dice sugar & cream	45.00	65.00	50.00		
5″ 2 hdld jelly	18.00		30.00		

#473 NARROW FLUTE WITH RIM Pattern (continued)

	crystal	moongleam	flamingo	hawthorne	vaseline
9″ oval	25.00		40.00		
6″ combination relish	25.00	35.00	30.00		
NOT ILLUSTRATED:					
6″ oval plate	15.00				150.00 (See Vaseline in Color Section)
7″ pickle tray (472)	15.00		35.00		

Page 77:   #500 OCTAGON Pattern

	crystal	moongleam	flamingo	sahara	marigold	moongleam handles
cream	15.00	25.00	20.00	30.00		35.00
sugar	15.00	25.00	20.00	30.00		35.00
6″ oblong tray	12.00	22.00	20.00			
frozen dessert	12.00	22.00	18.00		35.00	
6″ nappy	15.00	25.00	20.00		45.00	
ice tub	35.00	80.00	80.00	95.00	150.00	
5″ basket	80.00	130.00	110.00		300.00	

Page 78:

	crystal	moongleam	flamingo	sahara	marigold	dawn
ice tub	35.00	80.00	80.00	95.00	150.00	
12″ oblong variety tray	50.00	100.00	90.00	125.00		250.00

Page 79:   #1170 PLEAT & PANEL Pattern

	crystal	moongleam	flamingo	amber
4¾″ marmalade	12.00	20.00	20.00	
hotel cream	15.00	30.00	25.00	
hotel sugar & cover	15.00	30.00	25.00	
6½″ grape fruit or cereal	12.00	20.00	20.00	
3 oz oil	30.00	65.00	50.00	500.00+
5″ 2 hdld jelly	15.00	25.00	25.00	
8″ vase	25.00	55.00	45.00	
5″ lemon dish & cover	20.00	45.00	40.00	
6″ low ftd comport & cover	35.00	65.00	55.00	
5″ high ftd compotier & cover	45.00	85.00	70.00	

Page 80:

	crystal	moongleam	flamingo	hawthorne
4″ chow chow	12.00	15.00	15.00	
5″ bouillon cup & plate	15.00	35.00	30.00	
cup & saucer	25.00	45.00	35.00	
8″ nappy	20.00	40.00	30.00	
8″ plate	12.00	15.00	15.00	
9″ vegetable dish	20.00	40.00	30.00	
10½″ cheese & cracker	25.00	35.00	35.00	
10″ spice tray	25.00	55.00	45.00	$125.00+
12″ oval platter	20.00	30.00	30.00	

	crystal	moongleam	flamingo	sahara
12 oz ice tea	15.00	35.00	30.00	
8 oz tumbler	15.00	35.00	30.00	
5 oz sherbet	12.00	20.00	20.00	
5 oz saucer champagne	15.00	35.00	30.00	
7½ oz luncheon goblet	15.00	35.00	30.00	
3 pt jug	55.00	100.00	85.00	
8 oz goblet	15.00	35.00	30.00	
3 pt ice jug	65.00	125.00	100.00	175.00

Pages 81,82:   #1184 YEOMAN pattern

	crystal	moongleam	flamingo	sahara	hawthorne
8″ crescent salad plate	20.00	45.00	30.00	45.00	
#1186 puff box with insert (less without insert)	40.00	100.00	65.00		125.00

	crystal	moongleam	flamingo	marigold	sahara	vaseline
4½″ nappy	10.00	12.00	12.00		15.00	
6″ vegetable dish	10.00	12.00	12.00			
13″ celery tray	15.00	25.00	20.00	35.00	25.00	
9″ oval baker	15.00	25.00	20.00	35.00	25.00	
8″ oyster cocktail plate	10.00	20.00	15.00		20.00	60.00
9″ vegetable dish & cover	35.00	70.00	60.00	140.00		
12″ oblong tray	20.00					
12″ oval platter	20.00	35.00	30.00	50.00	35.00	

Page 83:

	crystal	moongleam	flamingo	marigold	sahara	cobalt	amber	moongleam handles
10½″ oval tray, 2 comp	25.00	40.00	35.00					40.00
8″ plate d/o	10.00	12.00	12.00	20.00	15.00	45.00	35.00	
13″ relish, 3 comp	15.00	30.00	22.00	35.00	30.00	(plain)	(plain)	
10½″ hdld sandwich	20.00	40.00	35.00					
11″ hdld tray, 3 comp	30.00							
11″ plate, 4 comp	20.00	40.00						

#1184 YEOMAN Pattern (continued)

	crystal	moongleam	flamingo	marigold	sahara	vaseline
5″ oval lemon dish	15.00					150.00
5″ round lemon dish	15.00	20.00	20.00		20.00	
9″ oval fruit	20.00					
6″ preserve	15.00					
5″ round lemon & cover	25.00	35.00	35.00		40.00	
6½″ grape fruit plate	10.00	12.00	12.00	20.00	15.00	
8″ pickle & olive	25.00	35.00	30.00			
ftd grape fruit	20.00	30.00	25.00		30.00	
2 hdld cheese plate	12.00					

Page 84:

	crystal	moongleam	flamingo	marigold	sahara	hawthorne
4 oz oil bottle	25.00	65.00	45.00	100.00	80.00	
French dressing boat & plate	30.00	55.00	50.00			
5″ low ftd jelly	15.00					
marmalade jar & cover	25.00					
ftd banana split	15.00	30.00	20.00	45.00	45.00	
7 oz saucer ftd syrup	45.00					
6″ low ftd comport deep	20.00	30.00	25.00		30.00	
10″ low ftd salver	30.00					
5″ high ftd comport	20.00	30.00	25.00		50.00	

	crystal	moongleam	flamingo	hawthorne	sahara	marigold	vaseline
cream (1023)	15.00	25.00	20.00	40.00	25.00	45.00	
sugar & cover (1023)	18.00	35.00	30.00	45.00	35.00	55.00	
egg cup	20.00	30.00	30.00			50.00	
8″ soup plate	15.00					25.00	
cup & saucer	20.00	25.00	25.00	35.00	25.00	35.00	
ftd bouillon & plate	25.00	40.00	30.00		40.00	55.00	200.00
cream soup & plate	20.00	35.00	25.00	50.00	35.00	50.00	
after dinner coffee cup/saucer	25.00	40.00	30.00		40.00	55.00	
8½″ 2 hdld berry dish	20.00	30.00	25.00				
finger bowl & plate	15.00	22.00	20.00		22.00		

Page 85:

	crystal	moongleam	flamingo	sahara
4½″ coaster plate	10.00			
coaster	8.00			
tumbler cover	20.00			
2¾ oz oyster cocktail	12.00	20.00	15.00	20.00
2½ oz bar (236)	10.00	15.00	12.00	15.00
8 oz tumbler	10.00	15.00	12.00	15.00
4½ oz soda	12.00	20.00	15.00	20.00
12 oz soda, cupped	10.00	15.00	12.00	15.00
12 oz soda, straight	10.00	15.00	12.00	15.00
8 oz goblet	15.00	25.00	25.00	25.00
6 oz saucer champagne	15.00	25.00	25.00	25.00
3½ oz sherbet	10.00	15.00	12.00	15.00
3 oz cocktail	15.00	25.00	25.00	25.00
5 oz parfait	15.00	25.00	25.00	25.00
quart jug	55.00	95.00	75.00	

	crystal	moongleam	flamingo	marigold	sahara	hawthorne	alexandrite
4″ hdld ash tray	20.00	40.00	35.00				
6½″ hdld bon bon	20.00	40.00	35.00			45.00	
5½″ 2 hdld bon bon	15.00	20.00	20.00	30.00			
cigarette ash tray	30.00	85.00	65.00				
8″ hdld mint, 3 comp	25.00	45.00	40.00	55.00			
6″ candy box & cover	25.00	65.00	55.00	100.00			
6″ candy box & cover, deep	30.00	70.00	60.00	110.00	90.00		500.00
8½″ hdld candy dish	20.00	45.00	40.00	85.00			
12″ floral bowl	20.00	30.00	25.00				
bridge smoking set	50.00	90.00	80.00	115.00	120.00	115.00	

Page 86:

	crystal	moongleam	flamingo	sahara	marigold	cobalt	hawthorne
cigarette box & ash tray cov	30.00	55.00	45.00	55.00			
#1023 hotel cream	15.00	25.00	20.00	25.00	45.00		40.00
#1023 hotel sugar & cover	18.00	35.00	30.00	35.00	55.00		45.00
indiv salt	15.00	30.00	25.00			200.00	
tumbler cover	20.00						
7x10″ relish tray	25.00	50.00	40.00	50.00			
finger bowl	12.00	18.00	15.00	18.00			
3½x4½″ relish tray insert	10.00	15.00	15.00	15.00			
4 oz fruit cocktail d/o	12.00	18.00	15.00	18.00			
2 oz oil #1 stopper	30.00	70.00	50.00	75.00	100.00		
13″ hors d'oeuvre base, center & cover	80.00						

#1184 YEOMAN Pattern (continued)

	crystal	moongleam	flamingo	marigold	sahara	cobalt	hawthorne
12 oz ftd soda, d/o	15.00	22.00	20.00	22.00			

NOT ILLUSTRATED:

	crystal	moongleam	flamingo	marigold	sahara	cobalt	hawthorne
6" plate*	10.00	12.00	12.00	20.00	15.00		
7" plate	10.00	12.00	12.00	20.00	15.00	45.00	20.00
9" plate	10.00	12.00	12.00	20.00	15.00		
10½" plate	35.00	50.00	45.00	55.00	50.00		60.00
14" plate	25.00	35.00	30.00	40.00	35.00		
15" oval platter	25.00	35.00	30.00	40.00	35.00		
9" celery d/o	15.00	25.00	20.00	30.00	25.00		
7" oval plate	12.00	20.00	15.00				

*amber $35.00

	crystal	moongleam	flamingo	marigold	sahara	cobalt	hawthorne
French dressing plate	12.00	20.00	15.00				
10 oz goblet d/o	15.00	25.00	25.00		25.00		
claret d/o	15.00	25.00	25.00				
8 oz soda, straight d/o	10.00	15.00	12.00		15.00		
10 oz soda, straight or cupped d/o	10.00	15.00	12.00		15.00		
28 oz mixing glass & metal top	90.00				180.00	300.00	
9" grill plate	20.00	40.00	35.00				
8" nappy, deep	15.00	22.00	20.00		22.00		
4½ oz sherbet d/o	10.00	15.00	12.00		15.00		
5 oz ftd soda d/o	12.00	20.00	15.00		20.00		
indiv cream d/o	25.00	40.00	35.00		40.00	(See Color Section-Sahara)	
mustard & cover d/o	45.00	90.00	80.00		90.00	(See Color Section-Sahara)	

Page 87:   #1229 OCTAGON Pattern

	crystal	moongleam	flamingo	marigold	sahara	hawthorne
5½" jelly	10.00	20.00	15.00	35.00	20.00	30.00
6" bon bon	10.00	20.00	15.00	35.00	20.00	30.00
6" cheese dish	10.00	20.00	15.00	35.00	20.00	30.00
6" mint	10.00	20.00	15.00	35.00	20.00	30.00
muffin plate (10", 12")	20.00	35.00	30.00	60.00	35.00	50.00
sandwich plate (10", 12")	15.00	30.00	25.00	60.00	30.00	50.00

Page 88:

	crystal	moongleam	flamingo	marigold	sahara	hawthorne	tangerine
13" hors d'oeuvre	20.00	35.00	30.00	60.00	35.00		
5½" ftd mayonnaise	12.00	25.00	20.00	40.00	25.00	35.00	750.00+
indiv nut	15.00	28.00	22.00	50.00	30.00	60.00	
8" ftd bowl	20.00	35.00	30.00	60.00			
8" oval dessert dish	20.00	30.00					

#1231 RIBBED OCTAGON Pattern

Page 89:

	crystal	moongleam	flamingo	sahara	cobalt
Water jug (rum pot)	300.00	950.00	950.00	950.00	1000.00

With #92 stopper value is more

Page 90:

	crystal	moongleam	flamingo	sahara	hawthorne
9" celery tray (12")	15.00	25.00	20.00		
12½" salad bowl	25.00	35.00	30.00		60.00
8" plate	12.00	15.00	15.00		
10½" sandwich plate	25.00	35.00	30.00	40.00	
12¾" oval platter	20.00	30.00	25.00		

	crystal	moongleam	flamingo	sahara
hotel cream	15.00	25.00	20.00	25.00
hotel sugar	15.00	25.00	20.00	25.00
6½" grape fruit	10.00	15.00	15.00	
after dinner coffee cup/saucer	20.00	30.00	25.00	
cup & saucer	15.00	25.00	20.00	
2 hdld cream soup & plate	15.00	25.00	20.00	
9" vegetable dish	15.00	25.00	20.00	
3" candlestick, pr	35.00	70.00	60.00	
9" soup plate	15.00	25.00	20.00	

Page 91:   #1252 TWIST Pattern

	crystal	moongleam	flamingo	marigold
cup (1252½)	15.00	25.00	20.00	40.00
indiv cream	20.00	30.00	25.00	55.00
indiv sugar	20.00	30.00	25.00	55.00

#1252 TWIST Pattern (continued)

Page 92:	crystal	moongleam	flamingo	marigold	sahara
8″ nappy	20.00	35.00	30.00	45.00	
7″ pickle tray	12.00	30.00	20.00	40.00	
8″ plate	10.00	18.00	15.00	27.00	25.00
12″ 2 hdld muffin plate	25.00	35.00	30.00	40.00	
10″ celery tray	20.00	35.00	30.00	45.00	35.00
12″ oval platter	25.00	35.00	30.00	40.00	
12″ 2 hdld sandwich plate	20.00	30.00	25.00	35.00	

	crystal	moongleam	flamingo	marigold	sahara
6″ 2 hdld jelly	15.00	20.00	18.00	25.00	
indiv nut dish	15.00	20.00	18.00	40.00	
indiv bon bon	18.00	30.00	25.00	50.00	
6″ 2 hdld bon bon	12.00	20.00	15.00	25.00	
3 cornered mint & cover (1253)	30.00	40.00	35.00	50.00	45.00

	crystal	moongleam	flamingo	marigold	sahara
ftd almond (indiv sugar)	20.00	30.00	25.00	55.00	
6″ 2 hdld cheese	12.00	20.00	15.00	25.00	
8″ Kraft cheese plate	20.00	30.00	25.00	40.00	
6″ 2 hdl mint	15.00	20.00	18.00	25.00	
10″ utility plate, 3 feet	25.00	35.00	30.00	50.00	
13″ relish, 3 comp	20.00	30.00	25.00	40.00	35.00

Page 93:	crystal	moongleam	flamingo	marigold	sahara
cream	20.00	30.00	25.00		
sugar & cover	25.00	35.00	30.00		
cream soup or bouillon & plate	22.00	30.00	25.00	45.00	
oval hotel cream	20.00	30.00	25.00	45.00	40.00
oval hotel sugar	20.00	30.00	25.00	45.00	40.00
cup & saucer	20.00	30.00	25.00	45.00	
ftd grape fruit	15.00	25.00	20.00	35.00	30.00
ftd cream	25.00	35.00	30.00		
ftd sugar	25.00	35.00	30.00		
9″ oval baker	20.00	30.00			

	crystal	moongleam	flamingo	marigold	sahara	moongleam ft crystal bowl	alexandrite
mayonnaise	22.00	40.00	30.00	55.00		50.00	
mayonnaise (1252½)	20.00	35.00	25.00	50.00	40.00		
4 oz oil bottle	30.00	90.00	65.00	135.00	90.00		
French dressing bottle	30.00	75.00	65.00	100.00	90.00		
8″ low ftd bowl	25.00	45.00	35.00	55.00			
mustard & cover	35.00	70.00	55.00	100.00	90.00		
ice tub	35.00	75.00	60.00	125.00	100.00		275.00
salt & pepper (#54) pr.	30.00	40.00	35.00	75.00	60.00		
7″ high ftd comport	30.00	70.00	55.00	100.00			

Page 94:	crystal	moongleam	flamingo	marigold
8 oz tumbler	15.00	25.00	20.00	45.00
12 oz ice tea	15.00	25.00	20.00	45.00
3 oz oyster cocktail	15.00	25.00	20.00	30.00
5 oz sherbet	15.00	25.00	20.00	30.00
3 oz cocktail	15.00	25.00	20.00	30.00
12 oz ftd ice tea	18.00	30.00	22.00	30.00
9 oz goblet	20.00	35.00	30.00	50.00
9 oz luncheon goblet	20.00	35.00	30.00	50.00
5 oz saucer champagne	18.00	30.00	22.00	40.00
2½ oz wine	20.00	35.00	30.00	60.00
3 pt jug	45.00	90.00	70.00	125.00

	crystal	moongleam	flamingo	marigold	sahara	alexandrite
9″ floral bowl, flared	25.00	35.00	30.00	60.00		
2″ candlestick, pr	40.00	80.00	75.00	125.00		
9″ floral bowl, rolled edge	25.00	35.00	30.00	60.00		
12″ floral bowl, oval	30.00	45.00	35.00	80.00	50.00	
12″ floral bowl, round	30.00	45.00	35.00	80.00	50.00	350.00
8″ nasturtium bowl	30.00	60.00	50.00	90.00	60.00	350.00

NOT ILLUSTRATED:

	crystal	moongleam	flamingo	marigold	sahara	tangerine/ amberina
2 comp relish	40.00	55.00	55.00		55.00	
4½″ plate	10.00	15.00	12.00	20.00	18.00	
6″ plate	10.00	18.00	15.00	27.00	25.00	550.00+
7″ plate	10.00	18.00	15.00	27.00	25.00	
9″ plate	15.00	25.00	20.00	30.00	28.00	
10½″ plate	25.00	40.00	35.00	60.00	50.00	
12″ plate	25.00	40.00	35.00	60.00		

Page 95:   #1401 EMPRESS Pattern

	crystal	moongleam
jug (without dolphin feet)		250.00
Plate (variant with ribs)		
(8055)	30.00	

Page 96:

	crystal	moongleam	flamingo	sahara	alexandrite	cobalt
8″ nappy	15.00	30.00	25.00	25.00		
10″ salad bowl	35.00	60.00	60.00	50.00		
8″ plate	12.00	20.00	20.00	20.00	60.00	55.00
6″ ftd comport	35.00	45.00	40.00	40.00		
8″ square plate (1401½)	25.00	50.00	50.00	50.00		

	crystal	moongleam	flamingo	sahara	alexandrite	cobalt	tangerine
7½″ ftd nappy	18.00	30.00	30.00	25.00			
6″ grapefruit, square	12.00	18.00	15.00	15.00			
7″ triplex relish	15.00	45.00	45.00	35.00	225.00		
13″ hors d'oeuvre	25.00	50.00	45.00	45.00			
8″ square plate	12.00	25.00	20.00	20.00	65.00	55.00	150.00
10″ oval dessert	35.00	60.00	60.00	50.00			

Page 97

	crystal	moongleam	flamingo	sahara	alexandrite	tangerine
cup & saucer (1401½)	25.00	40.00	40.00	35.00	115.00	
after dinner coffee cup & saucer	35.00	50.00	50.00	45.00		
cup & saucer	20.00	35.00	35.00	30.00	85.00	600.00+
bouillon & plate	30.00	40.00	35.00	35.00	125.00	
13″ celery tray	20.00	35.00	30.00	30.00	175.00	
14″ oval platter	25.00	45.00	40.00	40.00		
cream soup & plate	30.00	40.00	35.00	35.00	180.00	

	crystal	moongleam	flamingo	sahara	alexandrite	marigold	tangerine
indiv nut dish	15.00	30.00	30.00	25.00	125.00		
6″ ftd jelly, 2 hdld	15.00	25.00	25.00	20.00			
5½″ ftd mayonnaise	20.00	45.00	45.00	35.00	175.00		
6″ ftd mint	15.00	25.00	25.00	20.00			
6″ bon bon*	15.00	25.00	25.00	20.00			
salt/pepper	30.00	100.00	100.00	90.00	300.00	350.00+	400.00
5″ preserve, 2 hdld	15.00	25.00	25.00	20.00			
mustard & cover	25.00	60.00	60.00	50.00			
6″ candlestick, pr	200.00	400.00	300.00	250.00	600.00		
13″ pickle & olive, 2 comp	18.00	25.00	20.00	20.00			
4 oz oil #83 stopper	40.00	100.00	100.00	85.00			

*zircon 100.00+

Page 98:

	crystal	moongleam	flamingo	sahara	alexandrite	tangerine
ftd cream	15.00	40.00	40.00	35.00	250.00	450.00
indiv cream	15.00	35.00	35.00	25.00		
indiv sugar	15.00	35.00	35.00	25.00		
ftd sugar, 3 hdld	15.00	40.00	40.00	35.00	250.00	450.00
12″ 2 hdld sandwich plate	30.00	45.00	45.00	40.00	175.00	
12″ sq sandwich tray, cent hdl	35.00	60.00	60.00	50.00		
12″ 2 hdld muffin plate	30.00	45.00	45.00	40.00		

	crystal	moongleam	flamingo	sahara
15″ ftd punch bowl	450.00	900.00	900.00	900.00

Page 99:

	crystal	moongleam	flamingo	sahara	alexandrite
2½ oz oyster cocktail	1?.??	25.00	25.00	20.00	
4 oz sherbet	2?.00	30.00	30.00	25.00	
4 oz saucer champagne	25.00	55.00	55.00	50.00	
9 oz goblet	25.00	75.00	75.00	60.00	
9″ ftd vase D.F.	55.00	125.00	100.00	100.00	350.00
8 oz tumbler	15.00	35.00	35.00	30.00	
12 oz soda	15.00	35.00	35.00	30.00	
3 pt ftd jug	70.00	175.00	200.00	150.00	

	crystal	moongleam	flamingo	sahara	alexandrite	cobalt	tangerine
9″ floral bowl, rolled edge	20.00	40.00	40.00	40.00			
8½″ ftd floral bowl, 2 hndl	30.00	60.00	50.00	50.00			
7½″ ftd nasturtium bowl	40.00	100.00	100.00	90.00			
11″ ftd floral bowl	45.00	110.00	90.00	75.00	450.00	450.00	600.00

Page 100:

	crystal	moongleam	flamingo	sahara	alexandrite	cobalt	tangerine
cup with sq saucer	20.00	35.00	35.00	30.00	120.00		600.00+
10″ oval vegetable dish	20.00	35.00	35.00	30.00			
13″ sq sandwich plate, 2 hdld	30.00	50.00	45.00	40.00			
ash tray	40.00	350.00	125.00	250.00	350.00	400.00	
grape fruit & sq plate	20.00	35.00	35.00	30.00			
10″ sq salad bowl	35.00	60.00	60.00	50.00			1000.00

428

#1401 EMPRESS Pattern (continued)

	crystal	moongleam	flamingo	sahara	alexandrite	cobalt	tangerine
4 oz custard	15.00	35.00	35.00	30.00			
salt/pepper, pr*	40.00	100.00	100.00	90.00	250.00		400.00
6½″ oval lemon & cover	35.00	85.00	85.00	75.00			
8 oz ftd tumbler	50.00	115.00	110.00	110.00			
6″ candy box & cover	50.00	135.00	100.00	95.00		400.00	
cream soup & sq plate	30.00	40.00	35.00	35.00	180.00		
7″ oval comport	35.00	65.00	60.00	60.00			
ice tub & hdl	50.00	125.00	110.00	110.00			
6″ compotier D.F.	90.00	160.00	160.00	140.00			

*marigold 250.00+

Page 101:

	crystal	moongleam	flamingo	sahara
8″ vase, flared	40.00	100.00	90.00	80.00
7″ hdl triplex relish	35.00	75.00	65.00	65.00
marmalade & cover	50.00	95.00	85.00	85.00
condiment tray	20.00	40.00	35.00	35.00
10″ floral bowl, (Lion)	175.00	500.00	400.00	500.00
9″ floral bowl, flared	40.00	110.00	100.00	100.00

	crystal	moongleam	flamingo	sahara
16″ buffet relish, 4 comp	45.00	105.00	110.00	90.00
10″ hors d'oeuvre, 7 comp	35.00	95.00	85.00	85.00
2 hdld candlestick (nappy) pr	50.00	95.00	80.00	80.00
6 in square comport	40.00	80.00	70.00	70.00
frappe bowl & center	30.00	60.00	60.00	45.00
10″ combination relish, 3 comp	35.00	75.00	70.00	60.00

Page 102:

	crystal	moongleam	flamingo	sahara	alexandrite	zircon
7″ triplex relish, center hdl	35.00	75.00	85.00	85.00		
10″ comb. relish 3 comp	35.00	75.00	70.00	60.00		
10″ triplex relish	30.00	60.00	50.00	50.00		
7″ triplex relish	25.00	45.00	35.00	35.00	150.00	200.00+
13″ hors d'oeuvre	35.00	60.00	55.00	55.00		

NOT ILLUSTRATED:

	crystal	moongleam	flamingo	sahara	alexandrite	tangerine	cobalt
4½″ plate	7.00	12.00	10.00	10.00			
6″ plate	7.00	15.00	15.00	15.00	40.00	135.00	
7″ plate	10.00	15.00	15.00	15.00			
9″ plate	12.00	20.00	20.00	20.00			
10½″ plate	75.00	125.00	125.00	125.00	200.00		
12″ plate	30.00	55.00	50.00	55.00			
6″ plate, sq	7.00	20.00	15.00	15.00	40.00	135.00	
7″ plate, sq	10.00	20.00	15.00	15.00	50.00	135.00	55.00
10½″ plate, sq	75.00	125.00	125.00	125.00	200.00	300.00	
15″ plate, round	35.00	75.00	65.00	65.00			
12″ sandwich plate, sq 2 hdl	30.00	55.00	55.00	50.00		400.00+	
8″ mint, ftd	25.00	45.00	40.00	40.00			
5 oz soda	10.00	20.00	20.00	20.00			

Page 103:   #1404 OLD SANDWICH Pattern

	crystal
round cream & sugar	55.00 pr

Page 104:

	crystal	moongleam	flamingo	sahara	cobalt	tangerine
4 oz claret	20.00	40.00	35.00	35.00		
2½ oz wine	25.00	50.00	50.00	45.00		
3 oz cocktail	20.00	35.00	35.00	35.00		
4 oz oyster cocktail	25.00	40.00	35.00	35.00	100.00	500.00+
6 oz sundae	15.00	25.00	20.00	25.00		
10 oz low ftd goblet	20.00	45.00	40.00	35.00		
5 oz saucer champagne	20.00	45.00	35.00	35.00		
4½ oz parfait	20.00	40.00	40.00	35.00		
4 oz sherbet	15.00	20.00	20.00	20.00		
6″ square plate	15.00	20.00	20.00	20.00		600.00+
10 oz low ftd tumbler	15.00	30.00	25.00	25.00	110.00	
½ gal ice jug	60.00	150.00	150.00	175.00		
½ gal jug	60.00	150.00	150.00	175.00		

#1404 OLD SANDWICH Pattern (continued)

Page 105:	crystal	moongleam	flamingo	sahara	cobalt	tangerine
oval cream	20.00	30.00	30.00	30.00		
oval sugar	20.00	30.00	30.00	30.00		
cup & saucer	25.00	35.00	35.00	35.00		
8 oz soda or ice tea*	15.00	25.00	25.00	25.00		600.00+
1½ oz bar	25.00	60.00	60.00	60.00	110.00	
6½ oz toddy	15.00	25.00	25.00	25.00		
8 oz tumbler	15.00	30.00	25.00	25.00		
12 oz ftd soda or ice tea	15.00	30.00	25.00	25.00	110.00	
6″ candlestick, pr	75.00	210.00	195.00	185.00	450.00	
6″ comport	35.00	80.00	80.00	80.00		

*zircon 600.00+

Page 106:	crystal	moongleam	flamingo	sahara	cobalt
salt/pepper, pr	30.00	95.00	65.00	95.00	
indiv ash tray	10.00	45.00	45.00	35.00	65.00
2½ oz oil #85 stopper	40.00	110.00	110.00	90.00	
catsup bottle #3 stopper	35.00	100.00	100.00	85.00	
11″ round floral bowl, ftd	40.00	90.00	90.00	85.00	
#22 floral block	20.00	30.00	30.00	25.00	
12″ oval floral bowl, ftd	35.00	100.00	100.00	95.00	
finger bowl	15.00	30.00	30.00	25.00	

Page 107:	crystal	moongleam	flamingo	sahara	cobalt	amber
18 oz cream	35.00					
12 oz cream	30.00					
14 oz cream	32.00					
14 oz beer mug	55.00	250.00	400.00	160.00	350.00	350.00
18 oz beer mug	70.00	300.00	500.00	175.00	400.00	500.00
12 oz beer mug	35.00	310.00	325.00	150.00	300.00	350.00
cigarette holder	100.00			200.00		
1 pt decanter #98 stopper	100.00		400.00	200.00	325.00	
ftd pop corn bowl, cupped	75.00	225.00	225.00	175.00		

NOT ILLUSTRATED:

	crystal	moongleam	flamingo	sahara	tangerine	zircon
7″ plate, sq	12.00	20.00	20.00	20.00		
8″ plate, sq	15.00	25.00	25.00	25.00	800.00+	
5 oz soda, straight or cupped	17.00	30.00	30.00	30.00		
10 oz soda, straight or cupped	15.00	25.00	25.00	25.00	800.00+	500.00+
12 oz soda, straight or cupped	15.00	25.00	25.00	25.00		
10 oz beer mug, sham	95.00			150.00		

Page 108:   #1405 IPSWICH Pattern

	crystal
Cologne with #91 stopper	150.00

Page 109:	crystal	moongleam	flamingo	sahara	alexandrite
finger bowl & 6″ plate	15.00	30.00	30.00	25.00	
4 oz sherbet	12.00	25.00	30.00	20.00	
sugar	25.00	50.00	55.00	40.00	
cream	25.00	50.00	55.00	40.00	
2 oz oil, ftd #86 stopper	50.00	180.00	200.00	150.00	
10 oz tumbler	20.00	40.00	45.00	25.00	
4 oz saucer champagne	20.00	30.00	35.00	25.00	
7″ sq plate	15.00	25.00	25.00	20.00	
4 oz oyster cocktail	12.00	25.00	30.00	20.00	
8 oz ftd soda	20.00	30.00	35.00	25.00	
12 oz schoppen	20.00	30.00	35.00	25.00	
10 oz goblet	20.00	55.00	60.00	40.00	600.00+

Page 110:	crystal	moongleam	flamingo	sahara	cobalt
11″ floral bowl	45.00	90.00	90.00	90.00	225.00
ftd center piece w/vase pr	150.00	450.00	425.00	400.00	850.00
6″ candlestick, pr	175.00	200.00	200.00	200.00	
½ lb candy jar & cover	80.00	275.00	250.00	240.00	
1 qt cocktail shaker	150.00			300.00	
½ gal jug, stuck hdl	100.00	175.00	175.00	175.00	

NOT ILLUSTRATED:

	crystal	moongleam	flamingo	sahara
8″ plate, sq	15.00	25.00	25.00	20.00
5 oz soda, ftd	22.00	35.00	40.00	30.00
12 oz soda, ftd	20.00	30.00	35.00	25.00
¼ lb candy jar & cover	70.00	250.00	200.00	250.00

Page 111: #1415 TWENTIETH CENTURY Pattern

	crystal	moongleam	flamingo	sahara	cobalt	dawn
cereal bowl & 7" plate	30.00	60.00	60.00	60.00		
1 pt milk pitcher	40.00	85.00	85.00	85.00		125.00
12 oz ftd soda	20.00	45.00	45.00	45.00		45.00
9 oz ftd tumbler	20.00	45.00	45.00	45.00	90.00	45.00
5 oz ftd soda	20.00	45.00	45.00	45.00		45.00
4 oz ftd sherbet	20.00	35.00	35.00	35.00	75.00	40.00

Page 113: #1425 VICTORIAN Pattern

	crystal	sahara	cobalt
8" nappy	25.00	65.00	225.00
10½" floral bowl	45.00	75.00	275.00
13" sandwich plate	30.00	65.00	225.00
2 lt candlestick pr	125.00	250.00	600.00
cheese holder	25.00	50.00	95.00
7" plate	12.00	35.00	75.00
12" cracker plate	30.00	65.00	200.00

Page 114:

	crystal	sahara	cobalt
sugar	20.00	55.00	250.00
cream	20.00	55.00	250.00
indiv cigarette holder/ash tray	25.00	60.00	125.00
salt/pepper, pr	35.00	90.00	200.00
12" celery tray	20.00	60.00	125.00

Page 115:

	crystal	sahara	cobalt	moongleam	flamingo
4 oz claret	15.00	45.00	100.00		
3 oz cocktail	15.00	45.00	100.00		
2½ oz wine	20.00	70.00	130.00		
finger bowl & 6" plate	25.00	45.00	95.00		
8 oz old fashion cocktail	15.00	40.00	95.00		
2 oz bar	20.00	50.00	125.00		
10 oz ftd tumbler	15.00	50.00	110.00		
5 oz saucer champagne	15.00	50.00	110.00		
5 oz oyster cocktail	15.00				
5 oz sherbet	15.00	45.00	110.00	50.00	50.00
12 oz soda	18.00				
12 oz ftd soda	18.00	80.00	130.00		
9 oz high ftd goblet	22.00	80.00	130.00	75.00	75.00
9 oz goblet	22.00	70.00	120.00		

Page 116:

	crystal	sahara	cobalt
French drsg bottle #7 stopper	40.00		
6" ftd vase	35.00		
4" vase	25.00	50.00	90.00
5½" vase	25.00		
6" cigarette box & cover	40.00		
3 oz oil & #7 stopper	50.00		
4" cigarette box & cover	35.00		
27 oz rye bottle #99 stopper	90.00	200.00	300.00
9" ftd vase	50.00		

Page 117:

	crystal	zircon	sahara
5" comport	35.00		
triplex bowl	45.00		
11" 3 comp relish	40.00	700.00	
#1425½ condiment tray set	85.00		
rose bowl	50.00		200.00
10½ floral bowl	45.00		
¼ lb butter dish & cover	45.00		

Page 118:

	crystal
punch bowl	200.00
5 oz custard	12.00
21" buffet plate	70.00

Page 119: #1428 WARWICK Pattern

	crystal	moongleam	flamingo	sahara	cobalt	alexandrite
9" horn of plenty vase	35.00	325.00	325.00	225.00	350.00	650.00+
2 lt horn of plenty candle, pr	70.00	225.00	200.00	175.00	250.00	
horn of plenty indiv vase	20.00			50.00	125.00	
horn of plenty indiv candle, pr	40.00	150.00	300.00	100.00	150.00	
11" horn of plenty floral bowl	65.00			150.00	325.00	
horn of plenty cigarette hdl	20.00			50.00	125.00	

Page 121:   #1447 ROCOCO Pattern

	crystal	sahara	limelight
9½″ shallow hand nappy	30.00	75.00	
8″ handled nappy	30.00	75.00	
roll tray	35.00	75.00	
6″ comport	60.00	120.00	
4½″ nappy	20.00	50.00	
7″ plate	20.00	40.00	
comb mayonnaise & relish & cover	90.00	200.00	300.00
cracker plate & ftd cheese	75.00	175.00	

Page 122:

	crystal	sahara
bon bon	25.00	50.00
12″ celery	25.00	60.00
salt/pepper pr	65.00	110.00
cream & sugar pr	50.00	200.00 pr
cigarette box & cover	65.00	130.00
2 lt candlestick, pr	300.00	650.00
12 oz ftd soda	75.00	135.00
12″ floral bowl, oval	70.00	150.00
jelly	45.00	90.00

Page 123:   #1463 QUAKER Pattern

	crystal
8″ nappy	25.00
9″ plate	25.00

Pages 124,125:   #1469 RIDGELEIGH Pattern

	crystal	amber
roly poly with rest	60.00	
salt & pepper (#1469½)	30.00	350.00

Page 125

	crystal	sahara	zircon
coaster or cocktail rest	25.00		
sq ash tray	8.00	35.00	50.00
cigarette box & cover, oval	55.00		
round ash tray	20.00		
indiv oval jelly	18.00		
6″ plate	15.00		
4½″ nappy	10.00		
8″ sq plate	30.00		
cigarette holder, round	15.00	45.00	80.00
8″ round plate	25.00		

Page 126:

	crystal
12″ celery tray	25.00
12″ celery & olive tray	25.00
salt/pepper, pr	30.00
1 pt decanter #1469 stopper	95.00
7″ candelabra/bobeche, pr	150.00
13″ torque plate	45.00
2½ oz bar	25.00
6″ vase	20.00

Page 127:

	crystal
14″ oblong floral bowl (swan)	250.00
11½″ floral bowl	45.00
12″ fruit bowl	45.00
13½″ sandwich plate	35.00
9″ salad bowl	35.00

Page 128:

	crystal
4½″ nappy	10.00
4½″ nappy, scalloped	10.00
5″ nappy, sq	20.00
6″ plate	15.00
8″ round plate	20.00
14″ round plate	45.00
8″ sq plate	30.00

Page 129:

	crystal
13″ torte plate	45.00
13½″ sandwich plate	45.00
14″ torte plate	45.00

#1469 RIDGELEIGH Pattern (continued)

Page 130:	crystal		
8½″ berry bowl cupped	35.00		
10″ dessert, 2 hdld	35.00		
11″ salad bowl	40.00		
9″ salad bowl	35.00		
12″ fruit bowl	55.00		
11″ cone beverage bowl	75.00		

Page 131:	crystal	sahara	zircon
12″ oval floral bowl	35.00	80.00	175.00
8″ floral box	45.00		
11½″ floral bowl	35.00		
13″ cone floral bowl	55.00		
14″ oblong floral bowl	55.00		

Page 132:	crystal	exp. blue
10½″ oblong tray, 3 comp	30.00	
10½″ oblong tray	30.00	
11″ relish, 3 comp	40.00	
10″ relish, 5 comp (star)	45.00	500.00
12″ celery & olive	35.00	
12″ celery tray	35.00	

Page 133:	crystal
indiv vase #1, #2, #3, #4, #5	25.00
6″ vase	25.00
3½″ vase	25.00
hors d'oeuvre, oval	35.00

Page 134:	crystal	sahara	zircon
7″ ball vase, flared top	55.00		
7″ ball vase	55.00		
6″ candle vase, pr	45.00	135.00	175.00
10″ vase	50.00		
9″ vase	55.00		
9″ vase, flared	55.00		

Page 135:	crystal
indiv cream & sugar tray	25.00
indiv jelly, oval	20.00
jelly, 3 hdl	20.00
indiv sugar, oval	15.00
indiv cream, oval	15.00
sugar	20.00
cream	20.00
mayonnaise	25.00
marmalade & cover	55.00
mustard & cover	50.00

Page 136:	crystal
salt/pepper, pr	30.00
indiv salt	12.00
3 oz oil #103 stopper	35.00
French dressing bottle #100 stopper	50.00
5″ lemon dish & cover	40.00
6″ comport, low ft flared	25.00
6″ comport, low ft & cover	45.00

Page 137:	crystal
ice tub, 2 hdld	45.00
1 qt cocktail shaker	125.00
½ gal ice jug	110.00
1 pt decanter #95 stopper	125.00
½ gal jug	115.00
ice tub plate, 2 hdld	35.00

Page 138:	crystal	zircon
beverage cup	15.00	
coaster or cocktail rest	20.00	
cup & saucer	25.00	
2″ candlestick (sq), pr	45.00	150.00
7″ candelabra/bobeche, pr	150.00	
5 oz bitters bottle	50.00	
Rock & rye bottle #104 stopper	115.00	

Page 139:	crystal
2 lt candlestick/bobeche, pr.	150.00
2 lt candelabra A prisms, pr	300.00

433

#1469 RIDGELEIGH Pattern (continued)

Page 140:	crystal	sahara	zircon
ash tray, diamond	20.00		
ash tray, heart	20.00		
ash tray, club	20.00		
ash tray, spade	20.00		
ash tray, round	15.00		
bridge ash tray	15.00		
ash tray, sq	10.00	35.00	50.00
cigarette holder, sq	15.00	45.00	
cigarette holder, round	15.00	45.00	80.00
4 oz cologne bottle #105			
stopper	65.00		
6″ ash tray, sq	35.00		
oval cigarette box & cover	55.00		
4″ cigarette box & cover	35.00	70.00	100.00

Page 141:	crystal
goblet	25.00
saucer champagne	20.00
sherbet	15.00
oyster cocktail	15.00
cocktail	20.00
wine	25.00
claret	20.00
12 oz soda, ftd	20.00
2½ oz bar	25.00
8 oz old fashion	20.00
10 oz tumbler (#1469¾)	20.00
5 oz soda (#1469¾)	20.00

Page 142:	crystal
5 oz perfume bottle #1469	
stopper	65.00
punch cup or custard	10.00
11″ punch bowl	125.00
orange bowl	60.00

Page 143:   #1469¼ RIDGELEIGH Pattern

	crystal
8″ vase (triangular)	50.00
oval cigarette holder & ash tray, 2 comp	65.00

#1469½ RIDGELEIGH Pattern

	crystal
4″ ash tray	20.00
indiv nut	15.00
indiv nut, 2 comp	15.00
3″ candlestick (cylinder), pr	45.00
6″ bon bon	20.00
6″ cheese	20.00
6″ jelly	20.00
6″ jelly, 2 comp	20.00
7″ relish, 2 comp	30.00
8″ centerpiece	45.00

Page 144:	crystal	sahara	zircon
8″ vase	55.00	135.00	185.00
12 oz soda, cupped or flared	20.00		
cigarette holder & cover	35.00		
3½″ coaster	10.00	25.00	40.00
13½″ ftd torte plate	45.00		
14″ ftd salver	45.00		

Page 145:	crystal
5″ nappy	20.00
5″ puff box	45.00
8″ plate	20.00
1 lt. candelabra & prisms, pr	135.00

Page 147:   #4069 RIDGELEIGH Pattern - not marked

	crystal
8 oz goblet	50.00
8 oz luncheon goblet	40.00
5 oz saucer champagne	30.00
5 oz sherbet	25.00

#4069 RIDGELEIGH Pattern - not marked (continued)

	crystal
4 oz oyster cocktail	25.00
4 oz claret	35.00
3½ oz cocktail	30.00
2½ oz wine	45.00
2 oz sherry	45.00
1 oz cordial	100.00
5 oz soda	25.00
finger bowl (3335)	15.00

#1483 STANHOPE Pattern

Page 149:	crystal
7″ plate	15.00
4½″ nappy or porringer	15.00
3 oz oil bottle	75.00
12″ torte plate, 2 hdl	45.00
15″ torte plate	40.00

Page 150:	crystal	sahara
12″ relish, 2 hdl, 5 comp	45.00	
12″ celery tray, 2 hdl	35.00	250.00
11″ floral bowl, 2 hdl	45.00	
11″ salad bowl	40.00	
15″ plate	40.00	

Page 151:	crystal
6″ mint, 2 comp, 2 hdl	25.00
mayonnaise, 2 hdl	25.00
6″ mint, 2 hdl	25.00
6″ jelly, 3 comp, 1 hdl	25.00
6″ jelly, 1 hdl	25.00
12″ relish, 4 comp, 2 hdl	45.00
11″ triplex relish, 2 hdl	50.00

Page 152:	crystal
sugar, 2 hdl	25.00
cream, 1 hdl	25.00
cup & saucer	30.00
ice tub, 2 hdl	45.00
9″ vase, 2 hdl	50.00
7″ ball vase	50.00

Page 153	crystal	experimental light blue
salt/pepper, pr	50.00	
indiv nut	25.00	
indiv ash tray	20.00	
2 lt candelabra w A prisms, pr	250.00	4500.00+
cigarette box & cover	60.00	
6″ candy box & cover	65.00	

Page 154:	crystal
9 oz goblet	30.00
5½ oz saucer champagne	25.00
3½ oz cocktail	25.00
2½ oz wine	35.00
12 oz soda, ftd	25.00

Page 155: #4083 STANHOPE Pattern (blown stemware) - not marked

	crystal	zircon s/o
10 oz goblet	30.00	80.00
4 oz claret	30.00	80.00
5½ oz saucer champagne	25.00	70.00
2½ oz wine	35.00	85.00
5 oz soda	20.00	45.00
3½ oz cocktail	25.00	80.00
4 oz oyster cocktail	25.00	50.00
finger bowl (4080)	10.00	40.00
NOT ILLUSTRATED:		
8 oz soda	20.00	70.00
12 oz soda	25.00	80.00
1 oz cordial	75.00	275.00

Page 157: #1485 SATURN Pattern

	crystal	zircon
5″ nappy	15.00	45.00
7″ plate	15.00	45.00
15″ torte plate	35.00	75.00
11″ salad bowl	35.00	85.00
12″ fruit bowl	35.00	85.00

#1485 SATURN Pattern (continued)

	crystal	zircon
NOT ILLUSTRATED:		
6" plate	10.00	40.00
6¾" plate, rolled edge	10.00	40.00
8" plate	10.00	50.00
13" torte plate	30.00	75.00

Page 158:	crystal	zircon
cup/saucer	25.00	75.00
sugar	20.00	60.00
cream	20.00	60.00
tid-bit tray	20.00	75.00
5" whipped cream	20.00	70.00
baked apple	20.00	70.00
mayonnaise	20.00	70.00
violet vase	25.00	125.00
marmalade & cover	30.00	85.00
8½" vase, flared or straight	35.00	135.00

Page 159:	crystal	zircon
10 oz goblet	20.00	80.00
6 oz saucer champagne	15.00	60.00
4½ oz sherbet	10.00	40.00
3 oz cocktail	15.00	60.00
5 oz parfait	15.00	60.00
4 oz fruit cocktail	10.00	40.00
8 oz old fashion	15.00	60.00
12 oz soda	15.00	60.00
10 oz tumbler	15.00	60.00
9 oz luncheon tumbler	15.00	60.00
finger bowl	12.00	50.00

Page 160:	crystal	zircon
7" comport	35.00	150.00
2 lt candleblock, pr	125.00	400.00
mustard & paddle cover	40.00	250.00
2 oz oil #1 stopper	35.00	250.00
13" floral bowl	35.00	85.00
rose bowl	40.00	95.00
2 lt candelabra & E ball drops, pr	175.00	750.00
NOT ILLUSTRATED:		
7" relish, 2 comp hdl	40.00	175.00 (See Color Section-Zircon Odd Shades)
5 oz soda	15.00	60.00

Page 161: #1486 COLEPORT Pattern

	crystal
ice tub	60.00
floral bowl, oval	50.00

Page 162:	crystal	dawn
2 oz bar	20.00	
7 oz old fashion	20.00	
8" nappy	35.00	
10 oz tumbler	20.00	50.00(1487)
8 oz soda	20.00	

Page 163:	crystal
8 oz goblet	40.00
5½ oz saucer champagne	30.00
5½ oz sherbet	30.00
4 oz oyster cocktail	30.00
3 oz cocktail	35.00
2½ oz wine	40.00

Page 165: #1488 KOHINOOR Pattern

	crystal	zircon	sahara
14" floral bowl	50.00	250.00	
2 lt candelabra & D prisms, pr	200.00	800.00	
15½" fruit bowl	40.00	175.00	
13" floral bowl	35.00	175.00	200.00
cigarette holder	35.00	125.00	
17" hors d'oeuvres	50.00	200.00	
bridge ash tray	25.00	85.00	
ash tray	20.00	80.00	

Page 167: #4085 KOHINOOR Pattern

	crystal	zircon	exp. lt. blue
9 oz goblet	35.00	90.00	
9 oz goblet, low ft	35.00	90.00	550.00
5½ oz sherbet	25.00	70.00	
4½ oz claret	30.00	80.00	
2½ oz wine	30.00	120.00	
1 oz cordial	60.00	250.00	
3 oz cocktail	30.00	80.00	
6 oz Rhine wine	75.00	200.00	
4½ oz cocktail, tall stem	45.00	120.00	
5½ oz saucer champagne	30.00	80.00	
4 oz oyster cocktail	20.00	70.00	
12 oz soda	20.00	70.00	
12 oz soda (4085½)	20.00	80.00	
finger bowl (3335)	10.00	40.00	
6" ball vase	40.00	150.00	
32 oz jug (4161)	85.00	250.00	
11" salad bowl	35.00	150.00	

Page 169: #1495 FERN

	crystal	zircon	dawn
15" cheese & cracker plate & cover	60.00	200.00	
13" sandwich plate	30.00	100.00	
13" torte plate, hdl	30.00	100.00	
15" plate hdl	35.00	120.00	200.00

Page 170:

	crystal	zircon	dawn
2 lt. candlestick, bobeches & F prisms, pr	95.00	750.00	
relish, ftd, 2 hdl, 3 comp	35.00	125.00	
11" oval floral bowl, hdl	40.00	130.00	
13" fruit bowl, hdl	30.00	100.00	200.00
11" salad bowl, hdl	30.00	100.00	
sauce bowl	20.00	50.00	

Page 171:

	crystal	zircon
6" cheese, hdl	15.00	50.00
6" bon bon, hdl	15.00	55.00
4½" nappy	15.00	40.00
6" tid bit, hdl	15.00	40.00
6" mint, hdl	15.00	40.00
6" jelly, hdl	15.00	40.00
twin mayonnaise	25.00	70.00
sugar	25.00	70.00
cream	25.00	70.00
indiv sugar	25.00	80.00
indiv cream	25.00	80.00
jello dish 2 hdl & ftd	25.00	100.00
whipped cream or mayonnaise hdl & 8" plate	35.00	125.00

Page 175: #419 SUSSEX - marked on stem just below bowl

	crystal	moongleam	flamingo	cobalt
12 oz soda	20.00	35.00	30.00	
8 oz goblet	not listed	75.00	70.00	150.00
finger bowl	15.00	25.00	25.00	70.00
NOT ILLUSTRATED:				
10 oz goblet	not listed	75.00	70.00	150.00
5½ oz saucer champagne	not listed	60.00	60.00	80.00
5½ oz sherbet	not listed	40.00	40.00	60.00
2½ oz cocktail	not listed	60.00	60.00	80.00
5 oz soda	15.00	35.00	30.00	
8 oz soda	15.00	35.00	30.00	

#1306 COMET LEAF - marked on bottom of foot

	crystal	sahara	alexandrite
9 oz goblet	45.00	100.00	600.00+
NOT ILLUSTRATED:			
5 oz saucer champagne	35.00	50.00	
5 oz sherbet	30.00	40.00	
12 oz soda, ftd	35.00	50.00	

#1423 SWEET AD-O-LINE - marked inside of bowl

	crystal	moongleam	flamingo	cobalt
14 oz goblet	200.00	350.00+	350.00+	500.00+

Page 177: #2516 CIRCLE PAIR - not marked

	crystal	moongleam	flamingo
goblet	20.00	55.00	55.00

#3379 PYRAMID - may be marked on underside of foot

	moongleam	flamingo	NOT LISTED IN CRYSTAL
5 oz soda, ftd	60.00	50.00	
saucer champagne	60.00	50.00	
NOT ILLUSTRATED:			
10 oz goblet	90.00	80.00	
12 oz soda, ftd	60.00	50.00	

#4067 LOREN - not marked

	crystal
goblet	175.00+

#7005 DOUBLE RING

goblet	150.00+

Page 179:   #1408 (#7043) PANEL & DIAMOND POINT - marked on upper stem

	crystal	moongleam	sahara
goblet	175.00+	350.00+	400.00+

#8005 GALAXY - marked

	crystal	moongleam	flamingo	sahara
goblet	40.00	60.00	60.00	60.00
NOT ILLUSTRATED:				
sherbet	30.00	40.00	40.00	40.00

#8021 RIB IN RING - marked on upper stem

	moongleam
cocktail	300.00+

#3361 CHARLOTTE - marked on one panel of stem below hexagonal knop

	moongleam foot & stem hawthorne bowl
goblet	500.00+
saucer champagne (illus)	300.00+

Page 181:   #3304 UNIVERSAL Pattern Pull Stem - not marked

	crystal	amber
2 oz sherry	15.00	
1¼ oz pony brandy	20.00	
1 oz cordial	30.00	
1 oz pousse cafe	30.00	
finger bowl	10.00	
4 oz oyster cocktail (3389)	10.00	
3½ oz cocktail	15.00	
3 oz burgundy	15.00	
2½ oz creme de menthe	15.00	
2½ oz wine	15.00	
5½ oz saucer champagne	20.00	
5 oz parfait	15.00	50.00
5½ oz sherbet	15.00	
6 oz Rhine wine	20.00	
4½ oz claret	20.00	
10 oz goblet	20.00	
10 oz pilsner	30.00	
6½ oz champagne	15.00	
6 oz champagne, hollow stem	20.00	

Page 182:   #3311 VELVEDERE Pattern - not marked

	crystal	moongleam	flamingo
1½ oz sherry	20.00		
5½ oz ftd sherbet	15.00		
5" fruit salad	15.00	30.00	25.00
3½ oz cocktail	15.00		
7 oz parfait	15.00		
10 oz goblet	20.00		
4 oz claret or grape juice	15.00		
2 oz wine	20.00		
1 oz cordial	35.00		
5½ oz saucer champagne	15.00		
10 oz ftd tumbler	15.00		

Page 183: #3312 GAYOSO Pattern - not marked

	crystal	moongleam ft/hdl	flamingo	marigold
5½ oz sherbet	10.00		20.00	35.00
5½ oz saucer champagne	15.00		20.00	35.00
3½ oz cocktail	15.00		20.00	35.00
5 oz Russan coffee cup	20.00	35.00	30.00	90.00
2 oz sherry	20.00		25.00	
5 oz parfait	15.00		25.00	35.00
11 oz goblet	15.00		25.00	80.00
4½ oz claret	15.00		20.00	35.00
3 oz burgundy	15.00			
2½ oz wine	15.00		20.00	100.00
1 oz cordial	35.00		60.00	150.00
4½ oz hollow stem champagne	20.00		40.00	

Pages 184,185:   #3316 BILTMORE Pattern - not marked

	crystal	moongleam foot
PHOTO: indiv almond	15.00	25.00
3 oz burgundy	15.00	
1 oz pousse cafe	30.00	
finger bowl (4075)	10.00	
5½ oz sherbet	10.00	
6 oz saucer champagne	10.00	
3 oz cocktail	15.00	
10 oz goblet	15.00	
4½ oz grape juice or claret	15.00	
10 oz ftd tumbler or lun-cheon goblet	15.00	

Page 187:   #3318 WALDORF Pattern - not marked

	crystal
2½ oz wine	25.00
3 oz burgundy	20.00
1 oz cordial	50.00
¾ oz pony brandy	50.00
finger bowl (4080)	10.00
6 oz low ftd sundae	15.00
5 oz low ftd sherbet	15.00
3½ oz cocktail	15.00
4 oz oyster cocktail (3389)	15.00
5 oz low ftd fruit, shallow	15.00
11 oz tall stem goblet (3318½)	25.00
11 oz goblet	25.00
4 oz claret	25.00
4 oz grape juice	25.00
5 oz saucer champagne	20.00

Page 188:   #3324 DELAWARE Pattern - not marked

	crystal	flamingo	hawthorne	exp. blue
finger bowl	10.00	15.00		
4 oz oyster cocktail	15.00	30.00	40.00	
3½ oz cocktail	20.00	40.00	40.00	
4½ oz parfait	20.00	40.00		
9 oz goblet	25.00	50.00	80.00	500.00+
9 oz luncheon goblet	25.00	40.00		
6½ oz saucer champagne	20.00	30.00	50.00	
6½ oz sherbet	20.00	30.00	40.00	

Page 189:   #3325 RAMPUL Pattern - not marked

	crystal	flamingo	hawthorne	moongleam
9 oz goblet (illus)	30.00	70.00	100.00	70.00
3 oz cocktail	20.00	50.00	60.00	
6 oz saucer champagne	20.00	50.00	60.00	
6 oz sherbet	15.00	25.00	35.00	
4½ oz oyster cocktail	15.00	25.00	35.00	
parfait	30.00		90.00	

Page 191:   #3333 OLD GLORY Pattern - marked at top of stem near bowl

	crystal	hawthorne
2 oz wine	45.00	75.00
1 oz cordial	50.00	200.00
¾ oz pousse cafe	50.00	200.00
5½ oz sundae or sherbet	17.00	30.00
4½ oz oyster cocktail (3542)	17.00	30.00
3 oz burgundy	30.00	50.00
3 oz cocktail	30.00	50.00

#3333 OLD GLORY Pattern - marked at top of stem near bowl (continued)

	crystal	hawthorne
2 oz sherry	45.00	125.00
5½ oz saucer champagne	30.00	50.00
9 oz goblet	35.00	75.00
6 oz grape juice	40.00	55.00
4½ oz parfait	35.00	55.00
4½ oz claret	30.00	50.00

Page 192:

	crystal
12 oz ftd ice tea, hdl (3476)	30.00
6" high ftd comport	60.00
12 oz ftd soda (3476)	20.00
finger bowl (3309)	10.00
ftd grape fruit	30.00

Page 194:   #3350 WABASH Pattern -- marked upper stem below rings

	crystal plain w/o	moongleam ftd w/o or d/o	flamingo plain	hawthorne d/o	marigold bowl d/o
1 oz cordial	40.00	100.00	100.00	150.00	300.00
4 oz oyster cocktail	15.00	20.00	20.00	40.00	40.00
6 oz sherbet	15.00	20.00	20.00	40.00	40.00
3 oz cocktail	15.00	20.00	20.00	40.00	40.00
5 oz parfait	25.00	40.00	40.00	75.00	90.00
4 oz claret	20.00	25.00	25.00	50.00	65.00
6 oz saucer champagne	20.00	25.00	25.00	50.00	65.00
2½ oz wine	30.00	45.00	45.00	70.00	100.00
10 oz goblet	25.00	35.00	35.00	75.00	110.00
10 oz ftd tumbler	20.00	25.00	25.00	50.00	55.00
12 oz ftd soda or ice tea	20.00	25.00	25.00	60.00	65.00
12 oz ftd soda, hdl	25.00	30.00	30.00	75.00	95.00

Page 195:

	crystal	moongleam ft	flamingo	hawthorne	marigold bowl	sahara	alexandrite
3 pt ftd jug	100.00	150.00	160.00	200.00	400.00		
6" ftd comport & cover*	55.00	85.00	85.00	110.00	175.00		
#4132 peg grape fruit center	10.00						
#4139 ftd grape fruit center	10.00						
6" grape fruit	20.00	35.00	35.00	60.00	75.00		
finger bowl (4071)**	10.00	15.00	15.00	30.00	30.00	15.00	
6" plate	8.00	10.00	10.00	15.00	18.00	15.00	35.00
3 pt ftd tankard, cut neck	150.00	200.00	200.00				

*6" ftd comport offered with moongleam foot and knob
**75.00 for tangerine

Page 197:   #3555 FAIRACRE Pattern - marked on upper stem above ball

	crystal	moongleam ft	flamingo ft	moongleam	flamingo
4½ oz claret	15.00	30.00	30.00		
2½ oz wine	30.00	50.00	50.00		
3¾ oz oyster cocktail	15.00	30.00	30.00		
1 oz cordial	60.00	150.00	150.00		
finger bowl (4074)	10.00	15.00	15.00		
5 oz parfait	20.00	40.00	40.00		
10 oz luncheon goblet	20.00	40.00	40.00		
6½ oz saucer champagne	15.00	30.00	30.00		
6½ oz sherbet	15.00	30.00	30.00		
3½ oz cocktail	15.00	30.00	30.00		
12 oz ftd ice tea	15.00	30.00	30.00		
12 oz ftd ice tea, hdl	25.00	35.00	35.00		
10 oz goblet	20.00	40.00	40.00		
54 oz ftd jug	125.00	200.00	200.00	250.00	250.00

Page 199:   #8046 QUEEN GUINEVERE Pattern - marked on upper stem

	crystal
goblet	100.00

#3357 KING ARTHUR Pattern - marked on upper stem above ball

Page 201:

	crystal	moongleam ft	flamingo	flamingo ft	moongleam
2½ oz wine	35.00	50.00	50.00	50.00	
3½ oz cocktail	15.00	30.00	30.00	30.00	
1 oz cordial	60.00	150.00	150.00	150.00	
3¾ oz oyster cocktail	15.00	30.00	30.00	30.00	
finger bowl (4080)	10.00		20.00		20.00
6½ oz saucer champagne	15.00	30.00	30.00	30.00	
54 oz ftd jug (3355)	125.00	200.00	250.00	200.00	250.00
6½ oz sherbet	15.00	30.00	30.00	30.00	
12 oz ftd ice tea	15.00	30.00	30.00	30.00	

#3357 KING ARTHUR Pattern - marked on upper stem above ball (continued)

	crystal	moongleam ft	flamingo	flamingo ft
12 oz ftd ice tea, hdl	25.00	35.00	35.00	35.00
10 oz luncheon goblet	20.00	40.00	40.00	40.00
5 oz parfait	20.00	40.00	40.00	40.00
10 oz goblet	20.00	40.00	40.00	40.00

Handled items also come with colored handles.

Page 202: #3359 PLATEAU Pattern - not marked

	crystal	flamingo	marigold	moongleam	hawthorne	cobalt
finger bowl	10.00	20.00	30.00	20.00		
4 oz oyster cocktail	12.00	25.00	45.00			
6½ oz sherbet	12.00	25.00	45.00			275.00+
9 oz tumbler (pat. #73031)	10.00	20.00	30.00			
5½ soda	10.00	20.00	30.00			
8 oz soda	10.00	20.00	30.00			
12 oz soda or ice tea	15.00	25.00	35.00			
8½ oz goblet	15.00	35.00	65.00			
3 oz cocktail*	12.00	25.00	45.00	*Captions in catalog in error		
6½ oz saucer champagne*	12.00	25.00	45.00			
8 oz luncheon goblet*	15.00	35.00	65.00			
½ gal jug	120.00	150.00	200.00	150.00	200.00	
NOT ILLUSTRATED:						
6" rose bowl	35.00	70.00	150.00	75.00	125.00	

Page 203: #3360 PENN CHARTER Pattern - marked under swirl at top of stem

	crystal	flamingo*	hawthorne**
1½ oz sherry	35.00		
3 oz cocktail	20.00	40.00	50.00
4 oz oyster cocktail	20.00	40.00	50.00
finger bowl (3309)	10.00		
6 oz sherbet	20.00	40.00	50.00
2½ oz ftd bar (3381)	20.00		
6 oz saucer champagne	20.00	40.00	50.00
10 oz goblet	25.00	60.00	70.00
12 oz soda	20.00		
5 oz parfait	25.00	50.00	70.00
4½ oz claret	20.00		
NOT ILLUSTRATED:			
8½ oz goblet	25.00	60.00	70.00

*diamond optic and checker optic
**checker optic

Page 204: #3362 CHARTER OAK Pattern - marked on stem just below bowl

	crystal	moongleam	flamingo	marigold	hawthorne
4½ oz parfait	17.00	35.00	30.00	55.00	
3 oz cocktail	15.00	30.00	25.00	35.00	
3½ oz oyster cocktail	12.00	25.00	20.00	30.00	
finger bowl	10.00	20.00	20.00	30.00	
10 oz tumbler	12.00	25.00	20.00	30.00	
12 oz ice tea	12.00	25.00	20.00	30.00	
8 oz goblet	20.00	40.00	40.00	60.00	110.00
8 oz luncheon goblet	20.00	40.00	40.00	60.00	
7" high ftd comport	35.00	75.00	60.00	90.00	150.00
6 oz sherbet	15.00	25.00	25.00	35.00	
6 oz saucer champagne	15.00	25.00	25.00	35.00	
NOT ILLUSTRATED:					
½ gal jug	60.00	150.00	150.00	300.00+	

Page 205: #3365 RAMSHORN Pattern - marked on bulge of stem just below wafer. Ramshorn optic crystal known in plain also

	crystal	flamingo	moongleam foot
5" fruit salad	15.00	20.00	20.00
1½ oz bar	25.00	40.00	
8 oz ftd soda	20.00	30.00	
5 oz ftd soda	20.00	30.00	
9 oz goblet	35.00	60.00	
2½ oz wine	40.00	60.00	
3 oz cocktail	30.00	40.00	
6 oz sherbet	20.00	30.00	
6 oz saucer champagne	30.00	50.00	
4½ oz parfait	35.00	50.00	
NOT ILLUSTRATED:			
12 oz ftd soda	20.00	30.00	

Page 207:   **#3366 TROJAN Pattern - diamond optic - marked on stem beneath wafer**

	crystal	moongleam stem	flamingo	hawthorne
4½ oz parfait	25.00	40.00	40.00	65.00
1½ oz bar	20.00	40.00	40.00	55.00
3 oz oyster cocktail	10.00	20.00	20.00	40.00
8 oz soda	10.00	20.00	20.00	35.00
12 oz soda or ice tea	15.00	25.00	25.00	35.00
7″ ftd comport	40.00	60.00	60.00	95.00
8 oz goblet	25.00	50.00	50.00	75.00
3 oz cocktail	20.00	30.00	30.00	50.00
2½ oz wine	25.00	50.00	50.00	75.00
10 oz ftd tumbler	10.00	20.00	20.00	35.00
5 oz sherbet	15.00	25.00	25.00	45.00
5 oz saucer champagne	18.00	35.00	35.00	60.00
NOT ILLUSTRATED:				
4 oz claret	15.00	30.00	30.00	60.00
1 oz cordial	55.00	110.00	110.00	185.00
5 oz ftd soda	10.00	20.00	20.00	40.00

Page 208:   **#3368 ALBEMARLE Pattern - marked on upper stem below hexagonal knob**

	crystal	moongleam stem	flamingo	marigold bowl	sahara	alexandrite
3 oz cocktail	15.00	25.00	25.00	35.00		
2½ oz wine	30.00	55.00	55.00	75.00		
5 oz sherbet*	15.00	25.00	25.00	40.00		
1 oz cordial	55.00	125.00	125.00	275.00		
finger bowl (3309)	10.00	20.00	20.00	40.00		
10 oz ftd tumbler	10.00	20.00	20.00	40.00		
3 oz oyster cocktail	15.00	20.00	20.00	30.00		
7″ high ftd comport	45.00	60.00	60.00	100.00	100.00	325.00
1½ oz ftd bar	20.00	40.00	40.00	65.00		
12 oz soda or ice tea	15.00	25.00	25.00	35.00		
8 oz goblet**	25.00	50.00	50.00	90.00		225.00
4 oz claret	15.00	25.00	25.00	50.00		
4½ oz parfait**	25.00	40.00	40.00	75.00		
5 oz saucer champagne	25.00	50.00	50.00	75.00		

*5 oz sherbet 500.00-600.00 exp. lt. blue stem and foot
NOT ILLUSTRATED:
**In all marigold, 4½ oz parfait, 150.00; 8 oz goblet, 175.00

	crystal	moongleam stem	flamingo	marigold bowl		
5 oz ftd soda	10.00	20.00	20.00	30.00		
8 oz ftd soda	10.00	20.00	20.00	35.00		

Page 209:   **#3440 PORTSMOUTH Pattern - unmarked**

	crystal	moongleam foot	flamingo	tangerine
7 oz sherbet	15.00	25.00	25.00	
7 oz saucer champagne	15.00	25.00	25.00	
3½ oz cocktail	15.00	25.00	25.00	
9 oz goblet	20.00	35.00	35.00	500.00+

#3370 AFRICAN Pattern - unmarked

	crystal	moongleam foot	flamingo
8 oz goblet	30.00	50.00	50.00
3 oz wine	30.00	50.00	50.00
4 oz cocktail	25.00	45.00	45.00
6 oz sherbet	25.00	45.00	45.00
6 oz saucer champagne	25.00	45.00	45.00

NOTE: #3365 Ramshorn or #3366 Trojan sodas may be used with #3370

Page 211:   **#3376 ADAM Pattern - not marked**

	crystal	flamingo
finger bowl	10.00	20.00
10 oz ftd tumbler	20.00	35.00
4 oz oyster cocktail	20.00	35.00
5 oz ftd soda	20.00	35.00
12 oz ftd soda	20.00	35.00
11 oz goblet	30.00	60.00
4 oz claret	20.00	40.00
3½ oz cocktail	20.00	40.00
3 oz wine	30.00	60.00
6 oz saucer champagne	20.00	40.00
6 oz sherbet	20.00	35.00
NOT ILLUSTRATED:		
8 oz ftd soda	20.00	35.00

Page 213: #3380 OLD DOMINION Pattern - marked under hexagon wafer at top of stem

	crystal	moongleam bowl	moongleam stem	flamingo	marigold bowl	sahara	alexandrite	marigold stem
2 oz bar	20.00	40.00	30.00	30.00	80.00	40.00	125.00	60.00
1 oz cordial	50.00	180.00	150.00	150.00	350.00	180.00	350.00	300.00
4 oz oyster cocktail	12.00	25.00	25.00	25.00	35.00	40.00	65.00	
finger bowl (4075)	10.00			20.00	30.00	35.00	65.00	
6 oz saucer champagne (tall)	20.00	40.00	35.00	35.00	55.00	40.00	125.00	65.00
2½ oz wine	25.00	50.00	45.00	40.00	75.00	60.00	135.00	80.00
6 oz saucer champagne (short)	20.00	35.00	30.00	30.00	60.00	50.00	110.00	65.00
3 oz cocktail	20.00	35.00	30.00	35.00	60.00	50.00	95.00	60.00
6 oz sherbet	20.00	30.00	30.00	35.00	60.00	50.00	85.00	60.00
ftd grape fruit	20.00	35.00	30.00	35.00	60.00	50.00	125.00	65.00
10 oz goblet (tall)	25.00	45.00	40.00	45.00	65.00	55.00	150.00	75.00
10 oz goblet (short)	25.00	45.00	40.00	45.00	65.00	55.00	150.00	75.00
4 oz claret	20.00	40.00	30.00	30.00	45.00	35.00	85.00	55.00
5 oz parfait	20.00	40.00	30.00	30.00	45.00	35.00	95.00	55.00
12 oz soda or ice tea	15.00	30.00	25.00	25.00	30.00	30.00	75.00	30.00
10 oz ftd tumbler	12.00	30.00	25.00	25.00	30.00	30.00	75.00	30.00
NOT ILLUSTRATED:								
5 oz ftd soda	12.00	25.00	25.00	20.00	30.00	25.00	75.00	30.00
8 oz ftd soda	12.00	25.00	25.00	20.00	30.00	25.00	75.00	30.00
16 oz ftd soda	15.00	30.00	25.00	20.00	35.00	30.00	85.00	30.00
7" comport	45.00	75.00	60.00	60.00	100.00	60.00	275.00	120.00
5 oz frappe, short	15.00	30.00	25.00	25.00	40.00	30.00	65.00	25.00
5 oz frappe, tall	15.00	30.00	25.00	25.00	40.00	30.00	65.00	25.00

A few items are found in all marigold. A rare champagne is known in zircon. Also made 1 oz. bar.

Page 215: #3381 CREOLE Pattern - unmarked - not made in all crystal

	alexandrite bowl crystal stem	alexandrite	Pat. #82151 sahara bowl crystal stem
2½ oz ftd bar	175.00	175.00	150.00
1 oz cordial	300.00	350.00	400.00
5 oz oyster cocktail	100.00	125.00	65.00
ftd finger bowl	85.00	85.00	55.00
7 oz saucer champagne, tall	125.00	150.00	125.00
7 oz saucer champagne, short	125.00	150.00	125.00
2½ oz wine	150.00	165.00	150.00
7 oz sherbet	125.00	150.00	125.00
4 oz cocktail	125.00	150.00	125.00
ftd grape fruit	125.00	150.00	125.00
11 oz goblet, tall	175.00	195.00	150.00
11 oz goblet, short	175.00	195.00	150.00
5 oz parfait	100.00	125.00	65.00
12 oz ftd soda	100.00	125.00	65.00
10 oz ftd tumbler	100.00	125.00	65.00

Page 217: #3386 DIAMOND ROSE Pattern - marked on stem just below bowl

	crystal	flamingo	moongleam stem & foot	moongleam bowl	marigold bowl	sahara	cobalt bowl
11 oz goblet	50.00	75.00	90.00	90.00	125.00	75.00	
NOT ILLUSTRATED:							
6½ oz saucer champagne	30.00	50.00	50.00	50.00	75.00	50.00	
7 oz sherbet	30.00	50.00	50.00	50.00	75.00	50.00	
cocktail	30.00	50.00	50.00	50.00	75.00	50.00	
8 oz pilsner	45.00					125.00	250.00
10 oz pilsner	45.00					125.00	250.00
12 oz pilsner	45.00					125.00	250.00

Page 219: #3389 DUQUESNE Pattern - unmarked

	crystal	sahara bowl	sahara	tangerine bowl (w/o)
3 oz cocktail	25.00	40.00	40.00	200.00
5 oz parfait	25.00	40.00	40.00	225.00
2½ oz wine	30.00	50.00	50.00	275.00
1 oz cordial	50.00	180.00	180.00	700.00
finger bowl (4071)	10.00		20.00	100.00
ftd grape fruit	20.00	40.00	40.00	200.00
4 oz oyster cocktail	20.00	35.00	35.00	200.00
5 oz sherbet	20.00	35.00	35.00	200.00
10 oz ftd tumbler	10.00	20.00	20.00	175.00
9 oz goblet	25.00	65.00	65.00	275.00
4 oz claret	25.00	50.00	50.00	200.00
12 oz ftd soda	10.00	20.00	20.00	200.00
5 oz saucer champagne	25.00	50.00	50.00	200.00

Page 221:   #3390 CARCASSONNE Pattern - marked beneath bowl

	crystal	moongleam ft	flamingo	sahara	cobalt bowl	alexandrite bowl	amber
3 oz oyster cocktail	20.00	30.00	30.00	30.00	80.00	100.00	
2½ oz wine	30.00	50.00	50.00	50.00	120.00	150.00	
2 oz ftd bar	30.00	50.00	50.00	50.00	120.00	150.00	
6 oz sherbet	20.00	40.00	40.00	40.00	70.00	90.00	
11 oz goblet, short	25.00	50.00	50.00	50.00	100.00	125.00	
6 oz saucer champagne	20.00	35.00	35.00	35.00	70.00	100.00	650.00+
4 oz claret	20.00	35.00	35.00	35.00	70.00	90.00	
3 oz cocktail	20.00	35.00	35.00	35.00	70.00	90.00	
12 oz ftd soda or ice tea	20.00	35.00	35.00	35.00	70.00	100.00	
11 oz goblet, tall	25.00	50.00	50.00	50.00	100.00	125.00	
10½ oz morning after	25.00	60.00	60.00	60.00	180.00	180.00	
12 oz flagon	25.00	60.00	60.00	60.00	150.00	200.00	
NOT ILLUSTRATED:							
1 oz. cordial	30.00	100.00	100.00	110.00	200.00	325.00	

Page 222:

	crystal	moongleam ft	flamingo	sahara	cobalt bowl	alexandrite bowl	zircon bowl
cigarette holder	25.00	45.00	45.00	45.00	100.00	125.00	
ftd finger bowl	15.00	30.00	30.00	35.00	50.00	75.00	
8″ ftd vase	35.00	90.00	90.00	90.00	200.00	300.00	650.00+
1 pt ftd decanter #84 stopper	80.00	250.00	250.00	250.00	500.00	1500.00	
3 pt ftd jug	80.00	200.00	200.00	200.00	400.00	1500.00	

Page 223:   #3394 SAXONY Pattern - not marked

	crystal	sahara
12 oz goblet, tall stem	40.00	80.00
NOT ILLUSTRATED:		
12 oz goblet, short stem	35.00	65.00
5½ oz saucer champagne	20.00	40.00
5½ oz sherbet	20.00	40.00
4 oz oyster cocktail	20.00	40.00
3 oz cocktail	20.00	40.00
2½ oz wine	45.00	65.00
1 oz cordial	110.00	200.00
5 oz ftd soda	20.00	40.00
8 oz ftd soda	20.00	40.00
12 oz ftd soda	20.00	40.00
9 in vase, ftd	60.00	120.00
finger bowl (4074)	10.00	20.00

Page 224:   #3397 GASCONY Pattern - sometimes marked in middle of base on underside

	crystal	sahara	tangerine bowl	cobalt bowl	moongleam	flamingo
cream	40.00	80.00				
sugar	40.00	80.00				
ftd oval floral bowl	60.00	125.00	850.00+			
5″ candlestick #138 pr	100.00	175.00			200.00	200.00
10″ ftd floral bowl	100.00	200.00	1000.00	650.00		
NOT ILLUSTRATED:						
8″ vase			750.00			

Page 225:

	crystal	sahara	tangerine bowl	cobalt bowl	moongleam base & stopper	amber base
5 oz ftd soda	25.00	40.00	175.00			
4 oz oyster cocktail	25.00	50.00	175.00			
3 oz cocktail	25.00	50.00	175.00			
2½ oz wine	35.00	75.00	300.00	200.00		
6 oz sherbet	25.00	50.00	200.00			
1 pt decanter #88 stopper	100.00	300.00	2000.00+	500.00	400.00	
tomato juice pitcher	70.00	175.00				
11 oz goblet, low ft	60.00	120.00	400.00			600.00+
10 oz ftd tumbler	45.00	100.00	300.00			
6 oz saucer champagne	50.00	100.00	350.00			
12 oz ftd soda	50.00	100.00	350.00			

Rare items are found with an amber base or a gray base with crystal bowls.

Page 227: #3404 SPANISH Pattern - if marked, mark is on stem just above foot

	crystal	cobalt bowl	sahara bowl	tangerine bowl	exper. light blue	amber
3½ oz cocktail	40.00	125.00	175.00	350.00		
2½ oz wine	60.00	175.00				
1 oz cordial	90.00	250.00	400.00			
finger bowl (3335)	10.00	70.00				
3½ oz oyster cocktail	40.00	80.00	125.00	350.00		
12 oz ftd soda	30.00	70.00	125.00	350.00		
10 oz ftd tumbler	30.00	70.00	125.00			
5 oz ftd soda	30.00	60.00	80.00	275.00		
5½ oz sherbet	30.00	75.00	90.00		500.00+	
10 oz goblet	50.00	120.00	325.00	550.00		
4 oz claret	40.00	125.00	175.00	550.00		
5½ oz saucer champagne	40.00	125.00	175.00	550.00		600.00+
6" comport	90.00	300.00	350.00			

Page 229: #3408 JAMESTOWN Pattern - marked under swirled knob at top of stem

	crystal	sahara	moongleam	flamingo	cobalt	tangerine	amber
2 oz wine	45.00	200.00					
1½ oz sherry (3360)	45.00	200.00					
1 oz cordial	45.00	250.00					
finger bowl (3309)	10.00	35.00					
9 oz ftd tumbler	12.00	35.00					
12 oz beer mug (hdl colored)	60.00	140.00	140.00	275.00	200.00	325.00+	325.00
6 oz sherbet	20.00	80.00					
9" vase	60.00	225.00					
3 oz cocktail	20.00	80.00					
9 oz goblet	35.00	200.00	200.00	200.00	200.00+		
13 oz ftd soda	12.00	35.00					
4½ oz claret	20.00	80.00					
6 oz saucer champagne	20.00	80.00					

Page 231: #3409 PLYMOUTH Pattern - marked on upper stem

	crystal	sahara	cobalt
5 oz ftd soda	12.00	25.00	
6 oz sherbet	35.00	80.00	
3 oz oyster cocktail	12.00	25.00	
finger bowl (3335)	10.00	80.00	
6 oz saucer champagne	35.00	80.00	
3½ oz cocktail	35.00	80.00	
12 oz banquet goblet	65.00	225.00	
10 oz goblet	50.00	200.00	300.00+
12 oz ftd soda	12.00	35.00	
5 oz parfait	45.00	90.00	

Page 233: #3411 MONTE CRISTO Pattern - unmarked

	crystal	sahara
3½ oz cocktail	30.00	80.00
2½ oz wine	60.00	200.00
1½ oz sherry	65.00	200.00
1 oz cordial	75.00	250.00
finger bowl (3309)	10.00	20.00
3 oz oyster cocktail (3542)	15.00	25.00
5 oz ftd soda	15.00	25.00
7" comport	60.00	250.00
6 oz sherbet	30.00	80.00
9 oz goblet	40.00	200.00
4 oz claret	30.00	80.00
6 oz saucer champagne	30.00	80.00
9 oz ftd tumbler	15.00	35.00
12 oz ftd soda	15.00	35.00

Page 235: #3414 MARRIETTE Pattern - unmarked

	crystal
1 oz cordial	100.00
12 oz ftd soda	15.00
3 oz oyster cocktail (3409)	15.00
finger bowl (3335)	10.00
3½ oz cocktail	40.00
6 oz sherbet	40.00
10 oz ftd tumbler	15.00
1½ oz sherry	65.00
10 oz goblet	60.00
6 oz saucer champagne	40.00
3¾ oz claret	40.00
2½ oz wine	75.00

Page 237: #3416 BARBARA FRITCHIE Pattern - marked on stem under bowl

	crystal	sahara	alexandrite	cobalt
6 oz saucer champagne	40.00			
¾ oz brandy tall	100.00			
1 oz cordial, tall	125.00	400.00	400.00	400.00
2½ oz wine	85.00			
3½ oz cocktail	40.00			
1½ oz sherry, tall	75.00			
10 oz ftd tumbler	15.00			
18 oz brandy snifter	175.00			
6 oz sherbet	40.00			
finger bowl (3335)	10.00			
3 oz oyster cocktail (3409)	15.00			
10 oz goblet	60.00			
6 oz Rhine wine	150.00			
3¾ oz claret	50.00			
12 oz ftd soda (3409)	15.00			
10 oz goblet, low ftd	50.00			

NOTE: Only the bowls are in various colors, the stems and feet are crystal.

Page 239: #3418 SAVOY PLAZA Pattern - marked on top of stem

	crystal
1½ oz sherry	90.00
3½ oz oyster cocktail	30.00
1 oz cordial	100.00
finger bowl (4080)	10.00
3 oz wine	65.00
6 oz saucer champagne	40.00
3½ oz cocktail	30.00
10 oz goblet	50.00
12 oz ftd soda	30.00
5 oz ftd soda	30.00
4 oz claret	30.00

Page 241: #3424 ADMIRALTY Pattern - marked under bowl

	crystal
1 oz cordial	100.00
4½ oz oyster cocktail	30.00
finger bowl (3309)	10.00
5 oz ftd soda	30.00
2 oz sherry	90.00
3 oz cocktail	40.00
2 oz wine	75.00
9 oz goblet	50.00
12 oz ftd soda	30.00
4½ oz claret	40.00
5½ oz saucer champagne	40.00

Page 242: #4044 NEW ERA Pattern - marked on ring beneath bowl or underside of foot

	crystal	cobalt bowl
3 oz wine	40.00	200.00
3½ oz oyster cocktail	25.00	100.00
1 oz cordial	65.00	300.00
finger bowl (4080)	10.00	
6 oz saucer champagne	25.00	95.00
12 oz ftd soda	25.00	95.00
6 oz sherbet	25.00	95.00
3½ oz cocktail	25.00	95.00
10 oz goblet	30.00	200.00
12 oz pilsner	60.00	200.00
10 oz ftd tumbler	25.00	95.00
4 oz claret	25.00	95.00

Page 243:

	crystal	alexandrite
cup and saucer	45.00	
cream	30.00	
sugar	30.00	
after dinner cup and saucer	60.00	
indiv nut or ash tray	40.00	
2 lt. candlestick/bobeche pr	100.00	1200.00
5½ x 4½ bread & butter plate	20.00	
rye bottle & stopper	125.00	
13" relish, 3 comp	35.00	
13" celery tray	35.00	
9 x 7" plate	30.00	
11" floral bowl	60.00	

Page 245:   #4054 CORONATION Pattern - not marked

	crystal	dawn screen optic	limelight screen optic	zircon
2½ oz bar	20.00			any item:70.00+
3 oz cocktail	20.00			
4 oz cocktail, ftd	25.00			
8 oz old fashion	20.00	300.00+		
11 oz hot toddy	20.00			
30 oz martini mixer	75.00			
14 oz Slim Jim	40.00			
8 oz soda	20.00	300.00+	300.00+	
28 oz cocktail shaker	100.00			
½ gal jug	95.00			
½ gal ice tankard	125.00			

Page 247:   #4055 PARK LANE Pattern - not marked

	crystal
1½ oz sherry	50.00
2½ oz wine	50.00
1 oz cordial	100.00
3 oz cocktail	25.00
3 oz oyster cocktail	25.00
finger bowl (4080)	10.00
6 oz sherbet	20.00
6 oz saucer champagne	30.00
10 oz goblet	40.00
4 oz claret	25.00
13 oz ftd soda	20.00
5 oz ftd soda	20.00

Page 249:   #4090 COVENTRY Pattern - not marked

	crystal	zircon
10 oz goblet	40.00	150.00
10 oz goblet, low ftd	40.00	130.00
6 oz sherbet	30.00	65.00
6 oz saucer champagne	40.00	85.00
4½ oz claret	40.00	85.00
3 oz cocktail	40.00	75.00
4½ oz oyster cocktail	30.00	65.00
2 oz sherry	65.00	180.00
2½ oz wine	65.00	180.00
1 oz cordial	150.00	300.00+
¾ oz brandy	150.00	250.00+
12 oz ftd soda	40.00	65.00
finger bowl (4080)	10.00	40.00

Page 251: #4091 KIMBERLY Pattern - marked on stem below bowl

	crystal	zircon
10 oz goblet	40.00	130.00
10 oz goblet, low ft	30.00	130.00
5½ oz saucer champagne	30.00	100.00
4½ oz claret	30.00	100.00
3 oz cocktail	30.00	100.00
2 oz wine	55.00	140.00
1 oz cordial	85.00	300.00+
4½ oz oyster cocktail (3542)	10.00	60.00
5½ oz sherbet	25.00	95.00
finger bowl (3335)	10.00	40.00
12 oz ftd soda (4091½)	25.00	95.00

Page 253:   #4092 KENILWORTH Pattern - marked on stem below bowl

	crystal
10 oz goblet	50.00
5½ oz saucer champagne	40.00
3 oz cocktail	40.00
4½ oz claret	45.00
3 oz oyster cocktail	35.00
brandy snifter	175.00
6 oz Rhine wine	150.00
1 oz cordial, tall stem	100.00
¾ oz brandy tall stem	100.00
1½ oz sherry tall stem	75.00
2 oz wine	85.00
5½" comport	75.00
5 oz ftd soda (4092½)	25.00
5½ oz sherbet	25.00
finger bowl (3335)	20.00

447

MISCELLANEOUS STEMWARE

	crystal	moongleam	flamingo	sahara	cobalt	tangerine
1108 PENELOPE egg cup	30.00					
1229 BARNUM egg cup	30.00					
1108½ PENELOPE egg cup	30.00					
394 NARROW FLUTE Boston egg	20.00					
1228 RINGLING egg cup	30.00					
337 TOURAINE egg cup	15.00					150.00
1114 ARCADE high ball	15.00					
820 FIFTH AVENUE goblet	20.00					
414 TUDOR goblet	20.00					
1464 DRAPE goblet	100.00					
1437 FLINT RIDGE goblet	100.00				275.00	
811 ¾ HOFFMAN HOUSE 17 oz goblet	30.00	150.00	150.00	150.00		

Page 257:

	crystal	amber
4139 grapefruit center ftd	10.00	
4132 peg grapefruit center	10.00	
4052 NATIONAL sherbet (4051)	10.00	
4049 OLD FITZ hot whiskey	25.00	90.00
4052 NATIONAL goblet	20.00	
3800 TEXAS PINK grapefruit	20.00	
3801 TEXAS PINK grapefruit	20.00	75.00

Page 259: **ASH TRAYS**

	crystal	moongleam	flamingo	marigold	sahara	hawthorne	amber
356 WHITE OWL	35.00						
357 DUCK	85.00	175.00	165.00	500.00+			
358 SOLITAIRE	20.00	40.00	35.00	50.00	40.00		
359 CHESTERFIELD	25.00	50.00	40.00				
360 WINSTON	25.00	50.00	50.00				
361 IRWIN	50.00	95.00	95.00	175.00	105.00		
363 WINGS	20.00	40.00	35.00	50.00			
365 RHOMBIC	30.00	60.00	50.00				
366 SALEM	25.00	65.00	50.00				
439 FATIMA	20.00	35.00					
440 FACET	20.00						
442 MALTESE CROSS	20.00	40.00	35.00				
600 OLD GOLD	20.00						
1179 BOW TIE	20.00	40.00	35.00				
1180 TREFOIL	20.00	40.00	35.00				
1186 YEOMAN	15.00	30.00	30.00		50.00	60.00	90.00+
1187 YEOMAN	30.00	65.00					
1200 YEOMAN	10.00	20.00	20.00	40.00		40.00	
1286 CUPID & PSYCHE	30.00	60.00	50.00				
1386 IRISH SETTER	30.00	60.00	50.00				

Page 261

	crystal	moongleam	flamingo	marigold	sahara	cobalt	alexandrite
358 SOLITAIRE	20.00	40.00	35.00	50.00	40.00		
1454 DIAMOND POINT	10.00						
4044 NEW ERA	40.00						
355 QUATOR	15.00						
1425 VICTORIAN	25.00				60.00	125.00	
1424 LUCKY STRIKE	15.00						
1404 OLD SANDWICH	10.00	45.00	45.00		35.00	65.00	
439 FATIMA	20.00	35.00					
1184 YEOMAN	30.00	60.00	50.00		65.00		
1401 EMPRESS	40.00	350.00	250.00		125.00	400.00	350.00
353 MEDIUM FLAT PANEL	25.00		55.00				
1186 YEOMAN**	15.00	30.00	30.00		50.00		
1469½ RIDGELEIGH 4"	20.00						
1469 RIDGELEIGH round*	15.00						
1469¼ RIDGELEIGH 2 comp	65.00						
1469 RIDGELEIGH square*	10.00				35.00	zircon 50.00	
356 WHITE OWL	35.00						
365 RHOMBIC	30.00	60.00	50.00				
366 SALEM	25.00	65.00	50.00				
359 CHESTERFIELD	25.00	50.00	40.00				

Page 261 (continued)

	crystal	moongleam	flamingo
360 WINSTON	25.00	50.00	50.00
1201 PHILIP MORRIS	25.00	55.00	45.00
364 PEDESTAL	25.00	60.00	50.00
600 OLD GOLD	20.00		

Page 262

	crystal	moongleam	flamingo
441 GRAPE LEAF SQUARE***	35.00	75.00	65.00

*Captions in catalog reversed.   **hawthorne 60.00; amber 90.00+   ***hawthorne 100.00

Page 264:   #4224 STEEPLECHASE Pattern

	crystal	moongleam	flamingo	sahara
cocktail	60.00	100.00	100.00	100.00
cocktail mixer	120.00	350.00	300.00	300.00

Page 265:   DECANTERS

	crystal	flamingo	sahara	alexandrite	cobalt	moongleam ft & stop	flamingo ft & st
4026 SPENCER*	65.00	130.00					
2401 OAKWOOD	65.00						
3417 ADKINS	80.00						
3397 GASCONY**	100.00		300.00		500.00	400.00	
4027 CHRISTOS	90.00	250.00	250.00	1500.00	450.00	250.00	150.00
3390 CARCASSONNE	80.00	250.00	250.00	1500.00	500.00	250.00	

*4026 crystal/flamingo stopper 80, crystal, moongleam stopper 85.00, moongleam 130.00
** tangerine 1800.00

Page 266:

	crystal	moongleam	flamingo
4036 MARSHALL	75.00		
4033 MALONEY	85.00		
4035 BETHEL	85.00		
4028 ROBINSON	75.00	200.00	200.00

Page 267:

	crystal
4040 RYAN indiv	30.00
4038 DE KUYPEUR	175.00
4039 MARTIN	175.00
4037 CLARENCE	175.00

Page 269:   BEER MUGS

	crystal	sahara	cobalt
1426 CLOVER ROPE	300.00+	400.00+	500.00+
1434 TOM & JERRY	150.00	250.00+	

Page 270:

	crystal	moongleam handle	flamingo handle	sahara handle	cobalt handle	alexandrite handle	tangerine handle
3405 COYLE*	100.00	250.00+	250.00+	250.00+	300.00+		400.00+
3406 THRAN	100.00	250.00+	250.00+	250.00+	300.00+	400.00+	400.00+
3407 OVERDORF	100.00	250.00+	250.00+	250.00+	250.00+		400.00+

Some mugs are known with colored bodies and crystal handles. Those listed are known and others may possibly be found in moongleam, flamingo and sahara.
*alexandrite 1500+

	cobalt body	alexandrite body	tangerine body
3405 COYLE	300.00+	1500.00+	
3407 OVERDORF	300.00+		4500.00+

Page 271:   FOOTED & HANDLED SODAS, BEER MUGS & PILSNERS

	crystal	moongleam	flamingo	sahara	cobalt	tangerine	amber
3476 TEMPLE hdld soda	20.00						
2516 CIRCLE PAIR soda	30.00	60.00	50.00				
3476 TEMPLE soda	20.00						
3408 JAMESTOWN mug*	60.00	140.00	275.00	140.00	200.00	325.00+	325.00
4163 WHALEY mug* 16 oz	90.00	175.00	350.00+	175.00	175.00		
3386 DIAMOND ROSE pilsner	45.00			135.00	200.00		
4044 NEW ERA pilsner	35.00				200.00		
3420 MILWAUKEE pilsner	30.00						
3304 UNIVERSAL pilsner	30.00						

* colored handle, crystal body, red $500.00+

Page 273:

	crystal	moongleam foot	flamingo
3373 MORNING GLORY	NOT LISTED	85.00	100.00
3478 CONE	35.00		
3482 MONO-RING	35.00	45.00	

#2323 NAVY (Most items not illustrated)

	crystal with cobalt bases
2 oz bar	90.00
5 oz soda	50.00
6 oz soda	50.00
6 oz old fashion	55.00
7 oz soda	55.00
8 oz soda	55.00
8 oz old fashion	60.00
8 oz toddy	60.00
10 oz soda	65.00
12 oz soda	75.00
13 oz soda	80.00
6″ plate	75.00
7″ plate	125.00
8″ plate	125.00
bouillon plate	75.00
cup & saucer set	250.00
cream & sugar (set)	250.00

Page 277: #2351 NEWTON - made plain, wide optic, or diamond optic - Not marked

	crystal	moongleam	flamingo	marigold
2 oz bar, with & without sham	15.00			
6 oz toddy	15.00			
1 pt decanter (2401)	75.00			
8 oz toddy	20.00			
10 oz soda, ½ sham	15.00	30.00	30.00	45.00
10 oz soda, full sham	15.00			
10 oz soda, regular	15.00			

8 & 12 oz sodas, light made in moongleam, flamingo, marigold, hawthorne and sahara
Prices would be comparable to those above. Hawthorne 40.00
16 oz and 18 oz d/o in sahara 40.00

Page 279: #2401 OAKWOOD - not marked. Made plain, wide optic or diamond optic checker optic in hawthorne

All sodas in crystal	15.00
1 pt. decanter	75.00 crystal

	moongleam	flamingo	hawthorne	sahara
5 oz soda, light		30.00	40.00	
5½ oz soda, light	30.00	30.00		30.00

Page 281: SODAS

	crystal	moongleam	flamingo	marigold	sahara
2451	15.00				
2852	15.00				
3422	15.00				
2516 CIRCLE PAIR*	30.00	60.00	50.00	65.00	40.00
2512	15.00				
3417 ADKINS	15.00				
2352	15.00				
2351X NEWTON	15.00				
2405	15.00				

*made in 5, 8 and 12 oz sizes

Page 283: MISCELLANEOUS STEMWARE

	crystal	moongleam foot	flamingo	flamingo foot	hawthorne	zircon s/o	moongleam ft/flamingo bowl
3481 GLENFORD bar*	20.00	25.00	25.00	25.00	50.00		160.00
3480 KOORS bar	20.00	25.00	25.00				
3481 GLENFORD cocktail	15.00	20.00	15.00	20.00	45.00		
3480 KOORS cocktail	15.00	20.00	15.00				
3405 ALIBI cocktail	15.00	25.00					
3542 HAZELWOOD oyster	10.00		25.00		30.00	40.00	
in sahara	25.00						
3428 BRITTANY cocktail	20.00						
3419 COGNAC lg brandy	35.00						
in amber 125.00							
3481 GLENFORD soda	15.00	25.00	25.00	25.00	60.00		180.00
3421 AVIGNON champagne	20.00						
3480 KOORS soda 5 oz	15.00	20.00	20.00				
3480 KOORS soda 8½ oz	15.00	20.00	20.00				

alexandrite 175

Page 285: TUMBLERS - all unmarked

	crystal	moongleam	flamingo	marigold	sahara	hawthorne (d/o or checker optic)
2451	10.00					
2502	10.00					
2506	10.00					
2516 CIRCLE PAIR	30.00	60.00	50.00	65.00	40.00	
2930 PLAIN & FANCY	10.00					
2930 PLAIN & FANCY w/o	10.00	20.00				
2930 PLAIN & FANCY d/o	10.00	20.00	20.00	30.00	35.00	55.00
2931	10.00					
3004	10.00					
3359 PLATEAU	10.00		20.00	30.00		
3362 CHARTER OAK	15.00	25.00	20.00	25.00		
3517	10.00	20.00	20.00			
7007 ANGULAR CRISS CROSS	40.00		80.00			

Page 286: SODAS - unmarked

	crystal	moongleam	flamingo	marigold	sahara	hawthorne
2502	10.00					
2512 8 oz	10.00					
2512 12 oz	10.00					
2516 CIRCLE PAIR 5 oz	30.00	60.00	50.00	65.00	40.00	
2516 CIRCLE PAIR 8 oz	30.00	60.00	50.00	65.00	40.00	
2516 CIRCLE PAIR 12 oz	30.00	60.00	50.00	65.00	40.00	
2517 TEARDROP	20.00	45.00	35.00			75.00
2852 8 oz	10.00					
2852 12 oz	10.00					
3359 PLATEAU 5 oz	15.00	25.00	20.00	30.00		
3359 PLATEAU 12 oz	15.00	25.00	25.00	35.00		
3484 DONNA	15.00	30.00	25.00	45.00		

Page 287: BASKETS

	crystal
458 PICKET	125.00
459 ROUND COLONIAL	250.00

Page 288:

	crystal	moongleam	flamingo	hawthorne
461 BANDED PICKET	125.00	250.00	200.00	350.00
462 PLAIN HEXAGON	135.00			

Page 289:

	crystal	moongleam	flamingo
463 BONNET	150.00	250.00	250.00
467 HELMET (Pat. #51308)	175.00	250.00	225.00

Page 290:

	crystal	moongleam	flamingo	hawthorne	marigold
417 DOUBLE RIB & PANEL	80.00	125.00	110.00	250.00	
500 OCTAGON	80.00	130.00	110.00		300.00
465 RECESSED PANEL	100.00				

Page 292: CANDLESTICKS - priced per pair

	crystal	moongleam	flamingo	crystal with moongleam candleholder
1 GEORGIAN 9″	125.00		600.00	
2 OLD WILLIAMSBURG 7″	80.00	600.00		
5 PATRICIAN 9″	95.00	700.00 (candelabrum)		
16 CLASSIC 9″	110.00			
20 SHEFFIELD 9″	125.00			225.00

Page 293:

	crystal	moongleam	flamingo	vaseline
99 LITTLE SQUATTER	35.00	50.00	50.00	
33 SKIRTED PANEL 5″	65.00			
70 OCTAGONAL 9″	130.00			
71 OVAL 10″	210.00			
100 CENTENNIAL 9″	125.00	225.00	200.00	500.00 (6″)
101 SIMPLICITY 9″	150.00			

Page 295:

	crystal	moongleam	flamingo	sahara	cobalt
103 CUPPED SAUCER	40.00		65.00		
106 INVERTED SAUCER	40.00	80.00	90.00		
104 BERTHA	145.00	225.00	175.00		
102 BALLSTEM 9″	150.00				
105 PEMBROKE 9″	140.00	200.00	200.00		
107 WELLINGTON 10″	175.00	195.00	195.00		
108 THREE RING 7″	175.00				
109 PETTICOAT DOLPHIN 6″	250.00	450.00	400.00	550.00	750.00

Page 295 (continued)	crystal	moongleam	flamingo	hawthorne	marigold	sahara
113 MARS 3½"	35.00	50.00	45.00	125.00	145.00	120.00
112 MERCURY 3"	25.00	45.00	40.00	75.00		60.00
110 SANDWICH DOLPHIN	275.00	425.00	400.00			1200.00
cobalt 2000.00						
amber 2500.00						
zircon 3000.00						
111 CHERUB 11½"	350.00	950.00	750.00			
112 MERCURY 9"	175.00	250.00	250.00			

Page 299:	crystal	moongleam	flamingo	hawthorne	marigold	moongleam ft or top	flamingo ft or top
114 PLUTO 3½"	30.00	40.00	55.00	125.00	145.00		
116 OAK LEAF 3"	50.00	60.00	60.00	110.00		60.00	
118 MISS MUFFET 3"	35.00	55.00	50.00				
120 OVERLAPPING SWIRL	35.00	60.00	50.00	125.00			
121 PINWHEEL	30.00	55.00	50.00	75.00			
122 ZIG ZAG	30.00	55.00	50.00	75.00			
117 BAMBOO						275.00	265.00
123 MERCURY (insert)*	75.00	75.00	70.00	125.00			

*singles only

	crystal	moongleam	flamingo	marigold
126 TROPHY	75.00	125.00	125.00	
125 LEAF DESIGN	85.00	175.00	125.00	
129 TRICORN	150.00	275.00	250.00	375.00
130 ACORN	200.00	375.00	250.00	
127 TWIST STEM	125.00	250.00	250.00	
128 LIBERTY 3"	45.00	85.00	80.00	200.00
132 SUNBURST	45.00	75.00	60.00	150.00
600 SQUARE HDLD	70.00*			
1205 RAINDROP	45.00	90.00	85.00	
1231 RIBBED OCTAGON	35.00	70.00	60.00	
1252 TWIST	40.00	80.00	75.00	125.00

*single only

Page 301:	crystal	moongleam	flamingo	sahara	marigold	cobalt	alexandrite
1472 PARALLEL QUARTER	45.00						
1469½ RIDGELEIGH	45.00						
112 MERCURY 3"*	25.00	45.00	40.00	60.00			
99 LITTLE SQUATTER	35.00	50.00	50.00				
600 SQUARE HDLD	70.00						
132 SUNBURST	45.00	75.00	60.00		150.00		
1401 EMPRESS, nappy, ftd	35.00	65.00	60.00	60.00			
1404 OLD SANDWICH	75.00	210.00	195.00	185.00		450.00	
109 PETTICOAT DOLPHIN	250.00	450.00	400.00		550.00	650.00	
1401 EMPRESS, df	200.00	400.00	250.00	300.00			500.00
1405 IPSWICH	175.00	200.00	200.00	200.00			
2 OLD WILLIAMSBURG 7"	80.00	600.00					
135 EMPRESS	75.00	135.00	125.00	200.00	115.00	500.00	450.00
133 SWAN HANDLED	275.00	350.00	300.00	300.00	400.00		450.00
21 ARISTOCRAT 7"	95.00						

*hawthorne 75.00

Page 303:	marigold	crystal	moongleam	flamingo	sahara	cobalt	moongleam ft
129 TRICORN	375.00	150.00	275.00	250.00			250.00
134 TRIDENT*	250.00	50.00	175.00	125.00	150.00		150.00
1428 WARWICK 2 lt		70.00	225.00	200.00	175.00	250.00	
141 EDNA		375.00	600.00	600.00	600.00	700.00	
31 JACK-BE-NIMBLE		60.00	150.00	150.00	150.00		
1471 EMPIRE		350.00					
1433 THUMBPRINT & PANEL 2 lt		50.00	150.00	150.00	150.00	375.00	
4044 NEW ERA w/bobeche**		100.00					

*tangerine - 750.00; alexandrite - 600.00
**alexandrite - 1200.00

Page 305:	crystal	moongleam	flamingo	sahara	cobalt	alexandrite
1445 GRAPE CLUSTER 1 lt	150.00				750.00	
140 CROCUS	175.00	350.00	325.00	300.00	600.00	
1445 GRAPE CLUSTER 2 lt	250.00			750.00	1150.00	1500.00
142 CASCADE	75.00			200.00	600.00	
110 SANDWICH DOLPHIN*	275.00	425.00	400.00	1200.00	2000.00	

Page 305 (continued)	crystal	moongleam	flamingo	sahara	cobalt	alexandrite
1425 VICTORIAN	125.00			250.00	600.00	
1447 ROCOCO	300.00			650.00		
136 TRIPLEX	125.00	225.00	200.00	200.00	600.00	
1445 GRAPE CLUSTER l lt w/bobeche & prisms	175.00				650.00	

*amber - 2500.00; zircon - 3000.00

Page 306: #300 OLD WILLIAMSBURG Candelabra - priced per pair

	crystal	sahara
300 2 light	350.00	650.00
300 1 light	150.00	
300 1 light	175.00	300.00

Page 307: #300 OLD WILLIAMSBURG Candelabrum

	crystal	sahara
300 3 light	450.00	750.00

Page 308: #301 OLD WILLIAMSBURG candelabra - priced per pair

	crystal	sahara	alexandrite	cobalt
301 2 light	250.00	600.00	2500.00	2000.00
301 3 light	325.00	750.00	3000.00	2500.00

Page 309: #400, 401 & 402 Pattern Candelabra

	crystal	sahara	cobalt	cobalt ft
101 shelf support	50.00 ea.			
520 INNOVATION candle lamp	125.00 ea.			
300 OLD WILLIAMSBURG candle lamp/prisms	400.00 pr			

Page 311

	crystal	sahara	cobalt	cobalt ft
402 GOTHIC 2 light	300.00	850.00	1700.00	600.00
401 OLD WILLIAMSBURG	185.00			
400 OLD WILLIAMSBURG	300.00			

Page 312: WATER LAMPS - price for each

	crystal	moongleam ft	flamingo
4206 OPTIC TOOTH 8″	325.00	350.00	350.00
4206 OPTIC TOOTH 10″	350.00	375.00	375.00
4206 OPTIC TOOTH 12″	not made	400.00	400.00
4262 CHARTER OAK 10″	350.00	375.00	375.00
4366 TROJAN 9″	350.00	375.00	375.00

Page 313:	crystal	moongleam	flamingo	sahara
1183 REVERE candleblock, pr.	650.00			1500.00
1183 REVERE vase candlestick, pr.	200.00	350.00		
8040 EVA MAE candlestick, pr.	200.00	250.00	250.00	

Page 315: COLOGNES

	crystal	moongleam	flamingo	hawthorne
63 stopper	25.00	35.00	30.00	
64 stopper	25.00	35.00	30.00	
69 stopper	20.00	30.00	30.00	55.00
76 stopper	25.00	35.00	30.00	
77 DUCK stopper	35.00	60.00	60.00	
4034 SEVEN CIRCLE	60.00	140.00	140.00	
4035 SEVEN OCTAGON	75.00	155.00	155.00	
485 HEXAGON STEM	55.00	125.00	125.00	
487 HEXAGON STEM	65.00	125.00	125.00	
515 TAPER 1 oz	65.00			
515 TAPER ¼ oz	60.00	100.00	100.00	150.00
516 FAIRACRE 1 oz	75.00	175.00	160.00	200.00
517 CIRCLE PAIR ¼ oz	75.00	125.00	110.00	

Page 318-323: COLONIAL PIECES IN COLOR

	crystal	moongleam	flamingo	vaseline	sahara	cobalt	marigold
150 BANDED FLUTE 10″ tray	45.00	110.00	110.00				
299 toddy	15.00	45.00	40.00		40.00		
300 PEERLESS low ftd tumbler	20.00	110.00	100.00				
4½ oz low ftd sherbet, shallow	15.00		75.00				

	crystal	moongleam	flamingo	vaseline	sahara	cobalt	marigold
8 oz schoppen	15.00		65.00				
300½ PEERLESS							
2 oz bar, flared	15.00	75.00	75.00				
2 oz bar	15.00	75.00	75.00				
#2 water bottle	45.00				350.00		
8 oz tumbler	18.00	85.00	75.00				
11″ vase	35.00		150.00				
302 PEERLESS 12 oz ice tea	20.00		75.00				
339 CONTINENTAL water bottle	40.00		150.00				
341 PURITAN							
½ gal tankard	75.00		250.00				
3 oz low sherbet	15.00		75.00				
custard	10.00		30.00				
341½ PURITAN 1 pt squat jug	90.00	175.00	mglm hdl				
jug	125.00		850.00+				
350 PINWHEEL AND FAN							
punch bowl	175.00	600.00					
stand	50.00						
custard	35.00	40.00					
4″ nappy	15.00	75.00		175.00			
8″ nappy	45.00	250.00	250.00	450.00			400.00
tumbler	25.00						
odd shade yellow 100.00							
351 PRISCILLA							
4 oz ale	20.00		65.00				
12 oz ale	20.00	130.00	130.00		130.00	200.00	
14 oz ale*	25.00						
*tangerine 1000.00							
352 FLAT PANEL							
French dressing bottle with moongleam or	40.00		85.00				
flamingo stopper -	50.00						
*cigar jar	110.00	350.00					
Lavender jar	75.00	200.00	200.00				
finger bowl	15.00		30.00				
*zircon 600.00							

	crystal	moongleam	flamingo	sahara	hawthorne	vaseline
353 MEDIUM FLAT PANEL						
8″ vase	40.00		130.00		250.00	350.00
12″ ice cream tray	85.00		175.00			
toothbrush holder	45.00	100.00				
indiv almond (393)	15.00	30.00	25.00	35.00	60.00	
almond, lg	20.00	50.00	45.00		75.00	
354 WIDE FLAT PANEL						
stack set	50.00		100.00			
indiv butter	15.00		30.00	45.00		
hotel cream & sugar/oval	40.00	75.00	65.00	125.00	150.00	
16 oz sanitary syrup	50.00	100.00				
393 NARROW FLUTE						
bitters bottle	35.00	(350.00 in cobalt)				
indiv salt	20.00	40.00	35.00			
banana split	20.00		55.00			
indiv cream*	20.00	35.00	35.00	100.00		
indiv sugar	20.00	35.00	35.00	(100.00 in marigold)		
salt shaker pr	35.00	100.00	85.00			
*experimental light blue 600.00+						
394 NARROW FLUTE						
domino sugar	30.00	65.00	60.00	100.00		
12″ celery tray	20.00	40.00	30.00			
12″ combination relish 3 pt	25.00	50.00	45.00	(item not illustrated - same as celery tray but with 3 compartments)		
433 GRECIAN BORDER						
21″ punch bowl plate	125.00		300.00			
15″ punch bowl & foot	175.00		300.00			
4½ oz custard	18.00		45.00			
465 RECESSED PANEL						
½ lb candy jar & cover	45.00	600.00				650.00
473 NARROW FLUTE WITH RIM						
low ftd compote	25.00					175.00
small oval plate	20.00					150.00
468 OCTAGON WITH RIM						
12″ celery	20.00	40.00	35.00			

COLONIAL PIECES IN COLOR (continued)

	crystal	moongleam	flamingo	sahara	amber
527 TAPER 4½ oz soda	10.00	20.00	20.00	20.00	
588 3 oz soda	15.00		35.00		65.00
603					
5 oz soda, d/o	12.00		25.00		
12 oz soda, d/o	15.00		30.00		
1112 4½ oz sherbet d/o	10.00		30.00		
1216					
4½" nappy, cupped	10.00				50.00
Roman punch, n/o	25.00				75.00

Page 325: **COLONIAL PIECES IN ALEXANDRITE**

	crystal	alexandrite
300 PEERLESS low ftd goblet	15.00	500.00+
341½ PURITAN finger bowl	10.00	200.00
359 stemware		
7 oz goblet	15.00	600.00+
4 oz saucer champagne	10.00	400.00+
3 oz cocktail	10.00	400.00+
2 oz sherbet	10.00	275.00+
373 OLD WILLIAMSBURG		
goblet	20.00	600.00+
517 1 qt jug	40.00	400.00+
1000 marmalade & cover	75.00	400.00+
1150 COLONIAL STAR		
7" plate	15.00	200.00

Page 327: **MISCELLANEOUS HOTEL CREAMS & SUGARS**

	crystal	moongleam	flamingo	sahara	hawthorne	vaseline
414 TUDOR sugar/cov	50.00					
479 PETAL cream	20.00	30.00	25.00	50.00	65.00	
479 PETAL sugar	20.00	30.00	25.00	50.00	65.00	
1020 PHYLLIS cream	20.00	40.00	40.00			200.00
1021 CHRISTINE cream	25.00					
1021 CHRISTINE sugar/cov	30.00					
1020 PHYLLIS sugar	20.00	40.00	40.00			200.00

Page 328:

	crystal
1022 HARDING cream	30.00
1022 HARDING sugar/cov	35.00
1024 EILEEN cream	30.00
1024 EILEEN sugar/cov	35.00
1025 SHARON cream	30.00
1025 SHARON sugar/cov	35.00
1180 DEBRA cream	30.00
1180 DEBRA sugar/cov	35.00

Page 329: **MISCELLANEOUS CREAMS & SUGARS**

	crystal	moongleam	flamingo	sahara	hawthorne
360 CORBY cream (no illus.)	25.00	40.00	40.00	40.00	
360 CORBY sugar/cov (no illus.)	30.00	45.00	45.00	45.00	
1403 HALF CIRCLE cream	25.00	55.00	55.00	50.00	
1403 HALF CIRCLE sugar	25.00	55.00	55.00	50.00	
1001 CASWELL sugar sifter	30.00	55.00 ft	55.00		75.00
1001 CASWELL cream	30.00	55.00 ft	55.00		75.00

Page 331: FINGER BOWLS

	crystal	moongleam	flamingo	marigold	sahara	tangerine	alexandrite
3309 PETITE	10.00	20.00	15.00	30.00			
3311 VELVEDERE	10.00						
3312 GAYOSO	10.00	20.00	15.00	30.00			
3317 DRAKE	10.00		15.00				
3359 PLATEAU	10.00	20.00	20.00	30.00			
3481	10.00	20.00	20.00				
4071	10.00	20.00	20.00	30.00	20.00	100.00	
4072	10.00						
4074	10.00	20.00	20.00				
4075	10.00	20.00	20.00	30.00	20.00		75.00
4079	10.00						
4080*	10.00	20.00	20.00				

*zircon 40.00 s/o

Page 332:	crystal	moongleam	flamingo	marigold	sahara	tangerine	alexandrite
3390 CARCASSONNE*	15.00	30.00	30.00		35.00		75.00
3381 CREOLE					65.00		85.00
3397 GASCONY	25.00				50.00	175.00	
3311 VELVEDERE	10.00						
4080**	10.00	20.00	20.00				
4071	10.00	20.00	20.00	30.00	25.00	100.00	
3309 PETITE	10.00	20.00	20.00	30.00			
4074	10.00	20.00	20.00				
3312 GAYOSO	10.00	20.00	15.00	30.00			
3362 CHARTER OAK	10.00	20.00	20.00	30.00			
3335 LADY LEG***	10.00				25.00		
4075	10.00	25.00	20.00	30.00	25.00		75.00
3308 BOB WHITE	10.00						

*cobalt 90.00, bowl 100.00   **zircon 40.00   ***zircon 40.00; cobalt 70.00

Page 336:   FLORAL BOWLS & PLATEAUS

	crystal	moongleam	flamingo	hawthorne
10 GIBSON GIRL with frog	35.00	60.00	50.00	75.00
13 FLAT RIM	25.00	50.00	35.00	
45 FTD GIBSON GIRL	40.00	90.00	70.00	
116 OAK LEAF	35.00	55.00	45.00	75.00

Page 337:	crystal	moongleam	flamingo	hawthorne
1194 PAUL REVERE	25.00	50.00	35.00	
1195 PAUL REVERE, OPTIC	25.00	50.00	35.00	
1202 PANELED OCTAGON	25.00	50.00	35.00	75.00 11″
1202 PANELED OC-TAGON, rolled edge	25.00	50.00	35.00	75.00 11″

	crystal	moongleam	flamingo	hawthorne
1203 FLAT PANELED OCTAGON	35.00	55.00	45.00	75.00
1204 SWIRL	30.00	45.00	35.00	
1205 RAINDROP	35.00	45.00	35.00	
1206 SWIRL & RAINDROP	35.00	50.00	40.00	

Page 338:   FLORAL BOWLS

	crystal	moongleam	flamingo	sahara	alexandrite	marigold
1252 TWIST 12″ round	30.00	60.00	50.00	60.00	300.00	90.00
1401 EMPRESS 8½″ ftd	30.00	60.00	50.00	50.00		
1252 TWIST nasturtium	30.00	60.00	50.00	60.00	350.00	90.00
135 EMPRESS	40.00	90.00	75.00	90.00		
134 TRIDENT	35.00	85.00	70.00	80.00	300.00	
1401 EMPRESS nasturtium	40.00	100.00	90.00	100.00		

Page 339:	crystal	sahara	cobalt	moongleam	flamingo	zircon
1429 PRISTINE	50.00	100.00	450.00	175.00		
1440 ARCH	75.00	350.00	450.00			
1445 GRAPE CLUSTER	80.00	200.00	450.00	200.00		1000.00+
1425 VICTORIAN	45.00	75.00	275.00			
1433 THUMBPRINT & PANEL	50.00	100.00	275.00	100.00	250.00	
1428 WARWICK	65.00	150.00	325.00			

Page 340:	crystal	sahara	cobalt	tangerine
3397 GASCONY 10″ ftd	100.00	200.00	650.00	1000.00
4044 NEW ERA	60.00			
3397 GASCONY (no foot)	45.00		300.00	
1472 PARALLEL QUARTER	35.00			
1447 ROCOCO	70.00	150.00		
1471 EMPIRE	70.00			
3397 GASCONY, oval	60.00	125.00		850.00

Page 341:	crystal	moongleam	flamingo	sahara
50 ADENA	25.00	60.00	50.00	
133 SWAN HDLD	125.00	300.00	300.00	300.00

Page 343:   FLOWER BLOCKS

	crystal	moongleam	flamingo	hawthorne	marigold
2	10.00	20.00	20.00		
501 FOGG box & blocks	65.00	130.00	130.00		175.00
9	10.00	30.00	20.00	50.00 (#10 & 11)	
14 KINGFISHER	150.00	250.00	250.00	300.00	
15	20.00	40.00	40.00	75.00	
15 DUCK	150.00	225.00	225.00	275.00	
15 with 123 candle	85.00	150.00	150.00	200.00	

FLOWER BLOCKS (continued)

Page 344:	crystal	moongleam	flamingo	sahara
19 4″	10.00	30.00	20.00	30.00
20 5″	10.00	30.00	20.00	30.00
21 6″	10.00	30.00	20.00	30.00
18 (for 134 bowl)	30.00	60.00	60.00	60.00
17 (for 133 & 1469 bowl)	40.00	80.00	80.00	80.00
22 (for 1404 oval bowl)	30.00	60.00	60.00	60.00

Pages 346-347: HARVEY AMBER ITEMS

While these items often came in other colors, prices here are for amber only

	amber
12 SMALL EIGHT FLUTE salt	100.00 pr
201 HARVEY COLONIAL tumbler	50.00
300 PEERLESS Indiv decanter	60.00
337 TOURAINE	
goblet n/o	75.00
parfait n/o	65.00
5 oz juice n/o	35.00
337½ 4½ oz sherbet n/o	35.00
352 FLAT PANEL oil	400.00
353 MEDIUM FLAT PANEL	
1 qt jug	300.00
10″ tray	150.00
10 oz ftd soda	75.00
398 5″ nappy	30.00
586 12 oz soda, n/o	35.00
1106 HANDLELESS CUSTARD n/o	30.00
1125 STARBURST plate	40.00
1184 YEOMAN	
6¼″ plate	30.00
8″ plate	35.00
1217 finger bowl	45.00
1509 QUEEN ANN triplex relish	175.00
3304 UNIVERSAL parfait	45.00
3419 COGNAC brandy inhaler	125.00
3801 TEXAS PINK low comport	75.00
4049 OLD FITZ hot whiskey	90.00
4059 ALLEN water bottle	175.00
4165 SHAW 3 pt jug	250.00

Page 350: JUGS

	crystal	flamingo	marigold	moongleam handle	flamingo hdl/ft	hawthorne
2517 TEARDROP*	80.00	250.00		150.00		350.00
3350 WABASH 3 pt squat	150.00	250.00	450.00	200.00	175.00	300.00
2516 CIRCLE PAIR ½ gal	70.00	150.00		125.00	125.00	
3350 WABASH 3 pt tankard	150.00	200.00		200.00		

moongleam 450.00

	marigold	crystal	moongleam	flamingo	sahara	alexandrite	hawthorne
4165 SHAW*		45.00					
4164 GALLAGHER	500.00+	85.00	175.00	150.00	175.00	500.00	350.00
4163 WHALEY		75.00					
4166 BALDA		75.00					
4206 OPTIC TOOTH (colored foot & hdl)			150.00	125.00			
in hawthorne bowl/moongleam foot 400.00							

* amber 250.00; cobalt 300.00

Page 352:	crystal	moongleam	flamingo	marigold	sahara	hawthorne	moongleam hdl/ft
3484 DONNA	75.00	150.00	125.00	225.00			
4157 STEELE 1 pt	65.00						
4163 WHALEY	75.00						
3485 IRENE 3 pt	95.00	300.00	250.00		300.00		
4159 CLASSIC	75.00						
3480 KOORS*	75.00	150.00	150.00			200.00	150.00

*flamingo hdl/ft 150.00

	marigold	crystal	moongleam	flamingo	sahara	alexandrite d/o	hawthorne checker optic
4164 GALLAGHER	500.00+	85.00	175.00	150.00	175.00	500.00	350.00
3805 jug cover for 4164		30.00	60.00	55.00			
4165 SHAW*		45.00					
4163 WHALEY		75.00					
4166 BALDA		75.00					

*cobalt 300.00; amber 250.00

Page 355: MISCELLANEOUS PLATES

	crystal	moongleam	flamingo	alexandrite	amber	hawthorne
416 HERRINGBONE 8″	10.00	20.00	20.00			25.00
1125 STARBURST 8″	10.00				40.00	
1150 COLONIAL STAR 8″	15.00			200.00		
1128 PLAIN JANE 6″	10.00					
1130 HEISEY STAR 6½″	10.00					

	crystal	moongleam	flamingo
1218 SIMPLICITY 8″	6.00		
1219 SIMPLICITY WITH STAR	10.00		
1220 TWELVE SCALLOP 8″	15.00		
1222 FINE PLEAT 8″	15.00		
1223 FLUTED BORDER 8″	15.00	30.00	25.00

Page 357:	crystal	moongleam	flamingo	hawthorne
1224 HEXAGON SIX 8″	6.00	20.00	15.00	
1224 HEXAGON SIX d/o 8″	10.00	20.00	15.00	
1225 RIDGE & STAR 7″	15.00	30.00	25.00	40.00
1226 RIDGE BORDER 8″	15.00			
1227 PINWHEEL 8″	15.00			

	crystal	moongleam	flamingo	hawthorne
1228 SWIRL 7″	10.00	20.00		30.00
1228 SWIRL, marcel wave 7″	10.00	20.00		30.00
1230 FLUTED BORDER WITH RIB 8″	10.00			
1232 SPOKE 8″	15.00	30.00	25.00	
1233 PRESSED DIAMOND 7″	15.00		25.00	35.00

Page 359:	crystal	moongleam	flamingo	sahara	zircon	hawthorne
1238 BEEHIVE 8″	20.00	45.00	25.00	150.00	80.00	150.00
1241 OCTAGON SPIRAL 8″	15.00	30.00	25.00			
1245 SPIRAL 8″	15.00	30.00	25.00			
1242 OCTAGON SQUARE 8″	15.00	30.00	25.00			
1243 STEPPED OCTAGON 8″	10.00	20.00	15.00			

	crystal	moongleam	flamingo	hawthorne
1246 ACORN & LEAVES 8″	15.00	35.00	25.00	40.00
1248 PLAIN 7″	10.00			
1249 REVERSE SPIRAL 8″	15.00	30.00	25.00	40.00
1250 WIDE RIM PLAIN 8″	10.00	20.00	20.00	
1251 UNIQUE 8″	20.00			

Page 360:	crystal	moongleam	flamingo	sahara	alexandrite	marigold	hawthorne
4182 THIN 8″	10.00			20.00			
4182 THIN d/o 8″	10.00	20.00	20.00	20.00	45.00	30.00	30.00
4182 THIN w/o 8″	10.00						
4183 NARROW RIM PLAIN 7½″	10.00						
4184 SIX SCALLOP	10.00						

Page 361:

	crystal	moongleam	flamingo	hawthorne	marigold	cobalt
1223 FLUTED BORDER nappy	10.00	20.00	20.00			
1233 PRESSED DIAMOND cereal	15.00		25.00	35.00		

Page 361 (continued)

	crystal	moongleam	flamingo	hawthorne	marigold	cobalt
1223 FLUTED BORDER grapefruit	15.00	30.00	25.00			
1223 FLUTED BORDER baked apple & plate	20.00	30.00	25.00			
1233 PRESSED DIAMOND baked apple	15.00		25.00	35.00		
1223 FLUTED BORDER ice cream nappy	10.00	20.00	20.00			
1222 hot & cold liner	10.00					
1223 FLUTED BORDER hot & cold liner	10.00					
1241 OCTAGON SPIRAL nappy	15.00	30.00	25.00			
1243 STEPPED OCTAGON nappy	15.00	30.00	25.00			
1253 LEAF EDGE plate	20.00	40.00	40.00		60.00	
1254 CONCENTRIC RINGS plate	20.00	40.00	40.00		60.00	90.00

Pages 362-364

	crystal	moongleam	flamingo	sahara	cobalt
1234 STIPPLED DIAMOND	20.00	40.00	60.00		
1236 EAGLE	50.00	150.00			500.00+
1237 SANDWICH STAR	50.00	150.00			
1406 FLEUR DE LIS	45.00	90.00	90.00	90.00	
7093 BEADED ARROW	60.00				
7026 HEART & DRAPE		95.00	85.00		
1239 KATHIE	20.00				
1480 FAN RIB	20.00				
1432 CACTUS (no illus.)					250.00
8071 SANDWICH HAIRPIN (no illus.)	50.00				

Page 366:   SALTS & PEPPERS - priced per pair

	crystal	moongleam	moongleam foot	flamingo	flamingo foot	hawthorne	sahara
27 TALL SIX PANEL	30.00						
29 SHORT DOUBLE PANEL	30.00						
30 TALL DOUBLE PANEL	30.00						
42 ELEGANCE*	45.00		60.00	70.00			60.00
44 DETROIT	45.00						
45 PALMYRA	45.00						
46 CHESHIRE	45.00	90.00	80.00	80.00			
47 SPOOL	45.00	90.00		75.00			
48 KOORS	40.00	70.00	65.00	65.00	65.00		
49 YORKSHIRE	45.00	90.00	75.00	85.00	55.00	110.00	
50 LOUISISANA	45.00	90.00		115.00			
51 DRUM	45.00	125.00	110.00	100.00			
52 SHORT INDIVIDUAL	25.00	50.00		50.00		90.00	90.00
53 TALL INDIVIDUAL	30.00	60.00		60.00			

*marigold 125.00

Page 368:   MISCELLANEOUS SALTS OR PEPPERS

	crystal	moongleam	flamingo	sahara	cobalt	amber
12 SMALL EIGHT FLUTE	30.00	60.00	50.00	65.00	150.00	125.00
23 SHORT PANEL	20.00	45.00	40.00	50.00		
24 MEDIUM PANEL	20.00	45.00	40.00	50.00	150.00	125.00

Page 369:

	crystal	moongleam	flamingo	sahara	marigold	hawthorne	moongleam foot
25 TALL PANEL	20.00						
27 TALL SIX PANEL	30.00						
42 ELEGANCE	45.00		60.00	70.00	125.00		65.00
48 KOORS*	40.00	70.00	65.00				50.00
54 TWIST	35.00	70.00	65.00	80.00	100.00		
52 SHORT INDIVIDUAL	25.00	50.00	50.00	90.00		90.00	

*flamingo foot 65.00

Page 371:   VASES

	crystal	moongleam	flamingo	hawthorne	marigold	sahara
4203 EMOGENE	40.00	80.00	75.00	95.00		
2516 CIRCLE PAIR 12″	40.00	80.00	70.00			
4202 BAMBOO	45.00	95.00	85.00			
3359 PLATEAU rose bowl	45.00	90.00	75.00	110.00	110.00	
4157 STEELE rose bowl*	40.00	80.00	75.00	95.00		80.00
4191 OLYMPIA 8″	35.00	70.00 ft				

*also made in opaque tangerine slag and tangerine with yellow rim 900.00+

Page 371: VASES (continued)

NOT ILLUSTRATED: crystal
4191 OLYMPIA 6″   30.00 75.00 (moongleam foot)
4191 OLYMPIA 10″   45.00 95.00 (moongleam foot)

Page 372:

	crystal	moongleam	flamingo	hawthorne	marigold	moongleam foot	hawthorne moongleam
4204 JOYCE 9″	35.00	70.00	60.00	100.00	100.00		
4205 VALLI 8″	35.00	70.00	65.00	100.00	100.00		
4206 OPTIC TOOTH 8″	50.00		100.00	150.00	175.00	90.00	350.00
4207 MODERNE	40.00	80.00	70.00		110.00		
4209 OVAL 9″*	45.00	90.00	80.00		125.00		

*sahara 85.00

NOT ILLUSTRATED:

	crystal	moongleam	flamingo	hawthorne	marigold	moongleam foot	hawthorne moongleam
4206 OPTIC TOOTH 10″	60.00		80.00		150.00	70.00	350.00
4206 OPTIC TOOTH 12″	75.00		100.00	150.00	200.00	70.00	450.00
4209 OVAL 7″	30.00	60.00	55.00		90.00		

Page 373:

	crystal	moongleam	flamingo	marigold	sahara	alexandrite
4214 ELAINE swirl or d/o	45.00	70.00	85.00		90.00	
4215 DOROTHY d/o	30.00	60.00	55.00	70.00		
4217 FRANCES d/o 6″	40.00	80.00	75.00	90.00		
4211 LILAC 8½″	40.00	80.00	75.00	90.00		
4216 OCTAGON 9″	40.00	80.00	70.00		80.00	300.00
4218 MARILYN 9½″	40.00	85.00	85.00			
4219 LUCILE	45.00	90.00	80.00			

Page 374:

	crystal	moongleam	flamingo	hawthorne
516/1 7″ d/o	not listed	70.00	60.00	100.00
3480 KOORS 7″	not listed	70.00	60.00	100.00
516/2 6″ d/o	not listed	60.00	50.00	
516/3 9″ d/o	not listed	70.00	65.00	
2517 TEARDROP 12″	not listed	70.00	75.00	125.00
2517 TEARDROP 9½″	not listed	85.00	75.00	115.00

Page 375:

	crystal	moongleam	flamingo	moongleam foot	marigold	sahara	hawthorne
4160/1 ELLEN d/o	not listed	60.00	55.00				
4209 OVAL 9″	45.00	70.00	80.00		110.00	85.00	
4159/1 CLASSIC 9″	not listed	60.00	55.00				95.00
4196 RHODA 10″	not listed		90.00		85.00		

NOTE: Neither of the following vases was listed as being made in crystal.

Page 376:

	moongleam	flamingo	moongleam foot	flamingo foot
4162 GENIE (all variations)	65.00	60.00		
3355 FAIRACRE 12″		95.00	95.00	85.00

Page 377:   MISCELLANEOUS VASES

	crystal	moongleam	flamingo	hawthorne	sahara	cobalt	zircon s/o
4191 OLYMPIA 8″	35.00	70.00 ft.	70.00				
4157 STEELE rose bowl	40.00	80.00	75.00	75.00	80.00		
4202 BAMBOO 6″	45.00	95.00	85.00				
4045 BALL 9″*	60.00	550.00	750.00+		300.00	400.00	500.00+
4057 CECELIA 10″**	55.00						300.00

*6″ and 12″ made in tangerine Also 9″ listed as cobalt, plain. alexandrite 850.00 9″
**8″ vase in dawn $200.00+   **6″ vase in amber 200.00+

Page 379:

	crystal	moongleam	flamingo	sahara	alexandrite	cobalt	tangerine
4227, 4228, 4229, 4230, 4231, 4232 favor	80.00	300.00	325.00	200.00		150.00	600.00
4217 FRANCES**	40.00	80.00	75.00				
4224 IVY, plain & w/o	40.00	150.00	150.00	150.00		250.00	350.00
4222 HORSESHOE 6″	50.00	150.00		150.00			
4215 DOROTHY	30.00	60.00	55.00				
4220 JANICE 7″*	50.00	125.00	125.00	125.00	400.00		
4223 SWIRL 12″	100.00	250.00	200.00	250.00		450.00+	
4216 OCTAGON 9″	50.00	100.00	90.00	100.00	300.00		
4214 ELAINE 7″	45.00	70.00	85.00	90.00			

*also made 4½″ size, marigold 70.00
**marigold 85.00

Page 381,382:   MISCELLANEOUS ITEMS

	crystal	moongleam	flamingo	marigold	hawthorne	sahara	alexandrite
#2 liner, 3 pt	10.00	25.00	20.00	45.00			
6 mayonnaise ladle	20.00	40.00	35.00		70.00	50.00	100.00
10 CARTER ink	300.00						
10 OAK LEAF coaster	15.00	30.00	25.00		60.00	50.00	
500 MILK bottle top	15.00						
1010 DECAGON relish	20.00	40.00	40.00				
7089 CLOVERLEAF snack plate			50.00				
1245/3970 comport		75.00	75.00		125.00		

460

MISCELLANEOUS ITEMS (continued)

Page 384:	crystal	moongleam	flamingo	hawthorne	sahara
1180 BRAZIL nut dish	15.00	35.00	30.00		
1189 YEOMAN 13″ celery	20.00	40.00	35.00		
1186 YEOMAN cup/saucer	20.00	40.00	35.00		
1183 REVERE parfait	15.00				
1185 YEOMAN 12″ celery	20.00	40.00	35.00		
1186 YEOMAN 7″ comport	25.00	50.00	45.00	70.00	
1183 REVERE 6″ comport	25.00	50.00	55.00	70.00	
1181 cheese & cracker	45.00				
1186 YEOMAN 7″ com-port, deep	25.00	50.00	45.00		75.00

Page 385:	crystal	moongleam	flamingo	hawthorne	vaseline
1191 LOBE pickle & olive	20.00	40.00	35.00	70.00	
1194 PENTAGON relish	15.00	30.00	25.00		
1194 PENTAGON nut dish	15.00	35.00	30.00		
1193 INSIDE SCALLOP*	20.00	40.00	35.00		150.00
1187 YEOMAN 13″ tray	30.00				
1187 YEOMAN tray, 3 comp	35.00				
1201 LAVERNE 11″ bowl	25.00	60.00	55.00		250.00
1191 LOBE 9″ spice, hdld**	35.00	70.00	55.00	95.00	

*1193 INSIDE SCALLOP lg nappy also made in crystal 40.00 and vaseline 225.00
**also made without handle

Page 386:	crystal	moongleam	flamingo	marigold	hawthorne
1210 FROG cheese plate	75.00	175.00	145.00	425.00	
1210 duplex confection	40.00	85.00	70.00		
1210 2 hdld bonbon	40.00	80.00	70.00	90.00	
1216 PLAIN 8″ nappy	30.00				
1210 6″ relish	20.00	40.00	30.00	65.00	
1228 SWIRL baked apple & plate	20.00	40.00			60.00
1224 HEXAGON SIX salad bowl	30.00	65.00	60.00		
1221 STAR CENTER 10″ sandwich	20.00				

Page 388: MISCELLANEOUS SYRUPS, NAPPIES & PLATES

	crystal	moongleam	flamingo	sahara	marigold	alexandrite
1150 COLONIAL STAR 8″	15.00					250.00
1219 SIMPLICITY WITH STAR	10.00					
406 COARSE RIB 4½″ nappy	10.00	20.00	20.00			
*372 McGRADY 5 oz syrup	35.00	75.00	65.00	75.00		
398 HOPEWELL 4″	10.00					
1458 COURTHOUSE 8″	25.00					
4182 THIN PRESSED 7″	10.00	20.00	15.00	20.00	25.00	45.00
NOT ILLUSTRATED:						
*372 McGRADY 7 oz syrup	40.00	80.00	75.00	80.00		
372 McGRADY 12 oz syrup	45.00	90.00	80.00			

Page 389: MISCELLANEOUS CUSTARDS & FINGER BOWLS

	crystal	moongleam	flamingo	marigold	sahara
1101 STITCH custard	10.00	20.00 d/o	20.00 d/o		
1242 finger bowl	10.00	20.00	20.00		
1212 CRIM custard	10.00				
2 grapefruit, peg	10.00				
3 grapefruit, ftd	10.00				
5 mustard spoon	25.00	50.00	55.00	75.00	65.00
2 mustard spoon	25.00				
1 mustard spoon	25.00				
2 salad fork	50.00				
2 salad spoon	50.00				

Page 391: MISCELLANEOUS ITEMS

	crystal	moongleam	flamingo	sahara	cobalt
10 mustard paddle	25.00				
7 mayonnaise ladle	20.00	55.00	45.00	60.00	
10 muddler	20.00	55.00	50.00	70.00	125.00
11 muddler	25.00				
300½ PEERLESS #1 water bottle	55.00				
339 CONTINENTAL water bottle	55.00		135.00		
300½ PEERLESS #2 water bottle	55.00			150.00	

	crystal	moongleam	flamingo	hawthorne	sahara
354 WIDE FLAT PANEL ind sugar	20.00		35.00		
354 WIDE FLAT PANEL indiv cream	20.00		35.00		
354 WIDE FLAT PANEL indiv butter	15.00		30.00		55.00
417 DOUBLE RIB & PANEL carafe	100.00				
367 PRISM BAND decanter	95.00	300.00	250.00		
417 DOUBLE RIB & PANEL mustard	35.00	75.00	65.00	70.00	
394 NARROW FLUTE chow chow	15.00				

Page 393:	crystal	moongleam	flamingo	sahara	hawthorne
1115 BRADBURY bitters	45.00				
479 PETAL sugar	20.00	30.00	25.00	50.00	65.00
479 PETAL cream	20.00	30.00	25.00	50.00	65.00
485 HEXAGON STEM cologne	55.00	125.00	125.00		
473 NARROW FLUTE WITH RIM nut dish	20.00	35.00	25.00		50.00
1170 PLEAT & PANEL spice	25.00	55.00	45.00		125.00+
485 DUNHAM bowl	35.00				
485 DUNHAM plate	30.00				
1170 PLEAT & PANEL ice jug	65.00	125.00	100.00	175.00	

Page 395:	crystal	moongleam	flamingo	sahara	cobalt	alexandrite
1185 YEOMAN celery	20.00	40.00	35.00			
1189 YEOMAN indiv sugar/cover	45.00	90.00	90.00	90.00		
1189 YEOMAN indiv cream	45.00	90.00	90.00	90.00		
1222 hot & cold liner	10.00					
1224 hot & cold liner	10.00	25.00		25.00		
1186 YEOMAN cup/saucer	20.00	40.00	35.00			
1223 hot & cold liner	10.00					
1189 YEOMAN 9" celery	20.00	40.00	35.00			
1413 CATHEDRAL vase, hdld	75.00	175.00	150.00	175.00	300.00	
1404 OLD SANDWICH 8 oz pilsner	30.00			60.00 (10 oz)		
1413 CATHEDRAL Vase, straight	60.00	165.00	140.00	165.00	300.00	350.00

Page 397:	crystal	moongleam	flamingo	sahara	cobalt	amber
1417 ARCH tumbler	20.00	65.00	55.00	65.00	95.00	115.00
1454 DIAMOND POINT ind jelly	10.00					
1460 FLAME ftd tumbler	35.00				85.00	
1433 THUMBPRINT & PANEL 8½" vase	45.00	195.00	195.00	195.00	250.00	
1421 HI LO vase	80.00	325.00	325.00	325.00	325.00	
1430 ARISTOCRAT ½ lb, low ftd candy	100.00			350.00	500.00	
1420 TULIP vase	110.00	400.00	400.00	400.00	500.00	
1430 ARISTOCRAT ½ lt high ftd candy	100.00	325.00		325.00	500.00	
1466 STAR relish	55.00					
1433 THUMBPRINT & PANEL cheese & cracker	60.00			125.00	175.00	

*tangerine 2000.00

Page 399:	crystal	sahara	cobalt	moongleam	flamingo	tangerine
1473 BUTTRESS med center	25.00					
1473 BUTTRESS lg center	30.00					
1473 BUTTRESS corner	25.00					
1473 BUTTRESS sm center	25.00					
2000 Bobeche	25.00					
1479 BECKMAN sherbet	10.00					
4163 WHALEY pretzel jar	200.00	550.00				
4163 WHALEY 12 oz mug*	45.00	160.00	250.00	110.00	325.00	400.00+
3397 GASCONY 2 comp mayo	50.00	100.00				
1476 MORSE torque plate	50.00		300.00			

*handles only are in color

Page 402: MISCELLANEOUS ITEMS (continued)

	crystal
4056 CAESAR salad bowl	35.00
4266 custard	10.00
4058 custard	10.00
4058 PUMPKIN punch bowl & cover	350.00

Page 403:

	crystal	moongleam	flamingo	amber	crystal with cobalt stripes
4059 ALLEN water bottle	45.00			175.00	1500.00+
4061 McPEEK water bottle	45.00				
3417 ADKINS bitters	55.00				
4044 NEW ERA rock & rye	125.00				
3806 mushroom cover	25.00				
4056 FRYE water bottle	45.00				
4057 SCHNAIDT water bottle	45.00	175.00	150.00		

Page 404:

	crystal	moongleam	flamingo	sahara	alexandrite	marigold	cobalt
4121 GLENN marmalade/cov	45.00						
4122 WEAVER marmal/cov	55.00						
4002 AQUA CALIENTE	20.00	80.00	80.00	80.00			175.00
4225 COBEL 1 qt cocktail shaker	50.00	350.00	350.00	350.00			500.00
4182 THIN plate	10.00	20.00	15.00	20.00	45.00	25.00	
4225 COBEL Rock & Rye	100.00						
4222 HORSESHOE sugar*	30.00	70.00	60.00	55.00			
4222 HORSESHOE cream*	30.00	70.00	60.00	55.00			

*crystal with moongleam handles 40.00-50.00 each

Page 405: OIL BOTTLES

	crystal	moongleam	flamingo
2 BARNES	60.00		
1 PAULSON	60.00		
4042 REYNOLDS	45.00	90.00	85.00

Schroeder's Antiques Price Guide

Schroeder's Antiques Price Guide has climbed its way to the top in a field already supplied with several well-established publications! The word is out, *Schroeder's Price Guide* is the best buy at any price. Over 500 categories are covered, with more than 50,000 listings. But it's not volume alone that makes Schroeder's the unique guide it is recognized to be. From ABC Plates to Zsolnay, if it merits the interest of today's collector, you'll find it in Schroeder's. Each subject is represented with histories and background information. In addition, hundreds of sharp original photos are used each year to illustrate not only the rare and the unusual, but the everyday "fun-type" collectibles as well -- not postage stamp pictures, but large close-up shots that show important details clearly.

Each edition is completely re-typeset from all new sources. We have not and will not simply change prices in each new edition. All new copy and all new illustrations make Schroeder's THE price guide on antiques and collectibles.

The writing and researching team behind this giant is proportionately large. It is backed by a staff of more than seventy of Collector Books' finest authors, as well as a board of advisors made up of well-known antique authorities and the country's top dealers, all specialists in their fields. Accuracy is their primary aim. Prices are gathered over the entire year previous to publication, from ads and personal contacts. Then each category is thoroughly checked to spot inconsistencies, listings that may not be entirely reflective of actual market dealings, and lines too vague to be of merit. Only the best of the lot remains for publication. You'll find *Schroeder's Antiques Price Guide* the one to buy for factual information and quality.

No dealer, collector or investor can afford not to own this book. It is available from your favorite bookseller or antiques dealer at the low price of $12.95. If you are unable to find this price guide in your area, it's available from Collector Books, P. O. Box 3009, Paducah, KY 42001 at $12.95 plus $2.00 for postage and handling.

8½ x 11, 608 Pages $12.95

COLLECTOR BOOKS
A Division of Schroeder Publishing Co., Inc.